CALIFORNIA RAILROADS

CALIFORNIA RAILROADS

An Encyclopedia of Cable Car, Common Carrier, Horsecar, Industrial Interurban, Logging, Monorail, Motor Road, Short Lines, Streetcar, Switching and Terminal Railroads in California (1851-1992)

Alvin A. Fickewirth

Golden West Books

San Marino, California • 91118-8250

CALIFORNIA RAILROADS

Copyright ©1992 by Alvin A. Fickewirth
All Rights Reserved

Published by Golden West Books
San Marino, California 91118 U.S.A.

Library of Congress Catalog Card No. 92-12495
I.S.B.N. No. 0-87095-106-8

Library of Congress Cataloging-in-Publication Data

Fickewirth, Alvin A., 1912-
    California railroads: an encyclopedia of cable car, common carrier, horsecar,
industrial, interurban, logging, monorail, motor road, shortlines, streetcar,
switching and terminal railroads in California (1851-1992) / Alvin A. Fickewirth.

      p.   cm.
    Includes bibliographical references and index.
    ISBN 0-87095-106-8
    1. Railroads — California — Encyclopedias.   I. Title.
    TF24.C3F53   1992   92-12495
    385'.09794 — dc20   CIP

COVER PAINTING

Forty years ago, illustrator Lloyd Harting prepared this watercolor painting for a calendar cover, showing the arrival of a passenger train in 1876 at the Los Angeles & Independence Railroad station, in downtown Los Angeles. The depot site, located on San Pedro Street between 4th and 5th street, has long since been swallowed up by the sprawling "City of the Angels." This scene really illustrates the excitement and importance the railroad had on the city's early history.

It was 1846 before an American flag was first raised over Los Angeles. At that time, the population of Los Angeles was but a few thousand citizens. The Los Angeles & Independence Railroad was built from a wharf at Santa Monica to Los Angeles in 1875, and there were plans for an extension to the mining district of Independence. With the coming of the Southern Pacific from San Francisco on September 5, 1876, and the building of a line east toward Yuma, Los Angeles began to grow. One year after the cover scene took place, the Southern Pacific, in 1877, leased the LA&I and eventually absorbed it into its system. Also, in the same year, the first carload of oranges was sent east by rail. - *Donald Duke Collection*

TITLE PAGE ILLUSTRATION

Northwestern Pacific train No. 4, the Tiburon to Ukiah local passenger and mail train, passes through a treasure-trove of giant Sequoia trees while making its 106-mile run. Leaving the Tiburon ferry terminal at 3:30 P.M., train No. 4 often made as many as 30 station stops during its trip up the line before reaching Ukiah at 8:00 P.M. - *Donald Duke Collection*

Golden West Books
P.O. Box 80250
San Marino, California • 91118-8250

This book is dedicated to my son
John M. Fickewirth
and his company staff, who set
the data for *California Railroads*
on the computer.

UNION PACIFIC - The eastbound *Pacific Limited* races through the Southern California countryside, east of the East Los Angeles suburban station, in the late 1940's. Today this region is completely built up on both sides of the right-of-way. - *Donald Duke*

Preface

As a railroad historian and an afficianado of the steam locomotive, I felt quite honored when, in 1952, the El Monte Kiwanis Club asked me to speak to their group on the history of California railroads. As a school principal I had often given talks, but never on my favorite subject - railroads. I welcomed the idea of finally utilizing my vast knowledge about railroads, after all, I not only had an immense railroad library, but also a collection of railroad passes and other memorabilia.

The beginning of my speech to the group dealt with the information that California's first railroad was the Sacramento Valley Railroad between Sacramento and Folsom, built in 1855 by the father of California's railroads, Theodore T. Judah. Elaborating on this fact, I went on to tell them that at the time the citizens of California believed that Judah's proposed railroad, over the mighty Sierra in order to connect Sacramento to Omaha, was a crazy idea. However, Crazy Judah's line was built by the Central Pacific-Union Pacific and, in 1869, it became the nation's first

transcontinental railroad. I then elucidated on the coming of the second transcontinental line, the Atchison, Topeka & Santa Fe Railroad, and the eventual building of the Los Angeles to Salt Lake line by the San Pedro, Los Angeles & Salt Lake Railroad. To give them a more complete picture of the times, I presented the role of the short line railroad, the industrial carrier and the roads built to haul minerals. Explaining to them that Southern California's public transportation system began with the horsecar lines, advanced to the coming of cable cars, and that eventually the electric car took their place. At the conclusion of my program, the meeting was opened up for questions. Most of the inquiries proved to be rather mundane with the exception of one gentlemen who asked, ''How many railroads has California had or do they have?'' Believing at the time that the figure I was about to give was approximately right, I replied, ''At least a hundred!''

Upon arriving home that evening, I decided to sit down and list all the railroads that came to mind. Over a period

1

of several weeks, I kept adding to the list until I had nearly 300 railroads recorded. But as time went on, the question raised at the Kiwanis Club kept haunting me. Just exactly how many railroads did California have? It was then that I made the decision to reread my entire library and look through my files in search of the answer. Needless to say, my research found an additional 50 railroads.

In order to maintain these findings, I decided to catalog the information collected on each railroad by placing them on an index card. This included the full name of the railroad, where it was organized, the county where the organization took place and how many miles the railroad operated. Not only did I record the type of motive power used, but also if it was horse-drawn, run by a steam locomotive or operated by electricity, cable, etc. Along with this I noted if the railroad had merged into some other carrier, had been extended and, if so, to where or whether it was the result of a consolidation of several railroads. As I came across each new railroad, I filled out a new index card. By 1954 I had over 694 railroads on file.

In the meantime, several railroad historians of Southern California organized the Southern California Chapter of the Railway & Locomotive Historical Society. I became a charter member and a director of this august group. It was in April 1954 that the Chapter began the publication of a quarterly journal of California railroad history entitled the *Pacific Railway Journal*. I offered my California railroad list to the editor as I felt that by publishing it other unknown railroads might turn up. In order to be used, the list had to be transcribed from the index cards. This proved to be no easy task. It took several months to type and it became a spiral-bound book.

The editor of the *Pacific Railway Journal*, Donald Duke, had in his possession a near complete collection of railroad trade journals called the *Railroad Gazette* and *Railway Age*, dating from 1873 to 1954. While looking through these journals, Duke discovered that there was a wealth of information on new railroads in a column entitled "Railroad Construction" and "General Railroad News." Upon hearing this I decided I better take a look, and sure enough in the three years it took to plow through the 107 years of journals, I doubled my list of railroads.

A complete run of *Poor's Manual of Railroads*, 1860 to 1930, were also in Duke's library. From these volumes I was able to pick up additional information on railroads built and operated within California. He also had *Railway Review* from 1872 to 1904, and in 1905 it was renamed the *Railway & Engineering Review* and ran until 1929. While these journals tended to duplicate the *Railroad Gazette* and *Railway Age,* I still added to my list. I now had over 1,400 railroads that either ran, were proposed, surveyed or constructed within the state of California.

As the years rolled by I picked up additional new railroads from articles in the *Western Railroader, Pacific Rail News,* the *Pacific Lumberman* and the *Journal of Electricity, Power & Gas*. One summer I spent time at the California State Library researching the files of the California Railroad Commission, and paid a visit to the Secretary of State where I checked the incorporation of the state's railroads. Every stone was turned that might hide a railroad that was not already in my file.

I spent nearly two years typing the list all over again, and I also made a list of all the counties where a given railroad was organized. I had the sheets hardbound, ending up with three volumes. Here was an impressive collection of some 1,600 of the state's railroads. John Fickewirth, my son, decided that he would computerize the list. This in itself was another large undertaking. The end result was two huge loose-leaf binders, encompassing the whole list.

California Railroads has more that 1,672 railroads that were organized, built, operated and merged within the state. This list includes incline railroads, short lines, industrial-mineral carriers, horsecar lines, cable car lines, electric street and interurban railroads, main line carriers, etc. This book does not cover the 1,500 speculative or projected railroads that were the dream of some builder or real estate operator. To be included in this encyclopedia, a railroad had to be incorporated and have issued stock, although it may never have been built.

Every reasonable effort has been made to make this book as complete as possible. Although all information has been checked and double-checked against reliable sources, conflicting information is sure to crop up. The best information possible is presented here. Data for some railroads was found to be more detailed for some than for others, but for those with limited information that, unfortunately, was all that was found. In all probability, a reader may know of some obscure railroad that I have overlooked. It is my wish that if anyone finds some conflicting data, would he please let me know in care of the publisher. This has been a life-long effort on my part and, since I am not getting any younger, your early response would be appreciated. Needless to say, any added information or correction of a date will be incorporated in any future edition, making this history even more complete.

As you will see upon reading this book, it is bascially the culmination of 50 years of collecting and recording by this hobbyist so that he might answer the question initially raised at the Kiwanis Club over 40 years ago. "How many railroads has California had or do they have?"

Alvin A. Fickewirth

El Monte
May 1992

Foreword

California, more than any other part of the United States, has captured the imagination of men for a century and a half. It is a land of majestic mountain ranges, forbidding deserts and intimidating wilderness regions. Fringed by the Coast Range along its 800 mile coastline, it is separated by fertile inland valleys and is bordered on the east by the mighty Sierra Nevada Range. The Sacramento, San Joaquin and Imperial valleys quickly became the "bread basket" of the nation, producing cotton, vegetables, fruits and vineyards. California also became a land of instant wealth - a land of gold, oil and gigantic stands of timber. The state has the highest mountain peak in the contiguous United States with its majestic Mount Whitney rising 14,494 feet, and the lowest point in the nation with Death Valley at 282 feet below sea level. It was here in the "Golden State" that 1,672 railroads were either proposed, organized or built between 1854 and 1992.

As late as 1862 California was, for all intents and purposes, isolated from the rest of the United States. The distance from New York to California, by way of Cape Horn, was more than the entire circumference of the globe on the latitude of San Francisco, while the other route across the fever-infested Isthmus of Panama was as long as a direct line from New York to Pekin. Travelling by Overland Stage from St. Joseph on the Missouri River to Placerville on the western slope of the Sierra Nevada Range took 17 days, barring washouts, Indian attacks and other perils. When the rails of the Central Pacific and Union Pacific were joined at Promontory, Utah, in the spring of 1869, the pioneer days of California drew to a close.

This encyclopedia of California Railroads presents every known railroad that ever operated within the borders of the state. All railroads are listed in alphabetical order from "A" to "Y." In the appendix section is a listing of counties, presenting railroads that either began, had its home office or was organized in that particular county. Of all of California's 58 counties, only Alpine County never had a railroad passing through it or built within its borders. Trinity County runs a close second, with only a tip of the Northwestern Pacific Railroad crossing through it in its lower left-hand corner. However, two railroads were proposed within the county, but never built. Sutter County is without railroads, excepting for the passing through of the main lines of the Southern Pacific, Western Pacific and the interurban Sacramento Northern Railroad. The index to this book codes the railroad as to type, such as horsecar, cable car and electric railroad. It also shows whether the railroad is a main line, short line, industrial railroad or proposed railroad.

The bulk of California's railroads were built prior to 1905. After all, transportation was the first order of business in those days. Without railroads to transport goods to market, cities and population centers would never have developed. It is easy to understand how promoters of each railroad, horsecar line and electric railway believed he had a "sure thing." It even got to the point of calling it a bonanza since they felt it could be obtained with little effort. That simply by the laying of rails it would cause a steady stream of dollars to pour into the cash box. Thus, it is no surprise that 505 railroads were proposed, chartered and/or incorporated within California. All offered stock for sale with only a few actually beginning construction, but none of the 505 railroads were ever built. A like number of "dream" railroads were drawn up. They never were formally organized or incorporated and, consequently, are not listed in this encyclopedia.

Twenty-two transcontinental rail ventures were organized outside the state of California. However, they have been mentioned because it was their intent to terminate at a given point within the state. One of the railroads was the Denver, Colorado Canyon & Pacific Railroad. This railroad line planned to build west from Denver, following the Colorado River and terminating at San Diego. In all probability, one of the most farfetched railroad schemes was the San Francisco & Buenos Aires Railroad. It was organized and

3

stock was sold in order to build a railroad line south from San Francisco which would pass through Central America and continue on to Buenos Aires in South America.

The codes shown alongside the index listing best represents the type of railroad that it was. While they may not exactly fit the particular railroad, it best shows its catagory in the broadest of terms.

Public Transportation

Public transportation means the movement of people between two points within a city or metropolitan area. This catagory includes intercity and urban public transport which could be an electric interurban line, light rail system, rapid transit or subway line.

H - *Horsecar Lines* - California had 120 horsecar systems, many of which lasted no more than five years. A horsecar is a horse- or mule-driven streetcar running on rails within the streets of a city.

C - *Cable Car Lines* - The cable car was a technical advancement of the horsecar in which a streetcar is pulled along the streets by attaching itself to a moving cable under the street. Although invented in San Francisco, both Los Angeles and San Diego also had cable railway systems. Under this catagory, California had 33 cable systems which includes mostly incline railways operated by a cable running up and down hills, such as Angels Flight.

E - *Electric Streetcar and Interurban Lines* - The electric streetcar was a technological advancement of the cable car. It received its electric power from overhead wires which in turn was picked up by an overhead trolley pole that had wires running directly to motors mounted on the car's trucks. However, within the state there were three lines that operated by third-rail. This catagory includes streetcar lines, interurban lines, light rail systems, rapid transit and subway lines. Basically, it was any public convenience operated by electricity.

MO - *Motor Road* - In the 1880's self-propelled steam operated streetcars were nothing but a steam locomotive enclosed in a box-like affair. It is suggested that the reason it was done this way was so it would not scare horses. California had 16 motor road operations, mostly in metropolitan areas such as San Francisco, Oakland, Los Angeles and San Diego. The motor road proved impractical and the lines were either abandoned or converted to an electric operation. Motor roads were sometimes referred to as "Dummy" lines.

Common Carrier Railroads

A for-hire railroad that promises to serve the general public and that obtains a certificate of public convenience and necessity requiring that it charge reasonable rates, avoids undue or unjust discrimination, serves the public and delivers the goods. Railroads under this catagory are trunk line carriers that engage in intrastate and interstate movement of railroad cars. They can also be a short line railroad which operates over a short distance, a scenic or park railroad that, for the most part, handles tourists and terminal railroads that handle the switching at a pier or in specific yards.

M - *Main Line* or *Transcontinental Railroads* - In the 142 year history of California, the state has had only four transcontinental railroads. The Atchison, Topeka & Santa Fe Railway, the Southern Pacific, the Union Pacific and the Western Pacific. However, within this catagory the total number of railroads is 63. This includes the lines merged or consolidated to form the four transcontinental carriers. It also includes construction railroads which were incorporated by the carrier to build a specific segment of the system. Such as, i.e., the San Bernardino & Los Angeles Railway built from San Bernardino to San Dimas to connect with the Los Angeles & San Gabriel Valley Railroad in order to provide the Santa Fe with entrance into Los Angeles. After it was built the San Bernardino & Los Angeles Railway was sold to the Atchison, Topeka & Santa Fe Railway. This catagory also includes reorganization of common carrier railroads such as the Atchison, Topeka & Santa Fe Railroad. After its regorganization the only change was its official name from "Railroad" to "Railway."

SL - *Short Line Railroad* - A railroad with a few miles of track that connects with a trunk line. It serves towns or industries not considered to be a profitable operation for a trunk line. An originating carrier only hauls a load 16 miles while a trunk line may haul a car clear across the United States. The short line also receives a higher percentage of a through rate. California has had 220 railroads which fall in this catagory. As trunk line railroads are slimming down, unprofitable branch lines are fast becoming short line railroads which can operate under less restrictive rules than those governing the transcontinental railroads.

T - *Terminal - Switching Railroads* - A short line railroad that tends to operate in a manufacturing district, at a pier or in a specific yard, transferring cars between industrial sidings, providing pick-up and delivery service and interchanging with a trunk line or transcontinental carrier. A perfect example is the Howard Terminal Railway of Oakland or the Los Angeles Junction Railway at Vernon.

A - *Scenic or Park Railroads* - These are railroads, such as the Mount Tamalpais & Muir Woods Railroad, that were operated for the handling of tourists traveling to scenic attractions. The Mount Lowe Railroad was another perfect example. There were

6 such railroads like this in California. The Napa Valley Wine Train, Inc. also falls within this catagory.

Industrial-Commerical Railroad

An industrial or commercial railroad is a short line railroad that was built to strictly haul an owner's product. It could be either an industrial carrier, a logging railroad or one developed to haul ore from a quarry to a reduction mill.

I - *Industrial Railroad* - California has had 155 railroads that served steel mills and provided in-house switching services. It could be a mineral line such as the Ludlow & Southern which hauled ore from the mine at Bagdad to an interchange at Ludlow.

L - *Logging or Lumber Railroads* - For over 100 years logging and lumbering have been big business in California. Over the years, California has had 340 logging railroads. Some with only a few miles of track, while others had nearly a 100 miles. Most logging railrods were not built to the high standards of the common carrier railroads and their tracks were built on the ground without cut and fill grading. Their only purpose was to haul logs to the mill.

MO - *Monorails* - Railroads operating trains on a single rail whose vehicle straddled on both sides of the rail. A perfect example is the Epsom Salts Monorail which operated near Trona, crossing Searles Lake and operating through Wingate Pass to a mine. Other monorails were tried in more populated areas, however, it became complicated to cross a monorail route.

Proposed Railroads (P)

As already mentioned, California had 505 railroads that were proposed, but never built. These are often called a paper railroad. A perfect example is the American High-Speed Rail Corporation of Los Angeles which was proposed less than 10 years ago. This corporation was organized to build a "Bullet Type" high-speed railroad from Los Angeles International Airport to downtown Los Angeles and then on to San Diego. It was to be either above ground or in a cut and there were to be no grade crossings the entire distance. The firm organized, made plans, incorporated and sold stock. It was never built and was killed by the Environmental Impact Reports. At the turn of the century a number of street railways and short lines were proposed to serve a given community or industry, but were never built. To be included in this catagory a railroad had to have been proposed, incorporated or formal structure developed and stock offered for sale. In a limited number of cases some right-of-way was graded and a certain amount of rolling stock purchased. Several paper or proposed railroads were merged or consolidated into other carriers in order to obtain their franchise.

Track Gauge

The completion of the transcontinental railroad in 1869 not only solved the transportation problem across the American West, but it helped to settle America's rail gauge problem. Since the first railroad was built in this country, nearly every railroad chose its own width of track; in fact, it was thought to be an advantage to differ in gauge so that another railroad could not steal its business. As America continued to grow this became very impractical since most all freight was carried beyond the scope of a single railroad, thus requiring transshipment between various railroads of differing gauges.

When the Central Pacific-Union Pacific was being planned, President Lincoln was asked to fix the width of track, making it a standard gauge for the United States. Congress set the standard at 4 feet 8 1/2 inches between the heads of the rails. Legend has it that this width was the exact distance between the wheel-treads of a Roman Imperial Chariot's wheels. In the meantime, Great Britian had also chosen this as their standard gauge for its railroads.

The majority of California's railroads accepted standard gauge. At least those who wished to interchange cars between railroads. The second choice was narrow-gauge or three feet between rail heads. Thus, anything smaller than standard gauge became known as narrow-gauge while all gauges larger were referred to as broad gauge.

California's first railroad, the Sacramento Valley Railroad, was built to five feet 3 1/2 inch gauge. However, once the Central Pacific made a connection with it, the railroad was quickly converted to standard gauge. The California Central was originally a 5-foot gauge railroad, and it also immediately converted to standard gauge. The Antioch Railroad was built to 26-inch gauge and remained so its entire life. By 1880 nearly all railroads in California were either standard or narrow-gauge.

Most horsecar lines were either built to 3-foot 6-inch gauge or five-foot gauge. Cable railroads seemed to standardize on 3-foot 6-inch between rails, however, the electric railroads within the state set 4 feet 8 1/2 inches between the rails. For city streetcar lines that did not interchange, they were established as 3 feet between rails or 3 feet 6 inches. For some unknown reason, San Diego's City & University Heights Motor Road chose 3 feet 8 1/2 inches between rails.

The Arcata & Mad River Railroad, an early logging line, pondered the matter of its gauge in 1881. It finally decided that the most comfortable width for the single horse-drawn vehicles was a track gauge of 3 feet 9 1/2 inches. Logging railroads seemed to vary a great deal depending on the mountain country in which they operated. The Little River Redwood Company chose 3 feet 9 1/4 inches while the Warren Creek Railroad's line was built to 4 feet 9 1/4 inches. Many industrial or mining railroads that were service-oriented and did not interchange railcars chose 24- or 26-inch gauge.

When the Bay Area Rapid Transit (BART) was built, it chose 5 feet 6 inch gauge, throwing 70 years of standardization out the window.

SAN FRANCISCO MUNICIPAL RAILWAY - Car No. 1 was retired from active service in 1951, demotorized, and stored. This car was restored to its original condition for a 1962 celebration and placed in excursion service. It is shown here climbing the grade through Mission Park on the "J" Line on a rail enthusiasts excursion. - *Jim Wren*

Table of Contents

ATCHISON, TOPEKA & SANTA FE RAILWAY - The last offical run of a steam locomotive over Cajon Pass took place on February 6, 1955. No. 3759 was brought out of storage to power this Railway Club of Southern California's excursion entitled the "Farewell to Steam." In this view, No. 3759 races across the Mojave Desert west of Helendale. - *Donald Duke*

ALAMEDA BELT LINE RAILROAD

Organized 1917 - Steam - Standard Gauge

Located Alameda, Alameda County. Built by the city of Alameda along Clement Avenue from near Broadway to Grand Street. Distance 1.205 miles. At this time, operations were by the Southern Pacific Company. The Alameda Belt Line, Inc. purchased the properties and planned to extend the tracks to Morton Street (Encinal Terminals) and westward to the San Francisco Bay, a distance of 2.65 miles. Acquired by the Atchison, Topeka & Santa Fe R.R. and the Western Pacific R.R. January 12, 1925.

ALAMEDA BELT LINE - A switching railroad located around Encinal Terminal in Alameda. This joint Santa Fe/Western Pacific operation used 0-6-0 switchers before converting to diesel engines. - *Donald Duke Collection*

ALAMEDA COUNTY RAILWAY COMPANY

Organized November 1887 - Steam 1888-1895 - Electric 1895-1936 - Standard Gauge

Located Alameda, Alameda County. Began operations January 10, 1888 from Fruitvale to Laundry Farm Canyon via Leona Heights. Became the Oakland, Alameda & Laundry Farm R.R. Sold to the California Railway. Incorporated August 16, 1890. Extension built into Alameda to Park Street Bridge in 1896. Sold to the Oakland Traction Company in 1901. Consolidated into the San Francisco-Oakland Terminal Rys. 1912. Was electrified in 1895 and became the first electric railway in California to handle steam railroad equipment in interchange service. Became part of the Key System Transit Co. June 6, 1923. Abandoned June 10, 1936.

ALAMEDA COUNTY TERMINAL RAILWAY COMPANY

Incorporated August 8, 1889 - Electric - Standard Gauge

Located Alameda, Alameda County. Organized to take over a section of the Alameda County R.R. and to extend trackage to Custer Valley and stone quarries. Distance 14.75 miles. Merged into the Key System Transit Company June 6, 1923. Abandoned June 10, 1936.

ALAMEDA & HAYWARDS RAILROAD ALAMEDA RAILROAD COMPANY

Organized 1863 -

Located Alameda, Alameda County. Built from Bay Front to Howards. Distance 15.00 miles. Completed 1869.

ALAMEDA & OAKLAND HORSECAR RAILROAD COMPANY

Franchise granted 1870 - Horsecar 1874-1893 - Electric 1893-1936 - Standard Gauge

Located Alameda, Alameda County. Construction began in 1874 and built along Webster Street to Fassking's Park. Extended track to Park Street in 1876 and continued on High Street to Fruitvale Avenue in 1877. Crossed San Antonio Creek at Webster Street and began service to Oakland in 1882. Sold to the California Railway Company July 5, 1892. Electrified and renamed Alameda, Oakland & Piedmont Electric Railroad Company January 6, 1893. Became part of the Key System Transit Company June 6, 1923. Abandoned June 10, 1936.

ALAMEDA, OAKLAND & PIEDMONT ELECTRIC RAILROAD COMPANY

Began operations January 6, 1893 - Electric - Standard Gauge

Located Oakland, Alameda County. Purchased the California Railway Co. Became part of the Key System Transit Co. June 6, 1923. Abandoned June 10, 1936.

ALAMEDA, OAKLAND & PIEDMONT RAILWAY COMPANY

Chartered October 4, 1870 - Horsecar - 3 ft. Gauge

Located Oakland, Alameda County. Proposed to build to Alameda. Distance 7.55 miles. Steam power was to be used. Became a local Oakland street railway. Operated 5.00 miles of trackage.

ALAMEDA & SAN JOAQUIN VALLEY RAILROAD COMPANY

Incorporated May 1, 1895 - Steam - Standard Gauge

Located Stockton, San Joaquin County. Proposed to build a railroad from the coal mines of the San Francisco & San Joaquin Coal Co. at Corral Hollow via Lathrop and Tracy to the San Joaquin River near the dividing line between San Joaquin and Contra Costa counties. First contract for construction let July 29, 1895. Completed to Tesla via Carbona June 19, 1895. Distance 36.60 miles. Sold to the Western Pacific R.R. July 25, 1903. Section Carbona to Stockton became part of the Western Pacific main line. Trackage to Tesla abandoned January 1916.

ALAMEDA VALLEY RAILROAD

Organized 1863 or 1864 - Steam

Located Alameda, Alameda County. Built south to Villages Mill. Junction was to be made with the Western Pacific Railroad. Began operations in 1864.

ALBION LUMBER COMPANY RAILWAY

Organized May 26, 1891 - Steam - Standard Gauge

Located Albion, Mendocino County. Built a logging railroad from Albion to Christine. Distance 12.00 miles. Sold to the Albion & South Eastern R.R. January 17, 1905. Sold to the Northwestern Pacific R.R. Co. January 8, 1907. Ceased operation January 16, 1930. Dismantled December 10, 1937.

ALBION RIVER RAILROAD

Incorporated September 24, 1885 - Steam - Standard Gauge

Located Albion, Mendocino County. Built a logging railroad from Albion on the coast to timber. Distance 7.00 miles. Sold to the Albion & Southeastern Railway May 9, 1902. Sold to the Fort Bragg & Southeastern R.R. January 17, 1905. Sold to the Northwestern Pacific R.R. January 8, 1907. Ceased operations January 16, 1930. Dismantled December 10, 1937.

ALBION & SOUTHEASTERN RAILWAY

Incorporated May 8, 1902 - Steam - Standard Gauge

Located Albion, Mendocino County. Purchased the Albion River R.R. and the Albion Lumber Company R.R. Operated a railroad from Albion, at the mouth of the Albion River, to Boonville following the course of the Albion River. Distance 35.00 miles. Sold to the Fort Bragg & Southeastern Railroad Company January 17, 1905. Sold to the Northwestern Pacific Railroad Company January 8, 1907. Ceased operations January 16, 1930. Dismantled December 10, 1937.

ALBION & WETHERBEE COMPANY

Operated in 1880's - Standard Gauge

Located Albion, Mendocino County. Built ten miles of trackage from mill to timber.

ALCATRAZ ISLAND RAILROAD

Organized 1865 - Steam - Standard Gauge

Located Alcatraz Island, San Francisco County. Began operations in 1865 or 1866. Built from dock to interior of prison building. Distance .25 miles. Operated by Department of Army from 1868 to 1933. Transferred to Department of Justice in 1933. Ceased operations in 1963.

ALHAMBRA & PASADENA STREET RAILWAY COMPANY

Incorporated June 6, 1887 - Steam - 3 ft. 6 in. Gauge

Located Alhambra, Los Angeles County. Built from the Southern Pacific Company's Alhambra Station on Garfield Avenue north to Raymond Station on Fair Oaks Avenue and then to Colorado Street. Distance 5.00 miles. Began operation June 6, 1888. Converted to horsecar operation 1893. Abandoned 1893.

ALMADEN BRANCH RAILROAD COMPANY

Incorporated April 14, 1887 - Steam - 3 ft. Gauge

Located Campbell, Santa Cruz County. Built to New Almaden. Distance 9.60 miles. Completed 1886. Consolidated with South Pacific Coast R.R. May 23, 1887. Abandoned 1937.

ALMANOR RAILROAD COMPANY

Organized 1944 - Steam - Standard Gauge

Located Chester, Plumas County. Purchased 13.20 miles of the Red River Lumber Company R.R. trackage between Clear Creek Junction (Red River Junction) and Chester.

ALPINE LUMBER COMPANY

Organized 1908 - Steam - Standard Gauge

Located Santa Cruz, Santa Cruz County. Built 2.00 miles of trackage. Abandoned 1913.

ALTADENA RAILWAY

Incorporated February 19, 1887 - Horsecar - Standard Gauge

Located Altadena, Los Angeles County. Constructed a 7.00 mile horsecar street railway to Pasadena. Became Los Angeles, Pasadena & Glendale R.R. November 1889 and purchased the Los Angeles & Glendale R.R. Sold to the Los Angeles Terminal R.R. 1890. Now part of the Union Pacific R.R.

AMADOR BRANCH RAILROAD COMPANY

Incorporated July 3, 1875 - Steam - Standard Gauge

Located Galt, Sacramento County. Built to Ione. Opened for traffic December 3, 1876. Consolidated with the Northern R.R. Co. May 15, 1888. Consolidated with Southern Pacific Co. April 14, 1898. Trackage is now known as the Ione Branch of the Southern Pacific Co., connecting at Ione with the Amador Central R.R. Co.

AMADOR CENTRAL RAILROAD COMPANY

Incorporated September 24, 1908 - Steam - Standard Gauge

Located Martell, Amador County. Purchased the Ione & Eastern R.R. at a foreclosure sale August 22, 1908. Distance Ione 12.00 miles. Trackage from junction with the Southern Pacific Co. at Ione to Martell.

AMADOR RAILROAD COMPANY

Incorporated November 27, 1893 - Steam

Located Amador, Amador County. Stock issue placed on sale November 2, 1895, in Amador City. Project abandoned 1896.

AMADOR CENTRAL RAILROAD - A 12-mile short line operating off the Southern Pacific at Ione to Martell. This scene shows an excursion train leaving Ione in 1948. *- Arthur Lloyd*

AMARGOSA VALLEY RAILROAD COMPANY

Incorporated April 27, 1907 - Steam - Standard Gauge

Located San Bernardino County. Proposed to build from a point near Dumont on the Tonopah & Tidewater R.R. to a location across the Amargosa Valley. No construction work was done.

AMERICAN BORAX COMPANY

Organized 1901 - Steam - 3 ft. Gauge

Located Daggett, San Bernardino County. Built to the Columbia Mines. Distance 7.00 miles. One mile of track belonging to the Waterloo Mine R.R. was used. Ceased operation November 1907.

AMERICAN BULK LOADING ENTERPRISES

Located in San Pedro, Los Angeles County. Operates four miles of switching road at the Outer Harbor Bulk Terminal at a wharf at San Pedro's coal terminal.

AMERICAN CANYON RAILROAD

Steam - Standard Gauge

Located Auburn, Placer County. Built from a junction with the Southern Pacific Company west of Auburn to a quarry on the north fork of the American River.

AMERICAN COLONY RAILWAY COMPANY

Organized August 20, 1882 - Horsecar - Narrow-Gauge Steam - Standard Gauge

Located Long Beach, Los Angeles County. Built from Willmore Station on the Southern Pacific near Wilmington to Willmore City (Long Beach). Distance 1.15 miles. Was popularly called the "G.O.P." or the "Get Out and Push R.R." Horsecar line replaced in 1886 by a new standard gauge line built beside the narrow-gauge tracks. Taken into the Southern Pacific Co. July 19, 1887.

AMERICAN FRUIT GROWERS, INC.

Organized 1920 - Steam - Standard Gauge

Located Macdoel, Siskiyou County. Purchased the properties of the Dwinnell Lumber Company. Abandoned 1922.

AMERICAN HIGH SPEED RAIL CORPORATION OF LOS ANGELES

Organized December 1981

Located Los Angeles, Los Angeles County. Proposed to build a "bullet train type" of high speed railroad from Los Angeles south to San Diego. A branch line would be built to the Los Angeles International Airport. This section would be elevated and built along the shoulder of Interstate Highway 5 to the Los Angeles City station. Project abandoned November 13, 1984.

AMERICAN PACIFIC RAILROAD COMPANY

Incorporated September 15, 1897 - Steam -Standard Gauge

Incorporated in Kansas. Board members were men from California, Kansas and Georgia. Proposed to build a system of railroads from Savannah, Georgia and Jacksonville, Florida, west through Georgia, Alabama, Louisiana, Texas, New Mexico and Arizona to San Diego, California, with a north and south branch from Velasco, Texas north through Oklahoma, Kansas, Nebraska and South Dakota to the Canadian border in North Dakota. Another line was projected through Texas into Mexico ending at Topolobampo Bay. A railroad was to be incorporated in California to build eastward to Yuma, Arizona from San Diego.

AMERICAN RAPID TRANSIT COMPANY OF SOUTHERN CALIFORNIA

Incorporated April 16, 1887 - Electric

Located Alhambra, Los Angeles County. Planned to build to Los Angeles with branch lines to Pasadena, El Monte, Pomona, Long Beach and Santa Monica. Cars were to be suspended on overhead rails. A 14-foot clearance was to be standard. No construction work was done.

AMERICAN REDWOOD COMPANY

Organized 1915 - Steam - Standard Gauge

Located Gualala, Mendocino County. Purchased the Empire Redwood Co. properties. Distance 22.00 miles. Sold to the National Redwood Company 1920. Abandoned 1923.

AMERICAN RIVER, LAND & LUMBER COMPANY

Organized 1892 - Steam - 3 ft. Gauge

Located Folsom, El Dorado County. Built from mill to timber. Sold to the El Dorado Lumber Co. 1901. Sold to the Michigan California Lumber Co. 1911. Abandoned 1950.

AMTRAK

Organized January 18, 1970 - Diesel - Standard Gauge

On January 18, 1970 the Department of Transportation announced the formation of RAILPAX, a quasi-public corporation concept, for the operation of the nation's intercity passenger trains. By the time RAILPAX was to start on May 1, 1971, taking over specific popular routes for a basic system, the name was changed to AMTRAK. Within California, on the Southern Pacific, the Los Angeles to New Orleans route, the Los Angeles to Portland route, and San Francisco to Ogden route, were taken into the basic system. On the Santa Fe, the Los Angeles to Chicago route, the Los Angeles to San Diego commuter corridor were selected. Since the basic system has been established, the Santa Fe's Oakland-Bakersfield service has been reinitiated, and Union Pacific's Los Angeles to Ogden connection with service to Chicago.

AMTRAK - One of the ''Jewels'' of Amtrak operations is the Los Angeles-San Diego service with two scheduled runs extending to Santa Barbara. This train was photographed along the shores of the blue Pacific Ocean at San Clemente. - *Donald Duke*

ANAHEIM CITY & INTERURBAN RAILWAY

Incorporated May 1, 1912 - Electric - Standard Gauge

Located Anaheim, Orange County. Proposed to build an electric railway connecting Anaheim with Santa Ana, Fullerton, Orange and Los Angeles.

ANAHEIM, OLINDA & POMONA RAILROAD COMPANY

Incorporated January 10, 1888 - Standard Gauge

Located Anaheim, Orange County. Proposed to build from Alamitos Bay via Anaheim, Olinda, Carlton, Chico Ranch, Riverside and Colton to San Bernardino. A branch was to be built to Pomona. Total distance planned 96.00 miles. Grading completed 9.55 miles. Construction suspended January 1, 1889.

ANAHEIM RAILWAY

Incorporated November 1870 - Steam - Standard Gauge

Located Anaheim, Orange County. Proposed to build to Anaheim Landing on the Pacific Ocean. Project abandoned 1871.

ANAHEIM - SAN BERNARDINO RAILROAD

Incorporated September 5, 1868 - Steam - Standard Gauge

Located Anaheim, Orange County. Proposed to build a railroad from San Bernardino to Anaheim Landing on the Pacific Ocean via the town of Anaheim. Project abandoned.

ANAHEIM STREET RAILWAY COMPANY

Incorporated February 1, 1887 - Horsecar

Located Anaheim, Orange County. Built 1.50 miles of street railway.

ANAHEIM STREET RAILWAY - Anaheim's first city rail service carried passengers down Center Street from the Santa Fe to Southern Pacific station, circa 1890. - *First American Title Insurance Co.*

ANAHEIM - TUSTIN RAILROAD

Steam - Standard Gauge

Located Anaheim, Orange County. Built to Tustin. The official name of the Southern Pacific Anaheim-Tustin branch during organization and construction.

ANDERSON & BELLA VISTA RAILROAD

Organized 1909 or 1910 - Steam - Standard Gauge

Located Anderson, Shasta County. Built from Anderson on the Southern Pacific to Bella Vista. Distance 16.00 miles. Sold to the California, Shasta & Eastern Ry. 1913. Abandoned 1927.

ANDERSON & MIDDLETON LUMBER COMPANY

Organized 1902 - Steam - Standard Gauge

Located Bear Harbor, Mendocino County. Built 36 miles of trackage. Road abandoned 1904 or 1905.

ANGELS FLIGHT RAILWAY - Built as the Los Angeles Incline Railway in 1910, this 335-foot cable line carried passengers between Hill and Olive streets for 59 years. - *Donald Duke Collection*

ANGELS FLIGHT RAILWAY COMPANY

Incorporated November 11, 1912 - Cable - 2 ft. 6 in. Gauge

Located Los Angeles, Los Angeles County. Franchise granted May 20, 1910, to the Los Angeles Incline Ry. to build a 335-foot long cable car line between Olive and Hill streets on Bunker Hill. Became Angels Flight Ry. Co. November 11, 1912. Last run May 18, 1969. Dismantling began May 19, 1969.

ANTIOCH & GRANGERVILLE RAILROAD COMPANY

Incorporated 1880

Located in Contra Costa County. Proposed to build a prismoidal railroad from Moore's Landing on the San Joaquin River to Hill's Ferry a distance of 50.00 miles. Project abandoned 1881.

ANTIOCH & VISALIA RAILROAD

Proposed in 1870 or 1871. -

Located in Contra Costa County.

ANTIOCH RAILROAD COMPANY

Organized in 1899 - Steam - 26 in. Gauge

Located Antioch, Contra Costa County. Resulted from the reorganization of the Empire Coal Mine & Railroad Company. Operated trackage to Empire Coal Mines on Mt. Diablo. Distance 6.75 miles. Abandoned in 1901.

AQUEDUCT CONSTRUCTION PROJECT - CITY OF LOS ANGELES

Constructed 1907 - Steam - 3 ft. Gauge

Located in Los Angeles, Los Angeles County. Built along sections of the Los Angeles Aqueduct during construction period. Completed November 5, 1913. Abandoned 1914.

ARCADIA & MONROVIA RAILWAY COMPANY

Incorporated May 7, 1887 - Steam - Standard Gauge

Located Arcadia, Los Angeles County. Proposed to build from County Road and First Avenue to Orange Avenue and Falling Leaf Avenue, Monrovia. Distance 3.10 miles. Grading began in Arcadia April 1887. Project abandoned May 1887.

ARCATA & MAD RIVER RAILROAD COMPANY

Incorporated July 22, 1881 - Steam - 3 ft. 9 ¼ in. Gauge - Standard Gauge

Located Korbel, Humboldt County. Organized to take over the properties of the Arcata Transportation Company and proposed to extend the trackage from the Wharf in Humboldt Bay to Mad River. Reached Korbel (North Fork) in 1882. Distance 12.90 miles. Standard gauged tracks between junction with the Northwestern Pacific R.R. at Korblex to Korbel in 1925. Distance 7.50 miles. Narrow-gauge tracks from Wharf to Korblex removed 1942.

ARCATA MILL & LUMBER COMPANY

Organized 1887 or 1889 - Steam - Standard Gauge

Located Arcata, Humboldt County. Operated one mile of track around mill.

ARCATA & MAD RIVER RAILROAD - At the turn of the century, a two-car passenger train is ready to leave Arcata for Korbel. One of a few California logging railroads that had passenger service. - *W.C. Whittaker Collection*

AQUEDUCT CONSTRUCTION PROJECT - A mule-operated railway was used to distribute pipe along sections of the Los Angeles Aqueduct. The railway operated for seven years. - *Los Angeles Dept. of Water & Power*

ARCATA TRANSPORTATION COMPANY

Incorporated June 15, 1878 - Steam - 3 ft. 9 ¼ in. Gauge

Located Arcata, Humboldt County. Organized to take over the Union Plank Walk & Railroad Co. Extended trackage to Isaac Minor Mill on Warren Creek. Total mileage operated 6.26 miles. Deeded to Arcata & Mad River R.R. July 22, 1881.

ARIZONA & CALIFORNIA RAILROAD COMPANY

Incorporated September 10, 1903 - Steam - Standard Gauge

Located Matthie, Arizona. Built from A & C Junction on the Santa Fe, Prescott & Phoenix R.R. near Wickenburg, Arizona to Cadiz, California. Completed to Salome, Arizona July 10, 1905. Distance 50.03 miles. Completed from Salome, Arizona to Parker, Arizona June 17, 1907. Distance 56.81 miles. Completed from Parker, Arizona to Cadiz, California July 1, 1910. Distance 83.43 miles. First train from Phoenix, Arizona to Los Angeles, California over the Arizona & California R.R. tracks July 1, 1910. Sold to the California, Arizona & Santa Fe R.R. and leased to the Santa Fe R.R. December 28, 1911.

ARIZONA & CALIFORNIA RAILROAD COMPANY

Incorporated 1991 - Diesel - Standard Gauge

Located Parker, Arizona. Operated former Santa Fe Railway trackage purchased by David Parkinson between Cadiz, San Bernardino County to Matthie, AZ, over a distance of 249.3 miles. A branch line from Rice, San Bernardino County runs to Ripley, Riverside County, a distance of 49.4 miles. Total mileage is 244.6 miles. The road has obtained trackage rights over the Santa Fe Railway from Matthie to Phoenix, a distance of 54.1 miles. The road is operated by nine diesel locomotives. The first train operated on May 9, 1991.

ARROWHEAD & WATERMAN RAILROAD

Incorporated 1891 - Steam - Standard Gauge

Located San Bernardino, San Bernardino County. Proposed to build into the San Bernardino Mountains to Arrowhead Springs and Waterman. No work done.

ATCHISON, TOPEKA & SANTA FE RAILROAD COMPANY

Incorporated February 11, 1859 - Steam - Standard Gauge

Located National City, San Diego County. Ground broken December 20, 1880, for construction of the California Southern R.R. from National City to San Bernardino. Organized as a successor to Atchison & Topeka Railroad Company. Incorporated the California Southern R.R. October 12, 1880. Obtained a half interest in the Atlantic & Pacific Railroad Company. Organized eight companies which built or were formed to build branch lines in Southern California. Merged these eight companies into the California Central Ry. Company May 20, 1887. Built the Redondo Beach Railway Company incorporated April 23, 1888. All except the Atlantic & Pacific R.R. Company were consolidated into the Southern California Ry. Company November 7, 1889. Sold at auction in 1895 and reorganized as the Atchison, Topeka & Santa Fe Railway Company.

ATCHISON, TOPEKA & SANTA FE RAILWAY COMPANY

Incorporated December 12, 1895 - Steam - Standard Gauge

Located Southern California. Took over the assets of the Atchison, Topeka & Santa Fe Railroad Company which were purchased at the receiver's sale May 1895. Controlled the Southern California Railway Company and the half interest in the Atlantic & Pacific Railroad Company in California. Acquired the latter at receiver's sale and reorganized it as the Santa Fe Pacific R.R. Company in 1897. Latter was conveyed to the Atchison, Topeka & Santa Fe Ry. Company in 1902. Leased Southern California Railway Company in June 1904 and acquired it January 17, 1906. Built, leased, acquired or controlled wholly or jointly, and operated many roads in California including the San Francisco & San Joaquin Valley Ry. Company, Northwestern Pacific Railroad Company, California Eastern Ry. Company, Sunset Ry. Company, Arizona & Santa Fe Ry. Company and others.

ATLANTIC & PACIFIC RAILROAD COMPANY

Incorporated July 27, 1866 - Steam - Standard Gauge

Atchison, Topeka & Santa Fe R.R. Company and the St. Louis & San

ATLANTIC & PACIFIC RAILROAD - This Mastadon-type locomotive was one of several engines used to haul freight across Arizona and California before the line became the Santa Fe Railway. - *Donald Duke Collection*

Francisco Ry. Company joined in a partnership in 1879 to build the western section of the Atlantic & Pacific R.R. Company under the original charter, from south of Albuquerque, New Mexico Territory, to San Francisco and other California points on the 35th Parallel Route. Stopped by the Southern Pacific R.R. Company of California which built from Mojave to Needles and the Colorado River in 1883. Distance 242.5 miles. The Southern Pacific agreed to sell its line in 1884 but the Atlantic & Pacific R.R. Company had to accept a lease until the titles were cleared. Built from Beal, California, to the Colorado River. Opened May 10, 1890. Forced into receivership in 1895, terminating the partnership. Purchased by the Atchison, Topeka & Santa Fe Ry. May 3, 1897. Reorganized as the Santa Fe Pacific R.R. Company June 24, 1897. Conveyed to the Santa Fe Ry. July 1, 1902.

ATLAS - OLYMPIA COMPANY RAILROAD

Steam - Standard Gauge

Located Stanislaus County. A quarry road built from the end of the Atlas Branch of the Sierra Ry. Abandoned.

AUBURN BRANCH RAILROAD

Surveyed July 21, 1858 - Steam

Located Auburn, Placer County. Survey made to join the California Central Railroad at the most feasible point.

AUBURN STREET RAILWAY

Organized April 28, 1899 - Electric - Standard or 3 ft. Gauge

Located Auburn, Placer County. This company asked for a franchise to build a street railway in the town of Auburn. No construction work was done. Some surveys were made in 1901. The plan was reorganized April 6, 1912 and surveys were made to build from Aeolia Heights on the eastern city limits to the new Southern Pacific Company depot on Nevada Street.

AVENUE RAILROAD

Organized 1877 - Horsecar

Located Santa Cruz, Santa Cruz County. Purchased the Santa Cruz & Felton Railroad and extended it along Mission Street to the Pope House. In 1880 extended tracks along the beach, a distance of .25 miles. Became the Pacific Avenue Railroad in 1885. Electrified and became the Santa Cruz, Garfield Park & Capitola Electric Railroad in 1891.

AVILA & SUNSET RAILWAY COMPANY

Organized July 1902 - Steam - Standard Gauge

Located Guadaloupe, Santa Barbara County. Proposed to build a railroad in the vicinity of Santa Maria with two branches, one passing about two miles south of Santa Maria, the other through Arroyo Grande and the Avila Valley. Project abandoned in 1903.

AZUSA, POMONA & ELSINORE RAILROAD COMPANY

Incorporated 1895 - Steam - Standard Gauge

Located Pomona, Los Angeles County. This railroad proposed to build from Pomona to Lake Elsinore, and to construct a branch westerly to Azusa. The proposed length of this line was to be 57 miles, including the three mile Azusa Branch. The initial stock offering was for $1,500,000. With limited sale of the stock, the railroad folded up.

BAY AREA RAPID TRANSIT - Shortly after partial operations began on BART, a Concord bound train pulls into Lake Merritt station on October 17, 1972. Operation through the underwater bay tunnel to San Francisco did not begin until September 16, 1974. - *Harre Demoro*

B

BACK & FORTH RAILROAD

Built 1967 - Diesel - Standard Gauge

Located near Surf, Santa Barbara County. Built six miles south of Surf to the Southern Pacific Railroad station at Surf in the Space and Missile Test Center. (Santec of Vandenberg Air Force Base). Began operations March 1970.

BAJA CALIFORNIA & SONORA RAILROAD COMPANY

Proposed 1881 - Steam - Standard Gauge

Located National City, San Diego County. Proposed to build via Baja, California and Sonora, Mexico to Calabasas, Arizona Territory, north of Nogales, to connect the California Southern R.R. with the New Mexico & Arizona Ry. and the Sonora Ry. Ground broken in the Tijuana River Valley in 1882. No construction work done.

BAKERSFIELD & KERN ELECTRIC RAILWAY

Incorporated March 26, 1900 - Electric - Standard Gauge

Located Bakersfield, Kern County. Built 2.12 miles of electric street railway. Began operation February 17, 1901. Extended trackage to 7.50 miles by 1908. Extended to 10.51 miles between 1916 and 1917. Abandoned February 29, 1942.

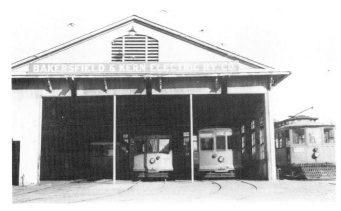

BAKERSFIELD & KERN ELECTRIC RAILWAY - The Bakersfield car barn as it appeared in 1935. The main route ran from the Southern Pacific depot at Sumner to the Santa Fe depot in the center of downtown. Four routes radiated into the residential area from the main route. - *Charles Smallwood*

BAKERSFIELD & LOS ANGELES RAILWAY COMPANY

Incorporated September 1898 - Steam - Standard Gauge

Located Bakersfield, Kern County. Proposed to build to Los Angeles by way of Tejon Pass. Company disbanded April 28, 1899.

BAKERSFIELD & SAN LUIS OBISPO RAILROAD COMPANY

Proposed October 30, 1875 - Steam - Standard Gauge

Located Bakersfield, Kern County. Proposed to build a railroad to the Pacific Coast at San Luis Obispo. Distance 125 miles. No construction work done.

BAKERSFIELD & VENTURA RAILWAY

Applied for franchise January 1902 - Electric - Standard Gauge

Located Fillmore, Ventura County. Proposed to build from "Brownstone Spur" on the Southern Pacific at Fillmore along Grand Avenue then north into Devil's Gate, the entrance to Sespe Canyon. Right-of-way was obtained through the Sespe Mts. to Mutah and Lockwood valleys, and along the Cuyanne River to Maricopa (Sunset).

BAKERSFIELD & VENTURA RAILWAY

Organized January 1902 - Steam - Standard Gauge

Located Oxnard, Ventura County. Took over the franchises of the Santa Clara Valley Electric Railway & Power Company March 1902. Proposed to build from a junction with the Southern Pacific at Fillmore to the entrance of Sespe Canyon then to Mutah and Lockwood valleys and on down the Cuyama Valley to Sunset (Maricopa). Surveys were begun April 1902. Reincorporated February 1903 as the Bakersfield & Ventura Ry. Company. The new franchise called for building a road from the San Fernando Valley north through Calabasas Pass to Triunfo and to Fillmore via Grimes Canyon. The original survey would be used to Sunset. From Sunset the road would run along the west side of the San Joaquin Valley to Pacheco Pass and then across the Santa Clara Valley and through the foothills to Santa Cruz. A grading camp was set up on the Patterson Ranch October 1903. Grading began on Oxnard streets December 13, 1903. Opened for traffic to Port Hueneme July 4, 1905. Sold to the Ventura County Railway in 1911.

BALLONA & SANTA MONICA RAILROAD COMPANY

Incorporated May 3, 1887 - Standard Gauge

Located Santa Monica, Los Angeles County. Built from a junction with the Southern Pacific Company on Railroad Street to Port Ballona. Distance 6.85 miles. Surveys finished January 5, 1889. Began operations 1892.

BARNWELL & SEARCHLIGHT RAILWAY COMPANY

Incorporated April 16, 1906 - Steam - Standard Gauge

Located Barnwell, San Bernardino County. Built to Searchlight, Nevada. Distance 23.22 miles. Construction began May 1906. Began operations April 1907. Purchased some right-of-way from the Searchlight & Northern R.R. Company. Leased to the Santa Fe Ry. 1907. Deeded to the Santa Fe Ry. December 28, 1911. Abandoned 1923.

BART - BAY AREA RAPID TRANSIT

Created June 4, 1957 - Electric - 5 ft. 6 in. Gauge

Located Oakland, Alameda County. Created by the California State Legislature in 1957 to build a rapid transit system to serve the nine counties surrounding San Francisco. BART is a 75-mile double-track system, connecting Richmond on the north, Concord on the east, and Fremont on the south with San Francisco and Daly City by means of a tunnel under San Francisco Bay. Partial operations began September 11, 1972, and full operation through the tunnel to San Francisco began September 16, 1974.

BAY & COAST RAILROAD COMPANY

Incorporated May 2, 1877 - Steam - 3 ft. Gauge

Located Alameda, Alameda County. Built from Newark via Mulford and across San Leandro Bay to High Street in Alameda and around Alameda via Encinal Avenue, Center Avenue, Alameda Point and Oakland junction to join the Oakland Township Ry. Distance 25.20 miles. Opened for service May 30, 1881. Sold to South Pacific Coast R.R. May 23, 1887. Leased to the Southern Pacific Company July 1, 1887. Standard gauged 1906.

BAY & COAST RAILWAY

Incorporated 1899 - Steam and Electric - 3 ft. Gauge

Located San Francisco, San Francisco County. The goal of this railroad was to build a line from San Francisco to Santa Cruz, a distance of 80 miles. No construction work done.

BAY COUNTIES ELECTRIC RAILROAD COMPANY

Incorporated December 1, 1905 - Electric - Standard Gauge

Located San Rafael, Marin County. Proposed to build to Napa, going from San Francisco by ferry across the bay to a point from Marin County and then through Sonoma and Napa counties to Napa City. Construction work began September 1907 by crews working from San Rafael and Towne Ranch. Distance 2.00 miles.

BAY COUNTIES POWER COMPANY

Organized January 1902 - Electric - Standard Gauge

Located Calistoga, Napa County. Proposed to build to Sausalito by way of St. Helena, Napa and Sonoma. At Sonoma a branch line was to be built to Santa Rosa, Healdsburg and Geyserville. No work done.

BAY POINT & CLAYTON RAILROAD COMPANY

Incorporated August 29, 1906 - Steam - Standard Gauge

Located Bay Point (Port Chicago), Contra Costa County. Built from Bay Point to Cowell. Distance 10.25 miles. Completed April 9, 1909. 8.00 miles sold to the U.S. Navy in 1941. Remaining 2.25 miles abandoned 1953.

BAY POINT & CLAYTON RAILROAD - An industrial railroad that ran from Bay Point (Port Chicago) to Cowell, a distance of 10.25 miles. - *Guy L. Dunscomb*

BAY SHORE & PACIFIC RAILROAD COMPANY

Incorporated September 22, 1905 - Steam - Standard Gauge

Located San Diego, San Diego County. Proposed to build from a point near the southern boundary of San Diego to Pacific Beach and La Jolla, and then to the northern boundary of San Diego. This was to be the first portion of a railroad that was to be built to Imperial and Humor. No construction work was done.

BAY SHORE RAILROAD COMPANY

Incorporated June 15, 1914 - Electric - Standard Gauge

Located San Diego, San Diego County. Proposed to build from Ocean Beach across the channel of False Bay and along the Strand to Bird Rock Beach in San Diego. Franchise granted July 18, 1914. Built from a junction with the Point Loma Railroad at Bacon and Voltaire streets, Ocean Beach, San Diego, north through Mission Beach to Pacific Avenue, Pacific Beach. Distance 2.00 miles. Sold to the San Diego Electric Ry. Company 1922.

BAYSHORE RAILWAY

Organized 1904 - Steam - Standard Gauge

Located San Francisco, San Francisco County. Built to San Bruno. Distance 11.84 miles. Opened for traffic 1907. This is the name under which the Southern Pacific Company built the Bayshore cut-off from San Francisco to San Bruno. Merged with the Southern Pacific Company June 30, 1908.

BAYSIDE LUMBER COMPANY

Incorporated January 6, 1905 - Steam - Standard Gauge

Located near Eureka, Humboldt County. Purchased the properties of the Bay Side Mill & Lumber Company. Operated logging road from mill to timber along Jacoby Creek. Ceased operations on Jacoby Creek 1913. Railroad leased to the Pacific Engineering & Construction Company December 1914 to 1915. Reorganized as Bayside Redwood Company 1920. 1.50 miles.

BAYSIDE MILL & LUMBER COMPANY

Organized January 1900 - Steam - Standard Gauge

Located near Eureka, Humboldt County. Built 9.00 miles of track from mill to

timber along Jacoby Creek. Sold to the Bayside Lumber Company January 6, 1905.

BAYSIDE REDWOOD COMPANY

Organized 1920 - Steam - Standard Gauge

Located near Eureka, Humboldt County. Resulted from the reorganization of the Bayside Lumber Company. Took back the trackage leased to the Pacific Engineering & Construction Company. Sold to the Humboldt Redwood Company 1929.

BEAR HARBOR & EEL RIVER RAILROAD
BEAR HARBOR LUMBER RAILROAD

Incorporated September 8, 1896 - Steam - Standard Gauge

Located Bear Harbor, Mendocino County. Built from a wharf in Bear Harbor to Andersonia located at a junction of Indian Creek and the Eel River. Distance 17.50 miles. Two different lumber companies operated over this road. The Bear Harbor Lumber Company, incorporated July 26, 1893, built the original track from wharf to Moody on Indian Creek. Distance 10.20 miles. The Bear Harbor Lumber Company incorporated the Bear Harbor & Eel River R.R. September 8, 1886. The Southern Humboldt Lumber Company was incorporated November 6, 1902. Extended trackage from Moody to Andersonia on the Eel River. Distance 7.80 miles. Completed September 1905. Ceased operations 1906 or 1907. Abandoned 1940.

BECHTEL - KAISER ROCK COMPANY
HENRY J. KAISER COMPANY

Began operations 1926 or 1927 - Steam - Standard Gauge

Located near Oroville on the Feather River, Butte County. Built trackage from the pits to the crusher. Abandoned January 1963.

BELT LINE RAILROAD COMPANY

Organized July 1890 - Electric - 3 ft. 6 in. Gauge

Located Los Angeles, Los Angeles County. Took over the operations of the Electric Rapid Transit Co. Acquired the Second Street Cable Ry. Company December 17, 1980. Deeded to the Los Angeles Consolidated Electrical Railway Co. Gauge changed on all lines that had standard gauge to 3 ft. 6 inch December 31, 1891. Sold to the Los Angeles Ry. Company August 18, 1895.

BELT RAILROAD COMPANY OF SAN FRANCISCO

Built 1891 - Steam - Standard Gauge

Located San Francisco, San Francisco County. Built by the Board of State Harbor Commissioners on state property in San Francisco. Reorganized as State Belt Railway of California.

BENDER BROTHERS

1901 - Steam - 3 ft. Gauge

Located Del Mar Landing, Sonora County. Sold to Glynn and Peterson Mill and Lumber Company 1903.

BENDIXEN SHIPBUILDING COMPANY

Located Eureka, Humboldt County. Operated 2 miles of trackage during the years 1908 to 1910.

BENICIA LAND & TERMINAL RAILWAY COMPANY

Franchised July 18, 1914 - Electric - Standard Gauge

Located Benicia, Solano County. Proposed to build an electric railway in Benicia and along certain county roads. The street railway was part of a plan to connect Vallejo, Benicia and Winters, via the Berryessa Valley.

BERKELEY BRANCH RAILROAD COMPANY

Incorporated September 25, 1876 - Steam - Electric -Standard Gauge

Located Berkeley, Alameda County. Built from Shell Mound via Shattuck Avenue to Vine Street (Berryman's). Distance 3.84 miles. Opened for service July 1, 1878. Consolidated with Northern Ry. Company May 15, 1888. Consolidated with Southern Pacific Company April 14, 1898. Electrified and trackage used by Southern Pacific Company interurbans from 1911 to 1940.

BERKELEY TRACTION COMPANY

Electric - Standard Gauge

Located Berkeley, Alameda County. Franchise granted for operation on College Avenue. Never operated independently. Merged with the Oakland Traction Consolidated to become the Oakland Traction Company.

BIG CREEK RAILROAD

Incorporated March 16, 1912 - Steam - Standard Gauge

Located El Prado, Fresno County. Built by Stone & Weber Construction Company from junction with Southern Pacific Company to Big Creek (Cascada). Sold to the San Joaquin & Eastern R.R. Company 1913. Abandoned 1933.

BIG FOUR ELECTRIC RAILWAY COMPANY

Incorporated May 18, 1912 - Electric - Standard Gauge

Located Tulare, Tulare County. Proposed to build eastward to Porterville via Woodville and Popular. A branch to be built to Visalia from Tulare. Distance 34 miles. Graded 4.50 miles on the Tulare to Visalia branch. 15.00 miles of right-of-way were obtained April 3, 1913. 7.00 miles were graded. Abandoned 1914.

BIG LAKES LUMBER COMPANY

Organized 1937 - Steam - Standard Gauge

Located Canby, Modoc County. Took over the properties of the Walker-Hovey Company. Operated over the tracks of the Canby R.R. Company. Sold to Ralph L. Smith Company in 1943. Abandoned 1948. Trackage removed 1951.

BIG PINES LIME & TRANSPORTATION COMPANY

Organized in 1910 - Electric - Narrow-Gauge

Located Big Pine Station (Pine Lodge Station after 1919), San Bernardino County. Proposed to build a narrow-gauge industrial line from a point on the Santa Fe just above Cajon Station to lime deposits. Distance 7.00 miles. Built a trackless trolley system that began operations in 1911.

BIRCH & SMART

Organized 1904 - Steam - 3 ft. Gauge

Located Smart, near Emigrant Gap, Nevada County. Built from a junction with the Southern Pacific Company. Constructed 5.01 miles of trackage. Sold to the Pacific Gas & Electric Company in 1910.

BLACK DIAMOND COAL & RAILROAD COMPANY

Began construction in 1868 - Steam - Standard Gauge - 36 in. Gauge

Located Pittsburg, Contra Costa County. Built to Nortonville on Mt. Diablo. Distance 5.90 miles. Mine operations were served by a 36-inch gauge railway. Mine ceased full operation in 1883. Operations discontinued in March 1923.

BLACK DIAMOND RAILROAD

Began operations 1868 - Steam - Standard Gauge

Located Contra Costa County. Built from the San Joaquin River to Nortonville River to Mt. Diablo. Distance 5.90 miles. Abandoned 1884.

BLACKWOOD LUMBER COMPANY

Organized 1921 - Steam - Standard Gauge

Logging road.

N.J. BLAGEN LUMBER COMPANY

Steam

Located Calpine, Sierra County. Operated in 1922-23.

BLAKE & BILGER COMPANY

Organized 1904 - Steam - 3 ft. Gauge

Located Oakland, Alameda County. Purchased the properties of the Oakland Paving Company including their narrow-gauge quarry railroad. Abandoned 1923.

BLAKE BROTHERS COMPANY

Organized 1914 - Steam - 3 ft. and Standard Gauge

Located Richmond, Contra Costa County. South of Castro Point on San Francisco Bay. Purchased the San Pablo Quarry Company and began operating one-fourth of a mile of 3 ft. gauge road. Narrow-gauge operations ceased in 1938 or 1939. Built a standard gauge railroad from Richmond & San Rafael Ferry Company pier at Castro Point to the rock crushing plant in 1924. Distance 1.75 miles. This trackage was built by Blake Brothers, Oakland Traction Company and Key System. Blake Brothers incorporated this trackage as the Castro Point Ry. & Term. Company. Key System owned .78 miles. Blake Brothers .09 miles and the Castro Point Ry. & Term. Company (point) .88 miles. This company was dissolved in 1962. Trackage and property sold to Standard Oil in June 1963. Leased to Quarry Products, Inc. in 1963.

BLAKE BROTHERS COMPANY - An industrial railroad that operated from a quarry to a rock crushing plant south of Castro Point. It connected with the Richmond Belt Line at Point Castro. - *W.C. Whittaker*

BLUE LAKE LOGGING COMPANY

Organized 1928 - Steam - Standard Gauge

Located Blue Lake, Humboldt County. Abandoned 1929.

BOCA & LOYALTON RAILROAD COMPANY

Incorporated September 24, 1900 - Steam - Standard Gauge

Located Loyalton, Sierra County. Began as a spur built from Boca on the Southern Pacific to Lewis Mills in 1897. Formal incorporation took place in 1900 and the trackage was extended to Beckwith. Total distance 39.50 miles. Amended articles of incorporation were filed March 26, 1904, authorizing construction of a railroad from Boca to Beckwith, Plumas County, and thence west along the Feather River, Spring Garden Creek and Spanish Creek to Quincy, Plumas County. Distance 80 miles. A branch road to run from main line, beginning three-fourths of a mile east of Beckwith, to Indian Creek via Red Clover, Squaw and Last Chance Valley, a distance of 35 miles. Another branch road was to be built from the main line at a point 2.50 miles west of Beckwith via Grizzly Creek for 18 miles. Abandoned December 1, 1916, except for 12.29 miles of trackage sold to the Western Pacific R.R. in 1905. A small section was sold to the Clover Valley Lumber Company.

BOCA & LOYALTON RAILROAD - A logging railroad that operated passenger service between the Southern Pacific and Lewis Mills in 1897. - *Donald Duke Collection*

BOCA MILL & ICE COMPANY

Narrow-Gauge

Located in Sierra County. Said to have operated .75 miles of narrow-gauge track railroad from mill to Truckee River.

BODIE & BENTON RAILWAY & COMMERCIAL COMPANY

Organized January 27, 1882 - Steam - 3 ft. Gauge

Located Bodie, Mono County. Organized to take over the operations of the Bodie Railway & Lumber Company. Reorganized in 1893 and given the original name of Bodie Railway & Lumber Company.

BODIE RAILWAY & LUMBER COMPANY

Organized February 18, 1881 - Steam - 3 ft. Gauge

Located Bodie, Mono County. Built to Mono Mills. Distance 32 miles. Completed November 14, 1881. Reorganized as Bodie & Benton Ry. & Commercial Company in 1882. Reorganized and given the original name of Bodie Ry. & Lumber Company in 1893. Renamed Mono Lake Ry. & Lumber Company December 23, 1906. Deeded to Mono Lake Ry. in 1907. Abandoned September 6, 1917. Track removal began September 1918.

Authority. Interurban Electric, Sacramento Northern, and Key System operated trains over this road. Trackage included East Bay Terminal in San Francisco, Bridge Yards (Oakland Army Base) and track between 26th Street and Bridge Yard. Interurban Electric used the 26th Street connection. 26th Street to Bridge Yard abandoned July 26, 1941. Later taken over by Oakland Terminal Railroad. Bridge line abandoned April 20, 1958.

BORATE & DAGGETT RAILROAD - Two Heisler locomotives, like the *Francis*, were used to haul Borate for the Pacific Coast Borax Co. - *Hugh Tolford Collection*

BODIE RAILWAY & LUMBER COMPANY - This narrow-gauge railroad carried mine timber from Mono Mills to Bodie between 1881 and 1917. - *Hugh Tolford Collection*

BONNIE CLAIRE & UBEHEBE RAILROAD

Proposed August 1906 - Steam - Standard Gauge

Located Bonnie Claire, Nevada. Proposed to build southwestward to the Ubehebe Mine in California, near Death Valley, Inyo County.

BORATE & DAGGETT RAILROAD COMPANY

Organized 1896 - Steam - 3 ft. and Standard Gauge

Located Daggett, San Bernardino County. Construction began 1898. Built from a junction with the Santa Fe Ry. at Daggett to Marion on Calico Lake. Completed July 1, 1898. This trackage used three rails so as to be both 3 ft. and standard gauge. Built 3 ft. gauge track from Marion to Borate in the Calico Mountains. Total distance 12.35 miles. Abandoned 1909.

BOULDER CREEK & PACIFIC RAILROAD

Steam

Located Boulder Creek, Santa Cruz County. Built northward to saw mill. Distance 11.60 miles.

BOULDER CREEK & PESCADERO RAILROAD

Steam

Located Santa Cruz County. Built from mill to timber in the Boulder Creek area. Distance 5.00 miles. Became part of the Wildwood Boulder Creek & Northern Railroad April 25, 1914.

BRIDGE RAILWAY

Began operations January 15, 1939 - Electric - Standard Gauge

Located San Francisco-Oakland Bay Bridge. Owned by the Toll Bridge

BROADWAY, BERKELEY & PIEDMONT RAILWAY

Organized 1876 - Horsecar - 5 ft. Gauge

Located Oakland, Alameda County. Built from 7th & Washington streets in Oakland to Mt. View Cemetery. Distance 6 miles.

BROADWAY & PIEDMONT HORSE RAILWAY

Located Oakland, Alameda County.

BROOKINGS LUMBER & BOX COMPANY RAILROAD

Organized 1897 - Steam - 3 ft. Gauge

Located Fredalba, San Bernardino County. Near Lake Arrowhead. Built from mill to timber northeast of Arrowbear Lake via Running Springs, and northwest into the timber along the present rim of the World Highway. The Highland section built around the mill and yards at Molino (near Highland) began operation in 1897. Abandoned 1912. Logging section in the San Bernardino Mountains from mill at Fredalba to timber began operations in 1899. Distance 5.75 miles. Ceased operations 1912. Dismantled 1914.

BROOKLYN AVENUE RAILWAY

Electric - 3 ft. 6 in. Gauge

Located Los Angeles. Operated along Brooklyn Avenue in Boyle Heights. Taken into the Los Angeles Railway in November 1911.

BROOKLYN & FRUIT VALE RAILROAD

Organized 1875 - Horsecar -

Located Oakland, Alameda County. Reorganized April 16, 1892 and named Highland Park & Fruit Vale Railroad. Built 2.25 miles of trackage. Sold to the Oakland Transit Company May 1887.

BUCKSPORT & ELK RIVER RAILROAD
BUCKSPORT & ELK RIVER RAILWAY

Incorporated July 22, 1884 - Steam - Standard Gauge

Located Bucksport, Humboldt County. Original company was the narrow-gauge Elk River Railroad, incorporated October 27, 1882. The Bucksport & Elk River Railroad organized July 22, 1884, standard gauged the road and built 7.67 miles of logging road by January 1, 1886. Reorganized May 14, 1932, as the Bucksport & Elk River Railway. Total distance 15 miles. Abandoned 1950. Dismantled 1953.

BURLINGAME RAILROAD COMPANY

Organized October 1914 - Electric - Standard Gauge

Located Burlingame, San Mateo County. Survey work begun November 1, 1914, for a railroad along the route of the storage-battery operated street railway from Easton to Burlingame Hills.

BURLINGAME RAILWAY

Franchise granted July 24, 1911 - Electric - Standard Gauge.

Located Burlingame, San Mateo County. Began construction of a street railway from the Southern Pacific Company station to Hillside Drive in the Burlingame Hills area. Distance 1.50 miles. A battery operated car was used. Abandoned November 19, 1917.

M.A. BURNS LUMBER COMPANY

Organized 1911 - Steam - Narrow-Gauge

Located Castella, Shasta County. Built from mill to woods. Distance 30 miles. Sold to Castle Crag Lumber Company. Abandoned 1936.

M.A. BURNS MANUFACTURING COMPANY

Steam - Standard Gauge

Located Eureka, Humboldt County. Operated 20 miles of trackage in 1923.

BUTTE COUNTY RAILROAD COMPANY

Franchise granted November 11, 1902 - Steam - Standard Gauge

Located Chico, Butte County. Incorporated February 24, 1903. Began construction April 1903. Regular service between Barber and Magalia began November 1, 1903. Opened for traffic to Sterling City April 15, 1904. Sold to the Southern Pacific Company November 27, 1903, who incorporated the Chico & Northern R.R. as a holding company for the Butte County R.R. Company properties. Leased back to the Butte County R.R. Company for operation. The Chico & Northern R.R. Company was not an operating company. Chico & Northern R.R. Company dissolved February 29, 1912. Butte County R.R. Company dissolved January 21, 1916. Trackage became the Southern Pacific's Chico-Sterling City branch.

BUTTE & PLUMAS RAILWAY

Incorporated October 29, 1902 - Steam - Standard Gauge

Located Oroville, Plumas County. Proposed to build along the north fork of the Feather River between Oroville and what was known as the East Branch of Indian Creek. Distance to be 53 miles. Began operations as a lumber carrier for Swayne Lumber Company and Truckee Lumber Company. Reincorporated June 1, 1901, to extend trackage to Stanwood. Total mileage operated 24.65 miles. Sold to Western Pacific Railroad June 1905. Abandoned 1939.

BRIDGE RAILWAY - The second or lower deck of the San Francisco-Oakland Bay Bridge was designed to carry commuter trains between Bridge Yards (Oakland Army Base) and Bay Bridge Transit Terminal in downtown San Francisco, as is shown here. Beginning on January 15, 1939, the double-track line across the bridge carried trains of the Interurban Electric Railway (Southern Pacific), the Key System and the Sacramento Northern. According to the California Toll Bridge Authority "Annual Reports," the bridge was designed to carry Santa Fe Railway passenger trains between Oakland and downtown San Francisco. Santa Fe terminated their trains at Oakland and used busses across the bridge to a modern bus station on Fourth Street. - *Donald Duke Collection*

CALIFORNIA WESTERN RAILROAD - Seven miles west of Willits, the rails of the California Western make a series of four gigantic loops as a means of gaining altitude between Shake City and Tunnel No. 2. In this scene rail motorcar No. M-200 ascends the first loop en route to Willits. - *Alan Krieg*

C

CAHUENGA VALLEY RAILROAD COMPANY

Incorporated March 26, 1888 - Steam - Electric - Narrow-Gauge

Located Los Angeles, Los Angeles County. Built from Diamond and Texas streets (now 1st and Belmont streets) to Santa Monica, via Hollywood. Distance 18 miles. Sold May 7, 1896 to the Pasadena & Pacific Railway Company and electrified. Sold to the Los Angeles-Pacific Railroad Company in 1902. Deeded to the Pacific Electric Railway in 1911.

CAHUENGA VALLEY RAILROAD - Built from the end of the Second Street Cable line to Hollywood. Used old cable cars and horsecars for passenger cars. - *Donald Duke Collection*

CALAVERAS CEMENT COMPANY

Built 1925 - Steam - Standard Gauge

Located Kentucky House, Calaveras County. Built from the end of the Southern Pacific Co. track to cement plant at Kentucky House, 3.95 miles. Sold to the Southern Pacific Co. April 28, 1929.

CALAVERAS COPPER COMPANY

Organized 1877 - Electric - 2 ft. Gauge

Located Copperopolis, Calaveras County. Built from mill to quarry. Distance 5.00 miles. Also operated by the Copperopolis Copper Mining Co. Abandoned 1927.

CALIFORNIA & ARIZONA RAILROAD

Incorporated December 27, 1870 - Steam - 3 ft. Gauge

Located Wilmington, Los Angeles County. Proposed to build from Wilmington to Wickenburg, Arizona. A branch was to be built into Owens Valley.

CALIFORNIA, ARIZONA & SANTA FE RAILWAY COMPANY

Incorporated December 21, 1911 - Steam - Standard Gauge

Incorporated as a holding company by the Santa Fe Railway Co. to negotiate the exchange of its New Mexico & Arizona Railway; Benson to Nogales, Arizona, the Sonora Railway Ltd. from Nogales to Guaymas, Sonora, Mexico, for the Mojave division, Mojave to Needles, of the Southern Pacific Company. Purchased the Ferris & Lakeview Railway Co., distance 8.00 miles, December 28, 1911 and leased it to the Santa Fe Railway until abandonment February 15, 1937. Took over the lease of the California Eastern Railway in 1911 until abandoned 1923. Acquired other lines in Arizona. Became part of Santa Fe May 19, 1928.

CALIFORNIA BARREL COMPANY

Organized 1916 - Steam - 3 ft. 9 ¼in. Gauge

Located McKinleyville, north of Eureka, Humboldt County. Built northward to timber. Distance 5.25 miles. Purchased the Humboldt Cooperage Co. 1918.

Moved to the North Fork Camp on Long Prairie Creek. 5.00 miles of trackage was built including a 6,300 foot incline. Closed down in 1932. Some limited activity in 1936. Abandoned 1938. Track removed 1941.

CALIFORNIA CENTRAL NARROW GAUGE RAILWAY COMPANY

Organized 1873 - Steam - 3 ft. Gauge

Located Benicia, Solano County. Proposed to build to Tehama with an extension to Red Bluff. Construction began May 1, 1873. Project abandoned 1874.

CALIFORNIA CENTRAL RAILROAD COMPANY

Incorporated March 20, 1912. - Steam - Standard Gauge

Located San Juan, San Benito County. Proposed to build from Hollister to San Juan with a junction with the San Juan Pacific Railway and then on to Watsonville, a distance of 29.80 miles. Took over the operations of the San Juan Pacific Railway May 21, 1912. Junction was made with the Southern Pacific Co. at Chittenden. Distance operated 8.00 miles. Ceased operations December 1937. Abandoned 1943.

CALIFORNIA CENTRAL RAILROAD

Incorporated July 1881 - Steam - Standard Gauge

Located Santa Cruz, Santa Cruz County. Proposed to build from the southern terminus of the San Francisco & Ocean Shore Railroad to Santa Cruz and then across Fresno County via McBride's Pass to the California state line.

CALIFORNIA CENTRAL RAILROAD COMPANY

Incorporated April 21, 1857 - Steam - 5 ft. Gauge

Located Folsom, Sacramento County. Proposed to build from the eastern terminal of the Sacramento Valley Railroad at Folsom northward to Marysville via Lincoln. Distance 41.50 miles. Construction began May 1858 at Folsom and built through Grider's Ranch (Roseville) to Lincoln. Distance 18.50 miles. Began service October 13, 1861. Sold to Central Pacific Railroad November 10, 1864. Standard gauged in 1865. Sold 8.20 miles to California & Oregon Railroad Company July 22, 1865. Abandoned 1868.

CALIFORNIA CENTRAL RAILWAY COMPANY

Incorporated May 20, 1887 - Steam - Standard Gauge

Located Southern California. Organized to consolidate eight companies which had built or proposed to build branches for the California Southern Railroad. These railroads were: Los Angeles & San Gabriel Valley Railroad Company which had built from Los Angeles to Pasadena in 1885 and extended to Mud Springs to 1886, 19.90 miles; San Bernardino & Los Angeles Railway which had built from San Bernardino to Mud Springs and began operations April 25, 1887, 38.80 miles; Los Angeles & Santa Monica Railway Company which proposed to build from Los Angeles via Redondo Junction and Inglewood to Port Ballona. Built by California Central September 23, 1887, 17.10 miles. Riverside, Santa Ana & Los Angeles Railway Company which had built from Highgrove to Riverside, opened January 8, 1886, and to Arlington March 15, 1886, 10.00 miles. Built by California Central from Arlington via Atwood and Orange to Santa Ana, May 20, 1887, 32.90 miles; and from Orange to Redondo Junction August 12, 1888, 29.50 miles; San Bernardino & San Diego Railway Company which proposed to build from Santa Ana to Fallbrook Junction August 12, 1888, 14.70 miles; San Diego Central Railway which proposed to build from San Diego, via El Cajon, Poway and Escondido to Escondido Junction. Built by California Central from Escondido Junction to Escondido December 31, 1887, 21.30 miles; San Bernardino Valley Railway Company which proposed to build from San Bernardino via Redlands to Mentone. Built December 31, 1887, 12 miles. San Jacinto Valley Railway Company proposed to build from Perris to San Jacinto. Built April 30, 1888, 19.40 miles. Leased the Redondo Beach Railway Company and California Southern Railroad Company to form Southern California Railway Company November 7, 1889. Leased to Atchison, Topeka & Santa Fe Railway Company June 1904.

CALIFORNIA CENTRAL RAILROAD - Built from the Sacramento Valley Railroad at Folsom to Lincoln, a distance of 41.50 miles. The locomotive *Lincoln* handles a passenger train across the American River north of Folsom. - *Donald Duke Collection*

CALIFORNIA COAL FIELDS RAILROAD

Incorporated July 1, 1920 - Steam - Standard Gauge

Located McKay, Monterey County. Took over the operations of the Stone Canyon & Pacific Railway Company. Distance 21.50 miles. Abandoned 1932.

CALIFORNIA COAL FIELDS RAILROAD - Operated a coal railroad from McKay to Stone Canyon, along the Southern Pacific, a distance of 21 miles. Coal was of low quality. - *Harre Demoro Collection*

CALIFORNIA COAST LINE RAILROAD

Organized May 1890 - Steam - Standard Gauge

Located Portland, Oregon. Organized to build a railroad southward along the Pacific Coast through California.

CALIFORNIA COMPANY

Incorporated January 20, 1909 - Electric - Standard Gauge

Located Petaluma, Sonoma County. Organized to take over the properties of the Lakeport & Richardson's Bay Railroad Company.

CALIFORNIA DEPARTMENT OF TRANSPORTATION (CALTRANS)

Organized 1979 - Diesel - Standard Gauge

Located San Francisco, San Francisco County. The California Department of Transportation purchased the commuter passenger services, formerly operated by the Southern Pacific, from San Francisco to San Jose. Funding for this service comes from Caltrans, the San Francisco Municipal Railway, the San Mateo County Transit District, the Santa Clara County Transit District, and from UMTA, the Federal Urban Mass Transportation Administration.

CALIFORNIA DEVELOPMENT COMPANY

Steam

Owned some trackage that was sold to the Imperial Irrigation District April 21, 1916.

CALIFORNIA DOOR COMPANY
CALDOR LUMBER COMPANY

Organized 1917 - Steam - 3 ft. Gauge

Located Caldor, El Dorado County. Built to Diamond Springs. Became Caldor Lumber Co. 1924. Operated 12.00 miles of track. Yard operations were transferred to Diamond & Caldor Railway in 1933. Some trackage abandoned 1933. Track removal completed September 1953.

CALIFORNIA EASTERN & NORTHERN RAILWAY

Incorporated June 9, 1917 - Steam - Standard Gauge

Located Rutherford, Napa County. Proposed to build from a junction with the San Francisco, Napa & Calistoga Railroad northeastward to Monticello.

CALIFORNIA EASTERN RAILWAY COMPANY

Incorporated October 30, 1895 - Steam - Standard Gauge

Located Goffs, San Bernardino County. Acquired the properties of the Nevada Southern Railway from Goffs to Barnwell (Manvel), 29.40 miles, April 17, 1896. Built from Barnwell to Leastalk, 8.30 miles. Extended from Ivanpah, 7.70 miles, in 1902. Leased to the Santa Fe Railway July 1, 1902. Assigned to the California, Arizona & San Francisco Railway in 1911. Barnwell to Ivanpah abandoned 1913. Remainder abandoned 1923.

CALIFORNIA ELECTRIC RAILWAY

Incorporated January 1, 1909 - Electric - Standard Gauge

Located San Francisco, San Francisco County. Proposed to build a cross-town street railway. Distance 2.50 miles. Taken over by the receivers April 1909. Surveys taken over by the United Railways of San Francisco in 1909.

CALIFORNIA FRUIT GROWERS EXCHANGE

Organized 1916 - Steam - Standard Gauge

Located Graeagle, Plumas County. Took over the operations of the Davis Box & Lumber Co. Railroad. Operated over 1,500 miles of track. Abandoned 1937.

CALIFORNIA GREAT TRUNK OF THE PACIFIC AND ATLANTIC RAILROAD CO.

Organized October 2, 1857 - Steam - Standard Gauge

Located San Francisco. Proposed to build to Oroville by way of San Mateo, Santa Clara, Alameda, San Joaquin, Sacramento, Placer, Yuba, and Butte counties.

CALIFORNIA, IDAHO & MONTANA RAILROAD COMPANY

Incorporated October 11, 1895 - Steam - Standard Gauge

Located Butte City, Montana. Proposed to build a railroad to San Francisco.

CALIFORNIA IMPROVEMENT COMPANY

Incorporated July 19, 1890 - Steam - Standard Gauge

Located Los Angeles, Los Angeles County. Incorporated in Illinois. Proposed to purchase the Los Angeles, Pasadena & Glendale Railroad and extend it to San Francisco. Project abandoned 1891.

CALIFORNIA INLAND EMPIRE RAILROAD

Organized December 1, 1905 - Steam - Standard Gauge

Located Boise City, Idaho. Proposed to build into California with branches touching the principal mineral, agricultural and grain belts of Washington and Oregon, with a terminus at Sausalito, California and ferry connections to San Francisco. Surveys completed Boise to San Francisco November 1906. Project abandoned 1907.

CALIFORNIA LUMBER COMPANY

Organized 1872 - Steam - Standard Gauge

Located Westport, Mendocino County. Began operations with ox power hauling logs over a tramway. Introduced steam power operations in 1889 or 1890. Operated from time to time over various short sections of track in the area. Sold to the Westport Lumber & Railroad Company in 1908. Company dissolved 1910. Part of the trackage used by Pollard Lumber Co. 1906 to 1918. Abandoned 1919.

CALIFORNIA MIDLAND RAILROAD

Organized February 1902 - Steam - Standard Gauge

Located San Francisco, San Francisco County. Proposed to build to a point near the mouth of the Kings Creek, a branch of the San Joaquin River, 200 miles, with a branch from a point on the main line near Madera to Bakersfield, 115 miles, also a branch into Yosemite Park, 70 miles long and a branch to Stockton, 20 miles. Total mileage 405 miles. No construction work done.

CALIFORNIA MIDLAND RAILROAD

Surveyed October 3, 1902 - Steam - Standard Gauge

Located Bakersfield, Kern County. Proposed to build to the coast at a point near the northern boundary line of Santa Barbara County. Distance 60 miles. No construction work done. Project abandoned 1903.

CALIFORNIA MIDLAND RAILROAD COMPANY

Organized 1892 - Steam - Standard Gauge

Located Sacramento, Sacramento County. Organized to build a road through the counties of Sacramento, San Joaquin, Merced, Fresno, Tulare and Kern to Bakersfield. Branches were to be built to Lathrop, Modesto, Stockton, and Antioch. This road was to parallel the Southern Pacific Company, but nearer to the foothills. Survey began April 17, 1892. Project abandoned in 1893.

CALIFORNIA MIDLAND RAILROAD COMPANY

Incorporated November 6, 1905 - Electric - Standard Gauge

Located Marysville, Yuba County. Proposed to build to Spenceville and from there two branches were built. One to Grass Valley and the other to Auburn. In Grass Valley a connection was to be made with the Nevada County Traction Company. This road was to be a 1,200 volt third-rail system. About 2.00 miles of track were laid in Marysville in 1906. The company paid $15,000 to Yuba County to strengthen the Yuba River levee on which the tracks were to be laid in October 1909. Secured an option to the Nevada County Narrow-Gauge Railroad from Colfax to Nevada City, October 1911. The gauge was to be changed to standard and the line electrified.

CALIFORNIA MIDLAND RAILWAY COMPANY

Incorporated April 26, 1902 - Steam - Standard Gauge

Located Burnells, Humboldt County. Organized to extend the Eel River & Eureka Railroad southeast to Burnells. Proposed to build 62.25 miles of trackage. Built to Carlotta. Distance 3.40 miles. Extended into woods 2.10 miles. Sold to the San Francisco & Northwestern Railway July 3, 1903. Became part of the Northwestern Pacific Railroad January 8, 1907.

CALIFORNIA & MT. DIABLO RAILROAD

Organized March 21, 1881 - Steam - 3 ft. Gauge

Located Emeryville, Alameda County. Proposed to build from San Francisco to Utah via Sonora Pass. Built from Emeryville (40th & San Pablo streets) through Berkeley to Richmond. Distance 9.85 miles. Sold to the California & Nevada Railroad Company. Trackage extended to city of San Pablo in 1886. Sold to Oakland & East Side Railroad and standard gauged in 1902. Became part of the Santa Fe Railway Company in 1904.

CALIFORNIA NARROW GAUGE RAILROAD & TRANSPORTATION COMPANY

Organized 1875 - Steam - 3 ft. Gauge

Located San Jose, Santa Clara County. Proposed to build from Dumbarton Pt., Alameda County to New Almaden via Alviso, Santa Clara and San Jose. A branch to be built from Santa Clara to Congress Springs. Total mileage 40.00 miles.

CALIFORNIA & NEVADA RAILROAD COMPANY

Began construction September 13, 1881 - Steam - 3 ft. Gauge

Located San Pablo, Alameda County. Purchased the California & Mt. Diablo Railroad February 1884. Built from Emeryville north to San Pablo then southeast to Bryant, a distance of 24.50 miles. Completed 10.25 miles of track by March 1885. Sold to the Oakland & East Side Railroad November 14, 1902. Built 11.80 miles of track from Oakland to Richmond 1904. Sold to the Santa Fe May 16, 1904. Santa Fe trackage between Richmond and Oakland abandoned June 1, 1979.

CALIFORNIA NORTHEASTERN RAILWAY

Incorporated July 6, 1905 - Steam - Standard Gauge

Located Weed, Siskiyou County. Built to Klamath Falls, Oregon. Distance 86.10 miles. Section Weed to Grass Lake acquired from Weed Lumber Co. July 29, 1905. Began construction September 1906. Completed May 1909. Sold to the Oregon Eastern Railway December 18, 1911. Sold to the Central Pacific Railway February 29, 1912. Section of Weed Lumber Co. abandoned after a new and shorter line was constructed April 17, 1927.

CALIFORNIA & NORTHEASTERN RAILROAD COMPANY

Incorporated November 18, 1892 - Steam - Standard Gauge

Located Anderson, Shasta County. Proposed to build to the Sacramento River.

CALIFORNIA & OREGON COAST RAILROAD COMPANY

Incorporated 1903 - Steam - Standard Gauge

Located Crescent City, Del Norte County. The purpose of this railroad was to run a line 91 miles long from Grants Pass, Oregon, to Crescent City, California. This Del Norte County railroad was set to have two branches. One branch was proposed to Chelco, a distance of 20 miles. The second branch was to run some 80 miles into Humboldt County.

CALIFORNIA & OREGON RAILROAD COMPANY

Incorporated June 30, 1865 - Steam - Standard Gauge

Located Marysville, Yuba County. Organized for the purpose of determining the practicability of a railroad from Marysville, California, to Portland, Oregon. Consolidated with Marysville Railroad Co. and California Central Railroad to form the California & Oregon Railroad Co. June 16, 1868. Consolidated with Central Pacific Railroad Co. August 22, 1870.

CALIFORNIA & OREGON RAILROAD - Organized by the Central Pacific to build a line from Marysville north to Portland, Oregon. The locomotives in this view are taking on wood for fuel in the Mount Shasta region. - *Donald Duke Collection*

CALIFORNIA & OREGON RAILROAD COMPANY

Incorporated January 16, 1868 - Steam - Standard Gauge

Located Roseville, Placer County. Built to Lincoln. Distance 10.30 miles. This trackage formerly belonged to the California Central Railroad Co. and the Marysville Railroad Co. Consolidated with the California and Oregon Railroad Co. Incorporated December 18, 1869. Consolidated with the Central Pacific Railroad August 22, 1870.

CALIFORNIA & OREGON RAILROAD COMPANY

Incorporated December 18, 1869 - Steam - Standard Gauge

Located Marysville, Yuba County. Consolidation of the California & Oregon Railroad Co. Operated from Marysville to Chico. Distance 75.33 miles. Consolidated with Central Pacific Railroad Co. August 22, 1870.

CALIFORNIA PACIFIC EASTERN EXTENSION COMPANY

Incorporated May 23, 1871 - Steam - Standard Gauge

Located Sacramento, Sacramento County. Organized by the California-Pacific Railroad to build 934 miles of railroad from Davisville (now Davis), Yolo County, to Oregon via Goose Lake into Oregon, Idaho and into Utah. No construction work done.

CALIFORNIA PACIFIC RAILROAD COMPANY

Incorporated January 10, 1865 - Steam - Standard Gauge

Located Sacramento, Sacramento County. Built from South Vallejo to Sacramento. Distance 60.40 miles. Began construction December 1866. Completed January 15, 1870, with a branch from Davis via Knights Landing to Marysville. Distance 44.10 miles. Completed March 15, 1870. Consolidated with the Sacramento & San Francisco Railroad Co. and the San Francisco & Marysville Railroad Co. Consolidated with California Pacific Railroad Co. December 29, 1869. Consolidated with Southern Pacific Co. April 14, 1898.

CALIFORNIA PACIFIC RAILROAD - Built from South Vallejo to Sacramento, with a branch from Davis to Marysville. Was consolidated with the Southern Pacific in 1898. - *Donald Duke Collection*

CALIFORNIA PACIFIC RAILROAD COMPANY

Incorporated December 29, 1869 - Steam - Standard Gauge

Located San Francisco, San Francisco County. Resulted from a consolidation of California Pacific Railroad Co. and the California Pacific Railroad Extension Co. Came under control of Central Pacific Railroad Co. August 1, 1871. Leased to the Central Pacific Railroad Co. July 1, 1876. Operated 113.50 miles of trackage. Consolidated with Southern Pacific Co. April 14, 1898. The section between Suisun and Sacramento is now commonly referred to as the "Cal-P." The California Pacific Extension Co. was incorporated May 23, 1871 to build over 900 miles of trackage to Oregon, Idaho and Utah. No work was done. Trackage from Marysville to Knights Landing. Distance 22.50 miles. Abandoned 1871.

CALIFORNIA PACIFIC RAILROAD COMPANY

Incorporated May 7, 1901 - Steam or Electric - Standard Gauge

Located Los Angeles, Los Angeles County. Proposed to build to San Pedro. Distance 17.50 miles. No construction work done.

CALIFORNIA PACIFIC RAILROAD EXTENSION COMPANY

Incorporated April 14, 1869 - Steam - Standard Gauge

Located San Francisco, San Francisco County. Acquired trackage from Napa Valley Railroad Co. June 9, 1869, from Napa Junction to Calistoga, Napa County. Distance 35 miles. Consolidated with the California Pacific Railroad Co. December 29, 1869.

CALIFORNIA PACIFIC RAILWAY COMPANY

Incorporated 1899 - Electric - 3 ft. 6 in. Gauge

Located Los Angeles, Los Angeles County. Began operations December 30, 1901. Sold to the Los Angeles Inter-Urban Railway Co. 1901. Standard gauged when taken into the Pacific Electric Railway and became their Torrance line.

CALIFORNIA PEACH GROWERS ASSOCIATION RAILROAD
CALIFORNIA PEACH & FIG GROWERS ASSOCIATION RAILROAD

Organized 1918 - Steam - Standard Gauge

Located Mather, Mariposa County. Built south from Mather on the Hetch-Hetchy Railroad. Distance 5 miles. Abandoned 1926.

CALIFORNIA RAILWAY COMPANY

Incorporated August 16, 1890 - Steam 1890-1895 - Electric 1895-1936 - Standard Gauge

Located Alameda, Alameda County. Took over the properties of the Alameda County Railway. (Oakland, Alameda & Laundry Farm). Electrified in 1895 and extended to Alameda at Park Street Bridge. Sold to the Oakland Traction Co. 1901. Consolidated into the San Francisco-Oakland Terminal Railway 1912. Became a part of the Key System Transit June 6, 1923. Abandoned June 10, 1936.

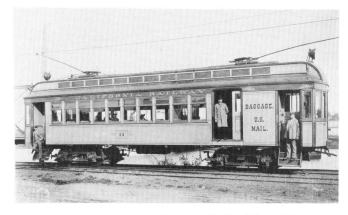

CALIFORNIA RAILWAY - A result of the merger of the Alameda County Railway and the Oakland, Alameda & Laundry Farm Railway. Became a part of the Key System in 1923. - *Donald Duke Collection*

CALIFORNIA RAPID TRANSIT RAILROAD COMPANY

Incorporated January 14, 1907 - Electric - Standard Gauge

Located San Francisco, San Francisco County. Proposed to build through Burlingame, San Mateo, Redwood City, Palo Alto, San Jose, Monterey to the southerly shore of Monterey Bay, and then to the Carmel River. Distance 140 miles. Near San Jose a branch was to be built through Alameda County to Martinez, Contra Costa County. Distance 75 miles. A branch to Redwood City from San Jose was also to be built. Distance 22 miles.

CALIFORNIA REDWOOD COMPANY

Organized 1882 - Steam - Standard Gauge

Located Trinidad, Humboldt County. Purchased the D.R. Jones & Company, the Cousins mill on Gunther Island, and the Hooper mill at Trinidad. Took control of the Trinidad Railroad and the Humboldt Logging Railway in 1883. Obtained partial control of the Bucksport & Elk River Railroad from Bucksport to the Dolber & Carson Lumber Company and to the Falk site of the Elk River Mill & Lumber Co. Operations of the railroad were suspended in 1886. The Excelsior Redwood Company was formed to take over the railroad trackage from Freshwater to the Humboldt Bay.

CALIFORNIA ROCK & GRAVEL COMPANY

Steam - Narrow-Gauge

Located Pleasanton, Alameda County. Industrial quarry road.

CALIFORNIA ROCK SALT COMPANY

Organized 1921 - Steam - 3 ft. Gauge

Located Saltus, near Amboy, San Bernardino County. Resulted from the reorganization of the Pacific Rock Salt Co. Reorganized as California Salt Co., 1950.

CALIFORNIA SALT COMPANY

Organized 1950 - Gas Engine - 3 ft. Gauge

Located Saltus, San Bernardino County. Result of the reorganization of the California Rock Salt Co. Took over operations of track from reduction mill to pits on Bristol Lake. Sold to Leslie Salt Co. 1960.

CALIFORNIA, SHASTA & EASTERN RAILROAD COMPANY

Incorporated July 12, 1912 - Steam - Standard Gauge

Located Anderson, Shasta County. Purchased the properties of the Anderson & Bella Vista Railroad organized in 1909. On September 4, 1913, the railroad operated from Anderson on the Southern Pacific to Bella Vista, a distance of 16 miles. Proposed to build on northward to Ingot. Abandoned 1927.

CALIFORNIA SHORT LINE RAILWAY COMPANY

Incorporated 1884 - Steam - Standard Gauge

Located Draper, Utah. Proposed to build to Pacific Coast. Built to Chester, Utah. Distance 8.00 miles. In 1885 graded 12.00 additional miles.

CALIFORNIA SOUTHERN EXTENSION RAILROAD COMPANY

Incorporated May 24, 1881 - Steam - Standard Gauge

Located Cajon Pass, San Bernardino County. Organized to extend the California Southern Railroad to a junction with the Atlantic & Pacific Railroad in California. Grading done in Cajon Pass sufficient to hold it. Merged with the California Southern Railroad Co. (of 1880) into the California Southern Railroad Co. January 4, 1882.

CALIFORNIA SOUTHERN RAILROAD COMPANY

Incorporated January 22, 1870 - Steam - Standard Gauge

Located Gilroy, Santa Clara County. Built to Salinas. Distance 45 miles. Consolidated with the Southern Pacific Co. October 12, 1870. Construction began 1871, completed November 1, 1872.

CALIFORNIA SOUTHERN RAILROAD COMPANY

Incorporated October 23, 1880 - Steam - Standard Gauge

Located National City, San Diego County. Proposed to build from National City via Temecula Canyon to San Bernardino. Construction began in National City in February 1881. Completed to Oceanside in December 1881. Distance 47 miles. Merged with California Southern Extension Railroad Co. January 4, 1882 forming the California Southern Railroad Co.

CALIFORNIA SOUTHERN RAILROAD - A Ten-Wheeler ready to assist a train from Oceanside to San Bernardino by way of Temecula Canyon, circa 1885. - *Donald Duke Collection*

CALIFORNIA SOUTHERN RAILROAD COMPANY

Organized December 1881 - Steam - Standard Gauge

Located San Diego, San Diego County. Articles of Incorporation filed January 4, 1882, as a merger of the California Southern Railroad Co. and the California Southern Extension Railroad Co. Completed building the road from Oceanside to Colton August 14, 1882, and to San Bernardino September 13, 1883. Distance 130.20 miles. Extended from San Bernardino to a junction with the Atlantic & Pacific Railroad at Barstow November 9, 1885. Distance National City to Barstow 211.20 miles. Operated the Los Angeles & San Gabriel Valley Railway and the San Bernardino & Los Angeles Railway until taken into the California Central Railway in 1887. Consolidated with California Central Railway Co. and Redondo Beach Railway Co. to form the Southern California Railway November 7, 1889. Became Atchison, Topeka & Santa Fe Railway January 17, 1906.

CALIFORNIA SOUTHERN RAILROAD COMPANY

Incorporated December 30, 1914 - Steam - Standard Gauge

Located Rice, Riverside County. Built from Rice to Ripley. Distance 49.90 miles. Leased to the Santa Fe Railway November 1, 1921. Purchased December 31, 1942.

CALIFORNIA STREET CABLE RAILROAD COMPANY
CALIFORNIA STREET RAILWAY

Began Operations April 9, 1878 - Cable - 3 ft. 6 in. Gauge

Located San Francisco, San Francisco County. Began as a cable car line from Kearney via California to Fillmore streets. Later extended to Central Avenue. Built a horsecar extension on California Street from Central to First Avenue. Became the California Street Cable Railroad Co. on July 31, 1884. Received a franchise for a steam dummy line extension to the beach. This was taken over by the Ferries & Cliff House Railway Co. The horsecar extension was given up when the Ferries & Cliff House dummy line began operations. Began operations of the O'Farrell, Jones and Hyde Street cable lines in 1890. Sold to the city and county of San Francisco 1951. Became part of the Municipal Railway of San Francisco.

CALIFORNIA STREET CABLE RAILROAD - An O'Farrell, Jones & Hyde Street cable car making a curve at Jones and Pine streets in downtown San Francisco, circa 1949. - *Donald Duke*

CALIFORNIA SUGAR REFINERY

Organized 1883 - Steam - 3 ft. Gauge

CALIFORNIA TERMINAL COMPANY

Incorporated September 12, 1911 - Electric - Standard Gauge

Located San Francisco, San Francisco County. Organized to take over the Lakeport & Richardson's Bay Railroad properties from The California Company.

CALIFORNIA TERMINAL RAILWAY COMPANY

Organized September 11, 1914 - Electric - Standard Gauge

Located San Francisco, San Francisco County. Application for charter made October 1, 1914. Proposed to build an electric railway. The plan called for taking a ferry from San Francisco to some point on the shore of San Francisco Bay or San Pablo Bay or San Rafael. Then take an electric train through Marin, Sonoma, Yolo and Sacramento counties. Branch lines to Petaluma and Napa were planned. Total distance of the electric railway was to be 90 miles. Project abandoned in 1915 or 1916.

CALIFORNIA TIE & TIMBER COMPANY

Organized 1929 - Steam - Standard Gauge

Located Pescadero, San Mateo County. Operated 1.00 mile of trackage. Abandoned 1933.

CALIFORNIA TIMBER COMPANY

Incorporated 1906 - Steam - 3 ft. Gauge

Located Boulder Creek, Santa Cruz County. Operated over 7.00 miles of trackage. Abandoned 1910 or 1911.

CALIFORNIA WESTERN RAILROAD

Organized 1884 - Steam - Standard Gauge

Located Fort Bragg, Mendocino County. Began construction 1885. Completed 1911. Sold June 1, 1987 to Mendocino Coast Railway, a subsidiary of Kyle Railways.

CALIFORNIA WESTERN RAILROAD

Incorporated December 19, 1947 - Steam - Standard Gauge

Located Fort Bragg, Mendocino County. Organized to take over the operation and properties of the California Western Railroad & Navigation Company. Sold to the Georgia Pacific Lumber Company in 1977. Railroad operations are by contract with the Mendocino Coast Railway.

CALIFORNIA WESTERN RAILROAD & NAVIGATION COMPANY

Incorporated June 30, 1905 - Steam - Standard Gauge

Located Fort Bragg, Mendocino County. Began as the Noyo & Pudding Creek Railroad in 1881. Became the Fort Bragg Railroad Co. in 1895. Organized as the California Western Railroad & Navigation Co. June 30, 1905. Built from Fort Bragg to Willits on the Northwestern Pacific Railroad. Became the California Western Railroad December 19, 1947.

CALIFORNIA WINE ASSOCIATION RAILROAD

Incorporated 1905 - Electric - Standard Gauge

Located Winehaven near Richmond, Contra Costa County. Operated over spurs in and around the Association plant and tracks on a pier into the San Francisco Bay. Abandoned 1930 or 1931.

CALIFORNIA & YOSEMITE SHORT LINE RAILROAD

Organized 1882 - Steam - Standard Gauge

Located Sacramento, Sacramento County. Proposed to build to Modesto and then over Tioga Pass to Mono Valley by way of either Lee Vining Canyon or Bennettsville. Surveys completed 1883.

CAMINO, PLACERVILLE & LAKE TAHOE RAILROAD COMPANY

Organized September 18, 1911 - Steam - Standard Gauge

Located Placerville, El Dorado County. Began operations in 1903 as the Placerville & Lake Tahoe Railroad. Built from Placerville on the Southern Pacific Co. to Camino, a distance of 8.05 miles. Last day of service June 21, 1986.

CAMINO, PLACERVILLE & LAKE TAHOE RAILROAD - A lumber and industrial railroad operating off the Southern Pacific at Placerville. The railroad was known for its Shay-geared steam locomotives. - *Donald Duke*

CAMP SAN LUIS OBISPO MILITARY RAILROAD

Built 1941 - Steam - Standard Gauge

Located San Luis Obispo, San Luis Obispo County. Railroad was built by the Southern Pacific Company for the U.S. Army from Goldtree near Stenner Creek to warehouses within the camp. The tracks paralleled State Highway 1 for some distance before entering the military property. Ceased operations 1969. Wye at Goldtree on the Southern Pacific Railroad removed 1983. Much of the original track is still in place.

CAMPBELL REDWOOD LUMBER COMPANY

Organized 1917 - Steam - Standard Gauge

Located Pescadero, San Mateo County. Operated 1.00 mile of track. Abandoned 1918.

CANBY RAILROAD COMPANY

Incorporated 1929 - Steam - Standard Gauge

Located Canby, Modoc County. Built southward to timber. Distance 20.00 miles. Over these tracks three different lumber companies operated: Walker-Hovey Co. 1929-1937, Big Lakes Lumber & Box Co. 1937-1943, and Ralph L. Smith 1943-1948. Trackage abandoned 1948. Rails removed 1951.

CARSON & COLORADO RAILROAD COMPANY
CARSON & COLORADO RAILWAY COMPANY

Incorporated May 10, 1880 - Steam - 3 ft. Gauge

Located Mound House, Nevada. Completed to Keeler, Inyo County, California August 1, 1883. Sold to the Carson & Colorado Railway Co. July 23, 1892. Distance 157.60 miles. The Carson & Colorado Railroad, Second Division, was incorporated November 23, 1881 and built from Filben, Nevada, to the Nevada-California state line via Montgomery Pass in 1882. The Carson & Colorado Railroad, Third Division, was incorporated November 23, 1881. Built from State Line to Keeler August 1, 1883. Sold to the Southern Pacific Co. May 11, 1905. Transferred to the Central Pacific Railway February 29, 1912, but was operated by the Southern Pacific Co. Merged with the Southern Pacific Co. June 30, 1959. Section from State Line to Benton abandoned 1938. Benton to Laws abandoned February 16, 1943. Laws to Keeler abandoned April 30, 1960.

CARSON RIVER RAILROAD

Organized 1867 or 1868 - Steam - Standard Gauge

Located Carson City, Nevada. Proposed to build southeast over Luthers Pass at Grass Lake in California and over Johnsons Pass to Tollgate where junction would be made with the San Francisco & Washoe Railroad

CARSON & COLORADO RAILROAD - This narrow-gauge railroad built south from Filben, Nevada, to the Nevada-California state line by way of Montgomery Pass. It eventually terminated at Keeler on Owens Lake. This train has just passed through the Montgomery Pass tunnel in California, circa 1893, the only tunnel on the line. - *Hugh Tolford Collection*

CASPER CREEK RAILROAD
CASPER & HARE CREEK RAILROAD
CASPER, SOUTH FORK & EASTERN RAILROAD COMPANY

Began construction 1874 - Mule Power/Steam - Standard Gauge

Located Casper, Mendocino County. Built from Casper Lumber Co. to Jug Handle Creek. Distance 1.50 miles. Changed to steam power June 1875. Extended trackage .5 miles into timber by 1878. Extended 3.50 miles by 1880. Casper Lumber Co. incorporated November 4, 1880. The railroad became the Casper & Hare Creek Railroad in 1885. Distance operated 6.00 miles. Extended to a distance of 8.00 miles by May 1890. Incorporated as the Casper, South Fork & Eastern Railroad July 8, 1903. Built to Camp 5 by 1912. Distance 18 miles. Reached Camp 20 by December 1945. Distance 35 miles. Abandoned 1947.

CASPER, SOUTH FORK & EASTERN RAILROAD - The Casper Lumber Co. operated this logging line to haul redwood timber to the lumber mill. The railroad used this novel 2-6-6-2 mallet-type engine called the *Trojan*. - *Donald Duke Collection*

CASTLE CRAG LUMBER COMPANY

Organized 1929 - Steam - Narrow-Gauge

Located Castella, Shasta County. Took over the properties of the M.A. Burns Lumber Co. Operated 14 miles of the original 30 miles. Abandoned 1936.

CASTRO POINT RAILWAY & TERMINAL COMPANY

Incorporated August 26, 1911 - Steam - Electric - Standard Gauge

Located Winehaven, Contra Costa County. Proposed to build from a junction with the Richmond Belt Line Railway to a quarry. No construction work done. Reincorporated by Blake Brothers Co. in 1924. Built with Key System and Oakland Traction Co. to Blake Brothers rock processing plant onto a pier of the Richmond & San Rafael Ferry Co. Distance 1.75 miles. Key System owned .78 miles, Blake Brothers .09 miles and the Castro Point Railway & Terminal Co. owned .88 miles. Blake Brothers used steam power for their operations. Key System used electric power. Key System discontinued

operations December 1933. Company dissolved as a common carrier 1962. Sold to Standard Oil June 1963.

CAZADERO LUMBER COMPANY

Organized 1889 - Steam - Narrow-Gauge

Located Cazadero, Sonoma County. Sold to D.H. McEwen Lumber Co. 1906. Sold to M.S. Wagy 1909. Abandoned 1910 or 1911.

CEMENT, TOLENAS & TIDEWATER RAILROAD COMPANY

Incorporated October 3, 1911 - Steam - Standard Gauge

Located Tolenas, Napa County. Built to Cement. Distance 2.00 miles.

CENTRAL & BOYLE HEIGHTS RAILROAD COMPANY

Organized in 1885 - Horsecar - 3 ft. 6 in. Gauge

Located Los Angeles, Los Angeles County. Operated 6.50 miles of horsecar street railway. Was an extention of City Railroad.

CENTRAL AVENUE RAILROAD COMPANY
CENTRAL AVENUE RAILWAY COMPANY

Franchise granted October 1889 - Electric - 3 ft. 6 in Gauge

Located Oakland, Alameda County. Planned to build a cable railway on 12th Street (also called Central Avenue). Franchise amended March 5, 1891, to use electric power. January 21, 1892, the Central Avenue Railway Co. was incorporated. Began operations July 19, 1893. Consolidated with the Oakland Transit Co. March 22, 1898.

CENTRAL CALIFORNIA RAILWAY COMPANY

Incorporated October 4, 1904 - Steam - Standard Gauge

Located San Francisco, San Francisco County. Built from Niles Junction across lower San Francisco Bay (Dunbarton Bridge) to Redwood Junction. Distance 16.24 miles. Opened to traffic May 1909. Deeded to the Central Pacific Railway February 29, 1912.

CENTRAL CALIFORNIA TRACTION COMPANY

Chartered August 7, 1905 - Electric - Standard Gauge

Located Stockton, San Joaquin County. Built to Sacramento. Distance 55.68 miles. Opened for service to Lodi September 2, 1907. Completed to Sacramento September 1, 1910. Sold to the Southern Pacific Co., Santa Fe Railway Co. and Western Pacific Railroad Co. January 1, 1928. Sold street railway lines in Stockton to the Stockton Electric Railroad Co. December 29, 1929. Interurban service discontinued February 5, 1933. Electrification ceased December 1946.

CENTRAL CALIFORNIA TRACTION - This interurban line ran between Stockton and Sacramento via Lodi, a distance of 52 miles. Electric passenger service was discontinued in 1933 and CCT became an electric freight only line. - *Charles Smallwood Collection*

27

CENTRAL PACIFIC RAILROAD - Building east from Sacramento to the California state line in 1863-1864, the railroad crossed Auburn Ravine near Newcastle. - *Donald Duke Collection*

CENTRAL PACIFIC RAILROAD OF CALIFORNIA
CENTRAL PACIFIC RAILROAD COMPANY

Incorporated June 28, 1861 - Steam - Standard Gauge

Located Sacramento, Sacramento County. Began construction January 8, 1863. Reincorporated as the Central Pacific Railroad of California October 8, 1864. Consolidated with Western Pacific Railroad Co. June 23, 1870. Completed to Promontory, Utah, May 10, 1869. Distance 690 miles. Became Central Pacific Railroad Co. Incorporated June 23, 1870 and consolidated August 22, 1870 with the California & Oregon Railroad; San Francisco, Oakland & Alameda Railroad; and San Joaquin Valley Railroad to form the Central Pacific Railroad Company.

CENTRAL PACIFIC RAILROAD
CENTRAL PACIFIC RAILWAY

Incorporated July 29, 1870 - Steam - Standard Gauge

Located Sacramento, Sacramento County. The Central Pacific Co. was the successor company of the Central Pacific Railroad Co. Reorganized as the Central Pacific Railway June 29, 1899. Purchased the Nevada & California Railway; Sacramento Southern Railroad; Central California Railway; Fernley & Lassen Railway; Goose Lake & Southern Railway; Modoc Northern Railway; Oregon & Eastern Railway and Chico & Northern Railroad. Merged with the Southern Pacific Co. June 30, 1958.

CENTRAL RAILROAD COMPANY

Organized 1861/Incorporated July 3, 1862 - Horsecar - 5 ft. Gauge

Located San Francisco, San Francisco County. Ran on Turk Street between Taylor and Lone Mountain Cemetery. Distance 6.0 miles. Began operations September 1883. Consolidated with Market Street Railway 1893.

CENTRAL RAILROAD COMPANY

Incorporated April 10, 1884 - Horsecar

Located Los Angeles, Los Angeles County. Organized to take over the operation of the Los Angeles & Aliso Street Railroad and the Spring & West Sixth Railroad.

CENTRAL RAILWAY OF CALIFORNIA

Incorporated 1902 - Steam - Standard Gauge

Located Bakersfield, Kern County. Proposed to build to Los Angeles. Distance 133 miles.

CENTRAL SACRAMENTO VALLEY RAILROAD COMPANY

Organized 1859 - Steam - Standard Gauge

Located Oroville, Butte County. Proposed to build from Oroville to Sacramento. Never incorporated.

CENTRAL STREET RAILWAY

Franchise granted 1867 - Horsecar - Standard Gauge

Located Sacramento, Sacramento County. Began service August 20, 1870. Ran from Front and K streets, the Central Pacific Station (freight), to 20th and G streets by way of J and 10th streets. Extended along 10th Street from K to the City Cemetery 14 blocks to the east and on Front Street north to the Central Pacific depot in 1880. Electrified with battery power in 1887. Electrified by steam-driven electric generators 1890's. Deeded to Sacramento Power & Light Company 1892. Deeded to Sacramento Electric Gas & Railway Co. June 1896. Taken over by the Pacific Gas & Electric Co. 1906. Sold to Pacific City Lines (part of the National City Lines Corp.) October 31, 1943. Named Sacramento City Lines. Took over the operations of the Central California Traction Co and the Sacramento Northern Railroad operations in 1944. Total miles operated 27.40. Last run January 1947.

CENTRAL STREET RAILWAY

Horsecar - Narrow-Gauge

Located Sacramento, Sacramento County. Operated 7.00 miles of street railway.

CENTRAL STREET RAILWAY

Charter 1891 - Horsecar - 3 ft. 6 in. Gauge

Located Santa Rosa, Sonoma County. Began operations March 1892, with 3.50 miles of horsecar line. Sold to the Santa Rosa Street Railways in 1902. Sold to Petaluma & Santa Rosa Railroad 1903.

CHANDLER, HENDERSON & COMPANY

Organized 1884 - Steam - Standard Gauge

Located Blue Lake, Humboldt County. Operated 1.00 mile of track.

CHARLES LUMBER COMPANY

Organized 1952 - Diesel - Standard Gauge

Located Boonville, Mendocino County. Operated 8.00 miles of trackage. Abandoned 1957.

CHICO & COLUSA RAILROAD

Surveyed 1875 - Steam - Standard Gauge

Located Chico, Butte County. Proposed to build from Chico to Colusa. Distance 35 miles. Survey began in 1875, but not completed.

CHICO ELECTRIC RAILWAY COMPANY

Incorporated August 15, 1904 - Electric - Standard Gauge

Located Chico, Butte County. Built 4.50 miles of street railway. Began operations January 1, 1905. Sold to Northern Electric Company August 1, 1905.

CHICO & NORTHERN RAILROAD COMPANY

Incorporated November 11, 1903 - Steam - Standard Gauge

Located Chico, Butte County. Incorporated by the Southern Pacific Co. as a holding company for the properties of the Butte County Railroad Co. Distance 30.57 miles. Leased the property back to the Butte County Railroad Co. The Chico & Northern Railroad dissolved February 29, 1912. Title of property conveyed to Central Pacific Railway. Title transferred to Southern Pacific Co. 1914. Butte County Railroad Co. dissolved January 1, 1916. Trackage now known as Southern Pacific Chico-Sterling City Branch.

CHINO VALLEY RAILWAY COMPANY

Completed April 27, 1888 - Steam - 3 ft. 6 in. Gauge

Located Chino, San Bernardino County. Proposed to build from Chino to a junction with the Anaheim, Olinda & Pomona Railroad at Carlton and then on to the coast. Built to Ontario. Distance 7.00 miles. Reached Harrington April 27, 1888. Distance 10 miles. Sold 1895 and standard gauged. Franchise abandoned 1901.

CHINO VALLEY RAILWAY - Built a steam dummy rail line between Ontario and Chino in 1888, a distance of seven miles. In this view a train is ready to leave Ontario for Chino. - *Gerald M. Best*

CHOWCHILLA PACIFIC RAILWAY COMPANY

Organized June 1, 1913 - Steam - Standard Gauge

Located Chowchilla, Madera County. Built from a junction with the Southern Pacific Co. to Dairyland. Distance 10.50 miles. Sold to the Visalia Electric Railroad Co. June 24, 1924. Leased to the Southern Pacific Co. January 1, 1936. Trackage east from Dairyland. Distance 5.57 miles. Abandoned 1956 Remainder of trackage retained as siding.

CHUCAWALLA VALLEY RAILROAD

Organized April 1910 - Steam - Standard Gauge

Located Blythe, Riverside County. Organized as a supplemental service of the irrigation project of the Chucawalla Development Co. Proposed to build 52 miles of track from Blythe on the Parker cutoff of the Santa Fe through the Chucawalla Valley.

C.W. CHUBBUCK

Organized 1884 - Tramway - Narrow-Gauge

Located Bijou, El Dorado County. Operated 4.00 miles of wooden tramway. Sold to Lake Valley Railroad Co. 1886. Abandoned 1898.

CITIZENS TRACTION COMPANY

Incorporated April 16, 1896 - Electric - 3 ft. 6 in. Gauge

Located San Diego, San Diego County. Acquired the properties of the San Diego Cable Railway Co. Electrified the road and equipment. Began operations July 28, 1896, over the cable car route from L Street on Sixth Street, C Street, Fourth Street, University Avenue, Normal Street, Park Avenue to Mission Cliff Park. Distance 4.70 miles. Deeded to the San Diego Electric Railway Co. March 23, 1898.

CITY OMNIBUS COMPANY

Began operations 1868 - Horsecar - Standard Gauge

Located Sacramento, Sacramento County. Horsecar line operating on the city streets. Renamed City Railway June 13, 1870.

CITY PARK BELT MOTOR ROAD
PARK BELT LINE

Organized 1887 - Horsecar - Steam - Standard Gauge

Located San Diego, San Diego County. Organized to take over the City & University Heights Motor Road and the University Heights Motor Road. Built a standard gauge railroad from 18th and A streets, San Diego, through City (Balboa) Park, crossed Wabash Canyon to Marlborough Street to University Avenue in East San Diego. Returned meandering west to near Robinson Street at Fifth Avenue and down Fifth to Fir Street. Operated in conjunction with the San Diego Street Car Company. A horsecar of the latter ran to 18th and A streets. The car was picked up by a steam dummy or motor of the Coronado Railroad which pulled it around the loop to Fifth Avenue and Fir Street. A horse handled the car to Broadway. Distance approximately 10.00 miles. First run made July 6, 1888. Operated intermittently until 1890. Assets were acquired by the San Diego Electric Railway Co. January 30, 1892. Abandoned April 23, 1949.

CITY RAILROAD COMPANY

Incorporated May 16, 1863 - Horsecar - 5 ft. Gauge

Located San Francisco, San Francisco County. Built 5.50 miles of horsecar street railway. First street railway on Market Street. Began operations in July 1869. Consolidated with the Market Street Railway Co. 1893.

CITY RAILROAD COMPANY

Incorporated July 5, 1883 - Horsecar - 5 ft. Gauge

Located Los Angeles, Los Angeles County. Consolidated May 1, 1886 with the Central Railroad.

CITY RAILWAY

Organized June 13, 1870 - Horsecar

Located Sacramento, Sacramento County. Began operations in 1868 as the City Omnibus Company.

CITY RAILWAY COMPANY OF LOS ANGELES

Incorporated November 30, 1910 - Electric - 3 ft. 6 in. Gauge

Located Los Angeles, Los Angeles County. Organized to construct extensions and new lines for the Los Angeles Railway.

CITY RAILWAY COMPANY OF PASADENA

Organized November 20, 1886 - Horsecar - 3 ft. 8 1/2 in. Gauge

Located Pasadena, Los Angeles County. Built in 1887 from Chestnut Street to Mountain View Street. Operated 3.00 miles of main line and 2.25 miles of branches. Electrified 1891. Deeded to Pasadena & Los Angeles Electric Railway Co. September 1894. Deeded to the original Pacific Electric Railway in 1903.

CITY STREET RAILROAD COMPANY

Organized January 1, 1885 - Horsecar - Standard Gauge

Located San Bernardino, San Bernardino County. Built from the Santa Fe Station, 3rd and K streets, east on 3rd to E Street and north on E Street to Hooperville near Base Line Street. Distance 1.50 miles. Ceased operations 1901. Rail removal began December 29, 1902. Company dissolved October 22, 1904.

CITIZENS TRACTION COMPANY - Acquired the San Diego Cable Railway and converted the cable cars to electric cars. Became a part of the San Diego Electric Railway in 1898. - *Donald Duke Collection*

29

CITY & UNIVERSITY HEIGHTS MOTOR ROAD

Organized 1886 - Steam Motor - 3 ft. 8 1/2 in. Gauge

Located San Diego, San Diego County. Proposed to build a railroad in San Diego. Placed orders for four steam dummy type engines. Two engines received became Coronado Railroad. Combined with City Park Belt Motor Road 1887. Built the Park Belt Line. Began operations July 6, 1888. Ceased operations 1890. Acquired by San Diego Electric Railway Co. January 30, 1892.

CLAREMONT ELECTRIC RAILROAD COMPANY

Franchise Granted January 4, 1894 - Electric - Standard Gauge

Located Pomona, Los Angeles County. Proposed to build from Pomona to Claremont. The route was to be from 2nd Street and Garey Avenue, north on Garey Avenue to Holt Avenue and east on Holt to the city limits. Another line was to be built on San Antonio Avenue north from Holt to Central Avenue and then east to the city limits. Construction began in February or March of 1894. Project abandoned in December 1894.

CLAREMONT, UNIVERSITY & FERRIES RAILROAD

Organized May 21, 1891 - Horsecar - 3 ft. Gauge

Located Berkeley, Alameda County. Started at Shattuck Avenue and ran west on Addison Street to Sacramento Street and then to the Southern Pacific Station. Abandoned 1903.

CLAY STREET HILL RAILROAD COMPANY
CLAY STREET HILL RAILROAD

Franchise granted August 3, 1870 - Cable - 3 ft. 6 in. Gauge

Located San Francisco, San Francisco County. Built on Clay Street from Kearney to Leavenworth streets. Began operations August 1, 1873. Extended rails on Van Ness Avenue. A branch line drawn by horses ran from Clay and Leavenworth streets to Larkin and Chestnut streets by way of Leavenworth, Vallejo Hyde, Union and Larkin streets. Abandoned in 1942.

CLEAR LAKE ELECTRIC RAILWAY COMPANY

Organized March 1903 - Electric - Standard Gauge

Located Cloverdale, Sonoma County. Proposed to build to Lakeport, Lake County. Distance 40.00 miles. Franchise granted October, 1903.

CLEAR LAKE LUMBER COMPANY
CLEAR LAKE RAILROAD COMPANY

Incorporated May 22, 1911 - Electric - Steam - Standard Gauge

Located Hopland, Mendocino County. Took over the projected right-of-way of the Clear Lake Northern Railway Co. Proposed to build to Lakeport by building a road up Dooley Creek through Sanel Valley thence across a range of hills to the Burns Stock Farm, then across McDowell Valley to the foot of the main range of mountains and then to Lakeport by running along the Pieta toll road to Highland Springs. Distance 23.50 miles. Granted the right to issue stock and bonds October 31, 1913. Surveys completed July 1913. The electric portion was not built. The Clear Lake Lumber Company built and operated 6.00 miles of steam powered railroad until 1917.

CLEAR LAKE & NORTHERN RAILROAD

Organized March 1891 - Steam - Standard Gauge

Located Lakeport, Lake County. Began grading from Low Gap 3.75 miles north of Ukiah on the San Francisco & North Pacific Railroad to Lakeport by way of Cole Creek Pass (Scotts Valley). Total distance to have been 20.00 miles.

CLEAR LAKE & NORTHERN PACIFIC RAILROAD

Incorporated 1889 or 1890 - Steam - Standard Gauge

Located Lakeport, Lake County. Proposed to build to Clear Lake. Distance 19.85 miles. Location surveys begun November 21, 1890.

CLEAR LAKE NORTHERN RAILWAY COMPANY

Incorporated January 20, 1909 - Steam - Standard Gauge

Located Lakeport, Lake County. Proposed to build from Pieta on the Northwestern Pacific Railroad east to Highland Springs, and then northwest via Kelseyville to Lakeport. Project abandoned in 1910. Part of the projected right-of-way incorporated into the Clear Lake Railroad in 1911.

CLEAR LAKE RAILROAD COMPANY

Organized 1908 - Electric - Standard Gauge

Located Yolo County.

CLEAR LAKE RAILROAD & ELECTRIC POWER COMPANY

Organized March 1904 - Electric - Standard Gauge

Located Hopland, Mendocino County. Proposed to build northeast to Lakeport. Distance 10.00 miles. No construction work begun.

CLEAR LAKE & RUSSIAN RIVER RAILROAD

Organized October 1892 - Steam - Standard Gauge

Located Lakeport, Lake County. A reorganization of the Clear Lake & Northern Railroad.

CLEAR LAKE & SOUTHERN RAILROAD

Incorporated October 5, 1906 - Steam - Standard Gauge

Located San Francisco, San Francisco County. Proposed to build through Marin, Sonoma, Napa and Lake counties to Lakeport. Connections to be made with San Francisco by ferryboats from the terminus on the Marin County shore. A branch to be built from San Rafael to San Quentin and another branch to the town of Reclamation, Sonoma County, to Petaluma.

CLEAR LAKE SOUTHERN RAILROAD COMPANY

Organized January 1907 - Electric - Standard Gauge

Located San Francisco, San Francisco County. Proposed to build north to Lakeport. Distance 130.00 miles. Surveys begun January 11, 1907. Project abandoned 1908.

CLEAR LAKE SUSPENDED MONORAIL COMPANY

Incorporated March 23, 1916 - Electric - Monorail

Located Hopland, Mendocino County. Proposed to buy the Clear Lake T.R. Company and to build a suspended electric driven car monorail for freight and passengers to Lakeport via Kelseyville. Distance 24.00 miles. Applications denied by the Railroad Commission of California June 1, 1916.

CLEAR LAKE TRAFFIC COMPANY

Incorporated December 1, 1908 - Steam - Standard Gauge

Located Lakeport, Lake County. Proposed to build to a junction with the Northwestern Pacific Railroad at or near Pieta. Distance 25.00 miles.

CLEONE LUMBER COMPANY

Organized 1900 - Steam - Narrow-Gauge

Located Fort Bragg, Mendocino County. Operated 1.00 mile of trackage on a lumber wharf at Cleone Landing.

CLINTON NARROW-GAUGE RAILROAD

Began operations September 1, 1878 - Steam - 3 ft. Gauge

Located Clinton, Placer County. Built along the west side of Juniper Creek at Clinton near the Truckee River. This was the name given to the trackage of the Pacific Lumber & Wood Co. By 1892 a total of 10.35 miles of track was laid. Abandoned 1901.

CLIO LUMBER COMPANY

Organized 1907 - Steam - Narrow-Gauge

Located Clio, Plumas County. Abandoned 1914.

CLIPPER MILL TRAMWAY

Began operations 1869 - Horsecar - Narrow-Gauge

Located Stewart's Point, Sonoma County. Began operations over the Platt Mill Co. tramway 1869. Suspended operations 1879. Sold to Richardson Brothers.

CLOVER VALLEY LUMBER COMPANY RAILROAD

Organized 1917 - Steam - Standard Gauge

Located Loyalton, Sierra County. Purchased the Boca & Loyalton Railroad Co. and the Roberts Lumber Co. Purchased properties of the Marsh Lumber Co. 1920. This section had been a narrow-gauge operation. Total operations 55.00 miles. Abandoned 1957.

CLOVER VALLEY LUMBER COMPANY - Built a 55-mile logging railroad north from Loyalton into the Grizzly Peak National Forest. In this view a log train approaches the mill at Loyalton. - *Donald Duke Collection*

CLOVERDALE & UKIAH RAILROAD COMPANY

Organized August 17, 1886 - Steam - 3 ft. Gauge

Located Cloverdale, Sonoma County. Proposed to build to Ukiah. Distance 28.50 miles. Sold to the San Francisco & North Pacific Railroad after completion of 24.50 miles of trackage. Consolidated into the Northwestern Pacific Railroad January 8. 1907.

COAST LINE RAILROAD COMPANY

Incorporated April 15, 1905 - Steam - Standard Guage

Located Santa Cruz, Santa Cruz County. Proposed to build to San Francisco along the coast by way of Pescadero. Distance 80.00 miles. A branch line was to be built from Pescadero to Boulder Creek. Distance 20.00 miles. Construction began September 1905. Completed to Davenport July 8, 1907. Distance 11.90 miles. Deeded to Southern Pacific Company August 24, 1917. Became known as the Davenport Branch of the Southern Pacific Company.

COAST MOTOR COMPANY

Organized 1889 - Steam - Standard Gauge

Located Oceanside, San Diego County. Proposed to build a steam motor line from Oceanside south to Carlsbad and an extension to Encinatas. Unable to obtain a franchise in Oceanside. The ties and rails were sold.

COAST REDWOOD COMPANY

Organized 1936 - Standard Gauge

Located Fairhaven, Del Norte County. Took over the operation of Hobbs, Wall & Company operations in and around Crescent City. Line was dismantled in 1941.

COGGINS BROTHERS LUMBER COMPANY

Organized December 1899 - Steam - Standard Gauge

Located Coles, Siskiyou County. Built from a junction on the Southern Pacific Co. to mill. Distance 6.00 miles. Surveyed January 1900. Opened for traffic May 1900. Abandoned 1906.

COLORADO & PACIFIC RAILWAY COMPANY

Incorporated January 1889 - Steam - Standard Gauge

Located Grand Junction, Colorado. Proposed to build from Grand Junction, Colorado, to San Francisco, Los Angeles and San Diego. No construction work done.

COLORADO RIVER & GULF RAILROAD

Incorporated 1901 - Steam - Standard Gauge

Located Needles, San Bernardino County. This railroad was incorporated for the sole purpose of serving the mines along the Colorado River. The terminus of the railroad was announced as Yuma, Arizona.

COLORADO RIVER LAND COMPANY

Organized September 1924 - Steam - Standard Gauge

Located Calexico, Imperial County. Proposed to build westward to Labamba on the coast, then southward parallel to the coast line to San Felipe, Mexico. Distance 135 miles. Took over the construction of a projected road from Mexicali, Mexico, to a point on the Gulf of California January 1925. Distance 75.00 miles. Reorganized as the Mexicali & Gulf Railroad April 25, 1925. Construction began May 1925. No track was laid in California after construction began.

COLORADO RIVER VALLEY ELECTRIC RAILWAY COMPANY

Incorporated February, 1914 - Electric - Standard Gauge

Located Parker, Arizona. Proposed to build from Blythe, Riverside County, California. Distance 50.00 miles. Was to build through the Colorado River Indian Reservation and then along the Colorado River to Blythe. Reorganized as the Parker & Colorado Electric Railway October 1914. Received a franchise from the Department of the Interior October 17, 1914.

COLORADO STREET RAILWAY COMPANY

Began operations November 16, 1886 - Horsecar - Electric - Standard Gauge

Located Pasadena, Los Angeles County. Built a horsecar street railway on Fair Oaks to the city limits. Electrified in 1894. Sold to the West Pasadena Railway Co. in 1893. Sold to the Pasadena & Los Angeles Electric Railway Co. in 1894. Sold to the original Pacific Electric Railway March 1902. Abandoned 1923.

COLTON & SAN BERNARDINO RAILWAY COMPANY

Chartered May 21, 1888 - Horsecar - Standard Gauge

Located San Bernardino, San Bernardino County. Built 3.50 miles of horsecar street railway. Opened for service July 1, 1888. Abandoned December 31, 1888.

COLUMBIA MATERIALS COMPANY

Standard Gauge

Located Declezville, San Bernardino County. Operated 1.88 miles of quarry road.

COLUSA & HAMILTON RAILROAD COMPANY

Incorporated July 29, 1911 - Steam - Standard Gauge

Located Harrington, Colusa County. Built to Hamilton. Construction began 1912. Completed in 1917. Distance 61 miles. Deeded to the Southern Pacific Railroad October 9, 1917.

COLUSA & LAKE RAILWAY COMPANY

Organized June 8, 1886 - Steam - 3 ft. Gauge

Located Colusa, Colusa County. Purchased the Colusa Railway November 27, 1886. Extended the road to Sites. Total operating distance 22.45 miles. Passenger service discontinued August 5, 1914. Abandoned February 26, 1916.

COLUSA RAILWAY COMPANY

Incorporated July 23, 1885 - Steam - 3 ft. Gauge

Located Colusa, Colusa County. Built from Colusa Junction on Southern Pacific to Colusa. Distance 10.00 miles. Sold to Colusa & Lake Railway November 27, 1886. Abandoned February 26, 1916.

CONKLIN MILL

Organized 1935 - Standard Gauge

Located Adin, Modoc County. Built 10.00 miles of trackage. Abandoned 1940.

CONSOLIDATED ELECTRIC COMPANY

Organized 1896 - Electric - 3 ft. Gauge

Located Santa Barbara, Santa Barbara County. Purchased the Santa Barbara Street Railway, a mule car line. Electrified October 1, 1896.

CONSOLIDATED PACIFIC CEMENT PLASTER COMPANY

Organized April 1909 - Steam - Standard Gauge

Located Funsten, near Amboy, San Bernardino County. Purchased the Pacific Cement Plaster Co. mule line. Rebuilt the line for steam power. Sold to the United States Gypsum Co. September 2, 1919. Abandoned 1924.

CONSOLIDATED PIEDMONT CABLE COMPANY

Organized 1889 - Cable - Electric - Standard Gauge

Located Oakland, Alameda County. Began operations August 1, 1890, from 24th and Harrison up and over Piedmont Hills to Blair Park. Purchased the Piedmont Cable Railway. Electrified in 1893. Sold to the Piedmont & Mountain View Railway April 1, 1895. Sold to Realty Syndicate in November 1897.

CONSOLIDATED ROCK PRODUCTS COMPANY

Steam - Standard Gauge

Located Azusa, Los Angeles County. Quarry roads built at various company locations: Largo Plant, Azusa, 3.50 miles; Irwindale Plant, 2.10 miles; San Fernando Plant, 1.20 miles; Claremont Plant, 3.00 miles (abandoned 1950); and El Monte to Baldwin Park, 4.15 miles. Began operations 1924. Abandoned 1936.

CONSOLIDATED ROCK PRODUCTS - An industrial quarry company which operated sites a Azusa, Claremont, El Monte, Irwindale and San Fernando. The railroad was used to haul rock to the crusher. - *Donald Duke*

CONSOLIDATED SALT COMPANY

Organized 1914 - Gas Engines - Narrow-Gauge

Located Mojave. Kern County. Line operated from Saltdale quarry at Koehn Lake near Mojave. Purchased the Diamond Salt Co. Deeded to Long Beach Salt Co. in 1927.

CONSUMER SALT COMPANY

Organized 1916 - Steam - 3 ft. Gauge

Located Saltus, near Amboy, San Bernardino County. Took over the properties of the Crystal Salt Co. Sold to Pacific Rock Salt Co. 1918.

CONTRA COSTA STEAM NAVIGATION COMPANY

Incorporated August 31, 1852 - Steam - 3 ft. and Standard Gauge

Located Petaluma, Sonoma County. Owned a right-of-way to San Rafael. Deeded all property to the Sonoma & Marin Railroad Co. March 23, 1875. Some construction work was done. Sold to the San Francisco & North Pacific Railroad October 27, 1876. Constructed 21.50 miles of standard gauge railroad. Became part of the Northwestern Pacific Railroad Co. January 8, 1907.

JOHN COOK LUMBER COMPANY

Organized 1892 - Steam - Narrow-Gauge

Located Hornbrook, Siskiyou County. Took over the operations of the Klamath River Lumber & Improvement Company three miles south of Hornbrook. In 1889 a mill was built and railroad organized in 1892 to extend in the Upper Klamath River basin to bring in the timber to the mill. Suffering severe losses in the Panic of 1893, Cook sold his interest to Harvey Lindley. Operation abandoned in 1902.

C.A. & KENNETH COPEN

Located Loyalton, Sierra County. Operated some trackage between 1950 and 1952.

COPPER BELT RAILWAY & POWER COMPANY

Incorporated January 24, 1902.

Located Copperopolis, Calaveras County. Organized to build a railroad between the Trinity Copper Mine and the Bully Hill Mine. Distance 24.00 miles.

COPPEROPOLIS COPPER MINING COMPANY

Electric - 2 ft. Gauge

Located Copperopolis, Calaveras County. Operated quarry road from mine to mill. Distance 5.00 miles. This property was also operarted by Calaveras Copper Co. Abandoned 1927.

CORN PRODUCTS COMPANY

Diesel - Standard Gauge

Located Stockton, San Joaquin County. Industrial railroad.

CORONA & SANTA FE RAILWAY COMPANY

Incorporated March 3, 1926 - Steam - Standard Gauge

Located Porphyry (near Corona), Riverside County. Built to Alberhill. Distance 15.37 miles. Leased to the Santa Fe Railway March 5, 1927.

CORONADO BEACH RAILROAD COMPANY

Organized 1886 - Horsecar - Steam Dummy - Standard Gauge

Located Coronado, San Diego County. Built from the Ferry Landing via Orange Avenue to Ocean Front, site of Hotel del Coronado. Distance 1.40 miles. Horsecar used until a steam dummy arrived August 19, 1886. Built from the Coronado Ferry landing, around Glorietta Bay, down the peninsula to Coronado Heights. Completed December 15, 1887. Distance 7.60 miles. Rails were being extended around San Diego Bay when the road was renamed Coronado Railroad Co. in March 1888.

CORONADO BEACH RAILROAD - Operated a steam dummy railroad line from the ferry terminal to Hotel del Coronado. Passenger cars were former horsecars which operated on the line until the arrival of the steam dummy. - *Donald Duke Collection*

CORONADO RAILROAD COMPANY

Incorporated April 15, 1886 - Steam - Standard Gauge

Located Coronado Island, San Diego County. Built from the Coronado Ferry Landing via Orange Avenue to the site of the Hotel del Coronado. Distance 1.40 miles. A horsecar was used until a steam dummy was delivered August 1886. Trackage was built south down the peninsula (Silver Strand) to Coronado Heights December 1887. Articles of incorporation amended March 1888, to include the building of a belt line around the head of San Diego Bay and north to San Diego from the Coronado Ferry Landing via Pomona Avenue to the Strand line below the hotel. The Belt Line was opened for service June 14, 1888. Distance 20.30 miles. The Peninsular Railroad of Lower California and the San Diego & Phoenix Railway Co. proposed to use the Coronado Railroad Co. tracks to enter San Diego. The Orange Avenue line was electrified in 1893. Steam division was leased to the National City & Otay Railway Co. August 1, 1906. Merged with the National City & Otay Railway Co. to form the San Diego Southern Railway Co. July 1, 1908. Electric division was sold to the San Diego Electric Railway Co. July 1, 1908.

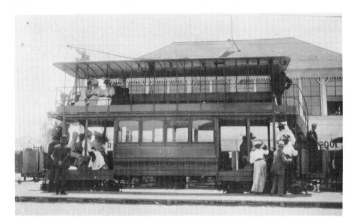

CORONADO RAILROAD - This double-deck trolley replaced the steam dummy line service between the ferry terminal and Hotel del Coronado. - *Donald Duke Collection*

CORRAL HOLLOW RAILROAD COMPANY

Organized August 10, 1895 - Steam - Standard Gauge.

Located Stockton, San Joaquin County. Proposed to build to coal fields 10.00 miles east of Stockton. No work done.

COTTENEVA LUMBER COMPANY

Organized 1911 - Steam - Standard Gauge

Located Hardy, Humboldt County. Operated 5.20 miles of logging road. Purchased the properties of the Hardy Creek & Eel River Railroad Co.

COULTERVILLE LUMBER COMPANY

Diesel - Standard Gauge.

Located Coulterville, Mariposa County. Operated a short amount of trackage around the mill 1948-1949.

COURT FLIGHT INCLINE RAILROAD

Began operations December 31, 1901 - Cable - 2 ft. 6 in. Gauge

Located Los Angeles, Los Angeles County. Built a 335-foot incline cable car line between Broadway and Court Street. Operated up a 46 percent grade. Ceased operations October 1, 1942. Dismantled 1944.

COVINA ELECTRIC RAILROAD COMPANY

Construction began November 5, 1903 - Electric - Standard Gauge

Located Covina, Los Angeles County. Proposed to build an electric railroad from Covina to Riverside. Project abandoned 1904.

COWELL PORTLAND CEMENT COMPANY

Organized 1906 - Steam - Standard Gauge

Located Cowell, Contra Costa County. Built from cement plant to quarry. Distance 3.20 miles. Completed 1907. Abandoned 1953.

CRANE CREEK LUMBER COMPANY

Organized 1928 - Steam - Standard Gauge

Located Willow Ranch, Modoc County. Built from a junction with the Nevada-California-Oregon Railroad southeasterly along Lasson Creek to the Warner Mountains. Distance 16.50 miles. Abandoned 1930. Tracks removed 1934.

CRESCENT CITY MILL & TRANSPORTATION COMPANY RAILROAD

Organized 1855 - Steam - Standard Gauge

Located Wakefield, on Lake Earl, Del Norte County. Built south to Crescent City. Sold to Hobbs, Wall Lumber Co. 1903. Abandoned 1941.

CRESCENT CITY RAILWAY COMPANY

Organized 1907 - Steam - Electric - Standard Gauge

Located Riverside, Riverside County. Built four miles of track in 1908 from Riverside Junction on the Salt Lake Route to the Crestmore Cement Plant of the Riverside-Portland Cement Company. First train operated May 1, 1908. The cement company leased out operations of the line to the Riverside & Arlington Railway Company during July 1908. The line was electrified. The route was extended north 2.40 miles to a connection with the Southern Pacific at Bloomington in April 1911. Operations were taken over by the Pacific Electric Railway on September 1, 1911 by purchase of the Riverside & Arlington Railway. Line was extended 3.30 miles further north to Rialto and a connection with the Santa Fe Railway. Total trackage from Riverside to Rialto was 9.585 miles. On March 1, 1915 the line was incorporated as the Riverside, Rialto & Pacific Railroad. Trackage was purchased by the Pacific Electric Railway on September 1, 1915. Trackage from Riverside Junction to Crestmore abandoned in 1936.

CRESCENT CITY & SMITH RIVER RAILROAD COMPANY
CRESCENT CITY, FORT DICK & SMITH RIVER RAILWAY

Organized 1906 or 1907 - Steam - Standard Gauge

Located Crescent City, Del Norte County. Known by both names. Built northward to Fort Dick and then on to timber along the Smith River. Distance 15.65 miles. Sold to the Del Norte Southern Railroad in 1912. Deeded to Hobbs, Wall & Co. in 1925. Abandoned 1940.

CROWN WILLIAMETTE PAPER COMPANY

Organized August 6, 1924 - Steam - Standard Gauge

Located Truckee, Placer County. Operated over the tracks of the Sierra Nevada Wood & Lumber Co. to Alder Creek. Distance 3.85 miles. Built from Alder Creek to woods. Distance 11.25 miles. Abandoned 1930.

CRYSTAL SALT COMPANY

Organized 1909 - Steam - 3 ft. Gauge

Located Saltus, near Amboy, San Bernardino County. Built from a spur on the Santa Fe Railway to salt beds on Bristol Lake. Distance 5.00 miles. Deeded to the Consumers Salt Co. in 1916. Sold to Pacific Rock Salt Co. in 1918. Reorganized California Rock Salt Co. in 1921. Reorganized California Salt Co. 1950. Sold to Leslie Salt Co. 1960.

DEATH VALLEY PRISMOIDAL RAILROAD - The famous "A" frame railroad is winding through Lawton Canyon en route to the mine. Mine timbers are the cargo for the day. The train has stopped for some unknown reason. - *Hugh Tolford Collection*

D

DAGGET & CALICO RAILROAD COMPANY

Organized March 1885 - Steam - Narrow-Gauge

Located Daggett, San Bernardino County. Proposed to build to the Oro Grande Co. mill and then to Calico. A branch was to be built to the Snow Bird Mine. Total distance 9.90 miles. Project abandoned 1886.

R.E. DANAHER LUMBER COMPANY
C.D. DANAHER PINE COMPANY

Organized 1911 - Steam - 3 ft. Gauge

Located Pilot Creek, El Dorado County. Built to Pino Grande. Distance 15.00 miles. Sold to El Dorado Lumber Co. 1915. Operated as R.E. Danaher Lumber Co. Became Michigan-California Lumber Co. January 1918. Abandoned 1951.

DARWIN DEVELOPMENT COMPANY

Organized April 3, 1917 - Electric - Standard Gauge

Located Darwin, Inyo County. Proposed to build an electric railway along the south shore of Owens Lake to a junction with the Southern Pacific Co. near Olancha.

DAVIS BOX & LUMBER COMPANY

Incorporated 1916 - Steam - Standard Gauge

Located Blairsden, Plumas County. Built 16.00 miles of trackage. Sold to California Fruit Exchange Growers in 1919. Abandoned in 1937.

A.B. DAVIS LUMBER COMPANY

Organized 1904 - Steam - Standard Gauge

Located Jenner, Sonoma County. Operated 2.00 miles of trackage.

DAVIS CREEK LUMBER COMPANY

Organized 1931 - Steam - Standard Gauge

Located Lookout, Modoc County. Built 3.00 miles of trackage. Abandoned 1938.

DAVIS-JOHNSON LUMBER COMPANY

Organized 1919 - Steam - Standard Gauge

Located Calpine, Sierra County. Built 15.00 miles of logging road. Abandoned 1936.

DEATH VALLEY MONORAIL COMPANY
DEATH VALLEY PRISMOIDAL
EPSON SALTS MONORAIL
AMERICAN MAGNESIUM COMPANY

Began construction 1922 - Gasoline Engine - A-Frame Monorail

Located Wingate Pass, San Bernardino County. Known by all four names. Built from Magnesia Spur on the Trona Railway. Crossed Searles Lake and then through Lawton Canyon and through Wingate Pass to the mine. Distance 28.00 miles. Completed 1924. Ceased operations June 1926. Road taken up in 1931.

DEATH VALLEY RAILROAD COMPANY

Incorporated January 26, 1914 - Steam - 3 ft. Gauge

Located Death Valley Junction, Inyo County. Built from a junction with the Tonopah & Tidewater Railroad to Ryan. Distance 20.10 miles. Opened for traffic December 1, 1914. Operations ceased March 15, 1931.

DEHAVEN LUMBER COMPANY
DEHAVEN RAILROAD COMPANY

Organized 1901 - Steam - Standard Gauge.

Located DeHaven, Mendocino County. The lumber company was organized in 1901. Later the railroad was reorganized as the DeHaven Railroad Co. Abandoned 1916 or 1917.

DEL MAR & SAN DIEGO RAILWAY COMPANY

Applied for franchise February 1888 - Steam - Standard Gauge

Located Del Mar, San Diego County. Proposed to build via La Jolla, Ocean Beach, Roseville to the foot of Market, then H Street in San Diego. Planned to take over the Roseville & Ocean Beach Railroad which had built 3.50 miles of trackage.

DEL NORTE & HUMBOLDT RAILROAD COMPANY

Incorporated 1903 - Steam - Standard Gauge

Located Eureka, Humboldt County. Proposed to build north to Crescent City. No construction work done.

DEL NORTE, MONTEREY & PACIFIC GROVE ELECTRIC RAILWAY COMPANY

Incorporated 1901 - Electric - Standard Gauge

Located Monterey, Monterey County. This railroad was incorporated to operate street railways in the Monterey County cities of Monterey and Pacific Grove, including adjacent areas.

DEL NORTE SOUTHERN RAILROAD

Organized 1912 - Steam - Standard Gauge

Located Crescent City, Del Norte County. Took over the properties of the Crescent City, Fort Dick & Smith River Railway. 15.65 miles of trackage. Extended the road a distance of 8.10 miles along the Smith River. Sold to Hobbs, Wall & Co. in 1925. Abandoned 1940.

DELONG MINING COMPANY RAILROAD

Organized September 1899 - Electric - Standard Gauge

Located Oroville, Butte County. Proposed to build by way of Pentz, Nelson Bar, Yankee Hill to the DeLong mines on the north fork of the Feather River. An extension to Quincy and possibly eastward through Beckwourth Pass was proposed. A branch was to be built to Briggs. Project never built.

DELTA FINANCE COMPANY

Steam - Standard Gauge

Located Alvarado, Alameda County. The name under which the track from Alvarado Junction on the Western Pacific Railroad to the plant of the Holly Sugar Co. at Alvarado is operated. Distance 2.70 miles.

DENVER, COLORADO CANYON & PACIFIC RAILROAD

Founded 1870 - Steam - Standard Gauge or 3 ft. Gauge

Located Grand Junction, Colorado. Proposed to build from a junction with the Denver & Rio Grande Railroad at Grand Junction, Colorado. The route would be along the Colorado River to the Gulf of California and then to San Diego, California. Survey began May 25, 1889, from Green River Station and along the course of the Green River. Survey completed to the Gulf of California April 28, 1890. Project abandoned in 1891.

DEPOT RAILWAY OF LOS ANGELES

Organized in 1888 - Horsecar - 3 ft. 6 in. Gauge

Located Los Angeles, Los Angeles County. A horsecar railway that ran on

Second Street from Spring Street to Santa Fe Avenue. Distance 3.50 miles. Sold to the Los Angeles Consolidated Electric Railway Co. May 8, 1891. Rebuilt and reopened as an electric street railway August 1, 1892. Deeded to the Los Angeles Railway Co. August 18, 1895.

DEPOT RAILWAY OF LOS ANGELES - A horsecar line that ran on Second Street between Spring and Santa Fe Avenue, connecting downtown with Southern Pacific's Arcade Station. - *Huntington Library*

DIAMOND MATCH COMPANY - A logging railroad that operated from Sterling City to Butte Falls, a distance of 45 miles. Part of the line was vacated in 1935 and completely abandoned in 1953. - *Guy L. Dunscomb*

DIAMOND SALT COMPANY

Organized 1911 or 1912 - Gas Engine - Narrow-Gauge

Located Saltdale Quarry at Koehn Lake near Mojave, Kern County. Deeded to Consolidated Salt Co. 1914. Sold to Long Beach Salt Co. 1927.

DIAMOND & CALDOR RAILWAY

Organized February 9, 1904 - Steam - 3 ft. Gauge

Located Diamond Springs, El Dorado County. Built from a junction with the Southern Pacific Co. to Caldor by way of Tiger Lily, Schoolhouse, Williams, Rodwell (Coles) and Leoni Meadow. Distance 34.69 miles. Completed October 1904. Ceased operations 1952. Track removal completed September 1953.

E.J. DODGE LUMBER COMPANY RAILROAD

Organized 1914 - Steam - Standard Gauge

Located Newberg, Humboldt County. Purchased the properties of the Eel River Valley Lumber Co. Railroad and extended it 1.00 mile for a total of 8.00 miles. Road ran from Newberg Junction on the Northwestern Pacific R.R. to Newberg and on into the woods. 2.00 miles of track abandoned in 1930. Road abandoned 1935. Dismantled 1943.

DIAMOND MATCH COMPANY RAILROAD

Organized August 8, 1902 - Steam - Standard Gauge and 39 3/4 in. Gauge

Located Sterling City, Butte County. Built to Butte Falls. Distance 45.00 miles. Most of this trackage was 39 3/4 in. gauge. 20.00 miles standard gauge rail was laid. Part was abandoned after 1935.. Total abandonment 1953. Proposed to build from Nelson on the Southern Pacific to timber. Distance 31.00 miles. A franchise was granted to build from Durham on the Southern Pacific 30.00 miles north of Marysville to Cherokee Ditch, Little Butte Creek, Magnolia and on to timber. Standard gauge section abandoned 1952. Last rail removed July 3, 1953.

DIAMOND & CALDOR RAILWAY - A narrow-gauge logging railroad which operated off the Southern Pacific at Diamond Springs and ran 34.69 miles to Caldor. Famous for its Shay-geared locomotives. - *Donald Duke*

DOLBEER & CARSON LUMBER CO.

Organized 1884 - Steam - Standard Gauge

Located Bucksport, Humboldt County. Took over the operations of the Bucksport & Elk River Railroad. Road ran from Bucksport to redwood timber on Elk Creek. Distance 15.00 miles. Trackage operated under the name of Dolbeer & Carson Lumber Co. in later years. Sold to the Pacific Lumber Co. in 1950. Built the Humboldt Northern Railway in 1905. This section ran from Fairhaven to Dows Prairie with a branch to Arcata. Sold to the Little River Redwood Co. in 1925. Sold to the Hammond Lumber Co. in 1931. Arcata branch sold to Simpson Logging Co. in 1950.

DOUGHERTY EXTENSION RAILROAD

Completed 1887 - Steam - Standard Gauge.

Located Dougherty Mill, Santa Cruz County. California Timber Co. Railroad at Dougherty Mill to handle freight cars from the Santa Cruz & Felton Railroad to the Waterman Creek Mill.

DOUGHERTY EXTENSION RAILWAY
DOUGHERTY LUMBER COMPANY

Steam - 3 ft./Standard Gauge

Located Boulder Creek, Santa Cruz County. Built from a junction with the South Pacific Coast Railway to timber, a distance of 8.15 miles. Abandoned 1918.

DUNCAN'S MILL, LAND & LUMBER ASSOCIATION

Incorporated 1880 - Steam - Standard Gauge

Located Duncan's Mill, Sonoma County. Built 5.00 miles of trackage in 1881 along Austin Creek. Abandoned 1917.

J. N. DURNEY LUMBER COMPANY

Organized 1906 - Steam - Standard Gauge

Located Weed, Siskiyou County. Built 4.00 miles of track from mill to timber in 1907. Abandoned 1912 or 1913.

DUTCH MINE RAILROAD

Steam - Narrow-Gauge

Located Quartz, Tuolumne County. Built from Quartz on the Sierra Railroad to a mine.

DWINNEL LUMBER COMPANY

Organized 1919 - Steam - Standard Gauge

Located Macdoel, Siskiyou County. Built 8.00 miles of track. Sold to American Fruit Growers, Inc. 1920. Abandoned 1922.

DOUGHERTY LUMBER COMPANY - A narrow-gauge logging railroad that operated off the South Pacific Coast Railway at Boulder Creek and extended into timber. When the South Pacific Coast Railway was taken over by the Southern Pacific, the line was converted to standard gauge and so was the Dougherty Lumber Company railway line. - *Donald Duke Collection*

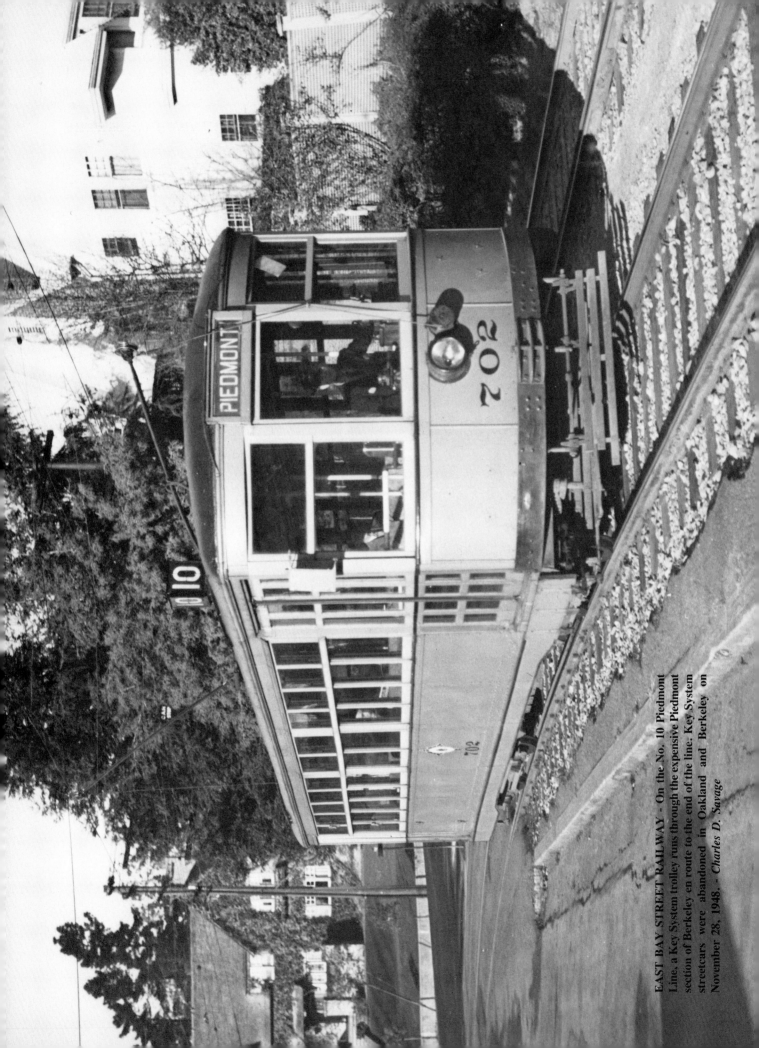

EAST BAY STREET RAILWAY - On the No. 10 Piedmont Line, a Key System trolley runs through the expensive Piedmont section of Berkeley en route to the end of the line. Key System streetcars were abandoned in Oakland and Berkeley on November 28, 1948. – *Charles D. Savage*

E

EAGLE MOUNTAIN RAILROAD COMPANY

Began operations July 29, 1948 - Diesel - Standard Gauge

Located Eagle Mountain, Riverside County. Built from Ferrum on the Southern Pacific Co. to the Iron Chief Mine. Distance 52.35 miles. Leased to the Southern Pacific Co. 1962. Last revenue run October 6, 1983.

EAST BAY STREET RAILWAYS, LTD.

Incorporated August 7, 1930 - Electric - Standard Gauge

Located Oakland, Alameda County. An operating company which operated the street railway lines of the Railway Equipment & Realty Co., Ltd. This was the street railway division of the former Key System Transit Co. In 1932 the East Bay Motor Coach Lines, Ltd., which took over the operations of the bus lines of the former Key System Transit Co., was merged with the East Bay Street Railway, Ltd. Became the East Bay Transit Company.

EAST BAY TRANSIT COMPANY

Organized 1932 - Electric - Standard Gauge

Located Oakland, Alameda County. Took over the operations of the East Bay Street Railways, Ltd. Operated over 288.58 miles of trackage in Oakland, Berkeley, Piedmont, Alameda, Albany, San Leandro, Hayward, Emeryville, El Cerrito and Richmond. Sold to the Key System 1941. Succeeded by the Key System Transit Lines 1947. Last day of operations November 28, 1948.

EAST LAKE PARK SCENIC RAILWAY

Built 1901 - Steam - 18 in. Gauge

Located East Lake Park (now Lincoln Park), Los Angeles, Los Angeles County. Ran through park and Seelig Zoo. Equipment leased to Venice Miniature Railroad in 1905.

EAST LOS ANGELES & SAN PEDRO STREET RAILWAY

Proposed in 1875 or 1876 - Horsecar - Standard Gauge

Located Los Angeles, Los Angeles County. A real estate promotion, but never built.

EAST OAKLAND STREET RAILWAY COMPANY

Chartered 1890 - Electric - Standard Gauge

Located Oakland, Alameda County. Organized June 18, 1892. Completed October 1892. Operated from 8th & Broadway, north on Broadway at 12th and then from 12th to 1st Avenue. Along 1st Avenue to a point near the intersection of what is now Excelsior Blvd. Consolidated with the Oakland Transit Co. April 10, 1899.

EAST OAKLAND STREET RAILWAY - A standard gauge street railway that operated on Broadway and in the residential sections of Oakland near the turn of the century. - *Harre Demoro Collection*

EAST SAN BERNARDINO RAILROAD

Incorporated January 19, 1888 - Steam Motor - 3 ft. Gauge

Located San Bernardino, San Bernardino County. Built along the public highway from the Santa Fe Station on Third Street between E and F streets to Orange Street in Redlands. Distance 10.12 miles. Became the San Bernardino & Redlands Railroad Company.

EAST SANTA CRUZ STREET RAILWAY

Incorporated 1890 - Horsecar - 3 ft. 2 1/2 in. Gauge

Located Santa Cruz, Santa Cruz County. Took over tracks located on Grant Street that were laid by an earlier line in 1877. Ran along Grant Street to Terminus at lower Plaza. Converted to steam dummy and operated until 1895. Electrified in 1893. Became Santa Cruz, Capitola & Watsonville Railroad in 1903 and extended line to Opal Avenue. Ceased operations December 8, 1924.

EAST SHORE & SUBURBAN RAILWAY COMPANY

Franchise granted August 13, 1900 - Electric - Standard Gauge

Located Richmond, Contra Costa County. Organized May 2, 1904 to build an electric street railway in Richmond. Incorporated December 16, 1904. Consolidated with the Oakland Traction Co., California Railway, San Francisco, Oakland & San Jose Consolidated Railway March 21, 1912 to become the San Francisco-Oakland Terminal Railways. Last operated as a part of the East Bay Street Railways, Ltd. Abandoned November 7, 1933.

EAST & WEST STREET RAILWAY COMPANY

Chartered in 1888 - Horsecar - Narrow-Gauge

Located Los Angeles, Los Angeles County. Started at 1st and Main streets in downtown Los Angeles. Ran out Main Street to Mission Road and to East Side Park (Lincoln Park). Was absorbed into the Los Angeles Cable Railway later in 1888.

EASTERN EXTENSION RAILROAD

Organized April 7, 1860 - Steam

Located Lincoln, Placer County. Proposed to build through Auburn Ravine to Auburn. Project rejected by voters June 27, 1860.

EASTERN SIERRA & PACIFIC RAILROAD COMPANY

Incorporated January 18, 1907 - Steam - Standard Gauge

Located San Luis Obispo, San Luis Obispo County. Consolidated with the Sierra Pacific Railroad. Proposed to build from Walker Pass westward to the coast. No construction work done.

EASTON RAILROAD

Organized January 5, 1913 - Electric - Standard Gauge

Located Easton (near Burlingame), San Mateo County. Built from Easton Station on the Southern Pacific in Easton to the foothills. Distance 4.00 miles. Began operations March 1, 1913. Proposed to extend its trackage to Burlingame.

EEL RIVER, EUREKA & PACIFIC RAILROAD COMPANY

Organized February 1903 - Steam - Standard Gauge

Located Pepperwood, Humboldt County. Projected south by way of Laribee to South Fork. Distance 12.00 miles. Construction begun by the Pacific Lumber Company March 1903. Sold to the San Francisco & Northwestern Company before completion May 15, 1903.

EEL RIVER & EUREKA RAILROAD COMPANY

Built 1882 - Steam - Standard Gauge

Located Eureka, Humboldt County. An extension of the South Bay Railroad Company. Built from Milford on Salmon Creek southward. Tunneled through Table Bluff to Loleta, and then on through the Eel River Valley to Alton and beyond to Van Duzen River. Distance 30 miles. Began service August 24, 1884, from Fields Landing south to Burnells. Distance 16.50 miles. Began operations to Eureka from South Bay July 6, 1885. Distance 6.30 miles. Purchased the California & Northern in 1901. Distance 9 miles. Sold to San Francisco & Northwestern 1903. Became part of the Northwestern Pacific in 1907. Became part of Eureka Southern Railroad in 1984.

EEL RIVER VALLEY LUMBER COMPANY

Organized 1891 - Steam - Standard Gauge

Located Fortuna, Humboldt County. Built into the Strong's Creek area. Distance 8.00 miles. Sold to the E.J. Dodge Lumber Co. in 1914.

EL DORADO LIME & MINERAL COMPANY

Steam - Narrow-Gauge

Located Bullard, El Dorado County. A 30-inch gauge crushed limestone hauler that carried minerals over two miles of track to a transfer at Bullard, on Southern Pacific's Placerville branch. Line operated by a Shay-geared locomotive until 1925, when replaced by a gasoline-driven Plymouth. Closest post office was Single Springs.

EL DORADO LUMBER COMPANY RAILROAD

Organized 1901 - Steam - 3 ft. Gauge

Located Camino, El Dorado County. Purchased the properties of the American River Land & Lumber Company. Extended the trackage to 34.00 miles. Sold to the Michigan-California Lumber Company 1917. Abandoned 1949-1950.

ELECTRIC RAPID TRANSIT COMPANY

Incorporated March 3, 1890 - Electric - Standard Gauge

Located Los Angeles, Los Angeles County. Incorporated to take over the properties of the Los Angeles Electric Railway Company. Tried operating horse-cars after a boiler explosion in the powerhouse. Became the Belt Line Railroad Company July 1890. Deeded to the Los Angeles Consolidated Electric Railway Co. November 3, 1891. Changed to 3 ft. 6 in. gauge December 31, 1891. Sold to the Los Angeles Railway Company August 18, 1895.

ELECTRIC RAPID TRANSIT STREET CAR COMPANY

Chartered March 1, 1887 - Electric - Standard Gauge

Located San Diego, San Diego County. Electrified the trackage of the San Diego & Old Town Street Railroad Co. from Kettner Blvd. and Broadway in San Diego to the Plaza in Old Town. Distance 2.85 miles. Began operations November 19, 1887. Electric motors pulled four-wheel trailers. In December the motors, trailers and overhead wire were transferred to a new line built from K Street on Fourth Avenue, University Avenue, Normal Street to Campus Avenue. Began operations December 31, 1887. Ceased operations June 1889. Franchise taken over by the San Diego Cable Railway Co.

ELK CREEK RAILROAD

Organized April 1889 - Steam - 3 ft. Gauge

Located Greenwood Creek, Mendocino County. Built to Elk Creek. Distance 20.00 miles. A branch was built down the right bank of Alder Creek. Distance 8.00 miles. Abandoned in 1913.

ELK REDWOOD COMPANY RAILROAD

Organized 1934 - Steam - 3 ft. Gauge

Located Elk, Mendocino County. Purchased from Goodyear Lumber Co. trackage from Elk to Alder Creek. Distance 28.00 miles. Trackage to Ponsalli Ranch. Distance 15.00 miles. Line from Elk to Alder Creek abandoned 1936. Line from Elk to Ponsalli Ranch abandoned 1938.

ELK RIVER MILL & LUMBER COMPANY

Organized 1885 - Steam - Standard Gauge

Located Elk River (Falk), Humboldt County. Built along Elk River to timber. Distance 6.00 miles. Abandoned 1937.

ELK RIVER RAILROAD

Incorporated July 22, 1882 - Steam - 3 ft. Gauge

Located Bucksport, Humboldt County. Sold to the Bucksport & Elk River Railroad. Converted to standard gauge in 1884. Reorganized as the Bucksport & Elk River Railway May 14, 1932. Abandoned 1950. Dismantled 1953.

ELKHORN & HUMBOLDT RAILROAD COMPANY

Organized May 10, 1875 - Steam - 3 ft. Gauge

Located Woodland, Yolo County. Proposed to build to Longview. Distance 16.00 miles.

ELMHURST STREET RAILWAY COMPANY

Incorporated May 1, 1910 - Electric - Standard Gauge

Located Elmhurst, Sacramento County. Proposed to build an electric street railway from the terminus of the Sacramento Electric, Gas & Railway Company to Manzanita and Helvetia avenues.

EL PASO, PHOENIX & CALIFORNIA RAILROAD COMPANY

Incorporated 1900 - Steam - Standard Gauge

Located El Paso, Texas. Proposed to build from El Paso, Texas, to Benson, Arizona, down the San Pedro Valley to the Gila River, to Florence, Phoenix and into California. No construction work was done.

ELSINORE, POMONA & LOS ANGELES RAILWAY COMPANY

Incorporated April 15, 1887 - Steam - Standard Gauge

Located Elsinore, Riverside County. Proposed to build from Los Angeles to San Jacinto via Pomona, South Riverside (Corona) to Elsinore. A branch to be built to Azusa and Lordsburg. Distance 57.33 miles. Built from Elsinore Junction to Alberhill. Distance 7.60 miles. Completed July 1, 1898. Rest of project abandoned March 1889. Leased to Southern California Railway 1896. Sold to the Santa Fe Railway January 17, 1906.

ELYSIAN PARK STREET RAILWAY COMPANY

Incorporated August 24, 1887 - Horsecar - 3 ft. 6 in. Gauge

Located Los Angeles, Los Angeles County. Built 3.14 miles of horsecar line. Sold to the Los Angeles Consolidated Electric Railway Co. November 16, 1891, and electrified. Deeded to Pasadena & Pacific Railway Co. November 15, 1895. Became part of the Los Angeles Railway Co.

EMERGENCY TRANSPORTATION COMPANY

Organized April 27, 1918 - Electric - Standard Gauge

Located Oakland, Alameda County. Proposed to build a single track street railway with a turnout on Chestnut Street in Oakland to Moore Shipbuilding Co. Upon completion the road was to be leased and operated by the San Francisco-Oakland Terminal Railways.

EMPIRE CITY RAILWAY

Organized 1910 - Steam - 30 in. Gauge

Located Empire City, Tuolumne County. Purchased the Stanislaus Railway. Extended trackage to Cold Spring Hill. Connection was made with the Sugar Pine Railway by an incline just above Lyon's Dam. Distance 12.00 miles. Operations were taken over by the Standard Lumber Co. in 1910.

EMPIRE COAL MINE & RAILROAD COMPANY

Organized June 23, 1877 - Steam - 26 in. Gauge

Located Antioch, Contra Costa County. Built to Empire Coal Mines on Mt. Diablo at Johnsonville. Distance 6.75 miles. Began construction August 25, 1877. Opened for traffic January 26, 1878. Ceased operations in 1897. Reorganized as Antioch Railroad in 1899. Very little activity under this name. Abandoned 1901.

EMPIRE REDWOOD COMPANY RAILROAD

Organized 1903 - Steam - Standard Gauge

Located Gualala, Mendocino County. Purchased the Gualala Milling Company Railroad. Distance 17.00 miles. Extended trackage 1.00 mile. Sold to the American Redwood Company 1915. Extended 4.00 miles. Sold to the National Redwood Company 1915. Abandoned 1923

ENID, SAN DIEGO & PACIFIC RAILROAD COMPANY

Chartered December 1, 1902 - Steam - Standard Gauge

Located Enid, Oklahoma. Proposed to build to San Diego. Distance 1,000 miles. Project abandoned 1903.

ESCONDIDO STREET CAR COMPANY

Began operations April 1, 1886 - Horsecar

Located Escondido, San Diego County. Organized by the Escondido Land & Town Company and laid track from the California Central (now Santa Fe) Station to a hotel site on Grand Avenue. Distance 1.00 mile.

EUREKA & EASTERN RAILROAD COMPANY

Organized January 6, 1902 - Steam - Standard Gauge

Located Eureka, Humboldt County. Proposed to build to Oregon and Idaho. A great deal of discussion on this project was held in Oregon and Idaho, but no construction.

EUREKA & EASTERN RAILWAY

Steam - Standard Gauge

Located Eureka, Humboldt County. The incorporation date of this railway, if in fact it was ever incorporated, is not known. What is known is that British investors, lead by Lord Thurlow, planned to build this Humboldt County railroad to run between Eureka and Redding. They also planned to connect with the Northern Pacific near Boise City, Idaho, and Oregon Short Line.

EUREKA & FRESHWATER RAILWAY

Incorporated 1900 - Steam - Standard Gauge

Located Freshwater, Humboldt County. Built from Freshwater Junction on the California & Northern Railway to Freshwater. Distance 14.35 miles. Began operations to timber along Maple Creek August 7, 1901. Some trackage purchased from the Humboldt Logging Company. Sold to Excelsior Logging Co. 1903. Sold to Pacific Lumber Company 1914.

EUREKA & KLAMATH RIVER RAILROAD

Incorporated January 12, 1896 - Steam - Standard Gauge

Located Vance, Humboldt County. Took over the operations of the Humboldt & Mad River Railroad (Vance Railroad) between Vance and Eureka. Began grading an extension between Eureka and Arcata April 14, 1899. Distance 7.50 miles. Completed construction to Arcata June 22, 1900. Proposed an extension from Arcata to Crescent City. Surveys for this extension began December 1900. Project abandoned 1901. Railroad extended to Samoa 1901. Sold to Hammond Lumber Co. 1900. Deeded to the Oregon & Eureka Railroad 1903. Section of the trackage was abandoned 1908. Sold to the Northwestern Pacific Railroad 1911.

EUREKA & RED BLUFF RAILROAD

Surveyed May 1892 - Steam - Standard Gauge

Located Eureka, Humboldt County. Surveyed the route for a railroad to Red Bluff, Tehama County. If the survey proved feasible the road was to be incorporated. Project abandoned January 1893.

EUREKA MUNICIPAL RAILWAY

Began operations December 23, 1921 - Electric - Standard Gauge

Located Eureka, Humboldt County. Successor to the Humboldt Transit Company. Municipal Railway and Eureka Street Railway were two terms the city of Eureka applied to the properties. Tickets and transfers were printed to read Eureka Street Railway. The cars were lettered Municipal Railway. Last day of operations was February 20, 1940.

EUREKA RAILROAD COMPANY

Organized 1852 - Steam - 5 ft. Gauge

Located Sacramento, Sacramento County. Proposed to build to Mormon Island. No construction work was done. The purchased right-of-way was laid with a plank road which was found to be cheaper.

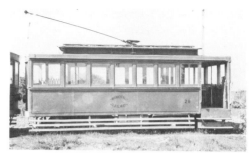

EUREKA MUNICIPAL RAILWAY - The city of Eureka took over the Humboldt Transit Company, thus forming the Eureka Municipal Railway in 1921. Trolleys operated until February 1940. - *Ted Wurm*

EUREKA SOUTHERN RAILROAD COMPANY

Incorporated 1983 - Diesel - Standard Gauge

Located Eureka, Humboldt County. Purchased the Eel River section of the Northwestern Pacific Railroad Company August 27, 1984. This included the trackage from Eureka to Mile Post 142, three miles north of Willits in Mendocino County. Distance 145 miles. Purchase also included the Carlotta, Korblex and Samoa branches. Operations began November 1, 1894. First passenger service inaugurated by the Redwood Coast Railway Company (Great Western Tours) May 17, 1985. Filed for bankruptcy on December 15, 1986. On November 12, 1991, a U.S. Bankruptcy Court ordered the sale of the company to a public agency, thus guaranteeing that the rail line will continue operating.

EUREKA SOUTHERN RAILROAD - A railroad organized in 1983 to take over the northern end of the Northwestern Pacific Railroad from Willits to Eureka. Tourist trains were operated by Great Western Tours. - *W.C. Whittaker*

EUREKA STREET RAILROAD COMPANY

Chartered October 14, 1887 - Horsecar - Standard Gauge

Located Eureka, Humboldt County. Built 3.46 miles of street railway. Began operations August 21, 1888. Ceased operations March 30, 1894.

EVERETT STREET RAILWAY

Organized May 1911 - Electric - Standard Gauge

Located Glendale, Los Angeles County. This company was promoted by the Glendale & Eagle Rock Railway to build an electric railway over certain streets in Glendale.

EXCELSIOR REDWOOD COMPANY

Organized 1891 - Steam - Standard Gauge

Located Eureka, Humboldt County. Built 15.00 miles of logging road from Freshwater to Maple Creek. Sold to the Freshwater Lumber Company 1903. Sold to the Pacific Lumber Company 1905.

EXPOSITION TERMINAL RAILWAY COMPANY

Organized May 2, 1913 - Steam

Located San Francisco, San Francisco County. Proposed to build and operate a railroad on the grounds of the Panama-Pacific Exposition. Operating trackage 10.00 miles.

FEATHER RIVER RAILWAY - A train of flatcars and boxcars loaded with lumber eases down the grade from the mill at Feather Falls to a junction with the Western Pacific at Land.

- Jim Wren

F

FAIRFAX INCLINE RAILROAD COMPANY

Began operations August 16, 1913 - Cable

Located Manor Hill, San Francisco, San Francisco County. Built 1,800-foot long incline cable car line. Abandoned 1929.

FAIRVIEW RAILROAD

Organized 1888 - Steam - Narrow-Gauge

Located Fairview, Orange County. Built from Southern Pacific Railroad near Costa Mesa. Distance 2.25 miles. Grading began January 1888. Completed March 23, 1888. Abandoned April 6, 1889.

FALK & MINOR LUMBER COMPANY

Built 1875 - Steam - Standard Gauge

Located Arcata, Humboldt County. Built 1.75 miles of track around the Dolly Vernon Mill. Abandoned 1875. Rebuilt 1876 around Jolly Giant Mill. Distance 1.50 miles. Abandoned 1880.

FALKES AERIAL RAILWAY

Organized March 15, 1912 - Electric

Located Santa Monica, Los Angeles County. Proposed to build on Fremont Avenue from Tidewater to Sawtell on the east. Applied for a franchise May 1, 1912.

FARALLON MIDLAND RAILWAY

Built 1880 - Mule Power - 3 ft. Gauge

Located Farallon Islands. Built from North Landing to Lighthouse Hill by the U. S. Coast Guard. The tram used wooden rails covered with strap iron, which were replaced by T-section rail in 1887. The tramway was extended to East Landing in 1887, for a total distance of 3,559 feet. The section of track from Lighthouse Hill to North Landing was abandoned in 1903. The tram is still in operation by the Point Reyes Bird Observatory, which has operated it in cooperation with the Wildlife Service since 1972. Motive power for the four-wheel cart is provided by man power. The island is 26 miles west of the entrance to San Francisco Bay.

FEATHER RIVER & BECKWOURTH PASS RAILROAD

Incorporated June 8, 1868 - Steam - Standard Gauge

Located Oroville, Butte County. Proposed to build along the North Fork of the Feather River over Beckwourth Pass to the California-Nevada border. Distance 145.00 miles. Project abandoned in 1871 or 1872.

FEATHER RIVER-CRESCENT MILLS RAILROAD

Incorporated December 15, 1902 - Steam

Located Crescent Mill, Plumas County. The projected route was from a point on the Feather River along Indian Creek to Crescent Mills.

FEATHER RIVER LUMBER COMPANY

Organized 1915 - Steam - 3 ft. Gauge

Located Portola, Plumas County. Built from mill to timber. Distance 30.50 miles. Abandoned 1943.

FEATHER RIVER PINE MILLS

Organized 1927 - Steam - Standard Gauge

Located near Oroville, Butte County. Organized to take over the properties of the Hutchinson Lumber Company including 32 miles of railroad. Purchased property April 22, 1927. Fire destroyed the mill near Oroville October 6, 1927. Operations discontinued. Properties sold to Feather River Railway Co. October 13, 1939, all but the trackage from Land to Feather Falls. Distance 17.57 miles. Abandoned 1950.

FEATHER RIVER RAILWAY COMPANY

Incorporated October 13, 1939 - Steam - Standard Gauge

Located Feather Falls, Butte County. Extends from junction with the Western Pacific Railway at Land to Feather Falls. Organized to acquire and operate the railroad owned by the Feather River Pine Mills. Built a mill at Feather Falls 22.00 miles east of the one that burned in 1927. Trackage between Bidwell Bar and Feather Falls became a common carrier. Rest of the trackage continued to operate as a logging road. All logging trackage abandoned October 1, 1966.

FELTON & PESCADERO RAILROAD COMPANY

Incorporated June 3, 1883 - Steam - 3 ft. Gauge

Located Near Felton, Santa Cruz County. Built to Boulder Creek. Distance 7.50 miles. Opened for service May 1, 1885. Consolidated with South Pacific Coast Railway May 23, 1887. Converted to standard gauge in 1905. Became part of the Southern Pacific Company. Abandoned by the Southern Pacific Company in 1934.

FERNLEY & LASSEN RAILWAY

Incorporated October 16, 1909 - Steam - Standard Gauge

Located Westwood, Lassen County. Proposed to build from Fernley, Nevada, via Susanville, California, to a junction with the Goose Lake & Southern Railway near Westwood. Distance 136.60 miles. Construction began June 1912. Completed to Westwood September 1, 1914. The section west from Wendel is known as the Westwood Branch.

FERRIES & CLIFF HOUSE RAILWAY COMPANY

Began operations July 1, 1888 - Steam - Cable - 3 ft. Gauge

Located San Francisco, San Francisco County. Took over the steam dummy line of the California Street Cable Railroad Co. Owned and operated the Powell Street Railway system which included a steam dummy line on California Street from Central Avenue (now Presidio Avenue) to the Cliff House. The steam dummy line projected as Park & Cliff House Railway Co. Cable portion named Powell Street Railway Co. These components consolidated into Ferries & Cliff House Railway Co. before operations commenced. Electrified in 1905. The cable cars of this company always were lettered "Powell Street Railway." Sold 1893 with first Market Street Railway Co. Became part of the Municipal Railway of San Francisco in 1951.

FIBERBOARD PRODUCTS, INC. (FIBERBOARD PAPER PRODUCTS CORPORATION)

Built 1946 - Diesel - Standard Gauge

Located Truckee, Nevada County. Built to Hobart Mills over the right-of-way of the former narrow-gauge Hobart Southern Railway. Abandoned 1955.

FIFTH STREET RAILWAY

Organized 1887 - Horsecar - Standard Gauge

Located Los Angeles, Los Angeles County. Authorized August 27, 1887 to build a horsecar line on East Fifth Street between Main and Wolfskill Avenue. Also to operate horsecars on Main Street between Fifth and First streets. Was later operated by Main Street & Agricultural Park Railroad Company. Became a part of the Pacific Electric Railway in 1911.

FINKBIND - GUILD COMPANY

Organized 1926 - Steam - Standard Gauge

Located Rockport, Mendocino County. Abandoned 1931.

FIRST STREET RAILROAD COMPANY

Organized October 17, 1871 - Horsecar - 3 ft. Gauge

Located San Jose, Santa Clara County. Built a street railway from San Pedro depot along Julian, First to Reed Street. Began operation April 5, 1872. Electrified and began electric car service December 1891. Consolidated into the San Jose Railroad in September 1894.

FIRST STREET & SAN PEDRO STREET RAILWAY

Horsecar

Located San Jose, Santa Clara County.

FIRST STREET & WILLOW GLEN RAILROAD COMPANY

Horsecar - 3 ft. Gauge

Located San Jose, Santa Clara County. Operated 7.50 miles of street railway.

FISK'S MILL

Organized 1860

Located Fisk's Mill Cove, Sonoma County. Sold 1874 to Fred Helmke. Moved to Cuffy's Cove, Mendocino County, near Elk 1875. Sold to L.E. White. Became Elk Redwood Company.

FOLSOM & PLACERVILLE RAILROAD COMPANY

Incorporated September 29, 1876 - Steam - Standard Gauge

Located Folsom, Sacramento County. Proposed to build from Folsom to a connection with the Sacramento Valley Railroad to Placerville, by way of Latrobe and Shingle Springs. Distance 40.00 miles. No construction work done. Consolidated with the Sacramento Valley Railroad to form the Sacramento & Placerville Railroad April 19, 1877.

FOLSOM STREET & FORT POINT RAILROAD & TUNNEL COMPANY

Franchise granted 1863 - Electric

Located San Francisco, San Francisco County. Proposed to build a street railway.

FORT BRAGG RAILROAD

Organized 1885 - Steam - Standard Gauge

Located Fort Bragg, Mendocino County. Took over the properties of the Noyo & Pudding Creek Railroad. Extended tracks into the woods, a total of 18.00 miles. Sold to the California Western Railroad & Navigation Co. June 30, 1905. Extended to Willits and junction with the Northwestern Pacific Railroad. Became California Western Railroad December 19, 1947.

FORT BRAGG & SOUTHEASTERN RAILROAD COMPANY

Incorporated March 25, 1903 - Steam - Standard Gauge

Located Albion, Mendocino County. Planned to build from Fort Bragg southward to Healdsburg. Purchased the Albion River Railroad January 17, 1905. Became Fort Bragg & Southeastern Railroad in 1903. Sold to Northwestern Pacific Railroad January 8, 1907. Extended trackage from Keene's Summit to Wendling. Also completed Clearbrook Branch. Ceased operations January 16, 1930. Dismantled December 10, 1937.

FORT ROSS LAND COMPANY

Organized 1910 - Steam - Standard Gauge

Located Fort Ross, Sonoma County. Built 1.00 mile of track. Sold to Redwood Lumber Company in 1911. Abandoned 1912 or 1913.

FORWARD BROTHERS LUMBER COMPANY

Located Manton, Tehama County. Operated 3.00 miles of trackage 1941.

FOSTER FARMS RAILROAD

Diesel - Standard Gauge

Located Turlock, Stanislaus County. Located Livingston, Merced County. Switching lines located off the Southern Pacific "San Joaquin Valley Route" in Central California. The lines are used to bring chicken feed into the chicken farms.

FOURTEENTH STREET RAILROAD (LETTERED 14TH ST. RAILROAD COMPANY)

Incorporated November 26, 1877 - Horsecar - 5 ft. Gauge

Located West Oakland, Alameda County. Began operations February 26, 1877. Ran from 7th and Washington streets north on Washington to 14th, west on 14th to Peralta Street, north on Peralta to 16th Street. Electrified 1893.

CHARLES H. FOWLER & COMPANY

Incorporated 1910 - Steam - Narrow-Gauge

Located Grass Valley, Nevada County. Operated 2.00 miles of trackage.

FREEPORT RAILROAD

Built 1858 - Steam - 5 ft. Gauge

Located Freeport (Newport), Sacramento County. Built from Freeport south of Sacramento to Perkins on the Sacramento Valley Railroad. Abandoned about 1865. Properties became part of the Sacramento & Placerville Railroad Co. on April 19, 1877. Became part of the Southern Pacific Company April 14, 1898.

FRESHWATER LUMBER COMPANY

Organized 1903 - Steam - Standard Gauge

Located Eureka, Humboldt County. Purchased the Excelsior Redwood Company and operated their railroad in the Freshwater and Maple Creek area. Sold to the Pacific Lumber Company in 1905.

FRESNO CITY, BELMONT & YOSEMITE RAILROAD COMPANY
FRESNO CITY, BELMONT & YOSEMITE RAILWAY COMPANY

Chartered October 1887 - Horsecar - Standard Gauge

Located Fresno, Fresno County. Construction began 1888. Built 1.50 miles of horsecar street railway. Reorganized in 1895. Sold to the Fresno City Railroad in 1901. Electrified in 1903. Sold to the Fresno Traction Company in 1903. Abandoned May 20, 1939.

FRESNO CITY RAILROAD COMPANY

Chartered May 1901 - Electric - Standard Gauge

Located Fresno, Fresno County. Purchased the Fresno City, Belmont & Yosemite Railroad. Electrified in 1903 and extended as a street railway. Distance 8.58 miles. Sold to Fresno Traction Co. 1903. Part sold to Pacific City Lines, Inc. March 20, 1939. Terminated operations May 20, 1939.

FRESNO & CLOVIS INTERURBAN RAILWAY
FRESNO, CLOVIS & ACADEMY INTERURBAN RAILWAY

Incorporated January 17, 1914 - Electric - Standard Gauge

Located Fresno, Fresno County. A franchise was granted by the Clovis City Council for the company to build on 5th Street from the east city limits to the west city limits. The completed line was to join the towns of Fresno, Clovis and Academy by electric railway. Distance 24.00 miles. February 28, 1914, the name was changed to Fresno, Clovis & Academy Interurban Railway.

FRESNO, COALINGA & TIDEWATER COMPANY
FRESNO, COALINGA & MONTEREY RAILWAY

Incorporated January 9, 1911 - Electric - Standard Gauge

Located Fresno, Fresno County. Organized to build from Fresno to Tidewater on Monterey Bay. Surveys began February 13, 1911, from Fresno to Monterey by way of Coalinga, Hollister and Salinas under the name of the Fresno, Coalinga & Monterey Railway. Distance 185.00 miles. Branch lines were proposed to be built to Bakersfield and oil fields, to San Jose and Santa Cruz. The total mileage to be 358.00 miles. First construction to be from Fresno to Coalinga. Distance 52.65 miles. Project abandoned 1914.

FRESNO COPPER COMPANY

Organized 1903 - Steam - Standard Gauge

Located Gordon, Fresno County. Built from a junction with the Southern Pacific Co. to mines. Distance 4.00 miles. Operations discontinued August 1910.

FRESNO COUNTY RAILWAY

Incorporated July 25, 1905 - Steam - Standard Gauge

Located Reedley, Fresno County. Built to Wahtoka. Construction began September 1905. Began operations August 1, 1906. Distance 6.68 miles. Leased to the Santa Fe Railway August 1, 1906. Deeded to Santa Fe Railway December 28, 1911.

FRESNO & EASTERN RAILROAD

Organized September 1911 - Electric - Standard Gauge

Located Fresno, Fresno County. Proposed to build to Shaver Lake. Distance 78.00 miles. Application for charter made November 1, 1911.

FRESNO, HANFORD & SUMMIT LAKE INTERURBAN RAILWAY

Incorporated September 24, 1908 - Electric - Standard Gauge

Located Fresno, Fresno County. Proposed to build to Sanger by way of Malaga, Fowler, Selma and Kingsburg. 28.00 miles of roadbed were graded before the project was abandoned in 1910. February 7, 1914 interest in this road was renewed and an applications was made to the Railroad Commission to build the road from Fresno to Selma. Project abandoned April 1916.

FRESNO INTERURBAN RAILROAD COMPANY

Incorporated April 4, 1914 - Electric - Standard Gauge

Located Fresno, Fresno County. Proposed to build to Clovis. Surveys completed May 1914. Began operations from J Street to McKinley Avenue in Fresno June 1, 1914. A Hall-Scott gasoline motor was used. Franchise obtained in Clovis August 1914. Reached Barton Vineyards December 1914. Began operations to State College in 1916. Electric operations used on this section. Trackage extended toward Centerville. Final trackage operated from Fresno via Fairview to Belmont. Distance 18.90 miles. Clovis section proposal abandoned in 1917. Steam operation over all sections except State College in 1917. Leased to Santa Fe Railway April 17, 1922. Controlled by stock ownership by Santa Fe Land Improvement Co. from 1922, but operated separately until May 15, 1926, when control passed to the Santa Fe Railway and property was leased to that company. Extended to Centerville 1927. Electric operations ceased in 1939.

FRESNO FLUME & IRRIGATION COMPANY
FRESNO FLUME & LUMBER COMPANY

Incorporated October 31, 1891 - Steam - Standard Gauge

Located Shaver, Fresno County. First incorporated as the Fresno Flume & Irrigation Co. Built from mill to timber a distance of 12.00 miles. Reincorporated as the Fresno Flume & Lumber Co. September 8, 1908. The railroad was named Shaver Lake Railroad in 1907. Railroad sold to the Southern California Edison Co. July 30, 1919. Abandoned 1927.

FRESNO & PINE RIDGE ROAD

Chartered April, 1889 - Steam - Standard Gauge

Located Fresno, Fresno County. Proposed to build to timberlands. Distance 52.00 miles. Surveys made from Fresno May or June 1889, for about 20.00 miles. Project abandoned September 1889.

FRESNO RAILROAD COMPANY

Organized 1889 - Horsecar - Standard Gauge

Located Fresno, Fresno County. Built 4.50 miles of horsecar street railway. Electrified in 1903. Sold to Fresno Traction Co. 1935. Operations terminated May 20, 1939.

FRESNO TRACTION COMPANY

Incorporated September 21, 1903 - Electric - Standard Gauge

Located Fresno, Fresno County. Proposed to build from Fresno to Wawona and from Fresno to Selma. Distance 196 miles. Operated 42.00 miles of street railway in and around the city of Fresno. Built a line from Biola Junction to Biola, distance 8.50 miles, which was immediately leased to the Southern Pacific Co. Company purchased by the Southern Pacific Co. 1910. Purchased the Fresno City Railway and the Fresno Railroad in 1935. Section Biola Junction to Biola deeded to Southern Pacific Co. October 26, 1936. Rest of trackage sold to Pacific City Lines April 1, 1939. All streetcar operations terminated May 20, 1939.

FRONT STREET, MISSION & OCEAN RAILROAD COMPANY

Incorporated 1862 - Horsecar - Narrow-Gauge

Located San Francisco, San Francisco County. Began operation November 1866. Built a horsecar line from Broadway and Battery to Broadway and Polk via Battery, Sutter and Polk streets. Converted to cable operation January 27, 1877. Operated for a time as Sutter Street Wire Cable Railway Co. Sold to United Railroad of San Francisco May 18, 1901.

FRUIT GROWERS SUPPLY COMPANY

Began operations 1909 - Steam - Standard Gauge

Located Hilt, Siskiyou County. Built from mill to timber of Red Mountain. Total of 50.00 miles built. 26.50 miles abandoned 1934, with the remainder in 1953. Susanville operations started 1921. Built 35.00 miles of track. Abandoned 1953. Westwood operations purchased trackage from Red River Lumber Co. in 1944. Abandoned 1953.

FRUIT GROWERS SUPPLY COMPANY - Operated two logging operations in California. One at Hilt and another at Susanville. The Hilt operation is portrayed in this view of two Shays moving a log train near Four Corners. Lumber was used for the making of fruit crates. - *John Signor Collection*

FULLERTON & RICHFIELD RAILWAY COMPANY

Incorporated February 18, 1910 - Steam - Standard Gauge

Located Fullerton, Orange County. Built to Richfield (now Atwood), Distance 5.10 miles. Deeded to Santa Fe Railway July 1, 1910.

FULTON & GUERNEVILLE RAILROAD COMPANY

Organized 1874 - Steam - Standard Gauge

Located Fulton, Sonoma County. Began construction in 1875. Was opened for traffic May 29, 1876 to Korbel's. Distance 12.00 miles. Extended to Guerneville and completed March 25, 1877. Incorporated May 23, 1877. Extended to Rio Campo. Total distance 18.18 miles. Became part of the San Francisco & North Pacific Railroad by consolidation July 12, 1877. Became part of the Northwestern Pacific Railroad January 8, 1907.

GRIZZLY CREEK LUMBER COMPANY - Operating in the Hazel Creek region of the Trinity Mountains, a logging train works its way past this logged-off section of mountainside. A connection to the Southern Pacific was made at Sims, 10 miles south of Dunsmuir. - *Donald Duke Collection*

G

GALT & IONE RAILWAY COMPANY

Organized October 9, 1875 - Steam - Standard Gauge

Located Galt, Sacramento County. Proposed to build into the Ione Valley in Amador County.

GARCIA & POINT ARENA RAILROAD

Organized 1870 - Steam - Narrow-Gauge

Located Point Arena, Mendocino County. Built from Arena Cove north to Flumeville. L. E. White took over the Garcia Mill in 1891 and in 1894 the railroad became a part of the L. E. White Lumber Company.

M.C. GARDNER LUMBER COMPANY

Organized 1875 - Steam - Standard Gauge

Located Camp Richardson, El Dorado County. Operated 40 miles of trackage from mill to timber. Abandoned 1885.

GARVANZA RAILROAD

Organized 1886 - Steam - Narrow-Gauge

Located Los Angeles, Los Angeles County. Proposed to build to Eagle Rock Valley via Garvanza. Built 1.25 miles of track. Project became bankrupt in 1889. Sold to Los Angeles, Glendale & Pasadena Railroad.

GEARY STREET MUNICIPAL RAILWAY

Began operations December 28, 1912 - Electric - Standard Gauge

Located San Francisco, San Francisco County. Took over the Geary Street, Park & Ocean Railroad Co. and electrified it. Became the Municipal Railway of San Francisco.

GEARY STREET, PARK & OCEAN RAILROAD COMPANY

Chartered November 5, 1878 - Steam - 5 ft. Gauge

Located San Francisco, San Francisco County. Began operations February 16, 1880, as a five-foot gauge double-track cable car line between Kearney and Central Avenue on Geary Street, with a steam dummy extension from Central Avenue via Point Lobos Avenue (now Geary Blvd.) and First Avenue to Golden Gate Park. Standard gauged in 1891 and extended from Central Avenue out Geary Blvd. to Fifth Avenue and via Fifth Avenue to Golden Gate Park. Steam dummy operation discontinued and First Avenue trackage abandoned. Other lines operated cable cars. Ceased operations May 5, 1912. Began electric operation as the Geary Street Municipal Railway December 28, 1912. Became part of Municipal Railway of San Francisco.

GEARY STREET, PARK & OCEAN RAILROAD - Began life as a 5-foot gauge cable car line on Geary Street between Kearney and Central Avenue. Had a steam dummy extension to Golden Gate Park. - *Harre Demoro Collection*

GEORGIA-PACIFIC CORPORATION

Organized 1956 - Diesel - Standard Gauge

Located Samoa, Humboldt County. Puchased the operations of the Hammond Lumber Co. Operated 31.00 miles of trackage. Took over the operations of the Humboldt Northern Railway in 1958.

GERSTLEY BORAX MINE RAILROAD

2 ft. Gauge

Located Shoshone, Inyo County. Built from a connection with the Tonapah & Tidewater Railroad to a mine. Distance 3.00 miles.

GIANT GAP & RUBICON RAILROAD COMPANY

Incorporated January 10, 1907 - Steam - Standard Gauge

Located Gorge, Placer County. Proposed to build from a junction with the Southern Pacific Co. at or near Gorge to a point near the Rubicon River, near Gerdners. Distance 50.00 miles. No construction work done.

GLADSTONE STREET RAILWAY COMPANY

Organized April 7, 1887 - Horsecar - Narrow-Gauge

Located Los Angeles, Los Angeles County. Operated on Citrus Avenue to a real estate development.

GLEN BLAIR REDWOOD COMPANY
GLEN BLAIR LUMBER COMPANY

Organized 1903 - Steam - Standard Gauge

Located Glen Blair, Mendocino County. Purchased the Pudding Creek Lumber Co. Railroad. Distance 5.00 miles. Built to Glen Blair from a junction with the California Western Railway & Navigation Co. Abandoned 1928. Dismantled 1941.

GLENDALE & EAGLE ROCK RAILWAY COMPANY

Organized 1909 - Electric - Narrow-Gauge - Standard Gauge

Located Glendale, Los Angeles County. Built from Glendale Junction with the Pacific Electric Railway Co. at Glendale and Wilson avenues by way of Wilson and Colorado Blvd. to Eagle Rock Blvd. in Eagle Rock. Began operations March 13, 1909. Distance 2.08 miles. Incorporated April 14, 1909. Trackage extended on Glendale Avenue and East Broadway to Brand Avenue. Built up Glendale Avenue to Verdugo Park. Completed July 3, 1910. Reached La Crescenta by way of Montrose in 1913. Section between Broadway and Brand Avenue in Glendale and the terminus in La Crescenta by way of Montrose was converted to standard gauge in 1914. Distance 6.22 miles. Total trackage operated 8.20 miles. Became the Glendale & Montrose Railway November 23, 1914.

GLENDALE, GLORETTA & SUNLAND RAILWAY COMPANY

Organized 1914 - Electric - 3 ft. 6 in. - Standard Gauge

Located Glendale, Los Angeles County. This was the name suggested for the Glendale & Eagle Rock Railway. It became the Glendale & Montrose Railway November 23, 1914.

GLENDALE MILL COMPANY
GLENDALE RAILROAD COMPANY

Organized 1893 - Steam - Standard Gauge

Located Glendale, near Arcata, Humboldt County. The Glendale Mill Co. built 1.00 mile of trackage. Deeded the property to the Minor Mill & Lumber Co. 1902. Incorporated as Glendale Railroad and extended 1.00 mile in 1903. Abandoned 1912.

GLENDALE & MONTROSE RAILWAY

Organized November 23, 1914 - Electric - Standard Gauge

Located Glendale, Los Angeles County. Took over the properties of the Glendale & Eagle Rock Railway, a single-track standard gauge electric railway from Glendale to La Crescenta. Distance 6.22 miles. A single track 3 ft. 6 in. gauge electric railway from Glendale to Eagle Rock. Distance 1.98 miles. Total miles operated main line 8.20 miles. Narrow-gauge section converted to standard gauge in 1917. Extended to Glendale Junction by use of Union Pacific trackage, thus extending passenger service along San Fernando Road to East Broadway. Abandoned passenger service December 3, 1930. Union Pacific continued to use the electric operation over the tracks from San Fernando Road to Glendale. Union Pacific Railroad abandoned its trackage in 1956.

GLENDALE & MONTROSE RAILWAY - An electric railway extending from Glendale Junction to La Crescenta, a distance of 6.22 miles. Handled freight to East Glendale by means of this electric locomotive. - *Jeff Moreau Collection*

GLENDALE & VERDUGO MOUNTAIN RAILWAY

Proposed in 1912 - Electric - Standard Gauge

Located Glendale, Los Angeles County. Proposed to build a two-mile long electric railway to connect Glendale with the summit of Verdugo Mountain. This was to be an inclined railway system invented and patented by Lewis Ginger of Glendale. The company was to operate six cars. Project abandoned June 1914, because of lack of financial backing.

GLYNN & PETERSON MILL & LUMBER COMPANY

Organized 1902 - Steam - 3 ft. Gauge

Located Del Mar, Santa Cruz County. Purchased Bender Brothers Mill 1903. Built 3.00 miles of track. Ceased operations in 1911.

GOLDEN GATE & CLIFF HOUSE RAILWAY

Located San Francisco, San Francisco County. Abandoned 1902.

GOLDEN GATE RAILROAD COMPANY

Chartered June 16, 1893 - Steam - Standard Gauge

Located San Pablo Bay, Sonoma County. Chartered to build northwesterly through various counties in California and Oregon with a number of branches. No construction work done.

GOLDEN STATE PORTLAND CEMENT COMPANY

Built 1915 - Steam - Standard Gauge

Located Oro Grande, San Bernardino County. Built from mill to quarry. Distance 1.75 miles. Sold to Riverside Cement Co. 1923. Ceased operations May 1, 1928. Scrapped 1941.

GOODYEAR REDWOOD COMPANY RAILROAD

Organized 1916 - Steam - 3 ft. Gauge

Located Elk, Mendocino County. Purchased 22.00 miles of trackage used by the L.E. White Lumber Co. Built from Elk to Alder Creek and from Elk to Ponsalli Ranch. Abandoned 1934.

GOOSE LAKE 55 RAILROAD

Authorized by Oregon Legislature January 16, 1986 - Diesel - Standard Gauge

Located Lakeland, Oregon. Purchased Southern Pacific Transportation Co. trackage from Lakeland, Oregon, to Alturas, Modoc County, California. Distance 55 miles. Original railroad organized March 31, 1888, as a 3 ft. gauge railroad from Reno, Nevada via Hackstaff, Wendel and Alturas, California, to Lakeland, Oregon. Distance 235.71 miles. Converted to standard gauge by Southern Pacific May 1928. Contract to run the railroad awarded to the Great Western Railway Co. of Loveland, Colorado, in March 1986.

GOOSE LAKE & SOUTHERN RAILWAY COMPANY

Incorporated April 30, 1908 - Steam - Standard Gauge

Located Alturas, Modoc County. Proposed to build from a connection with the proposed Oregon Eastern Railway Co. near Goose Lake to Anderson on the Central Pacific Railway. Project abandoned.

GOUGH STREET RAILROAD

Incorporated September 3, 1910 - Electric - Standard Gauge

Located San Francisco, San Francisco County. Organized to build a street railway from the corner of Gough Street and McAllister Street, extending south along Gough Street to Haight Street, then to connect with lines in San Francisco. Distance 1.00 mile. Began construction November 1910.

GRAEAGLE LUMBER COMPANY

Organized 1916 - Steam - 3 ft. Gauge

Located Blairsden, Plumas County. In the early 1920's built over the abandoned roadbed of the Sierra & Mohawk Railway. Abandoned 1935.

GRANITE MOUNTAIN ROCK QUARRY RAILROAD

Incorporated 1916 - Steam - Standard Gauge

Located Warren Creek, Humboldt County. Built along Warren Creek. Constructed to deliver rock to the Humboldt Bay jetties that were being built. Became Warren Creek Railroad in 1917. Ceased operations in 1917. Section of right-of-way sold to Arcata & Mad River Railroad in 1952.

GRAND VALLEY, COLORADO RIVER & SOUTHERN PACIFIC RAILROAD

Incorporated March 1904 - Steam - Standard Gauge

Located Grand Junction, Utah. Proposed to build down the Grand Valley to the Colorado River and then to the Pacific Coast. Project abandoned in 1905.

GRANITE ROCK COMPANY RAILROAD

Incorporated February 14, 1900 - Steam - 3 ft. and Standard Gauge

Located Logan, near Watsonville Junction, Santa Cruz County. Began operations as a narrow-gauge railroad from Milepost 95.2 on the Southern Pacific Railroad to Quarry in 1911. Distance 4.75 miles. Ceased narrow-gauge operations in 1961. Standard gauge operations designed to switch cars from the Southern Pacific Railroad to quarry bunkers began in 1920. Distance 4.82 miles.

GRANTS PASS - CRESCENT CITY RAILROAD COMPANY

Organized April 14, 1913 - Steam - Standard Gauge

Located Grants Pass, Oregon. Proposed to build southwest to Crescent City, California. Distance 98.50 miles. Surveys completed September 1913. 7.00 miles of roadbed graded from Grants Pass southward by December 1913. No construction work done in California.

GREAT NORTHERN RAILWAY COMPANY

Completed 1931 - Steam - Standard Gauge

Located Bieber, Lassen County. Built from the Oregon border southward to a junction with the Western Pacific Railroad. A branch was built from Lookout to Hambone in Modoc County to make a connection with the McCloud River Railroad.

GREAT WESTERN GOLD COMPANY

Organized June 29, 1906 - Steam - 3 ft. Gauge

Located Redding, Shasta County. Proposed to build to Ingot where a smelter was located. Survey begun July 1906. Distance 26.00 miles. Project abandoned March 15, 1907.

GREATER PACIFIC RAILROAD & NAVIGATION COMPANY

Application filed June 18, 1979 - Diesel - Standard Gauge

Location South Gate, Los Angeles County. Designed to serve the Lundy-Thagard Oil Co. on a right-of-way laid in the Rio Hondo flood control channel.

GREENHORN RAILROAD

Organized 1888 or 1889 - Steam - 3 ft. Gauge

Located Kitts Mill, Nevada County. Built from a point near You Bet Side Track on the Nevada Narrow-Gauge Railroad to Kitts Mill. Distance 5.00 miles. This road was also known as Kitts Railroad. Abandoned 1902.

GREENWOOD RAILROAD COMPANY

Incorporated 1890 - Steam - Narrow-Gauge

Located Greenwood, Mendocino County. Took over the operations of the Mendocino Railroad. Extended trackage from mill to timber. Distance 21.00 miles. Sold to the L.E. White Lumber Co. June 1916. Deeded to Goodyear Redwood Co. in 1916.

GRIZZLY CREEK LUMBER COMPANY

Organized 1921 - Steam - Standard Gauge

Located Castella, Shasta County. Built trackage into Hazel Creek area to haul out timber. Connection to the Southern Pacific was made at Sims, south of Dunsmuir.

GUALALA MILL COMPANY
GUALALA RIVER RAILROAD

Organized 1884 - Steam - 5 ft. 8 1/2 in. Gauge

Located Bowen's Landing, Mendocino County. Began as a bull dragline in 1872. Converted to steam operation 1884. Built from Bowen's Landing to timber. Distance 12.25 miles. Came under the ownership of the Empire Redwood Company in 1903. Sold to American Redwood Company in 1915. Sold to National Redwood Company in 1920. Ceased operations in 1924. Sold for scrap in 1937.

GUALALA MILLING COMPANY

Organized 1872 - Steam - Standard Gauge

Located Gualala, Mendocino County. Built as 5 ft. 8 in. gauge from Gualala to Valley Crossing, a distance of 17.10 miles. Converted to standard gauge. Sold to Empire Redwood Co. in 1903. Sold to American Redwood Co. in 1915 and extended 5.20 miles. Sold to National Redwood Company in 1920 and extended 1.00 mile. Abandoned 1923.

GUALALA RIVER RAILROAD COMPANY

Incorporated January 1891 - Steam - Standard Gauge

Located Bowen's Landing, Mendocino County. Built southward through the Gualala Valley and along the Gualala River. Distance 14.00 miles. Proposed to build on through Sonoma County to Cazadero with a branch line to Point Arena to the source of Pepperwood Creek, to Pile Creek and along Buckeye Creek and the Wheatfield Fork of the Gualala River. Total of 103.00 miles to be constructed. The 14.00 miles of track constructed were operated by the Empire Redwood Co. Some trackage was built around Cazadero. Road abandoned 1908 or 1909. Equipment moved to Empire Redwood Co. holdings at Gualala.

GUERNE & MURPHY RAILROAD

Organized April 1, 1892 - Steam - Standard Gauge

Located Guernewood Park near Guerneville, Sonoma County. Built to Finley. Distance 3.00 miles. Relocated and built up Mission Gulch in 1895 or 1896. Distance 2.50 miles. Became part of the San Francisco & North Pacific Railway in 1897.

GOODYEAR REDWOOD COMPANY - Purchased 22 miles of trackage of the the L.E. White Lumber Co. out of Elk in Mendocino County. The line was later extended to Alder Creek and Ponsalli Ranch. The railroad was abandoned in 1934 due to falling redwood lumber sales. The company's three Shay-geared locomotives were abandoned at Rockport and were not scrapped until World War II. - *Hugh Tolford Collection*

HOWARD TERMINAL RAILWAY - A switching railroad operating in the privately owned Howard Terminal in the western part of Oakland, and interchanged with the Southern Pacific and the Western Pacific. - *Jim Wren*

HALL'S ADDITION STREET RAILWAY COMPANY

Incorporated July 18, 1887 - Horsecar - Standard Gauge

Located Riverside, Riverside County. Built a horsecar line from 10th and Main streets south on Main to 14th, east to Park Avenue and then south along Park Avenue to Date Street. Eventually reached the foot of Victoria Hill. Total mileage 1.569 miles. Sold to Riverside & Arlington Railway Co. June 11, 1895.

HAMMOND & LITTLE RIVER REDWOOD COMPANY

Organized 1912 - Steam - Standard Gauge

Located Crannell, Humboldt County. Purchased the properties of the Hammond Lumber Co. 81 miles of trackage were in use. Sold to Hammond Redwood Lumber Co. in 1936. Sold to Georgia-Pacific Corp. in 1956.

HAMMOND LUMBER COMPANY

Organized 1912 - Steam - Standard Gauge

Located Samoa, Humboldt County. Purchased the Vance Redwood Lumber Co. interests. Built 10.00 miles of trackage beyond the terminus of the Humboldt Northern Railway. Sold to the Hammond & Little River Redwood Co. in 1931. Deeded to Hammond Redwood Lumber Co. in 1936. Sold to Georgia-Pacific Corp. in 1956.

HAMMOND REDWOOD LUMBER COMPANY

Organized 1936 - Steam - Standard Gauge

Located Samoa, Humboldt County. Took over the properties of the Hammond & Little River Redwood Co. 80.00 miles of trackage were in use. Operated the Humboldt Northern Railway. Purchased the Humboldt Redwood Co. 1937. Sold to the Georgia-Pacific Corp. in 1956.

HAMMOND REDWOOD LUMBER - At one time operated 80 miles of logging railroad in Humboldt County. Organized in 1938 as a consolidation of Hammond & Little River Redwood Co. and Humboldt Redwood Co. - *Harre Demoro Collection*

HANFORD & SUMMIT LAKE RAILWAY COMPANY

Incorporated June 25, 1910 - Electric - Standard Gauge

Located Hanford, Kings County. Proposed to build an electric railroad through Grangeville and Hardwick into the Summit Lakes region and return through Lemoore and Armona. An extension to be built to Laton. Distance 15.00 miles. Constructed trackage from Hardwick to Ingle via Riverdale. Distance 43.00 miles. Operated as a steam road until August 24, 1917, when the road was deeded to the Southern Pacific Co. Section from Hardwick to Riverdale abandoned in 1952.

HARBOR BELT LINE RAILROAD

Began operations June 1, 1929 - Steam - Standard Gauge

Located Los Angeles Harbor, Los Angeles County. Organized as the operating agency of the Atchison, Topeka & Santa Fe Railway, Union Pacific Railroad Co., Pacific Electric Railway Co. and the Southern Pacific Co. in and about the Los Angeles Harbor area.

HARDY CREEK & EEL RIVER RAILROAD COMPANY

Organized 1907 - Steam - Standard Gauge

Located Hardy, Humboldt County. Built 5.20 miles of logging road. Sold to the Cottoneva Lumber Co. in 1911.

JOHN HARFORD'S RAILROAD

Organized 1871 - Horse Power - 30 in. Gauge

Located San Luis Obispo, San Luis Obispo County. Built from near San Luis Obispo to a wharf near Point San Luis. Completed September 1873. Sold to San Luis Obispo & Santa Maria Valley Railroad. Became part of the Pacific Coast Railway September 25, 1882. Became the Port San Luis Transportation Company February 28, 1942. Abandoned October 19, 1942.

HARPSET & SPRING TRAMWAY

Organized - 1876 - Steam - Narrow-Gauge

Located Gannon Slough, near Eureka, Humboldt County. Built a logging road from mill to timber.

S.M. HASKINS

Organized 1905 - Steam - Narrow-Gauge

Located San Diego, San Diego County. Petitioned for a franchise January 1906 to build from the foot of 4th Avenue, through Middletown, around the bay to Roseville and La Playa in San Diego. No construction work done.

HASSLER LUMBER COMPANY

Organized 1950 - Standard Gauge

Located Hobart Mills, Nevada County. Operated 7.00 miles of trackage. Abandoned 1951.

A. HAUN & SONS

Organized 1907 - Steam - Standard Gauge

Located Branscomb, Mendocino County. Built in 1908. Operated 1.00 mile of track. Abandoned 1924.

HAZEL GREEN RAILROAD

Organized 1909 - Steam - Standard Gauge

Located Horse Shoe Bend, Mariposa County. Right-of-way surveyed in 1910 from Horse Shoe Bend through Buck Meadows to timber. No construction work done.

HEALD & GUERNE LUMBER COMPANY

Organized 1876 - Steam - Standard Gauge

Located Guerneville, Sonoma County. Logging road.

HEALDSBURG RAILWAY

Organized January 31, 1914 - Electric - Standard Gauge

Located Healdsburg, Sonoma County. Proposed to build through Dry Creek Valley and Alexander Valley to Geyserville.

HELM RAILWAY

Gasoline Engine - Standard Gauge

Located Laytonville, Mendocino County. Operated 1.00 mile of switching track in 1941.

HENEY'S RAILROAD

Organized 1892 - Horse Power - 30 in. Gauge

Located Southport, Humboldt County. Built around Table Bluff to Wait's Slough. Sold to the Pacific Lumber Co. to be part of their Humboldt Bay & Eel River Railroad November 17, 1882.

HERCULES POWDER COMPANY

Organized 1921 - Gasoline Engine - Narrow-Gauge

Located Richmond, Contra Costa County. Operated 11.00 miles of industrial trackage in and around the plant.

HETCH-HETCHY RAILROAD COMPANY

Began operations 1916 - Steam - Standard Gauge

Located Hetch-Hetchy Junction on the Sierra Railway, Tuolumne County. Built from Junction to O'Shaughnessy Dam. Completed October 1917. Shops were located at Groveland. Leased to the Sierra Railway June 1, 1934. Became their Hetch-Hetchy Division. Abandoned 1949.

HETCH-HETCHY & YOSEMITE VALLEY RAILROAD COMPANY

Incorporated August 28, 1900 - Steam - 3 ft. Gauge

Located Tuolumne, Tuolumne County. Operated over 25.00 miles of the West Side Lumber Co. trackage as a common carrier from Tuolumne to Thompson's Meadows. Reorganized and sold to the Pickering Lumber Co. in 1925. Reorganized as West Side Lumber Company in 1934. Common carrier company dissolved June 28, 1943. Trackage abandoned 1961.

HETCH-HETCHY RAILROAD - Built by the city of San Francisco to haul in supplies for the construction of O'Shaughnessy Dam. In this view a train of materials crosses the Tuolumne River en route to the dam. - *W.C. Whittaker*

J.C. HICKMAN & SON

Organized 1910 - Steam - Standard Gauge

Located Annapolis, Sonoma County. Operated 2.00 miles of track. Abandoned 1912.

HIGHLAND LUMBER COMPANY RAILROAD

Organized December 12, 1890 - Steam - Standard Gauge

Located San Bernardino, San Bernardino County. Began construction of a railroad grade up City Creek Canyon. In June 1891 the idea of a railroad was abandoned and a switchback wagon road was built up the mountain to the mill at Long Point.

HIGHLAND PACIFIC RAILROAD

Incorporated September 18, 1909 - Electric - Standard Gauge

Located Lakeport, Lake County. Organized to take over the Sonoma & Lake County Railroad. Proposed to build from Upper Lake to Lakeport, with a branch 3.00 miles from Kelseyville to the nearest point on the main line in Big Valley, and from Lakeport to Preston and on to Santa Rosa. Distance 70.00 miles. Proposed to secure control of the Petaluma & Santa Rosa Railway or secure trackage rights over it.

HIGHLAND PARK & FRUIT VALE RAILROAD

Organized 1875 - Horsecar - Narrow-Gauge

Located Oakland, Alameda County. Began as a horsecar line that was famous for its double-deck cars. Incorporated on April 16, 1892, as the Brooklyn & Fruit Vale Railroad, a horsecar line. Reorganized as the Highland Park & Fruit Vale Railroad. Taken into the Oakland Transit Co. May 1897. Became part of the Key System.

HIGHLAND RAILROAD

Organized 1887 - Steam - 3 ft. 6 in. Gauge

Located San Bernardino, San Bernardino County. Organized as the San Bernardino, Arrowhead & Waterman Railroad Co. Completed August 17, 1888. Built from a junction with the San Bernardino & Redlands Railroad to Patton State Institution via Harlem Springs and Highland. Sold to the San Bernardino Valley Traction Co. in 1903 and converted to standard gauge. Sold to the Pacific Electric Railway September 1, 1911.

HIGHLAND RAILROAD - A motor road built from the junction of the San Bernardino & Redlands Railroad to Patton State Hospital and Highland. - *Donald Duke Collection*

HIGHLAND RAILROAD COMPANY

Incorporated March 3, 1888 - Horsecar - 3 ft. 6 in. Gauge

Located Pasadena, Los Angeles County. Proposed to build from Los Angeles to Wilson's Peak via Pasadena. Construction was from Colorado Street and Euclid Avenue in Pasadena via Walnut Street to Highland Street near Altadena. Began operations July 1888. Extended to Raymond Station 1889. Total mileage 4.75 miles. Sold to Pasadena & Los Angeles Electric Railway 1894 and electrified. Deeded to the original Pacific Electric Railway 1903. Abandoned 1941.

F. A. HIHN LUMBER COMPANY

Organized 1874 - Steam - Narrow-Gauge

Located Loma Prieta, Santa Clara County. Operated in Loma Prieta during the 1880's.

HOBART ESTATE COMPANY

Organized 1917 - Steam - 3 ft. and Standard Gauge

Located Hobart, Nevada County. Purchased the Sierra Nevada Wood & Lumber Co. Standard gauge operations from Truckee to Hobart Mills. Narrow-gauge operations from mill to woods Operating mileage 32.00 miles. Organized section Truckee to Hobart Mills as the Hobart Southern Railroad Co. in 1932. Abandoned 1937.

HOBART SOUTHERN RAILROAD COMPANY

Organized 1932 - Steam - Standard Gauge

Located Hobart Mills, Nevada County. Operated over the standard gauge section of the Sierra Nevada Wood & Lumber Co. to Truckee. Purchased by the Hobart Estates Co. in 1917. Distance 6.50 miles. Abandoned December 1, 1937.

HOBART ESTATE - A photograph showing Hobart Mills shortly after the abandonment of the Hobart Southern Railroad, circa 1937. - *Guy L. Dunscomb*

Began operations October 1, 1904. Operated between El Centro and Seeley. Distance 8.73 miles. Acquired by the Southern Pacific Co. June 30, 1925.

HOLTON INTERURBAN RAILWAY - Built to connect Holtville with El Centro, a distance of 10.46 miles. Passenger service was operated by gas-electric cars. Never was electrified. - *Donald Duke Collection*

HOBART SOUTHERN - A lumber railroad operated on behalf of the Hobart Estate from Truckee to Hobart Mills. - *Harre Demoro Collection*

HOBBS, WALL & COMPANY

Organized 1886 - Steam - Standard Gauge

Located Crescent City, Del Norte County. Built to Smith River. Distance 15.65 miles. Organized as a common carrier and named Crescent City, Fort Dick & Smith River Railway. Renamed the Crescent City & Smith River Railroad Co. 1906 or 1907. Sold to Del Norte Southern Railroad in 1912. Common carrier status dissolved in 1925. Abandoned in 1940.

HOLLY SUGAR COMPANY RAILROAD

Steam - Standard Gauge

Located Tracy, San Joaquin County. Built from a junction with the Southern Pacific Co. to the Holly Sugar Plant.

HOLMES - EUREKA LUMBER COMPANY RAILROAD

Began construction 1904 - Steam - Standard Gauge

Located Carlotta, Humboldt County. Built from mill to timber. Distance 8.00 miles. Leased 7.00 miles of track on the Carlotta branch of the Northwestern Pacific Railroad in 1948. Abandoned in 1949.

HOLT & SAN ANTONIO AVENUE STREET RAILROAD COMPANY

Franchise granted February 15, 1887 - Horsecar - 3 ft. 6 in. Gauge

Located Pomona, Los Angeles County. Built from 2nd and Main streets north on Main to Holt, then east on Holt to San Antonio Avenue, north on San Antonio Avenue to San Bernardino Avenue. Distance 2.23 miles. Incorporated October 21, 1887. Completed February 5, 1888. Began operations February 10, 1888. Last car ran November 1890. Track removal began December 5, 1893.

HOLTON INTERURBAN RAILWAY COMPANY

Incorporated December 31, 1903 - Steam - Standard Gauge

Located Holtville, Imperial County. Built to El Centro. Distance 10.46 miles.

C. A. HOOPER COMPANY

Organized 1886 - Steam - Standard Gauge

Located Hardy, Mendocino County. Sold to the New York & Pennsylvania Redwood Co. Abandoned 1931.

HORTON BROTHERS RAILROAD

Organized 1902 - Steam - 38 in. Gauge

Located Loyalton, Sierra County. Built from mill to timber. Distance 15.00 miles. Sold to the Marsh Lumber Co. in 1908. Some sections were converted to standard gauge. Sold to Clover Valley Lumber Co. in 1920.

HOWARD CREEK LUMBER COMPANY RAILROAD

Built 1906 - Steam - Standard Gauge

Located Westport, Mendocino County. Built 2.00 miles of track.

HOWARD TERMINAL RAILWAY

Incorporated April 21, 1917 - Steam - Standard Gauge

Located Oakland, Alameda County. Built 1.64 miles of trackage in the private Howard Terminal in the western part of Oakland on an arm of San Francisco Bay. Interchanged cars with the Southern Pacific Company and the Western Pacific Railroad and switched the terminal tracks. Ceased operations June 1, 1978. Property sold to Port of Oakland.

HOVEY & WALKER

Organized 1929 - Steam - Standard Gauge

Located near Macdoel, Siskiyou County. Leased the trackage of the Pickering Lumber Co. and extended it 3.50 miles southward to timber.

HUENEME, MALIBU & PORT LOS ANGELES RAILWAY COMPANY
HUENEME, MALIBU & SOUTHERN RAILWAY

Incorporated September 1903 - Steam - Standard Gauge

Located Malibu, Los Angeles County. Construction began in 1906 on a proposed railroad from Santa Monica to Hueneme. Distance 55.00 miles. 16.00 miles were constructed from Malibu. Reorganized as the Hueneme, Malibu & Southern Railway January 25, 1916. Abandoned 1918.

HUMBOLDT & EASTERN RAILROAD COMPANY

Organized July 1908 - Electric - Standard or 3 ft. Gauge

Located Eureka, Humboldt County. Proposed to build from a point on Humboldt Bay to a point somewhere in the Sacramento Valley at or near Redding or Red Bluff. Distance 125 miles. Preliminary surveys began September 1909. Surveys completed December 1909. Included in the survey was a branch line to the copper district of Shasta County. Surveys for sources of electric power began in January 1910. Project abandoned May 1910.

HUMBOLDT BAY & EEL RIVER RAILROAD

Incorporated November 17, 1882 - Steam - Standard Gauge

Located Humboldt Bay, Humboldt County. Incorporated by the Pacific Lumber Co. Purchased Heney's Railroad that ran from Southport to Wait's Slough. Discontinued operations in 1883. Began construction from Alton Junction on the Eel River & Eureka Railroad to Forestville (Scotia). Completed August 20, 1884. Extended 6.00 miles south of Scotia by 1889. Sold to the San Francisco & Northwestern Railway in May 15, 1903.

HUMBOLDT BAY & MAD RIVER RAILROAD
HUMBOLDT BAY & TRINIDAD LOG & LUMBER COMPANY
HUMBOLDT BAY & TRINIDAD RAILROAD COMPANY

Organized 1875 - Steam - Standard Gauge

Located Vance, Humboldt County. John Vance began his lumbering operations on Mad River. He built a railroad from his mill to Mad River Slough north of Eureka on Humboldt Bay. The railroad was reorganized as the Humboldt Bay & Trinidad Log & Lumber Co. in 1891. Reorganized as Humboldt Bay & Trinidad Railroad Co. 1892. 13.50 miles of track constructed. Transferred to the Eureka & Klamath River Railroad 1896.

HUMBOLDT COOPERAGE COMPANY

Incorporated 1913 - Steam - Standard Gauge

Located Arcata, Humboldt County. Built from mill to timber. Distance 2.00 miles. Deeded to California Barrel Co. 1918. Abandoned 1927.

HOBBS, WALL & COMPANY - A 2-4-2 tank locomotive brings in logs to the at Crescent City, circa 1915. - *Henry Sorensen Collection*

HUMBOLDT & MAD RIVER RAILROAD - A train bringing a load of logs in from the Lindsay Creek area. A "Gypsy" engine is on the siding switching empties. - *Clarke Museum Collection*

HUMBOLDT COUNTY RAILROAD

Incorporated January 1903 - Steam - Standard Gauge

Located Alta Junction, Humboldt County. Proposed to build from the present Northwestern Pacific Railroad to Camp Grant. Project abandoned.

HUMBOLDT LOGGING RAILROAD

Began operations 1885 - Steam - Standard Gauge

Located Freshwater, Humboldt County. Built to Maple Creek. Distance 14.00 miles. Sold to the Freshwater Lumber Co. Sold to the Pacific Lumber Co.

HUMBOLDT LUMBER & MILL COMPANY

Organized 1882 - Steam - 3 ft. 9 1/2 in. Gauge

Located Korbel, Humboldt County. Built one mile of track. Extended trackage along Mad River to Canyon Creek in 1891. Distance 3.00 miles. Sold to Northern Redwood Lumber Co. in February 1903. Abandoned in 1956.

HUMBOLDT NORTHERN RAILWAY

Incorporated October 19, 1904 - Steam - Standard Gauge

Located Samoa, Humboldt County. Built by the Dolbeer & Carson Lumber Co. to haul logs to tidewater for its mill. The railroad functioned for several companies at different times: Dolbeer & Carson Lumber Co. 1905 to 1925, Little River Redwood Co. 1925 to 1931 and Hammond Interests 1931 to 1958.

HUMBOLDT RAILROAD

Incorporated March 13, 1901 - Steam - Standard Gauge

Located Dyerville, Humboldt County. Proposed to build northward to Crescent City. Distance 135 miles. No construction.

HUMBOLDT REDWOOD COMPANY

Organized 1929 - Steam - Standard Gauge

Located Carlotta, Humboldt County. Purchased the Bayside Redwood Company operations. Operated over 5 miles of trackage. Abandoned 1937.

HUMBOLDT, SISKIYOU & KLAMATH RAILROAD

Organized June 1, 1913 - Steam - Standard Gauge

Located Eureka, Humboldt County. Proposed to build to Klamath Falls, Oregon, by building along the Klamath River. Distance 350 miles.

HUMBOLDT TRANSIT COMPANY

Chartered July 31, 1903 - Electric - Standard Gauge

Located Eureka, Humboldt County. Built 11.13 miles of electric railway. Began operations September 15, 1903. Sold to the city of Eureka in December 23, 1921. Became Eureka Municipal Railway. Ceased operations February 20, 1940.

HUME-BENNETT LUMBER COMPANY

Organized 1908 - Steam - 3 ft. Gauge

Located Hume Lake, Fresno County. Took over the facilities of the Sequoia Railroad and moved them to Converse Basin. Two lines were in operation. One ran south along Ten Mile Creek from the log dump to a junction about a mile above the lake and then across Tornado Creek to timber. Abandoned 1915. The other continued south up Ten Mile Creek to Bearskin Meadow with several spurs to timber. Converted to standard gauge in 1914. Operations reincorporated as Sanger Lumber Co. in 1917. Ceased operations in 1918. Abandoned in 1930.

HUTCHINSON LUMBER COMPANY

Organized 1923 - Steam - Standard Gauge

Located near Oroville, Butte County. Built from mill to timber. Total mileage 35.00 miles. Company failed in 1927. Sold to Feather River Pine Mills in April 22, 1927.

INTERURBAN ELECTRIC RAILWAY - A Southern Pacific electric commuter train races along the 7th Street line in the southern section of Oakland. The large "2" was a means for towermen to select the proper track in San Francisco's Bay Bridge Terminal. - *Charles D. Savage*

I

IMPERIAL & GULF RAILROAD COMPANY

Incorporated March 11, 1902 - Steam - Standard Gauge

Located Niland, Imperial County. Built from Imperial Junction on the Southern Pacific to Imperial. Distance 29.35 miles. Contract for grading let May 2, 1902. Forfeited its charter to the Inter-California Railway Co. in December 14, 1905. Operated by the Southern Pacific Co. Assigned to the Southern Pacific Co. on May 31, 1935.

IMPERIAL IRRIGATION DISTRICT

Organized 1918 - Steam - Standard Gauge

Located Andrade, Imperial County. Operated just south of Araz Junction with the Southern Pacific Co. on the Inter-California Railroad. Granted trackage rights over the Inter-California Railroad to Volcano in Mexico. Distance 25.00 miles. Built from Volcano to Volcano Lake. Distance 5.48 miles. Extended to Cocapah Quarry in 1920. Distance 6.00 miles. Rails removed from Volcano to Cocopah Quarry in 1921. Trackage was laid on Ockerson Levee, Saiz Levee and other levees in Mexico until 45.50 miles of track were in operation. Operations ceased in 1938. Tracks were removed in 1939.

IMPERIAL IRRIGATION DISTRICT RAILROAD

Organized 1918 - Steam - Standard Gauge

Located Imperial, Imperial County. Used during the construction period of the Imperial Valley Irrigation District's canals.

INTER-COUNTIES RAILWAY

Application for charter April 1911 - Electric - Standard Gauge

Located Modesto, Stanislaus County. Proposed to build to Crow's Landing and Newman, and from Modesto to Turlock, Merced, Madera and Fresno.

IMPERIAL VALLEY GYPSUM & OIL CORPORATION
IMPERIAL GYPSUM COMPANY RAILROAD

Organized September 1920 - Steam - 3 ft. Gauge

Located Plaster City, Imperial County. Built from a junction with the San Diego & Arizona Eastern Railway to quarry. Distance 19.63 miles. Surveys started April 1921. Completed September 1922. Opened for traffic October 14, 1922. Sold to the Pacific Portland Cement Co. in 1924. Sold to U.S. Gypsum Co. in 1946.

INDIAN VALLEY RAILROAD COMPANY

Incorporated June 30, 1916 - Steam - Standard Gauge

Located Paxton, Plumas County. Built from a junction with the Western Pacific Railroad to Engels. Distance 21.50 miles. Completed September 1, 1917. Sold to the Western Pacific Railroad 1921. Abandoned March 1, 1938.

INDIAN VALLEY RAILROAD - Built from a junction with the Western Pacific at Paxton to Engels, a distance of 21.50 miles. A train bound for Engels passes through Crescent Mills. - *W.C. Whittaker*

INDUSTRIAL TERMINAL RAILWAY COMPANY

Organized January 4, 1915 - Steam - Standard Gauge

Located Los Angeles, Los Angeles County. Incorporated March 20, 1915. Built from Alameda Street north of Aliso Street, then east and north to Alhambra Avenue to the Los Angeles River. Distance 1.97 miles. This area now occupied by the Los Angeles Union Passenger Terminal. Operated by the Southern Pacific Company. Deeded to the Southern Pacific Co.

INTER-CALIFORNIA RAILWAY COMPANY

Incorporated June 15, 1904 - Steam - Standard Gauge

Located Niland, Imperial County. The development of California's Imperial Valley required access to rail transportation. Since SP's main line passed several miles to the northeast, a connecting link with the valley was built as the Imperial & Gulf Railroad. This road was incorporated March 11, 1902 and extended south from Old Beach (Imperial Junction, later Niland) into the valley and ended at El Centro. Since most of the vegetables moved east, it was decided to build a low grade line east to Yuma by way of the Republic of Mexico. The Inter-California Railway Company was incorporated on June 15, 1904, to build a line connecting El Centro with Araz Junction, six miles west of Yuma, a distance of 96 miles. The line was formally opened June 30, 1911 and leased to the SP in 1912. It was assigned to the Southern Pacific May 31, 1935. Trackage within Mexico was abandoned in 1959.

INTER-COUNTIES RAILWAY

Application for charter April 1911 - Electric - Standard Gauge

Located Modesto, Stanislaus County. Proposed to build to Crow's Landing and Newman, and from Modesto to Turlock, Merced, Madera and Fresno.

INTER-MOUNTAIN ELECTRIC RAILROAD COMPANY

Organized March 1904 - Electric - Standard Gauge

Located Clovis, Fresno County. Proposed to build to Sunnyside. Project abandoned.

INTER-URBAN ELECTRIC RAILWAY COMPANY

Incorporated November 14, 1934 - Electric - Standard Gauge

Located San Francisco, San Francisco County. Organized to be the operating company for the Southern Pacific Co. electric suburban service in Oakland, Berkeley, Alameda, San Leandro and San Francisco. Service over the San Francisco-Oakland Bay Bridge began January 15, 1939. Last train operated July 25, 1941. Approximately 40 miles of track had been in operation. Company dissolved August 3, 1949.

INTER-URBAN RAILWAY COMPANY

Incorporated May 16, 1901 - Electric - Standard Gauge

Located Santa Ana, Orange County. Resulted from the merger of the Santa Ana & Orange Motor Company and the Santa Ana, Orange & Tustin Street Railway Company. Deeded to the Pacific Electric Railway Company December 5, 1901. Deeded by Pacific Electric Railway Co. to Los Angeles Inter-Urban Railway Co. July 1, 1904.

INYO DEVELOPMENT COMPANY

Organized 1885 - Steam - 2 ft. Gauge

Located Keeler, Inyo County. Built 2.60 miles of track for their salt works on Owens Lake. Abandoned 1926.

IONE & EASTERN RAILROAD COMPANY

Organized May 1, 1904 - Steam - Standard Gauge

Located Ione, Amador County. Proposed to build to Sutter Creek. Distance 14.00 miles. Proposed to build a branch from Sutter Creek to Volcano. Distance 13.00 miles. Completed construction from Ione to Mountain Springs. Distance 6.50 miles. Sold to the Amador Central Railroad in 1908 and completed to Martell.

IRON MOUNTAIN RAILWAY - An industrial railroad built from a junction with the Southern Pacific at Keswick to Iron Mountain Mines. Small tank locomotives hauled the ore to a processing plant. - *John Signor Collection* (BELOW) A tank engine working its way out of the mine. - *Donald Duke Collection*

IONE RAILROAD

Organized October 1, 1875 - Steam - 3 ft. Gauge

Located Ione Valley, Amador County. Proposed to build a railroad in Ione Valley. No construction work done.

IRON MOUNTAIN RAILWAY COMPANY

Incorporated July 17, 1895 - Steam - 3 ft. Gauge - Standard Gauge

Located Keswick, Shasta County. Built from Iron Mountain Mines to Spring Creek (Keswick) 5.00 miles north of Redding. Distance 13.50 miles. A branch to Copley was built later. Distance 4.00 miles. Opened for traffic February 1, 1896. Standard gauge operations were from Keswick to a junction with the California & Oregon Railroad (Southern Pacific Co.). Distance 2.00 miles. Railroad abandoned February 5, 1927.

IRVINE & MUIR LUMBER COMPANY

Organized 1906 - Steam - Standard Gauge

Located Willits, Mendocino County. Built 13.00 miles of track. Abandoned 1928.

ISLAND MOUNTAIN RAILWAY

Built 1900 - Cable - 4 ft. Gauge

Located Avalon, (Catalina Island), Los Angeles County. Carried passengers from Avalon Bay near the amphitheater to the top of the hill and down the other side to Lover's Cove where they could board the glass-bottom boats, stopping for local passengers at terraces along the way. Distance 1,000 ft. Ceased operations 1918. Reactivated briefly in 1921 for Shriner's Convention. Abandoned in 1924.

J

JACKSON, SUTTER & AMADOR RAILWAY COMPANY

Incorporated 1890 - Steam - Standard Gauge

Located San Francisco, San Francisco County. This railroad was to run from Ione, on the Southern Pacific, to Martells, a distance of 13 miles. Branch lines were proposed to Sutter Creek, Amador City and Drytown, a total distance of 35 additional miles. Project abandoned.

JACOBY CREEK RAILROAD COMPANY

Built 1875 - Horse Power - Standard Gauge

Located Eureka, Humboldt County. Began operations as a logging railroad using horse-drawn cars. Converted to steam power operations in 1886 or 1887. Total distance 7.00 miles. Ceased operations in 1890. Taken over by the Bayside Mill & Lumber Co. Organized as a common carrier in 1900. Deeded to the Bayside Lumber Co. January 6, 1905. Ceased operations in 1913. Leased to Pacific Engineering & Construction Co. in December 1914. Reorganized as Bayside Redwood Co. in 1920. Sold to Humboldt Redwood Co. in 1929.

JAMESTOWN & YOSEMITE VALLEY RAILROAD

Incorporated February 4, 1905 - Steam - Standard Gauge

Located Jamestown, Tuolumne County. Proposed to build southeast to a point at or near Maricopa. Distance 40.00 miles. A branch was to be built into Yosemite Valley. Distance 35.00 miles. Project abandoned in 1907.

JENNER LUMBER CO.

Incorporated 1911 - Steam - Standard Gauge

Located Jenner, Sonoma County. Organized to take over the properties of the Western Redwood Lumber Co. Evicted by the owners of Myers Ranch.

JOHNSON - POLLOCK LUMBER COMPANY

Built 1915 - Steam - Narrow-Gauge

Located Macdoel, Siskiyou County. Built 6.00 miles of logging road from a junction on the Southern Pacific Co. to timber. Abandoned 1919.

JUNIPERO LAND & TOWN COMPANY

Surveyed 1888 - Motor Road - Standard Gauge

Located San Diego, San Diego County. Proposed to build a motor railroad up Mission Valley in San Diego to Grantville. Proposed to extend to Poway, Escondido and Elsinore. No construction work done.

KEY SYSTEM - An "A" train bound for San Francisco, passes Tower No. 2 before entering the main line en route to the tracks over the San Francisco-Oakland Bay Bridge. - *Donald Duke*

K

H.J. KAISER GRAVEL COMPANY

Gasoline Engine - Standard Gauge

Located Oroville, Butte County. Operated 2.00 miles of quarry road.

KANSAS CITY, LAWTON & PACIFIC RAILROAD COMPANY

Planned 1907 - Steam - Standard Gauge

Surveys were begun from Quanah, Texas, through Carlsbad, New Mexico, to San Diego.

KANSAS PACIFIC RAILROAD COMPANY

Steam - Standard Guage

Located Denver, Colorado. Reached Denver, Colorado, August 1870. Proposed to extend to the Pacific Coast. Route selected was to reach San Francisco via Walker Pass. A branch was to be built to San Bernardino and San Diego.

KAWEAH & GIANT FOREST RAILROAD

Organized 1888 - Steam - Standard Gauge

Located Three Rivers, Tulare County. Built 2.00 miles of logging railroad. Abandoned 1890.

KELLER & MORFEY COMPANY

Franchise granted June 1888 - Horsecar - Standard Gauge

Located San Diego, San Diego County. Proposed to build a double-track horsecar street railway from 31st Street via K Street, Sixth Avenue, C Street, India Street, Ivy Street, Union Street to C Street. Expected to convert to cable car operation. No construction work done.

KELLER - KERCKHOFF COMPANY

Organized 1906 - Electric - Standard Gauge

Located San Diego, San Diego County. Applied for a franchise December 31, 1906. Proposed to build from Los Angeles via Oceanside and Escondido to San Diego. Franchise granted in San Diego in 1908. Some grading was done from San Diego to north of Old Town. Some rail was laid. Franchise forfeited in 1910.

KESTERSON LUMBER COMPANY
KESPINE LUMBER COMPANY

Began construction 1925 - Steam - Standard Gauge

Located Dorris, Siskiyou County. Built from a junction with the Southern Pacific Co. to timber. Distance 15.00 miles. Kesterson Lumber Co. began operations in 1926. Abandoned in 1930. Kespine Lumber Co. operated in the same area. Built 7.00 miles of track in 1922 and operations were taken over by Kesterson Lumber Co. the same year.

KEY SYSTEM
KEY SYSTEM, LTD.
KEY SYSTEM TRANSIT COMPANY
KEY TERMINAL RAILWAY, LTD.
KEY ROUTE

Incorporated June 1, 1923 - Electric - Standard Gauge

Located Oakland, Alameda County. Key Route was the popular name used by the San Francisco, Oakland & San Jose Railway organized in June 1902. The term was used by its immediate successor, the San Francisco, Oakland & San Jose Consolidated Railway, which was the result of a merger in 1903 of the San Francisco, Oakland & San Jose Railway and the San Francisco & Bay Counties Railway. Key System was the popular name of the San Francisco - Oakland Terminal Railway's ferry and electric train division, which was also called the "Key Division." Key Route and Key System were officially spon-

sored "slogan names" as the management felt that the corporate titles were too long to be spoken. The name "Key Route" was used long after the San Francisco - Oakland Terminal Railway adopted the name Key System. The Oakland, Antioch & Eastern Railway called its San Francisco connection the "Key Route Ferry" for at least five years after the San Francisco - Oakland Terminal Railway began using "Key System" in place of "Key Route". Key System Transit Company was the immediate successor of the San Francisco - Oakland Terminal Railway. This was the first time that the corporate title contained the words "Key System." Incorporated in June 1, 1923. In 1929, this company failed. Its properties were taken over by the Railway Equipment & Realty Co., Ltd. This company was a holding company, not an operating company. Their holdings were:

KEY SYSTEM, LTD. The Transbay Division (Key Division) of the former Key System Transit Co. east of Keel Station.

KEY TERMINAL RAILWAY, LTD. The Key System train lines west of Keel Station (the Key Pier) and the ferryboat operations.

EAST BAY STREET RAILWAY, LTD. The former Key System Transit Company's streetcar division. This was the traction division of the San Francisco - Oakland Terminal Railway days.

EAST BAY MOTOR COACH LINES, LTD. The bus lines of the former Key System Transit Company.

KEY SYSTEM TRANSIT LINES. After the National City Lines purchased the Railway Equipment & Realty Company, Ltd. properties, the name Key System was changed to Key System Transit Lines.

Key System was the result of a consolidation February 26, 1935, of the Key System Ltd. and Key Terminal Railway, Ltd. Last electric streetcar operation April 20, 1958.

KIMSHEW RAILROAD

Organized 1910 - Steam - Standard Gauge

Located Sterling City, Butte County. Built 25.00 miles of logging railroad. Abandoned in 1912.

KING COAL COMPANY

Operated 1916 - 1920 - Steam - Standard Gauge

Located Oakland, Alameda County. Operated one locomotive lettered King Coal Company on the tracks of the Howard Terminal for moving coal cars on the terminal docks. Ceased operations in 1920.

KINGS RIVER RAILROAD
KINGS LAKE SHORE RAILROAD

Construction began 1910 - Steam - Standard Gauge

Located Corcoran, Kings County. Organized to build to Tulare Lake. Began construction as the Kings River Railroad in 1910. Built 10.05 miles of track. Incorporated May 7, 1917, as Kings Lake Shore Railroad. Completed 15.00 miles of track extended 17.40 miles from Corcoran on the Santa Fe to Liberty. Abandoned January 22, 1934.

KINGS RIVER RAILWAY COMPANY

Incorporated October 21, 1909 - Steam - Standard Gauge

Located Piedra, Fresno County. Built to Wahtoke. Distance 10.70 miles. Opened for service March 3, 1911. Sold to the Santa Fe Railway March 18, 1911.

CHARLES W. KITTS LUMBER COMPANY
KITTS RAILROAD

Organized 1888 or 1889 - Steam - 3 ft. Gauge

Located Greenhorn Creek, Nevada County. Built from a point near You Bet Side Track on the Nevada County Narrow-Gauge Railroad to Kitts Mill. Distance 5.00 miles. Also known as the Greenhorn Railroad. Abandoned 1902.

KEY SYSTEM - From 1903 to 1939 the hub of the commuter road was the Key Route Pier which extended out from land at Oakland into the deep water of San Francisco Bay. All San Francisco bound passengers detrained at the pier and boarded ferryboats for the remainder of their journey to the Ferry Building at San Francisco. In this view the San Francisco-Oakland Bay Bridge is nearing completion. Treasure Island, off Yerba Buena Island, is being filled in for the San Francisco International Exposition. - *Donald Duke Collection*

Passengers walked from their ferryboats to the Key System interurban trains waiting inside the Key Pier. This photograph was taken just prior to the opening of the San Francisco-Oakland Bay Bridge rail operations as route indications had been change to A, B, C, E, H, G, F and K as a simpler train control system for loading and unloading at the new San Francisco Bridge Terminal. - *Donald Duke Collection*

KLAMATH LAKE RAILROAD - A logging line built from the Southern Pacific at Thrall (north of Yreka) to timber. Line finally extended into Oregon, a distance of 24.32 miles. - *Donald Duke Collection*

KLAMATH - CALIFORNIA REDWOOD COMPANY

Built 1935 - Steam - Standard Gauge

Located Klamath, Del Norte County. Built one mile of track. Ceased operations in 1938.

KLAMATH LAKE RAILROAD COMPANY

Incorporated December 12, 1901 - Steam - Standard Gauge

Located Thrall, Siskiyou County. Built from a junction with the Southern Pacific Co. to Pokegama, Klamath County, Oregon. Distance 24.32 miles. Completed April 29, 1903. Sold to the Weyerhaeuser Timber Co. in 1905. Became the Oregon Southern Railroad in 1907. Leased to the Siskiyou Electric Power & Light Co. 1912 to 1913. Out of service from 1913 to 1916. Sold to the California - Oregon Power Co. 1916. Abandoned 1942.

KNOB PEAK LUMBER COMPANY

Built 1951 - Standard Gauge

Located Placerville, El Dorado County. Proposed to build ten miles of logging road in 1950 or 1951. Probably built some trackage but did not operate.

KYLE RAILWAYS

Organized 1979 - Diesel - Standard Guage

Located San Diego, San Diego County. Took over the operations of the San Diego & Arizona Eastern Railroad.

63

LAKE TAHOE RAILWAY & TRANSPORTATION CO. - A narrow-gauge rail line built from Truckee, on the Southern Pacific, to the west shore of Lake Tahoe at Tahoe City. Passengers detrained and boarded the *Glenbrook* for the trip to the east shore of the lake. - *Hugh Tolford Collection*

L

LAKE ARROWHEAD DAM CONSTRUCTION COMPANY
(ARROWHEAD RESERVOIR & POWER COMPANY)
Organized 1905 - Steam - 3 ft. Gauge

Located Lake Arrowhead, San Bernardino County. Built from quarry to dam construction site. Began operations in 1905. Ceased operations in 1921. Built a cable tramway up the side of mountain in Waterman Canyon. Grading completed February 21, 1906. First rails laid May 12, 1906. Distance 4,170 ft. Grade was about 45° from head of Waterman Canyon up to Skyland. Began operations July 31, 1906. Ceased operations 1921.

LAKE COUNTY LUMBER & BOX COMPANY RAILROAD
Steam - 3 ft. Gauge

Located Hopeland, Lake County. Built a narrow-gauge railroad for box timber from Hopeland to Lakeport on Clear Lake. Ceased operations during August 1940.

LAKE ELSINORE RAILROAD
Organized July 1887 - Electric - Standard Gauge

Located Elsinore, Riverside County. Proposed to build an elevated electric railroad around Lake Elsinore. Franchise granted July 1887. Project abandoned in 1889.

LAKE SHORE ELECTRIC RAILWAY COMPANY
Organized 1900 - Electric - Standard Gauge

Located Elsinore, Riverside County. A rejuvinated Lake Elsinore Railroad project for building an electric railroad around the shore to serve proposed real estate developments.

LAKE TAHOE NARROW-GAUGE RAILROAD
Organized 1878 - Steam - 3 ft. Gauge

Located Summit, Placer County. Built from a junction with the Southern Pacific Company to mines located in the neighborhood of Lake Tahoe. Distance 8.75 miles.

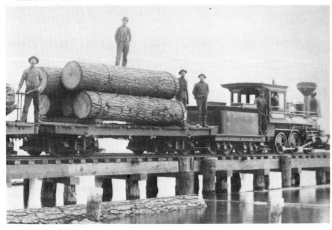

LAKE TAHOE NARROW-GAUGE RAILROAD - A logging and mining line that operated off the Southern Pacific and ran toward Lake Tahoe, a distance of 8.75 miles. - *Hugh Tolford Collection*

LAKE TAHOE RAILWAY COMPANY
Incorporated April 24, 1904 - Steam - Standard Gauge

Located Placerville, El Dorado County. Proposed to build northerly and eas-

terly to Pino Grande and then to Lake Tahoe at a point near Fallac. Distance 65.00 miles. No construction work done.

LAKE TAHOE RAILWAY & TRANSPORTATION COMPANY
Incorporated December 19, 1898 - Steam - 3 ft. Gauge

Located Truckee, Nevada County. Built to Tahoe City. Distance 16.00 miles. Began operations May 1, 1899. Leased to the Southern Pacific Co. October 16, 1925. Standard gauged and began operations May 15, 1926. Sold to the Southern Pacific Co. May 1933. Abandoned 1943.

LAKE VALLEY RAILROAD COMPANY
Organized 1886 - Steam - 3 ft. Gauge

Located Bijou, El Dorado County. Purchased the G.W. Chubbuck interests. Took over 4.00 miles of wooden tramway. Converted to rail operation in 1891. Extended the trackage 10.00 miles. Abandoned 1898.

LAKEPORT & RICHARDSON'S BAY RAILROAD COMPANY
Organized 1907 - Electric - Standard Gauge

Located Petaluma, Sonoma County. Proposed to build in Marin, Sonoma, Napa and Lake counties. January 1908 the name was changed to Napa, Sacramento & Richardson Bay County Railroad. April 1908 survey was begun from Petaluma to McNear's Point. Reorganized September 17, 1908, as The California Company and proposed to build either electric or steam railroad from San Francisco to Sacramento. Distance 90.75 miles. Purchased the Sacramento & Vallejo Railroad and Vaca Valley & Napa Railroad properties in 1909. Renamed the California Terminal Railway Company September 12, 1911. All projects abandoned in 1913.

LAKEPORT & SOUTHERN RAILWAY
Organized 1906 - Steam - Standard Gauge

Located Napa, Napa County. Proposed to operate between undesignated cities in Napa and Marin counties in conjunction with the San Francisco, Vallejo & Napa Valley Railroad. Project abandoned in 1907.

LA MOINE LUMBER & TRADING COMPANY
Organized 1898 - Steam - 3 ft. Gauge

Located Dunsmuir, Siskiyou County. Built from La Moine Lumber Company mill to Mountain Top. Distance 22.00 miles. Abandoned 1922.

LA MOINE LUMBER & TRADING CO. - Operated a logging railroad from the La Moine Mill, near Dunsmuir, to Mountain Top, a distance of 22 miles. - *John Signor Collection*

LASSEN LOGGING COMPANY RAILROAD

Organized 1918 - Steam - Standard Gauge

Located Mason, Lassen County. Built from a junction with the Southern Pacific Co. to mill. Distance 1.00 miles. Abandoned 1932.

LASSEN LUMBER & BOX COMPANY RAILROAD

Organized 1918 - Steam - Standard Gauge

Located Westwood Junction, Lassen County. Built from a junction with the Southern Pacific to mill and on to timber. Distance 18.00 miles. Abandoned 1938.

LATON LUMBER & INVESTMENT COMPANY

Organized 1906 - Steam - Standard Gauge

Located Markham, Sonoma County. Purchased the properties of the Markham Lumber Co. in 1906. Operated 3.00 miles of trackage. Abandoned 1910 or 1911.

LATON & WESTERN RAILROAD COMPANY

Incorporated August 8, 1910 - Steam - Standard Gauge

Located Laton, Fresno County. Built to Lanare. Distance 15.60 miles. Began passenger service February 22, 1911. Sold to the California, Arizona & Santa Fe Railway Co. in 1916. Deeded to the Santa Fe Railway Co. September 21, 1916.

LESLIE SALT COMPANY

Organized 1960 - Gas Engine - 3 ft. Gauge

Located Saltus, near Amboy, San Bernardino County. Purchased the properties of the California Salt Co. Operated 5.00 miles of trackage from mill to salt beds on Bristol Lake. Standard gauge connection made with the Santa Fe. Abandoned in 1979.

LIBERTY LUMBER COMPANY

Built 1920 - Steam - Standard Gauge

Located Duncans Mills, Sonoma County. Built 1.00 mile of track in and about the mill property. Abandoned 1923.

LILA C RAILROAD

Built 1910 - Steam - Standard Gauge

Located Lila C Mine, Inyo County. Built to Old Ryan. Distance 6.98 miles. Abandoned 1914. 3.50 miles of roadbed converted to 3 ft. gauge when the Death Valley Railroad was built to Ryan (New Ryan). Rebuilt to standard gauge between Lila C Mine and Horton 1924. Gas engine used in later years.

LIME KILN RAILROAD

Built 1892 - Monorail

Located Tres Pinos, San Benito County. Built an "A" frame type monorail from Tres Pinos on the Southern Pacific to Lime Kiln. Distance 12.00 miles. Abandoned September 1892.

LINCOLN & GOLD HILL RAILROAD

Surveys completed November 1, 1859 - Steam - 5 ft. Gauge

Located south of Lincoln, Placer County. Proposed to build from a point where the California Central Railroad was to cross Auburn Ravine to Gold Hill. Distance 7.00 miles. This road was also referred to as the Extension Branch Railroad. One mile of grading completed by December 31, 1859. The name Eastern Extension Railroad was also used by T.D. Judah in 1860. He expected to complete the railroad by December 1860 or January 1861. Project was not built.

LINCOLN NORTHERN RAILROAD

Chartered March 13, 1907 - Steam - Standard Gauge

Located Lincoln, Placer County. Proposed to build to Dairy Farm Mine. Distance 11.10 miles. Funds were to have been advanced by the Southern Pacific Co. No construction work was done.

LINCOLN, SAN FRANCISCO & EASTERN RAILROAD COMPANY

Organized January 1905 - Steam - Standard Gauge

Located Lincoln, Placer County. Began building from Vernon Landing in a northerly direction up the east bank of the Sacramento River to Nicholaus in Sutter County, thence east to Lincoln and then northeast through Spencerville and Grass Valley to Nevada City. Distance 68 miles. Grading completed for 10.00 miles by October 1903.

LINK BELT RAILWAY

Organized January 1, 1910 - Electric - Standard Gauge

Located Colfax, Placer County. Incorporated to build an electric railroad in an undisclosed area in Placer County.

LITTLE RIVER REDWOOD COMPANY

Organized 1908 - Steam - 3 ft. 9 1/4 in. Gauge

Located Crannell, Humboldt County. Purchased a branch of the Humboldt Northern Railway to Fair Haven. Extended the trackage from Bullwinkle to timber. Total mileage 17.95. Deeded to Hammond & Little River Redwood Co. 1931. Abandoned 1936.

LITTLE VALLEY LUMBER COMPANY CLEONE TRAMWAY

Began operations 1901 - Horse Power - Narrow-gauge

Located Cleone, Mendocino County. Began operations after building 2.50 miles of track for horse-drawn log cars. Trackage extended from Laguna Mill through Cleone to Laguna Chute. Abandoned 1904.

LOMA PRIETA LUMBER COMPANY

Incorporated May 28, 1910 - Steam - 30 in. Gauge

Located Molino, Santa Cruz County. Built to a point approximately halfway between Loma Prieta and old Monte Vista. Constructed a 2,250-foot rail incline up the side of Aptos Creek Canyon from a point on the Loma Prieta to Hinckley Ridge. Extended trackage along Hinckley Ridge and China Ridge. Distance 12.15 miles. Began operations in 1911. Was operated by the Loma Prieta Lumber Company and the Molino Timber Company. Abandoned in 1926.

LOMA PRIETA RAILROAD
LOMA PRIETA LUMBER COMPANY

Steam - 30 in. Gauge

Located Loma Prieta, Santa Cruz County. Proposed to build from a point halfway between Loma Prieta and Old Monte Vista. A 2,250-foot incline up the side of Aptos Creek Canyon from the Loma Prieta right-of-way to a point 657 feet up on Hinckley Ridge and into the forests on Hinckley and China ridges. Distance 4.75 miles. Incorporated May 28, 1910, by the Molino Timber Co.

LOMA PRIETA RAILROAD COMPANY

Incorporated July 10, 1882 - Steam - Standard Gauge

Located Aptos, Santa Cruz County. Built to Loma Prieta. Distance 3.70 miles. Opened for traffic November 13, 1883. Became part of the Pajaro & Santa Cruz Railroad July 3, 1884. Leased to the Southern Pacific Co. May 14, 1888. Abandoned 1928.

LONE PINE UTILITIES COMPANY

Organized January 1914 - Electric - Highway

Located Grava, San Bernardino County. Proposed to build from a station on the Santa Fe Railway in Cajon Pass to what was known as Upper Swartout Valley in Lytle Creek area. Distance 8.75 miles. Motive power was to be a trackless trolley system. Application for franchise was made February 3, 1914. Project reorganized to extend trolley wire a distance of 27.00 miles. Project abandoned 1916.

LONG BEACH & ALAMITOS BAY RAILWAY COMPANY

Organized June 22, 1891 - Steam - Standard Gauge

Located **Long Beach, Los Angeles County.** Organized by the Los Angeles & Ocean Railway Co. as an extension to Alamitos Bay from Long Beach. Consolidated with the Los Angeles & Ocean Railway September 8, 1891. No construction work done.

LONG BEACH RAILROAD COMPANY
Incorporated October 31, 1887 - Steam - Standard Gauge

Located **Long Beach, Los Angeles County.** Proposed to build from Long Beach Junction with the Los Angeles & Long Beach Railroad through Long Beach eastward to boundary line between Rancho Los Cerritos and Rancho Los Alamitos. Built by the Southern Pacific Co. from Thenard to Long Beach in 1888. Distance 4.00 miles. Consolidated with the Southern Pacific Co. May 14, 1888.

LONG BEACH SALT COMPANY
Organized 1927 - Gas Engine - Narrow-Gauge

Located **Saltdale, Kern County.** Organized to take over the operations of the Consolidated Salt Co. who operated a salt quarry at Koehn Lake near Mojave.

LONG BEACH & SAN PEDRO RAILWAY COMPANY
Incorporated April 9, 1888 - Steam - 3 ft. 6 in. Gauge

Located **Long Beach, Los Angeles County.** Proposed to build to San Pedro Harbor as an extension to the Los Angeles & Ocean Railroad. Distance surveyed 5.00 miles. No construction work done.

LONG BEACH, WHITTIER & LOS ANGELES COUNTY RAILROAD COMPANY
Incorporated December 17, 1887 - Steam - Standard Gauge

Located **Long Beach, Los Angeles County.** Proposed to build to Ramona via Whittier to a point between El Monte and Puente and then northeast to San Dimas Creek. Distance 60.00 miles. Construction began January 25, 1888, from Studebaker to Whittier. Distance 5.90 miles. Began operations March 6, 1888. Consolidated with the Southern Pacific Co. May 14, 1888. Abandoned 1942.

LONG-BELL LUMBER COMPANY
Organized 1926 - Steam - Standard Gauge

Located **Weed, Siskiyou County.** Purchased the Weed Lumber Co. 1905. Continued to operate under this name until 1926. Long-Bell Lumber Company operations were abandoned 1956. 60.00 miles of track were operated. Located Leaf, Siskiyou County. Operated eastward from a junction on the Southern Pacific to Modoc County. 89 miles of standard gauge track were built.

LONG-BELL LUMBER CO. - This logging company operated over 60 miles of logging railroad tracks in Northern California from 1905 to 1926. This locomotive operated in Siskiyou County. - *Donald Duke*

LOOKOUT MOUNTAIN PARK LAND & WATER COMPANY
Organized July 1, 1900 - Electric - Standard Gauge

Located **Los Angeles, Los Angeles County.** Proposed to build a scenic railway up Laurel Canyon and along the mountain rim of Lookout Mountain Park.

LOS ANGELES & ALISO STREET RAILROAD COMPANY
Incorporated February 15, 1876 - Horsecar - 3 ft. 6 in. Gauge

Located **Los Angeles, Los Angeles County.** Began operations February 13, 1877. Sold to the Central Railway Company in 1884 and electrified. Merged into the Los Angeles Railway in 1896. Abandoned March 31, 1963.

LOS ANGELES BOARD OF HARBOR COMMISSIONERS
Organized July 1925 - Steam - Standard Gauge

Located **San Pedro, Los Angeles County.** Proposed to build a municipally-owned terminal railroad around the Los Angeles harbor.

LOS ANGELES CABLE RAILWAY COMPANY
Incorporated July 8, 1887 - Cable - 3 ft. 6 in. Gauge

Located **Los Angeles, Los Angeles County.** Organized to take over the operation of the horsecar lines owned by the Central Railroad Co., City Railroad Co. and the East & West Street Railway Co. Operated from Jefferson Street north along Grand Avenue to Seventh Street, then east on Broadway, north to First Street, east on Spring Street and north to the Plaza, then along San Fernando Street over the Southern Pacific Railroad tracks and across a bridge over the Los Angeles River to Downey Avenue and out Downey Avenue to Gates Street.

LOS ANGELES CABLE RAILWAY - This spectacular viaduct carried the cable line up and over Southern Pacific railroad tracks on old San Fernando Street en route to the east side of the Los Angeles River. - *Huntington Library*

LOS ANGELES, CARLTON & EASTERN RAILROAD COMPANY
Incorporated February 9, 1888 - Steam - Standard Gauge

Located **Los Angeles, Los Angeles County.** Proposed to build to Carlton via Whittier. A junction was to be made with the Anaheim, Olinda & Pomona Railroad to serve the Olinda Ranch. Distance 24.50 miles. No construction work was done.

LOS ANGELES & CERRO GORDO NARROW-GAUGE RAILROAD
Incorporated May, 1874 - Steam - 3 ft. 6 in. Gauge

Located **Los Angeles, Los Angeles County.** Proposed to build by way of Mojave to Cerro Gordo Mines. Poor sale of stock resulted in it being merged into the Los Angeles & Independence Railroad plans.

LOS ANGELES & COAST RAILROAD
Organized 1874 - Steam - Standard Gauge

Located **Los Angeles, Los Angeles County.** Proposed to build a railway to the ocean in or near Santa Monica. Project abandoned.

LOS ANGELES CONSOLIDATED ELECTRIC RAILWAY COMPANY

Incorporated November 12, 1890 - Electric - 3 ft. 6 in. Gauge

Located Los Angeles, Los Angeles County. Purchased the Depot Railroad of Los Angeles. Trackage from 2nd Street along Spring Street to Santa Fe Avenue and Central Avenue. Opened for service May 8, 1891. Purchased the Los Angeles & Vernon Railroad operating from Central Avenue and 5th Street along Central Avenue to Slauson Avenue May 8, 1891. Secured the Belt Line Railroad Co. November 3, 1891. All gauges made 3 ft. 6 in. December 31, 1891. Sold to the Los Angeles Railway Co. August 18, 1895. Abandoned March 31, 1963.

LOS ANGELES COUNTY FLOOD CONTROL DISTRICT RAILROAD

Organized 1914 - Steam - Standard Gauge

Located Los Angeles, Los Angeles County. The winter of 1910-1911 saw devastating floods along the Los Angeles and San Gabriel rivers that destroyed bridges and inundated fertile farm lands. The Los Angeles County Flood Control District was formed in 1914 to control floods by cement lining the waterways and to build control check dams in the Sierra Madre Mountains. The railroad was used to haul cement, crushed rock and steel into the control channels and dams.

LOS ANGELES COUNTY LIGHT RAIL
LOS ANGELES COUNTY TRANSIT COMMISSION

Construction began December 10, 1986 - Electric - Standard Gauge

Located Los Angeles, Los Angeles County. Construction began in Long Beach December 10, 1986, toward Los Angeles along Long Beach Blvd. Study authorized December 17, 1986, for Pasadena - Los Angeles corridor through Lincoln Heights. Authorized study December 17, 1986, for work on the Century - El Segundo Rail Transit Project. Light Rail Transit Line Century Freeway route ground breaking November 13, 1986.

LOS ANGELES COUNTY RAILROAD COMPANY

Incorporated June 21, 1887 - Steam - Standard Gauge

Located Los Angeles, Los Angeles County. Purchased the Ostrich Farm Railroad and extended it to Santa Monica. Built from a junction on Griffith Park Avenue on Sunset Blvd. to Hoover Street and then to Vermont via Fountain to Orange. Reached Santa Monica via Santa Monica Blvd. Total mileage 28.55. Began operations February 23, 1889. Consolidated into the Los Angeles & Pacific Railroad April 29, 1895, and electrified. Became part of the Pacific Electric Railway in 1911.

LOS ANGELES, DAGGETT & TONOPAH RAILROAD COMPANY

Incorporated April 1903 - Steam - Standard Gauge

Located Daggett, San Bernardino County. Incorporated in Nevada. Proposed to build from Daggett to Tonopah, Nevada. To build in a north and south direction through the counties of San Bernardino and Inyo in California and Esmeralda and Nye counties in Nevada. Distance 235.00 miles. No construction work done.

LOS ANGELES & EAGLE ROCK VALLEY RAILROAD
LOS ANGELES, GARVANZA & EAGLE ROCK RAILROAD

Franchised April 25, 1887 - Steam - Standard Gauge

Located Los Angeles, Los Angeles County. Built from Avenue 20 and Pasadena Avenue, out Pasadena Avenue to Avenue 44 near Sycamore Grove. Continued along York Blvd., Eagle Rock Blvd. and Colorado Blvd. to Townsend Avenue. Built from Garvanza to Eagle Rock by December 1887. Distance 9.10 miles. Began operations May 10, 1888. Ceased operations May 20, 1888. Tracks removed April 14, 1889. Eventually parts of the right-of-way became part of the Los Angeles, Pasadena & Glendale Railroad.

LOS ANGELES & EASTERN RAILROAD COMPANY

Incorporated December 28, 1888 - Steam - Standard Gauge

Located Los Angeles, Los Angeles County. Proposed to build northeast through Pasadena to Kramer. Distance 97.00 miles. Surveys were made and work was expected to begin March 1889. No construction work was done.

LOS ANGELES ELECTRIC RAILWAY COMPANY

Incorporated September 11, 1886 - Electric - Standard Gauge

Located Los Angeles, Los Angeles County. Began operations on Pico Street January 4, 1887. Built on Maple Avenue to 30th Street. Built on 7th Street from Wall Street to Alameda Street in 1888. Horsecars took over operations June 8, 1888. Ceased operations April 1889. Reopened as the Electric Rapid Transit Co. March 1890. Became the Belt Line Railroad Company July 1890. Deeded to the Los Angeles Consolidated Electric Railway Co. November 3, 1891. Gauge changed to 3 ft. 6 in. December 31, 1891. Sold to Los Angeles Railway Co. August 18, 1895.

LOS ANGELES ELECTRIC RAILWAY - Southern California's first electric railway ran from the Plaza out Wall and Maple streets to 32nd Street. A branch line on Pico ran to the Electric Railway Homestead Assn. housing track. - *Huntington Library*

LOS ANGELES & GLENDALE ELECTRIC RAILWAY COMPANY

Incorporated May 7, 1903 - Electric - Standard Gauge

Located Los Angeles, Los Angeles County. Lines in Glendale deeded to the Los Angeles Inter-Urban Railway Company March 11, 1904.

LOS ANGELES & GLENDALE RAILROAD

Incorporated January 13, 1887 - Steam - 3 ft. 6 in. Gauge

Located Glendale, Los Angeles County. Resulted from the reorganization of the Los Angeles & Glendale Steam Railway Co. Built from the east bank of the Los Angeles River at the Downey Avenue crossing (now North Broadway) to Arroyo Seco Street (now Humboldt). Over this street to Wills Street (now Avenue 26), Columbus (Huron) Street and onto Cypress Avenue, which it followed to the city limits at Alice Street, then on private right-of-way to and along the north side of San Fernando Road onto Crow Avenue (Glendale Avenue) and then northward into the town of Glendale. Distance 7.00 miles. Completed February 15, 1888. Began operations March 24, 1888. Deeded to the Los Angeles, Pasadena & Glendale Railroad March 30, 1889.

LOS ANGELES & GLENDALE STEAM RAILWAY COMPANY

Incorporated January 8, 1887 - Steam - Standard Gauge

Located Glendale, Los Angeles County. Proposed to build an electric street railway to Hayes and Hoff streets. Distance 7.00 miles. Reorganized as the Los Angeles & Glendale Railroad Co.

LOS ANGELES HARBOR DEPARTMENT RAILROAD

Organized 1910 - Steam - Standard Gauge

Located Los Angeles, Los Angeles County. On December 9, 1907, the Los Angeles City Council created a Los Angeles Board of Harbor Commissioners and marked the absorption of the city of San Pedro into the city of Los Angeles and the founding of the Port of Los Angeles. A Los Angeles Harbor Department Railroad was formed in 1910 to build a railroad to haul rock in order to form a breakwater. Fifty percent of the rock was brought in on the Southern Pacific and Pacific Electric, and 50 percent was quarried on Catalina Island and hauled to ships by tank locomotives. In 1911, the first 8,500 foot section of the breakwater was completed. In 1913, the Los Angeles Harbor lighthouse called "Angel Gate" was built. The Los Angeles Harbor Department Railroad was abandoned following World War II.

LOS ANGELES HARBOR RAILROAD

Incorporated March 13, 1908 - Steam - Standard Gauge

Located Wilmington, Los Angeles County. Plans for a Harbor Railroad were taken over by the Harbor Belt Line Railroad in June 1929.

LOS ANGELES, HERMOSA & REDONDO RAILROAD COMPANY

Incorporated December 19, 1901 - Electric - Standard Gauge

Located Los Angeles, Los Angeles County. Purchased the Redondo & Hermosa Beach Railroad Co. on March 12, 1902. Consolidated with the Los Angeles - Pacific Railroad Co. and the Los Angeles - Santa Monica Railroad Co. on June 10, 1903 to form the Los Angeles Pacific Railroad Co. of California. Became part of the Pacific Electric Railway in 1911.

LOS ANGELES & HUENEME RAILROAD COMPANY

Incorporated April 10, 1889 - Steam - Standard Gauge

Located Los Angeles, Los Angeles County. Proposed to build through San Fernando and over Santa Susanna Pass to Hueneme. Distance 70.00 miles. Surveys completed May 10, 1889. No construction work done.

LOS ANGELES INCLINE RAILWAY

Franchise granted May 20, 1901 - Cable - 2 ft. 6 in. Gauge

Located Los Angeles, Los Angeles County. Building began August 2, 1901, as a 335 ft. long cable railway between Olive and Hill streets on Bunker Hill. Began operations December 30, 1901. Became Angels Flight Railway Co. on November 11, 1912.

LOS ANGELES & INDEPENDENCE RAILROAD COMPANY

Incorporated January 8, 1875 - Steam - 3 ft. 6 in. Gauge

Located Santa Monica, Los Angeles County. Proposed to build east then north through Cajon Pass to Independence, Inyo County. Work began at Santa Monica February 18, 1875, with the construction of a wharf. Grading began in the Cajon Pass March 20, 1875. By September 4, 1875, a change in route was proposed. The new route would be through Chino and Riverside to San Bernardino rather than Santa Monica to Cajon Pass. Built from 3rd Street in Santa Monica to 4th and San Pedro streets in Los Angeles. Grading completed October 17, 1875. Opened for service December 1, 1875. Some construction work was done in the Cajon Pass and a branch to the Panamint Mountains was surveyed. Leased to the Southern Pacific Company June 4, 1877. Leased to the Central Pacific Railroad Company which operated the property until March 1, 1888. Consolidated with the Southern Pacific Co. May 14, 1888. The passenger line Santa Monica to Los Angeles was transferred to the Los Angeles - Pacific Railway 1898. Deeded to the Pacific Electric Railway 1902.

LOS ANGELES INTER-URBAN RAILWAY COMPANY

Incorporated June 6, 1903 - Electric - Standard Gauge

Located Los Angeles, Los Angeles County. Purchased the Los Angeles Traction Co. and California Pacific Railway January 1904. Sold to the Pacific Electric Railway November 10, 1910.

LOS ANGELES & INDEPENDENCE RAILROAD - Proposed to build from Santa Monica to Cerro Gordo. Construction came to a halt at Los Angeles and the line eventually was purchased by the Southern Pacific. - *Gerald M. Best Collection*

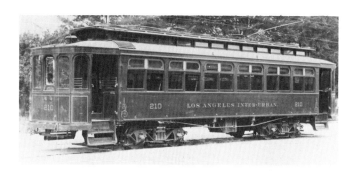

LOS ANGELES INTER-URBAN - This line was Henry E. Huntington's first venture into interurban transportation in Los Angeles. It merged to form the Pacific Electric in November 1910. - *Donald Duke Collection*

LOS ANGELES JUNCTION RAILWAY COMPANY

Incorporated May 26, 1923 - Steam - Standard Gauge

Located Vernon, Los Angeles County. Organized to handle the switching services in the central manufacturing district in and about the city of Vernon. A wholly-owned subsidiary of the Santa Fe Railway.

LOS ANGELES JUNCTION RAILWAY - A switching railroad serving the Los Angeles Union Stockyards and the warehouses of the Central Manufacturing District of Vernon. - *Donald Duke Collection*

LOS ANGELES & LONG BEACH RAILROAD

Built 1885 - Horsecar - 3 ft. Gauge

Located Dominguez, Los Angeles County. Built from a junction with the San Pedro & Los Angeles Railroad to Long Beach. Distance 3.70 miles. Rebuilt 1886 and steam dummy engine used. Rebuilt from Thenard to Long Beach on December 29, 1888. Deeded to the Southern Pacific Co. December 29, 1889.

LOS ANGELES METROPOLITAN TRANSIT AUTHORITY

Established March 5, 1958 - Electric - 3 ft. 6 in. and Standard Gauge

Located Los Angeles, Los Angeles County. Purchased the Pacific Electric Railway passenger service rail lines and the Metropolitan Coach Line (Los Angeles Railway). Last rail line abandoned March 31, 1963.

LOS ANGELES & LONG BEACH RAILROAD - A horsecar line which converted to this bizarre steam locomotive to operate the 3.5-mile line in Long Beach. Lacking proper traction, it was hard to maintain a schedule. - *Donald Duke Collection*

LOS ANGELES & MOUNT WASHINGTON RAILWAY COMPANY

Incorporated November 2, 1908 - Cable - 3 ft. 6 in. Gauge

Located Los Angeles, Los Angeles County. Built a 2,900 foot cable car line from Marmion Way at Avenue 43 to Hotel Mt. Washington. Began operations 1909. Abandoned January 9, 1919.

LOS ANGELES MUNICIPAL RAILROAD & TERMINAL COMPANY

Proposed August 1912 - Electric - Standard Gauge

Located Los Angeles, Los Angeles County. Proposed to build along San Pedro Street in Los Angeles and then to the harbor at San Pedro.

LOS ANGELES, NIAGRA & SAN DIEGO RAILROAD COMPANY

Incorporated April 15, 1887 - Steam - Standard Gauge

Located San Diego, San Diego County. Proposed to build from Puente, Los Angeles County via Chino, Rincon, La Sierra ranches to South Riverside, then via Niagra to San Diego. Distance 150 miles. No construction work done.

LOS ANGELES, OCEAN PARK & SANTA MONICA RAILWAY COMPANY

Incorporated December 8, 1902 - Electric - Standard Gauge

Located Los Angeles, Los Angeles County. Built the West Jefferson Street line. Proposed to build on to Ocean Park and then to Santa Monica. Deeded to the Los Angeles & Pacific Railroad of California June 14, 1904. Sold to the Pacific Electric Railway Company in 1910.

LOS ANGELES & OCEAN RAILWAY COMPANY

Incorporated September 14, 1887 - Steam - Standard Gauge

Located Long Beach, Los Angeles County. Proposed to build from Nadeau Park (Ballona/Santa Fe Junction) through Nadeau vineyard to Clearwater, then through Cerritos Ranch to Alamitos Bay. A branch was to be built through Long Beach to San Pedro. Distance 28.00 miles. Grading began February 3, 1888. About 25 miles of roadbed were graded by June 8, 1888. Consolidated with the Long Beach & Alamitos Bay Railway Co. September 8, 1891. Project abandoned 1891.

LOS ANGELES OSTRICH FARM RAILWAY COMPANY

Incorporated August 5, 1886 - Electric - 3 ft. Gauge

Located Los Angeles, Los Angeles County. Built from Beaudry and Sunset Blvd. along Sunset Blvd. to Griffith Park Drive, then crossed the Los Angeles River and continued to the Southern Pacific station in Burbank. Distance 9.85 miles. Sold July 9, 1887, to the Los Angeles County Railroad Co. Consolidated into the Los Angeles & Pacific Railroad Co. April 29, 1895. Merged into the Pacific Electric Railway Co. in 1911.

LOS ANGELES & OWENS RIVER RAILWAY COMPANY

Organized September 29, 1906 - Electric - Standard Gauge

Located Owens River Valley, Inyo County. Proposed to build southward to Los Angeles following the most opportune grades and alignments.

LOS ANGELES, OWENS VALLEY & UTAH RAILROAD COMPANY

Organized June 1893 - Steam - Standard Gauge

Located Mojave, Kern County. Proposed to build to Independence, Inyo County. No construction work done.

LOS ANGELES PACIFIC COMPANY

Organized October 2, 1905 - Electric - Standard Gauge

Located Los Angeles, Los Angeles County. This company was the result of the consolidation of the Los Angeles Pacific Railroad Company of California and the Santa Monica Canyon Railroad Company. Consolidated with the Santa Monica & Northern Railway Company March 30, 1907. Merged with the Pacific Electric Railway Co. September 1, 1911.

LOS ANGELES PACIFIC CO. - This interurban line ran from downtown Los Angeles to Santa Monica via Hollywood. It was merged into the Pacific Electric Railway on September 1, 1911. - *Donald Duke Collection*

LOS ANGELES PACIFIC RAILROAD COMPANY OF CALIFORNIA

Incorporated June 16, 1903 - Electric - Standard Gauge

Located Los Angeles, Los Angeles County. Organized to acquire through consolidation the Los Angeles - Pacific Railroad Company, the Los Angeles, Hermosa Beach & Redondo Railway Company and the Los Angeles - Santa Monica Railroad Co. Consolidated with the Santa Monica Canyon Railroad Co. to form the Los Angeles Pacific Co. October 2, 1905. Merged with the Pacific Electric Railway Co. September 1, 1911.

LOS ANGELES - PACIFIC RAILWAY COMPANY

Incorporated January 3, 1898 - Electric - Standard Gauge

Located Los Angeles, Los Angeles County. By incorporation, the following electric railways were brought under the control of one company: Los Angeles - Pacific Railway Co. (Arizona) Incorporated January 6, 1898; Los Angeles - Pacific Railway Co. (California) Incorporated May 16, 1898; Pasadena & Pacific Railway Co. (Arizona) Incorporated November 15, 1894; and the Pasadena & Pacific Railway Co. (California) Incorporated November 9, 1894. Purchased the Inglewood Branch of the Southern California Railway (Santa Fe) March 21, 1902. Reorganized June 9, 1902, as the Los Angeles - Pacific Railroad Company. Merged into the Pacific Electric Railway Co. September 1, 1911.

LOS ANGELES & PACIFIC RAILWAY COMPANY

Incorporated August 31, 1888 - Electric - Standard Gauge

Located Los Angeles, Los Angeles County. This was the first street railway to be incorporated as the Los Angeles & Pacific Railway Company. It was reorganized September 11, 1888, and became the second Los Angeles & Pacific Railway Company. Sold April 29, 1895, to the Pasadena & Pacific Railway Company.

LOS ANGELES & PASADENA ELECTRIC RAILWAY COMPANY

Incorporated 1894 - Electric - Standard Gauge

Located Pasadena, Los Angeles County. Organized to purchase all existing Pasadena street railways. Began electric operations May 1, 1895. Merged with the Los Angeles - Pasadena Traction Co. in 1900. Sold to the Pacific Electric Railway 1902. Abandoned October 17, 1942.

LOS ANGELES & PASADENA RAILWAY COMPANY

Organized June 29, 1888 - Electric - Narrow-Gauge

Located Los Angeles, Los Angeles County. Proposed to build from Franklin and Fort streets to North High Street and then along North Broadway to the Los Angeles River. Entry to Pasadena was to be made over the route of the Eagle Rock Valley Railroad. Line located July 2, 1888. 5.00 miles of track laid by July 31, 1888. Deeded to the Los Angeles, Pasadena & Glendale Railway Co.

LOS ANGELES & PASADENA RAPID TRANSIT COMPANY

Incorporated January 31, 1888 - Electric - Standard Guage

Located Pasadena, Los Angeles County. Proposed to build to Los Angeles by way of Ramona. Stock subscription began April 4, 1888. Project abandoned in 1889.

LOS ANGELES & PASADENA RAILWAY COMPANY

Incorporated June 24, 1884 - Steam - 3 ft. Gauge

Located Los Angeles, Los Angeles County. Proposed to build from the Southern Pacific Co. station via Garvanza to Pasadena at Fair Oaks and Colorado Blvd. Distance 11.90 miles. Some grading of right-of-way was done. Deeded to the Los Angeles & San Gabriel Valley Railroad Co. September 1884.

LOS ANGELES, PASADENA & ALTADENA RAILROAD COMPANY

Incorporated June 15, 1894 - Electric - Standard Gauge

Located Los Angeles, Los Angeles County. Proposed to build to Altadena by way of Pasadena. Surveys begun July 1894. Project abandoned 1894.

LOS ANGELES, PASADENA & GLENDALE RAILWAY COMPANY

Incorporated March 30, 1889 - Steam - Standard Gauge

Located Los Angeles, Los Angeles County. Incorporated February 19, 1887, as the Altadena Railway. Reincorporated March 30, 1889, as the Los Angeles, Pasadena & Glendale Railway Co. Purchased the Los Angeles & Glendale Railroad. Built an extension from Arroyo Seco and Wells Street along the route once used by the Pasadena branch of the Union Pacific Railroad. Construction work began on December 20, 1889. Completed to Pasadena and opened for traffic March 12, 1890. Took over the franchise of the Los Angeles & Pasadena Railroad Company. Constructed trackage along the proposed route of the Los Angeles & Pasadena Railway. Distance 10.00 miles. Extended trackage of Glendale line to Verdugo Park. Distance 9.00 miles. Operated from Raymond Station to Altadena. Distance 7.50 miles. Total trackage 26.50 miles. Sold to the Los Angeles Terminal Railway June 1890. Deeded to the San Pedro, Los Angeles & Salt Lake Railroad Co. in 1901.

LOS ANGELES - PASADENA TRACTION COMPANY

Organized 1900 - Electric - Standard Gauge

Located Pasadena, Los Angeles County. Merged with the Los Angeles & Pasadena Electric Railway Co. in 1900. Sold to the Pacific Electric Railway Co. March 1902. Abandoned October 17, 1942.

LOS ANGELES RAILWAY COMPANY
LOS ANGELES TRANSIT COMPANY

Incorporated March 19, 1895 - Electric - 3 ft. 6 in. Gauge

Located Los Angeles, Los Angeles County. Took over the properties of the Los Angeles Consolidated Electric Railway October 1, 1898. Consolidated with the Main Street & Agricultural Park Railroad Company. Purchased the Metro Street Railway and the San Pedro Railroad. Acquired the Los Angeles & Pasadena Electric Railway Co. January 1, 1899. Acquired the Pasadena & Mt. Lowe Railway in June 1900. Became Los Angeles Railway Corp. October 10, 1910. Became the Los Angeles Transit Lines January 10, 1945. Became part of the Los Angeles Metropolitan Transit Authority. Abandoned March 31, 1963.

LOS ANGELES RAILWAY - Henry E. Huntington's pride and joy was the Los Angeles Railway which was an amalgamation of several street railway systems. It remained as a part of the Huntington estate until 1945. - *Donald Duke*

LOS ANGELES RAILWAY CORPORATION

Incorporated October 22, 1910 - Electric - 3 ft. 6 in. Gauge

Located Los Angeles, Los Angeles County. Organized as successor to the Los Angeles Railway Co. Purchased all narrow-gauge operations of the Pacific Electric Railway Co. and the Los Angeles Inter-Urban Railway Co. in November 1911. This included the Temple Street Cable Railway, Brooklyn Avenue Railway and the Los Angeles Traction Company. Purchased all portions of the California Pacific Railway and the three divisions of the Los Angeles & Redondo Railway. Controlled under the ownership of the City Railway Company of Los Angeles.

LOS ANGELES & REDONDO RAILWAY COMPANY

Organized April 20, 1896 - Steam - 3 ft. Gauge

Located Los Angeles, Los Angeles County. Chartered as the Redondo Railway Co. April 11, 1889. Began operations 1890. Built a street railway from 48th Street to Arlington Avenue. Distance 1.74 miles. Built from Los Angeles to Strawberry Park. Distance 6.90 miles. Extended to Redondo. Total distance operated 17.00 miles. Electrified in 1902. Converted to standard gauge in 1909. Sold to the Pacific Electric Railway September 1, 1911.

LOS ANGELES & REDONDO RAILWAY - A narrow-gauge railroad built from Los Angeles to Strawberry Park and extended to Redondo Beach. The line was electrified in 1902 and converted to standard gauge in 1909. - *Donald Duke Collection*

LOS ANGELES, SALT LAKE & ATLANTIC RAILWAY COMPANY

Incorporated January 15, 1889 - Steam - Standard Gauge

Located Los Angeles, Los Angeles County. Proposed to build from Alamitos Bay and Rattlesnake Island terminals to Long Beach and then through Clearwater, Nadeau Winery to the east bank of the Los Angeles River. The road was to enter Los Angeles along the river. Secured right-of-way of the Los Angeles & Ocean Railroad. Surveys made, but no construction work was done. Franchise along the river bank graded to the Los Angeles city limits.

LOS ANGELES & SALT LAKE RAILROAD COMPANY

Organized 1916 - Steam - Standard Gauge

Located Los Angeles, Los Angeles County. Incorporated as the San Pedro, Los Angeles & Salt Lake Railroad Co. in 1901. When San Pedro was taken into the city of Los Angeles, the company was reorganized as the Los Angeles & Salt Lake Railroad Company. Full control acquired by the Union Pacific Railway Co. in 1921.

LOS ANGELES & SALT LAKE RAILROAD - Began life as the San Pedro, Los Angeles & Salt Lake Railroad, however, the name was shortened when San Pedro became a part of Los Angeles. It was known as the Salt Lake Route and the arrowhead formed a part of its emblem. - *Donald Duke Collection*

LOS ANGELES & SAN DIEGO BEACH RAILWAY COMPANY

Organized 1888 - Steam - Standard Guage

Located San Diego, San Diego County. Took over the operation of the San Diego, Old Town & Pacific Beach Railway Co. and the San Diego, Pacific Beach & La Jolla Railway Co. in La Jolla. Operating mileage 14.50 miles. Built and operated an electric streetcar line in San Diego in 1905, along Kittner Blvd. on C Street to Sixth Avenue and Waterfront to the San Diego, Cuyamaca & Eastern Railway depot at 10th Avenue and Commercial Street. Operated two McKeen Motor Cars from 1908 to 1916. Permission to abandon granted January 1919.

LOS ANGELES & SAN DIEGO RAILROAD COMPANY

Incorporated October 10, 1876 - Steam - Standard Gauge

Located Los Angeles, Los Angeles County. Proposed to build from Florence (So. Los Angeles) to Anaheim and then to San Diego. Distance 124 miles. Built from Florence to Santa Ana. Completed December 17, 1877. Distance 27.82 miles. Operated by the Central Pacific Railroad until March 1, 1885, and by Southern Pacific Co. until September 6, 1887. Consolidated with the Southern Pacific Co. May 14, 1888.

LOS ANGELES & SAN DIEGO BEACH RAILWAY - An amalgamation of two other railway lines. The carrier was operated by steam, electric, and motor car, such as shown above. Two McKeen Motor Cars ran the line from 1908-1916. - *Donald Duke Collection*

LOS ANGELES, SAN DIEGO & YUMA RAILROAD COMPANY

Incorporated April 23, 1889 - Steam - Standard Gauge

Located San Diego, San Diego County. Proposed to build from Los Angeles to Yuma via Del Mar, La Jolla, Ocean Beach, Roseville, Old Town and San Diego. Took over the franchises of the Del Mar & San Diego Railway, the Roseville & Ocean Beach Railroad and the San Diego & Eastern Terminal Railway. The Ocean Beach Railroad had built from Roseville to Ocean Beach. Opened for service April 23, 1887. Grading was done between Roseville and Old Town. The rails were attached and "stolen" by the Pacific Coast Steamship Company in June 1889. They were "restolen" and laid from Old Town towards Roseville. The steamship company tore them up in two days in January 1890 and shipped them away. San Diego & Eastern Terminal Railway laid some track on Atlantic Street, now Pacific Coast Highway. Organization replaced by the San Diego & Phoenix Railroad Company April 13, 1893.

LOS ANGELES & SAN FERNANDO ELECTRIC RAILWAY COMPANY

Incorporated June 2, 1911 - Electric - Standard Gauge

Located Los Angeles, Los Angeles County. Proposed to build to San Fernando via Griffith Park. Construction began on 6.00 miles of track in June 1911. Deeded to the Pacific Electric Railway March 19, 1912.

LOS ANGELES, SAN FERNANDO & HUENEME RAILROAD COMPANY

Surveyed September 29, 1887 - Steam - Standard Gauge

Located Los Angeles, Los Angeles County. Proposed to build through the San Fernando Valley and Simi Valley to Hueneme. Distance 63.00 miles. No construction work done.

LOS ANGELES, SAN FRANCISCO & SALT LAKE RAILROAD COMPANY

Incorporated October 26, 1894 - Steam - Standard Gauge

Located Los Angeles, Los Angeles County. Proposed to build toward Salt Lake City, Utah, through the counties of Los Angeles, San Bernardino, Inyo, Kern, Tulare, Fresno, Merced, Stanislaus, San Mateo, San Joaquin, Santa Clara and Alameda. Surveys from Los Angeles began November 1895. Project abandoned December 1895.

LOS ANGELES, SAN FRANCISCO SHORT LINE RAILROAD COMPANY

Incorporated February 18, 1908 - Electric - Standard Gauge

Located Los Angeles, Los Angeles County. Proposed to build to San Francisco. Surveys completed in March 1908. Proposed route by way of Hollister was to be 80.00 miles shorter than that of the existing Southern Pacific Co.

LOS ANGELES & SAN GABRIEL VALLEY RAILROAD COMPANY

Incorporated August 30, 1883 - Steam - Standard Gauge

Located Los Angeles, Los Angeles County. Built to Pasadena by way of Highland Park. Opened for service September 16, 1885. Extended to Duarte November 5, 1886. Distance 19.19 miles. Merged with the San Bernardino & Los Angeles Railway May 20, 1887. Merged into the California Central Railway Co. May 31, 1887. Became part of the Santa Fe Railway June 1904.

LOS ANGELES & SAN GABRIEL VALLEY RAILROAD - Built from Los Angeles to Pasadena by way of Highland Park. Was extended to San Dimas to meet Santa Fe's San Bernardino & Los Angeles Railway. Became a part of the Santa Fe System in 1904. - *Donald Duke Collection*

LOS ANGELES & SAN JOAQUIN VALLEY RAILROAD COMPANY

Organized September 1, 1913 - Electric - Standard Gauge

Located Los Angeles, Los Angeles County. Proposed to build northeastward across the San Fernando Valley by way of Olig and the Tejon Pass to Bakersfield.

LOS ANGELES & SAN PEDRO RAILROAD COMPANY

Incorporated February 18, 1868 - Steam - Standard Gauge

Located Los Angeles, Los Angeles County. Built to Wilmington. Distance 22.25 miles. Began operations October 26, 1868. This was the first railroad in Southern California. Consolidated into the Southern Pacific Co. December 18, 1874. Trackage is now the Harbor Subdivision of the Los Angeles Division of the Southern Pacific Company.

LOS ANGELES & SANTA MONICA RAILROAD

Proposed August 1873 - Steam - 3 ft. Gauge

Located Los Angeles, Los Angeles County. Proposed to build westward to Santa Monica. Distance 14.75 miles. Project abandoned 1874.

LOS ANGELES & SANTA MONICA RAILROAD COMPANY

Organized November 6, 1902 - Electric - Standard Gauge

Located Los Angeles, Los Angeles County. Built a street railway from Los Angeles to Santa Monica by way of the Soldier's Home. Became the Los Angeles Pacific Railway Company. Sold to the Pacific Electric Railway Co. in 1911.

LOS ANGELES & SANTA MONICA RAILWAY COMPANY

Organized January 6, 1886 - Steam - Standard Gauge

Located Los Angeles, Los Angeles County. Proposed to build from Los Angeles to Port Ballona by way of Inglewood. Merged into the California Central Railway Co. May 31, 1887. Construction work done by the California Central Railway. Opened for service September 23, 1887. Distance 17.10 miles. Became part of the Santa Fe Railway in 1904.

LOS ANGELES & SAN PEDRO RAILROAD - Southern California's first railway built from Wilmington to Los Angeles in 1868. Was traded to the Southern Pacific as a means of enticing the SP to extend their tracks to Los Angeles. (BELOW) A Los Angeles & San Pedro Railroad mixed train leaves the wharf at Wilmington bound for Los Angeles. - *Both Donald Duke Collection*

LOS ANGELES, SAN PEDRO & WILMINGTON HARBOR RAILROAD COMPANY

Organized January 1909 - Steam - Standard Gauge

Located Los Angeles, Los Angeles County. Proposed to build to Wilmington where dock facilities would be built.

LOS ANGELES SUBURBAN HOMES

Organized July 5, 1911 - Electric - Standard Gauge

Located Van Nuys, Los Angeles County. Began grading for an electric railway through Cahuenga Pass. Also proposed to build from Van Nuys to Owensmouth. Project abandoned in 1913.

LOS ANGELES TERMINAL EXCHANGE, INC.

Incorporated March 1929 - Electric - Standard Gauge

Located Los Angeles, Los Angeles County. Proposed to construct an independent terminal system and union station at the Plaza and Civic Center together with about twenty tracks about three miles each in a subway, to be operated with electric locomotives and to be connected with the tracks of all roads entering the city. Project abandoned November 2, 1929, due to lack of I.C.C. approval.

LOS ANGELES TERMINAL RAILWAY COMPANY

Incorporated August 27, 1890 - Steam - Standard Gauge

Located Los Angeles, Los Angeles County. Proposed to construct and acquire by lease, purchase or consolidation and operate a railroad with branches, in the counties of Los Angeles and Ventura. Proposed to build from San Pedro Bay to Los Angeles, then by way of the San Fernando Valley to Hueneme in Ventura County. One branch to run from Los Angeles by way of Pasadena to Altadena, another to run to Santa Monica. A branch was proposed to reach Glendale and the Verdugo Canyon. Another branch was to connect with the

Southern Pacific Company at Saticoy or Montalvo. The estimated mileage of construction would be 140.00 miles. On September 20, 1890, the company proposed to build a branch line from Los Angeles to the coal fields of southwestern Nevada. Purchased the Los Angeles, Pasadena & Glendale Railway Co. and the Altadena Railway Co. September 3, 1890. Secured the franchise of the Los Angeles, Utah & Atlantic Railroad October 1890. Opened for traffic from Los Angeles to Long Beach on November 8, 1891; to San Pedro on November 13, 1891. Glendale line changed to standard gauge December 21, 1891. Sold to the San Pedro, Los Angeles & Salt Lake Railroad Co. in 1901. Became the Union Pacific Pasadena Branch.

LOS ANGELES TERMINAL - A local Southern California railway that built from Los Angeles to Terminal Island via Long Beach. The LAT built a branch to Glendale and another to Pasadena-Altadena. In this view a LAT train is about to leave Terminal Island for Los Angeles. The route was purchased by the Salt Lake Route in 1901. - *Donald Duke Collection*

LOS ANGELES TRACTION COMPANY

Chartered February 25, 1895 - Electric - 3 ft. 6 in. Gauge

Located Los Angeles, Los Angeles County. Began operations August 29, 1895 from Fourth and Fresno streets to Adams and Arlington. Later built a branch line to Westlake Park. Completed 12.00 miles of street railway by December 1897. Sold to Los Angeles Inter-Urban Railway Co. January 2, 1904. Became part of the Pacific Electric Railway Co. September 1, 1911.

LOS ANGELES TRANSIT LINES

Organized January 10, 1945 - Electric - Narrow-Gauge

Located Los Angeles, Los Angeles County. In 1944 the Henry E. Huntington estate decided to sell their holdings in the Los Angeles Railway. Their stock was sold to American City Lines, a division of National City Lines, a bus operating company controlled by General Motors, Standard Oil, and Firestone Tire & Rubber Co. as a means of converting street railway lines to motor bus. The sale was consumated January 10, 1945 and the Los Angeles Railway became the Los Angeles Transit Lines. The new company began a wholesale abandonment of street car lines.

LOS ANGELES, TROPICO & GLENDALE RAILWAY COMPANY

Incorporated August 28, 1903 - Electric - Standard Gauge

Located Los Angeles, Los Angeles County. Proposed to build from a point on the Los Angeles River to Santa Barbara. Right-of-way secured across the Q.C.B. Richardson Ranch to Griffith Park. No construction work was done.

LOS ANGELES UNION PASSENGER TERMINAL

Organized 1937 - Steam - Standard Gauge

Located Los Angeles, Los Angeles County. Operational name for the 13.10 miles of track in the Los Angeles Union Passenger Terminal. Opened for service May 3, 1939. First train arrived May 7, 1939, at 6:00 A.M. All operations transferred to AMTRAK on April 1, 1977.

LOS ANGELES UNION PASSENGER TERMINAL - The last of the large metropolitan railway stations. Opened in May 1939 and operates 13 miles of track within the terminal facility. - *Union Pacific*

LOS ANGELES, UTAH & ATLANTIC RAILROAD COMPANY

Incorporated November 15, 1888 - Steam - Standard Gauge

Located Los Angeles, Los Angeles County. Proposed to build from San Pedro to Los Angeles and then north through San Bernardino, Kern and Inyo counties. To be the shortest route to the Atlantic. Project abandoned 1889. Franchise secured by the Los Angeles Terminal Railway in 1890.

LOS ANGELES & VERNON STREET RAILWAY

Chartered June 1887 - Horsecar - 3 ft. 6 in. Gauge

Located Los Angeles, Los Angeles County. Built along Central Avenue from Fifth Street to Slauson Avenue. Sold to the Los Angeles Consolidated Electric Railway Co. May 8, 1891. Became part of the Los Angeles Railway Co. August 18, 1895. Abandoned March 31, 1963.

LOS ANGELES & VERNON STREET RAILWAY - A horsecar line built from Vernon to downtown Los Angeles by way of Central Avenue. This barn was located at 22nd and Central Avenue in 1890. - *Huntington Library*

LOS ANGELES - WESTERN RAILWAY COMPANY

Incorporated October 27, 1910 - Electric - Standard Gauge

Located Hermosa Beach, Los Angeles County. Proposed to build inland from tidewater to Culver Station. Also to build 3.00 miles of branch lines. Total distance to be operated 7.25 miles. No construction work done.

LUDLOW & SOUTHERN RAILWAY COMPANY

Incorporated July 1902 - Steam - Standard Gauge

Located Ludlow, San Bernardino County. Built from a junction with the Santa Fe Railway to Bagdad (Steadman). Distance 7.50 miles. Construction began August 1902. Completed June 1903. Sold to the Pacific Mine Corp. 1910. Ceased operations as a commmon carrier 1916. Abandoned 1928. Tracks taken up 1936.

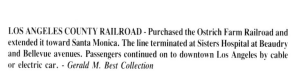

LOS ANGELES COUNTY RAILROAD - Purchased the Ostrich Farm Railroad and extended it toward Santa Monica. The line terminated at Sisters Hospital at Beaudry and Bellevue avenues. Passengers continued on to downtown Los Angeles by cable or electric car. - *Gerald M. Best Collection*

LOS ANGELES COUNTY FLOOD CONTROL DISTRICT - Used to haul cement and metal supports during the cement lining of the Los Angeles River, Arroyo Seco and other flood control channels. - *Donald Duke Collection*

LOMA PRIETA RAILROAD - A logging railroad that connected with the Southern Pacific at Loma Prieta in the redwood forest near Santa Cruz. Became a part of the Molino Lumber Company in 1910. - *Donald Duke Collection*

MARKET STREET RAILWAY - This railway operated an interurban line from 8th and Market streets in downtown San Francisco to San Mateo. As is evidenced by this scene at Broadway, between Sholim and San Mateo, their tracks paralleled the Southern Pacific for a short distance north of Burlingame. - *Donald Duke*

M

MADERA FLUME & TRADING COMPANY

Incorporated May 21, 1878 - Steam - 3 ft. Gauge

Located Soquel Mill, Madera County. Construction began in 1889 from mill to timber. Distance 4.00 miles. Acquired by Madera Sugar Pine Company in 1899.

MADERA RAILWAY COMPANY

Incorporated August 1, 1903 - Electric - Standard Gauge

Located Madera, Madera County. Built from Gowan Station to Knowles Spur. Distance 1.00 miles.

MADERA SUGAR PINE RAILROAD

Incorporated May 8, 1899 - Steam - 3 ft. Gauge

Located Sugar Pine, Madera County. Acquired the properties of the Madera Flume & Trading Company. Built northward to timber along Big Creek and on until just a few miles south of Wawona. Built north and west along Rush Creek and north and east toward Old Highway 41 by 1918. In 1919 rails were laid into the Raymond Mountain area. In 1927 track was laid to Hogan Mountain and Signal Peak region and into Mariposa County. Distance 25 miles. Suspended operations in 1931. Trackage from Sugar Pine to Signal Peak removed in 1934.

MADRONA LAND & LUMBER COMPANY

Built 1877 - Steam - Narrow-Gauge

Located Sonoma, Sonoma County. Built one mile of track.

MAIN & FIFTH STREET RAILWAY

Began operations March 1, 1888 - Horsecar - 3 ft. 6 in. Gauge

Located Los Angeles, Los Angeles County. Built and owned by Francisca Jesurum to connect downtown with Southern Pacific's new Arcade Station. Line ran from 1st Street South on Main to Fifth Street. East on Fifth Street to SP depot on Wolfskill (Central) Avenue. Line merged into the Main Street & Agricultural Park Street Railway Company.

MAIN, FIFTH & SAN PEDRO STREET RAILWAY COMPANY

Incorporated July 21, 1897 - Electric - 3 ft. 6 in. Gauge

Located Los Angeles, Los Angeles County. Began operations August 1, 1898, on San Pedro Street from Fifth Street to 30th Street. Sold to the Los Angeles Railway Co. October 1, 1898. Abandoned March 31, 1963.

MAIN STREET & AGRICULTURAL PARK HORSECAR LINE

Incorporated 1874 - Horsecar - 3 ft. 6 in. Gauge

Located Los Angeles, Los Angeles County. Built from Temple and Main Street, down Main to Washington Street. Reorganized as the Main Street & Agricultural Park Railroad Company.

MAIN STREET & AGRICULTURAL PARK RAILROAD COMPANY

Incorporated November 18, 1876 - Horsecar - 3 ft. 6 in. Gauge

Located Los Angeles, Los Angeles County. Operated 6.62 miles of horsecar line in Los Angeles. Ran south on Main from Temple to Jefferson, west on Jefferson to Figueroa, and south on Figueroa to Agricultural Park. Opened for service on July 1, 1875. Line electrified April 1, 1897. Sold to the Los Angeles Railway September 1897.

MAIN STREET & AGRICULTURAL PARK RAILROAD - Began life as a horse-car line in 1875 and converted to electricity in 1897. Line ran south on Main Street and south Figueroa to Agricultural Park (Exposition Park). - *Huntington Library*

MAMMOTH COPPER COMPANY RAILROAD

Organized December 7, 1906 - Steam - Narrow-Gauge

Located Kennett, Shasta County. Proposed to build from a spur on the Southern Pacific Railroad to Quarter Hill. Distance 4.00 miles. Project abandoned.

JOHNS-MANVILLE PRODUCTS CORPORATION

Electric - Standard Gauge

Located Lompoc, Santa Barbara County. Built seven miles of switching track from quarry to Celite Processing Plant.

MAPLE AVENUE ELECTRIC RAILWAY

Built 1887 - Electric - Narrow-Gauge

Located Los Angeles, Los Angeles County. Built from First and Main streets along Maple to Pico Street and west on Pico to Harvard Blvd. Ceased operations in 1888.

MARE ISLAND FREIGHT LINE COMPANY

Organized 1919 - Electric - Standard Gauge

Located Napa Junction, Napa County. Built by the San Francisco, Napa & Calistoga Railway Co. from Napa Junction to Mare Island Navy Yard. Began operations September 20, 1920. Sold to the U.S. Government and renamed August 15, 1956.

MARE ISLAND FREIGHT LINE - A line built by the Napa Valley Route interurban line to Mare Island following World War I. Line sold to the U.S. government in 1956. - *Harre Demoro Collection*

MARIN & NAPA RAILROAD COMPANY

Incorporated August 17, 1886 - Steam - 3 ft. Gauge

Located Marin, Marin County. Built to Sears Point. Distance 7.67 miles. Completed June 18, 1887. Leased to the Sonoma Valley Railroad June 30, 1888. Sold to the San Francisco & North Pacific Railway Co. December 19, 1888. Changed to standard gauge November 30, 1889. Completed April 9, 1890. Consolidated into the Northwestern Pacific Railroad January 8, 1907.

MARIN COUNTY ELECTRIC RAILWAYS

Incorporated December 24, 1913 - Electric - Standard Gauge

Located Mill Valley, Marin County. Proposed to build three rail lines from the Northwestern Pacific Railroad: Mill Valley Station on Throckmorton Avenue to the Cascades; to Blythedale Canyon; and one along the east side of Mill Valley to the high school. Project abandoned in 1916.

MARIN SHORE RAILROAD COMPANY

Incorporated March 17, 1904 - Steam - Standard Gauge

Located San Rafael, Marin County. Proposed to build northerly to Point Pedro and then to Ignacio. Distance 20.00 miles. Surveys completed July 1905. Project abandoned 1906.

MARIN TERMINAL RAILROAD COMPANY
MARIN TERMINAL ELECTRIC RAILROAD

Organized 1905 - Steam - Standard Gauge

Located Petaluma, Sonoma County. The Marin Terminal Electric Railroad was organized in 1906 to take over the surveys of the Marin Terminal Railroad Co. This project was proposed by the Petaluma & Santa Rosa Railway to connect it with the San Francisco, Vallejo & Napa Valley Railroad. This connection would provide Napa and Santa Rosa areas with a deepwater terminal where ferries could transport freight and passengers in a more direct route to San Francisco. Project abandoned January 1907.

MARKET STREET & FAIRMONT RAILROAD COMPANY

Cable - Standard Gauge

Located San Francisco, San Francisco County. A subsidiary of the Market Street Cable Railway. Built the Castro Street Cable Line running on Market Street to Valencia Street to Castro Street and over Castro Street to 26th Street. The portion of the line on Castro between 18th and 26th Street was run as a cable line until abandoned in March 1941, by the second Market Street Railway Co. The Castro Cable was the last standard gauge cable railway to operate in the United States.

MARKET STREET & WILLOW GLEN HORSE RAILROAD COMPANY

Incorporated February 23, 1876 - Horsecar - Standard Gauge

Located San Jose, Santa Clara County. Franchise granted February 11, 1876, for a horsecar line from Julian, along Market, San Fernando, San Salvador and Bird to Willow Street. Later extended on Julian to the Southern Pacific Depot. Began operations January 6, 1877. Became part of the San Jose Railroad December 22, 1909.

MARKET STREET RAILROAD

Organized 1869 - Horsecar - Narrow-Gauge

Located Oakland, Alameda County. Horsecar street railway operating in Oakland.

MARKET STREET RAILROAD COMPANY
MARKET STREET CABLE RAILWAY COMPANY

Chartered 1857 - Steam - Standard Gauge, 3 ft. Gauge - 3 ft. 6 in. Gauge and 5 ft. Gauge

Located San Francisco, San Francisco County. Built from California and Market streets to Valencia Street and 16th Street. Built down Market Street to the waterfront and extended tracks from 16th to 25th Street on Valencia in 1863. Grading for the Market Street Railroad Co. began in May 1859. The first rails were laid July 7, 1859. Operation began July 4, 1860. A branch line was built from Hayes Street to Laguna Street in 1864. All lines were converted to

MARKET STREET CABLE RAILWAY - The terminus of Market Street Railway's famous standard gauge cable car line known as the Castro Street Line. The line was operated by steam dummy power between 1880-1888. - *Charles D. Savage*

horsecars in 1868. Became the Market Street Cable Railway Company May 20, 1882. Began first operations as a cable railroad August 22, 1883, from ferries to 28th Street and Mission Street by way of Market Street to Valencia Street. Power was primarily by cable until the Castro Street line was built and a steam dummy was used. The steam dummy ran Market Street between Valencia Street and Castro Street from 1880 to 1888. A horsecar line operated on Fifth Street. Properties were reorganized as Market Street Railway Company in 1893. Properties deeded to the new company were: Horsecar lines, 4.11 miles; cable car lines, 44.29 miles; steam-operated lines, 11.80 miles; electric operated lines, 117.96 miles. After reorganization, electrification began on all lines where such power was practical. Reorganized February 16, 1921, and took over the operations of the United Railroad of San Francisco. Operations were merged into the Municipal Railway of San Francisco September 29, 1944.

MARKET STREET RAILWAY COMPANY

Organized 1893 - Electric - Standard Gauge

Located San Francisco, San Francisco County. Organized as a consolidation of the Market Street Cable Railway, Central Railroad Company, North Beach & Mission Railway Co., City Railroad Co., Potrero & Bay View Railroad Co., Park & Ocean Railroad Co., Ocean Beach Railway Co.,Southern Heights & Visitation Railway Co., Ferries & Cliff House Railway Co.,Omnibus Cable Co. and Market Street & Fairmont Railway Co. Took over the operations of the Metropolitan Railway Co. Deeded to the United Railroad of San Francisco in 1902. Deeded to the Market Street Railway Co. in 1920. Sold to the Municipal Railway of San Francisco in 1944.

ANDREW MARKHAM LUMBER COMPANY

Incorporated July 1886 - Horse Power - 3 ft. Gauge

Located Markham, Sonoma County. Built 1.25 miles of track from mill to timber. Changed to steam power and standard gauge by 1900. Sold to Laton Lumber & Investment Co. 1906.

MARSH LUMBER COMPANY

Organized 1908 - Steam - 3 ft. Gauge

Located Loyalton, Sierra County. Purchased the Horton Brothers operations. Distance 7.00 miles. Standard gauged some of the trackage. Sold to Clover Valley Lumber Co. 1920.

MARTIN-MARIETTA CARBON COMPANY

Steam - Standard Gauge

Located San Francisco, San Francisco County. Operated switching tracks within Martin-Marietta Carbon Company plant located northwest of Henry Ford Drawbridge.

MARTINEZ & CONCORD INTERURBAN RAILWAY COMPANY

Organized January 22, 1916 - Electric - Standard Gauge

MARSH LUMBER CO. - Built seven miles of logging railroad in and around Loyalton, Sierra County, operating for approximately 20 years. Was sold to the Clover Valley Lumber Co. in 1920. - *Donald Duke Collection*

Located Martinez, Contra Costa County. Proposed to build to Government Ranch by way of Escobar and Peyton Road. To connect with the Oakland, Antioch & Eastern Railway at Government Ranch. Distance 6.50 miles. Project abandoned 1917.

MARYSVILLE & BENICIA RAILROAD COMPANY

Incorporated 1851 - Steam - Standard Gauge

Located Marysville, Yuba County. Proposed to construct a railroad from Marysville to Benecia, or any point on the Sacramento River at or near Knights Ferry. Was absorbed by the San Francisco & Marysville Railroad in 1858 before any construction was done. Railroad was acquired because of railroad bridge privileges already obtained by the Marysville & Benicia Railroad Co.

MARYSVILLE & COLUSA RAILROAD COMPANY
MARYSVILLE - COLUSA RAILWAY

Organized November 1911 - Electric - Standard Gauge

Located Marysville, Yuba County. Proposed to build an electric railway to connect the towns of Meridian, Sutter City and Colusa. Reorganized as the Marysville & Colusa Railroad Company. Deeded to the Northern Electric Railway in 1915.

MARYSVILLE & GREAT EASTERN RAILROAD COMPANY

Organized 1907 - Electric - Standard Gauge

Located Marysville, Yuba County. Proposed to build to Downieville. A conference was held with the Northern Electric Railroad in January 1907, to obtain rights over part of the distance. A junction was to be made somewhere with the San Francisco, Vallejo & Vaca Valley Electric Railway & Steamship Company. Project abandoned in 1909.

MARYSVILLE & SUSANVILLE RAILWAY COMPANY

Incorporated April 8, 1904 - Steam - Standard Gauge

Located Marysville, Yuba County. Proposed to build to a point in the Honey Lake Valley near Susanville and from Susanville to a point on the boundary line between California and Nevada. Distance approximately 200.00 miles. Surveys begun June 1904. Project sold to Western Pacific Railroad October 2, 1905.

MARYSVILLE & YUBA CITY STREET RAILROAD COMPANY
MARYSVILLE & YUBA CITY RAILROAD COMPANY

Incorporated April 11, 1889 - Horsecar - 3 ft. 6 in. Gauge

Located Marysville, Yuba County. Built to Yuba City. Distance 3.26 miles. Construction began May 13, 1889 in Marysville. Began operations August 19, 1889. Operations were between the Southern Pacific Company station in

Marysville and the California Northern Railroad station in Yuba City. Sold to the Northern Electric Railway July 12, 1906. Rebuilt as a standard gauge road and electrified by the Northern Electric Co. between 1905 and 1907. Electric operations began in 1907. Company dissolved November 14, 1911. Road abandoned February 16, 1942.

MARYSVILLE RAILROAD COMPANY

Incorporated November 29, 1867 - Steam - Standard Gauge

Located Marysville, Yuba County. Proposed to build to some point on the Central Pacific Railroad between the American River and Roseville. No construction work done. Consolidated with the California & Oregon Railroad Co. June 16, 1869. (Second California & Oregon Railroad). Consolidated with Central Pacific Railroad Co. August 22, 1870.

MASSACK TIMBER & LUMBER COMPANY

Incorporated 1916 - Steam - 3 ft. Gauge

Located Spring Garden, Plumas County. Built 3.00 miles of track by 1917. Abandoned 1921.

MATEO STREET & SANTA FE AVENUE STREET CAR COMPANY

Organized 1895 - Horsecar - Narrow-Gauge

Located Los Angeles, Los Angeles County. A one-horse horsecar line operating south from Santa Fe's La Grande station at First and Mateo Street, to Santa Fe Avenue. South on Santa Fe Avenue to Slauson Avenue. Purchased by Abbot Kinney in 1896 and converted to a steam dummy line

MATTOLE LUMBER COMPANY

Built 1908 - Steam - 3 ft. Gauge

Located Mattole, Humboldt County. Built a logging road from the mouth of the Mattole River to timber. Distance 4.00 miles. Abandoned 1918.

MC CLOUD RIVER RAILROAD COMPANY

Organized 1896 - Chartered January 22, 1897 - Steam - Standard Gauge

Located McCloud, Siskiyou County. Began operations in 1897. Reached Upton by 1903. Distance 18.32 miles. Extended from Shasta to Slagger Creek. Distance 46.10 miles by 1908. Present operations from a junction with the Southern Pacific Co. at Mt. Shasta to Hambone with a junction with Western Pacific Railroad and the Great Northern Railway and a branch to Burney. Total operating mileage 77.90 miles.

McCLOUD RIVER RAILROAD - A logging line built to log the timber around Mount Shasta. Was extended east from McCloud and later built to a connection with the Great Northern at Hambone, a distance of 49.5 miles. Built a branch to Burney in the 1950's. - *Don Hansen*

MC CORMICK & HAUPMAN

Organized 1901 - Steam - Standard Gauge

Located Fieldbrook, Humboldt County. Built 1.00 mile of track in 1902.

CHARLES R. MC CORMICK LUMBER COMPANY
MC CORMICK STEAMSHIP COMPANY

Incorporated 1910 - Steam Motor - Standard Gauge

Located San Diego, San Diego County. Industrial railroad from wharf at the foot of Dewey Street to lumberyards. Succeeded by the McCormick Steamship Co. 1937. Abandoned 1942.

D.H. MC EWEN LUMBER COMPANY

Organized 1906 - Steam - Narrow Gauge

Located Cazadero, Sonoma County. Purchased the Cazadero Lumber Company in 1906. Sold to M.S. Wagy in 1909. Operated 6.00 miles of trackage. Abandoned 1910 or 1911.

MC KAY & COMPANY

Organized about 1891 - Steam - Standard Gauge

Located Eureka, Humboldt County. Took over the operations of the Occidental Milling Company. Extended the trackage from Eureka Slough to timber. Distance 10.50 miles. Abandoned 1934.

MC KAY & COMPANY LUMBER COMPANY

Steam - Narrow-Gauge

Located Eureka, Humboldt County. Slough to timber along Ryan Slough. Distance 6.15 miles.

MC KAY & COMPANY RAILROAD

Organized 1905 - Steam - Standard Gauge

Located Eureka, Humboldt County. Ryan Slough woods to the Occidental Mill on Humboldt Bay in Eureka between A and B streets.

MC KAY LUMBER COMPANY

Steam - 2 ft. Gauge

Located McKay, Tuolumne County. Built from mill to timber. Distance 5.00 miles.

MEMPHIS & EL PASO RAILROAD COMPANY
MEMPHIS, EL PASO & PACIFIC RAILROAD COMPANY

Chartered 1853 - Steam - Standard Gauge

Located El Paso, Texas. Originally chartered as the Memphis & El Paso Railroad Company. Reorganized as Memphis, El Paso & Pacific Railroad Co. to build from Texas over the 32nd parallel to San Diego in 1856. Contracted to take over land grants and franchise of the San Diego & Gila, Southern Pacific & Atlantic Railroad Co. February 1869. Route surveyed from San Diego to Fort Yuma, Arizona by way of National Ranch, Jamul, Campo, Jacumba, Carriso Canyon and Algodones. No construction work done in California.

MENDOCINO COAST RAILWAY

Began service June 1, 1987 - Diesel - Standard Gauge

Located Fort Bragg, Mendocino County. Purchased the California Western Railroad June 1, 1987. Distance 40.00 miles to Willits with junction with Northwestern Pacific and Eureka Southern.

MENDOCINO LUMBER COMPANY

Construction began 1900 - Steam - Standard Gauge

Located Big River, Mendocino County. Built from Perkin's Camp to Fraser's Landing. Distance 1.50 miles. Began operations August 18, 1900. 10.33 miles of track were built during the peak of operations. Ceased operations August 1936. Abandoned 1938.

MENDOCINO RAILROAD

Chartered October 22, 1875 - Steam - 3 ft. Gauge

Located Greenwood, Mendocino county. Built from Cuffy's Cove to Helmke's Mill on Donahue's Creek during 1875 and 1876. Distance 27.00 miles. Deeded to Greenwood Railroad Company in 1890. Sold to L. E. White Lumber Company. Deeded to Goodyear Redwood Company in 1916.

MERCED CANYON RAILWAY
MERCED CANYON RAILWAY COMPANY

Incorporated October 20, 1905 - Steam - 3 ft. Gauge

Located Merced, Merced County. Proposed to build to the western border of Yosemite Park. Trackage to follow along the Merced River. Distance 90.00 miles. Company dissolved November 30, 1909.

MERCED GOLD MINING COMPANY

Organized November 19, 1894 - Steam - 24 in. Gauge

Located Coulterville, Mariposa County. Built from the Mary Harrison Mine to the Potosi Mill. Distance 4.00 miles. Railroad completed in 1896. Ceased operations in 1904.

MESA & EL CAJON RAILROAD COMPANY

Organized July, 1887 - Steam Motor or Electric - Standard Gauge

Located San Diego, San Diego County. Proposed to build a steam motor or electric railway from a connection with the Electric Rapid Transit Company, then build on upper Fifth Avenue to El Cajon. Distance 15.00 miles. No construction work done.

METROLINK

Organized September 13, 1991 - Diesel - Standard Gauge

Located Los Angeles, Los Angeles County. The Southern California Regional Rail Authority (SCRRA) officially came into being September 13, 1991, when the counties of Los Angeles, San Bernardino, Ventura, Riverside, and Orange signed an agreement designing the agency to plan, design, construct, and operate nine passenger rail lines to be known as Metrolink. SCRRA recently obtained 56 miles of operating rights from the Union Pacific between Riverside and Los Angeles, and are negotiating with Santa Fe for an additional 240 miles.

METRO RAIL

Organized 1980 - Electric - Standard Gauge

Located Los Angeles, Los Angeles County. A 1980 referendum approved a 150-mile subway and light rail system for Los Angeles County. Ground was broken November 1, 1985 for a light rail line from Los Angeles to Long Beach. Line was opened for traffic on July 16, 1990.

METRO RAIL LOS ANGELES

Organized 1980 - Electric - Standard Gauge

Located Los Angeles, Los Angeles County. Work began in 1986 on a subway rapid transit line to run 18 miles from Los Angeles Union Station to North Hollywood. Ground breaking held September 29, 1986. First 4-mile section to be completed and in operation sometime in 1992.

METROPOLITAN COACH LINES

Organized 1953 - Electric - 3 ft. 6 in. and Standard Gauge

Located Los Angeles, Los Angeles County. Took over the passenger operations of the Pacific Electric Railway Co. and the Los Angeles Railway on October 1, 1953. Sold to the Los Angeles Metropolitan Transit Authority March 5, 1958.

METROPOLITAN REDWOOD COMPANY

Organized 1907 - Steam - Standard Gauge

Located Metropolitan, Humboldt County. Operated 4.00 miles of trackage. Abandoned 1929.

METROPOLITAN STREET RAILWAY

Incorporated February 21, 1891 - Horsecar - Cable - 5 ft. Gauge

Located San Francisco San Francisco County. Built from Market Street to Golden Gate Park. Began operations October 1892. Sold to the Market Street Railway Company in 1894.

METROPOTAN TRANSIT DEVELOPMENT BOARD

Organized 1976 - Electric - Standard Gauge

Located San Diego, San Diego County. Purchased the San Diego & Arizona Eastern Railroad. Began operations of San Diego Trolley in July 1981.

MEXICAN PACIFIC RAILROAD COMPANY

Organized 1888 - Steam - Standard Gauge

Located Phoenix, Arizona Territory. Proposed to build to San Diego by way of Yuma and south to Mazatlan and Tepic in Mexico. No construction work done.

MEXICO & SAN DIEGO RAILWAY COMPANY

Organized 1911 - Electric - Standard Gauge

Located San Diego, San Diego County. Acquired the assets of the South San Diego & Imperial Beach Railway. Operated ferry-motor car service from San Diego to Imperial Beach. Arranged trackage rights over San Diego & South Eastern Railway, former Coronado Belt Line, from National City & Otay Railway Company junction to South San Diego, then to Imperial Beach. Distance 3.00 miles. Abandoned after the floods in January 1916.

MEXICO & SAN DIEGO RAILWAY - Operated a battery rail car from San Diego to Imperial Beach which was later converted to electric power. Purchased the San Diego & South Eastern interurban line. Abandoned after floods of 1916. - *Donald Duke Collection*

MICHIGAN - CALIFORNIA LUMBER COMPANY

Organized 1917 - Steam - 3 ft. Gauge

Located Camino, El Dorado County. Purchased the holdings of the R.E. Danaher Company. The line from Camino to Pino Grande, including an aerial tramway, was built in 1911. Before abandonment 50 miles of trackage were in operation. Abandoned 1951.

MICHIGAN-CALIFORNIA LUMBER CO. - A narrow-gauge Shay locomotive operated logging line that ran over some 60 miles of line from Camino to Pino Grande. Abandoned in 1951. - *Donald Duke*

MIDLAND PACIFIC RAILROAD COMPANY

Organized 1901 - Steam - Standard Gauge

Located Bakersfield, Kern County. Proposed to build a railroad to the Pacific Coast. Incorporated March 16, 1906, to build to San Luis Obispo Bay by way of Sunset, Cuyama, and Santa Maria to Port Harford. Distance 140 miles. Grading completed for 10.00 miles. 12.00 miles of track laid by 1907. Reorganized August 22, 1908.

MID - PACIFIC RAILROAD

Organized 1929 - Steam - Standard Gauge

Located in California and Nevada. A plan proposed for the consolidation of the Tonopah & Tidewater Railroad Co., Tonopah & Goldfield Railroad Co., Nevada Central Railroad Co., Virginia & Truckee Railway Co., Nevada Copper Belt Railroad Co. and the Eureka Nevada Railway Co. into one operating company. Four new railroads were proposed to join the existing companies together. These new railroads were to be: Santa Fe Connecting Railroad Co., Nevada Southern Railroad Co., Los Angeles & Nevada Railroad Co. and the Nevada Central Extension Railroad Company. The project was abandoned in 1934.

MILL VALLEY & MT. TAMALPAIS SCENIC RAILWAY COMPANY

Chartered January 16, 1896 - Steam - Standard Gauge

Located Mt. Tamalpais, Marin County. Opened for service August 18, 1896. Became the Mt. Tamalpais & Muir Woods Railway in 1913. Abandoned in 1930.

MINARETS & WESTERN RAILWAY COMPANY

Organized March 3, 1921 - Steam - Standard Gauge

Located Pinedale, Fresno County. Construction began in 1922 from Pinedale to Pinedale Junction. From Pinedale Junction to El Prado trackage rights over the Southern Pacific Co. were used. Distance 9.24 miles. From El Prado the company built northward to Wishon. Distance 38.50 miles. Opened for service July 15, 1923. Abandoned March 16, 1934. Section Pinedale to Pinedale Junction sold to the Southern Pacific January 2, 1935. Dismantling of the rest of the railroad began in 1936.

MINKLER SOUTHERN RAILWAY

Incorporated May 22, 1913 - Steam - Standard Gauge

Located Minkler, Fresno County. Built from Minkler to Wyeth, Cutler to Exeter and Redbank to Woodlake. Distance 43.70 miles. Completed in 1914. Leased to the Atchison, Topeka & Santa Fe Railway Co. October 1, 1914. Built from Lindsay to Porterville. Distance 12.10 miles. Completed in 1917. Deeded to the Santa Fe Railway Co. January 1, 1918. Built from Porterville to Ducor and Gil Junction to Landco in 1920. Distance 15.20 miles. Leased to the Santa Fe Railway Co. July 15, 1920. Acquired by the Santa Fe Railway Co. December 31, 1942.

MINOR MILL & LUMBER CO. - Built three miles of logging railroad from Isaac Minor Mill into the redwoods. Became the Glendale Railroad in 1903. - *Donald Duke Collection*

MINOR, KIRK & COMPANY
MINOR MILL & LUMBER COMPANY

Organized 1890 - Steam - 4 ft. 9 in. Gauge

Located **Warren Creek, Humboldt County.** Issac Minor built a mill on Warren Creek and constructed 2.30 miles of logging railroad. Mill burned in 1885. Operations moved to Glendale. Three miles of logging road were constructed. Became the Glendale Railroad in 1903. Mill and railroad ceased operations in 1911. Abandoned in 1912. Rebuilt along Warren Creek in 1917 and named Warren Creek Railroad. Operated under the name Granite Mountain Rock Quarry Railroad. Ceased operations in 1917. Short section of right-of-way sold to the Arcata & Mad River Railroad in 1952.

MINTON MILLS

Organized 1919 - Steam - 3 ft. Gauge

Located **Duncan Mills, Sonoma County.** Operated 4.00 miles of trackage. Abandoned 1922.

MODESTO & EMPIRE TRACTION COMPANY

Incorporated October 7, 1911 - Steam - Standard Gauge

Located **Modesto, Stanislaus County.** Took over the properties of the Modesto Interurban Railroad organized in March 1909. Built to Empire and a junction with the Athcison, Topeka & Santa Fe Railway. Distance 5.186 miles. Began operations November 11, 1911. Passenger service discontinued in 1917.

MODESTO & EMPIRE TRACTION - Took over the Modesto Interurban Railroad and became a steam-powered switching road around the canneries of Modesto. Locomotive in this view waits under the Tidewater Southern electrified overhead in the southern section of Modesto. - *Allan Youell*

MODESTO INTERURBAN RAILROAD

Proposed 1908 - Motor Car - Standard Gauge

Located **Modesto, Stanislaus County.** Proposed to build from Modesto along McHenry Avenue for a distance. Then to Riverbank by the most direct route. Distance 9.50 miles. Incorporated March 23, 1909, to construct 5.23 miles of track from Modesto to Empire. Became Modesto & Empire Traction Company October 7, 1911. First train November 1, 1911. Abandoned passenger service in 1917.

MODESTO INTERURBAN RAILROAD COMPANY

Incorporated March 23, 1909 - Electric - Standard Gauge

Located **Modesto, Stanislaus County.** Built to Empire. Distance 5.22 miles. Sold to the Modesto & Empire Traction Co. October 7, 1911.

MODESTO, TUOLUMNE & MONO RAILROAD COMPANY
MODESTO & YOSEMITE VALLEY RAILROAD COMPANY

Incorporated May 1900 - Steam - Standard Gauge

Located **Modesto, Stanislaus County.** Proposed to build from Oakdale to Modesto. Then on to the Crows Landing and to Tidewater. Project abandoned in 1901.

MODOC NORTHERN RAILWAY COMPANY

Incorporated July 23, 1908 - Steam - Standard Gauge

Located **Alturas, Modoc County.** Proposed to build to Klamath Falls, Oregon. Distance 98.75 miles. Title transferred to the Central Pacific Railroad Co. on February 29, 1912. Trackage constructed by the Southern Pacific Co. Construction began August 1928. Completed July 13, 1929.

MOJAVE & BAKERSFIELD RAILROAD COMPANY

Incorporated October 11, 1910 - Steam - Standard Gauge

Located **Bakersfield, Kern County.** Proposed to build a new railroad between Bakersfield and Mojave. No work done. Merged with the Southern Pacific July 1917.

MOJAVE NORTHERN RAILROAD COMPANY

Construction began 1915 - Steam - Standard Gauge

Located **Victorville, San Bernardino County.** Began operations to quarry August 1916. Distance 3.35 miles. Trackage extended from Southwest Portland Cement Company plant to quarry at Black Mountain. Distance 16.35 miles. Common carrier status dissolved in 1925. Became a plant facility and operations taken over by the newly reorganized Southwestern Portland Cement Company.

MOJAVE NORTHERN RAILROAD - A quarry railroad between Victorville to Black Mountain, a distance of 16.35 miles. Near the end of steam, the line operated a great many railfan excursion trips. - *Donald Duke*

MOLINO TIMBER COMPANY

Operated 1890's - Steam - Narrow-Gauge

Located **Loma Prieta, Santa Clara County.**

MONO LAKE RAILWAY & LUMBER COMPANY
MONO LAKE RAILWAY

Organized December 23, 1906 - Steam - 3 ft. Gauge

Located **Bodie, Mono County.** Organized to take over the properties of the Bodie Railway & Lumber Company. Renamed Mono Lake Railway in 1907. Abandoned September 6, 1917. Tracks removed by September 1918.

MONOLITH RAILROAD
MONOLITH PORTLAND CEMENT COMPANY RAILROAD

Organized 1906 - Steam - 3 ft. Gauge

Located **Monolith, Kern County.** Built by the Los Angeles Metropolitan Water District in 1907 to haul rock from a quarry in the Tehachapi Mountains to the cement plant for construction work on the Owens Valley Water Aqueduct and dams. Distance 4.10 miles. Sold to the U.S. Potash Company in 1919. Sold to Monolith Portland Cement Company in 1920. Converted to diesel power. Electric mine engines used in mine shafts. Ceased operations December 1972. Abandoned in 1973.

MONORAIL RAPID TRANSIT COMPANY

Incorporated April 1912 - Electric - Standard Gauge

Located **San Francisco, San Francisco County.** Proposed to build a monorail system in the city of San Francisco.

MONROVIA, ARCADIA & PASADENA RAILROAD

Organized May 1887 - Electric - Narrow-Gauge

Located **Arcadia, Los Angeles County.** Proposed to build a street railroad on Olive Street in Arcadia.

MONROVIA STREET RAILWAY

Organized 1888 - Horsecar - Narrow-Gauge

Located **Monrovia, Los Angeles County.** Built a horsecar street railway from the Santa Fe Railway Station up Myrtle Avenue. Distance 1.00 mile. Ceased operation in 1891.

MONTECITO RAILWAY COMPANY

Incorporated July 25, 1914 - Electric - Standard Gauge

Located Los Angeles, Los Angeles County. Proposed to build from Griffin Avenue and Avenue 43 to Mount Gillig. The company planned to build an amusement park at the end of the line. Constructed 2.40 miles of track. Began operations March 21, 1915. When plans for the amusement park failed, the line ceased operations during June 1915. Tracks removed during February 1918.

MONTEREY & DEL MONTE HEIGHTS RAILWAY COMPANY

Chartered June 29, 1909 - Electric - Standard Gauge

Located Monterey, Monterey County. Built a line east from Monterey to Del Monte Heights, a distance of 2.86 miles. Began operations February 22, 1912. Real estate sales fell off and the line ceasesd operations October 31, 1914. Property conveyed to the Monterey & Pacific Railway. Due to limited sale of homesites, service discontinued July 20, 1923.

MONTEREY & EASTERN RAILROAD

Incorporated April 17, 1906 - Steam - Standard Gauge

Located Monterey, Monterey County. Proposed to build to Salinas.

MONTEREY EXTENSION RAILROAD COMPANY

Incorporated Janaury 6, 1888 - Steam - Standard Gauge

Located Monterey, Monterey County. Built to Lake Majella. Distance 4.30 miles. Consolidated with the Southern Pacific May 14, 1888. Construction finished August 1, 1889.

MONTEREY & FRESNO RAILROAD COMPANY

Incorporated January 1895 - Steam - Standard Gauge

Located Monterey, Monterey County. Proposed to build in a southeast direction through the towns of Salinas, San Juan and Hollister to Fresno. Distance 150.00 miles. Surveys began March 1893. Right-of-way secured in May 1893. Contract for the first 10 miles of track let May 26, 1893. Contract let to the California Construction Co. June 2, 1893. Grading began near Monterey in July 1894. Project abandoned in 1899.

MONTEREY, FRESNO & EASTERN RAILWAY COMPANY

Incorporated December 29, 1906 - Electric - Standard Gauge

Located Monterey, Monterey County. Proposed to build eastward to Fresno. Distance 140 miles. Began construction of a 1,500-foot wharf at Monterey Bay May 3, 1907. Purchased the Watsonville Transportation Co. in April 1907.

MONTEREY & PACIFIC GROVE STREET RAILWAY & ELECTRIC POWER COMPANY

Organized June 2, 1893 - Horsecar - 3 ft. Gauge

Located Monterey, Monterey County. Began operations as a privately owned horsecar line August 12, 1890. Sold to the Monterey & Pacific Grove Street Railway & Electric Power Co. in June 1893. Electrified in 1903. Became the Monterey & Pacific Grove Railway August 24, 1903. Operated 6.60 miles of street railway between Pacific Grove, Monterey and Del Monte.

MONTEREY & PACIFIC GROVE RAILWAY COMPANY
MONTEREY & PACIFIC GROVE STREET RAILWAY & ELECTRIC POWER COMPANY

Began operations August 5, 1891 - Horsecar - Narrow-Gauge

Located Pacific Grove, Monterey County. Built from Lighthouse Avenue and 17th Street to west gate of the Del Monte Hotel at 7th Street and Sloat Avenue, Monterey. The route was along Lighthouse, Fountain, and Central to Lighthouse in New Monterey, to Decacur Street, then to downtown Monterey up Alvarado Street, Munras, Pearl and Washington to Perry Street (Del Monte Avenue) on to Ocean Avenue, through Oak Grove to their car barn at Del Monte Terminus. On June 3, 1893, the company reorganized as the Monterey & Pacific Grove Street Railway & Electric Power Company. Electrified in 1902 and converted to standard gauge in 1905. An extension was built from Lighthouse and 17th Street in Pacific Grove to the city's Southern Pacific Railroad depot. Planned to build along the 17 Mile Drive along the coast to Carmel. Plan abandoned. Service discontinued July 20, 1923.

MONTEREY PENINSULA RAILROAD COMPANY

Organized 1977 - Electric - Standard Gauge

Located Monterey, Monterey County. Proposed to use the abandoned Southern Pacific's Monterey to Pacific Grove right-of-way. To build from Fisherman's Wharf to Cannery Row and between Cannery Row and Lover's Point.

MONTEREY RAILROAD COMPANY

Incorporated January 24, 1880 - Steam - Standard Gauge

Located Monterey, Monterey County. Took over the Monterey & Salinas Valley Railroad Company. Built from Monterey to Castroville (Del Monte) for the Pacific Improvement Company March 4, 1880. The Pacific Improvement Company had standard gauged 12.21 miles of trackage. Consolidated with the Southern Pacific Co. March 14, 1888.

MONTEREY & SALINAS VALLEY RAILROAD

Organized 1874 - Steam - 3 ft. Gauge

Located Salinas, Monterey County. Built to Monterey. Distance 19 miles. Intended to extend the railroad north to Soledad 35 miles.

MONTEREY & SALINAS VALLEY RAILROAD COMPANY

Incorporated March 5, 1874 - Steam - 3 ft. Gauge

Located Monterey, Monterey County. Built from Castroville (Del Monte Junction). Distance 15.12 miles. Opened for service October 1874. Sold by foreclosure December 22, 1879 to Pacific Improvement Company. Converted to standard gauge a distance of 12.21 miles in 1879. Conveyed to Monterey Railroad Company on March 4, 1880. Consolidated with the Southern Pacific Co. May 14, 1888. This was the first steam operated narrow-gauge railroad in California.

MONTEREY & SAN JOAQUIN RAILWAY

Organized January 1912 - Electric - Standard Gauge

Located Monterey, Monterey County. Organized to take over the properties of the Monterey & Del Monte Heights Railroad. Distance 3.00 miles and extend the trackage into the San Joaquin Valley. Project abandoned 1913 or 1914.

MOON LUMBER COMPANY

Organized 1921 - Steam - Narrow-Gauge

Located Hilt, Siskiyou County. Operated 3.00 miles of trackage. Operations ceased 1923.

MORAN BROTHERS COMPANY

Organized 1880 - Steam - 3 ft. Gauge

Located Reno, Nevada. Built to Amadee, California, near Honey Lake in Lassen County. Completed in 1890. Distance 83.00 miles. Sold in 1893 to Nevada-California-Oregon Railway.

MOUNT HUNTER RAILROAD

Organized 1904 - Electric - Standard Gauge

Located San Jose, Santa Clara County. Proposed to build in the vicinity of San Jose. Project abandoned.

MOUNT OLIVET CEMETERY'S ELECTRIC RAILWAY

Electric - Standard Gauge

Located San Francisco, San Francisco County. This was a long spur running from San Mateo Line to Mt. Olivet Cemetery. The cars on occasion ran over the tracks of the United Railroads of San Francisco to downtown San Francisco. Abandoned 1932.

MOUNTAIN COPPER COMPANY, LTD.

Constructed 1905 - Steam - 3 ft. Gauge - Standard Gauge

Located Mococo, Contra Costa County. Built 3.25 miles of narrow and standard gauged trackage in and about the company smelter and wharf in the Martinez region of San Francisco Bay.

MOUNTAIN QUARRIES RAILROAD

Organized 1909 - Steam - Standard Gauge

Located Flint, Placer County. At Flint, just west of Auburn on the westbound Southern Pacific "Donner Pass Route," the Mountain Quarries Railroad served a limestone deposit with an 8-mile line. Was later purchased by the Pacific Portland Cement Company. Ceased operations in 1940.

MOUNTAIN VALLEY RAILROAD
MOUNTAIN VALLEY & BAKERSFIELD RAILROAD COMPANY

Incorporated September 1900 - Steam - Standard Gauge

Located Bakersfield, Kern County. Proposed to build from a junction with the Southern Pacific Co. northwest along the Kern River to Weldon. The Mountain Valley Railroad was reincorporated November 1900, as the Mountain View & Bakersfield Railroad Company. Project abandoned in 1901.

MT. HEBRON LUMBER COMPANY

Organized 1918 - Steam - 3 ft. Gauge

Located Macdoel, Siskiyou County. Built from mill to timber. Distance 6.00 miles. Ceased operations in 1926.

MT. LOWE RAILWAY

Organized June 3, 1891 - Electric - 3 ft. 6 in. Gauge Cable Incline

Located Altadena, Los Angeles County. A portion of the Pasadena & Mount Lowe Railway which carried passengers from Altadena (Rubio Canyon) to the summit of Echo Mountain and a connection with the narrow-gauge electric line to Alpine Tavern.

MOUNT LOWE RAILWAY - The terminal of the standard gauge line from downtown Los Angeles was at Rubio station where the great incline took off, running 1,500 feet up a 48 percent grade to the summit of Echo Mountain. (LEFT) One of the major attractions on the Alpine Division (from Echo Mountain to Alpine Tavern) was the famous circular bridge, built on a 120 degree curve. - *Both Donald Duke Collection*

MUNICIPAL RAILWAY OF SAN FRANCISCO (Cable Car Division) - The center of San Francisco's cable car operation is at the corner of Powell and Market streets, where passengers assist in turning the cable cars around on the turntable. - *Donald Duke Collection*

MUNICIPAL RAILWAY OF SAN FRANCISCO - Was formed in 1912 to take over several streetcar and cable car lines in the city of San Francisco. Purchased the United Railway of San Francisco in 1915 and procured the Market Street Railway in 1944. In this view, two cars are operating on Geary Street, the original part of the line, in the 1950's. - *G.C. White*

MT. SHASTA CORPORATION CONSTRUCTION RAILROAD

Built 1921- Steam - Standard Gauge

Located Bartell Spur, Siskiyou County. Built by the Pacific Gas & Electric Co. from the McCloud River Railroad to Power House No. 1 on the Pitt River. Called the Pitt River Railroad Co. by some people.

MT. SHASTA PINE MANUFACTURING COMPANY

Organized 1887 - Steam - Standard Gauge

Located Mt. Shasta, Siskiyou County. Purchased the facilities of the Pioneer Box & Lumber Company. Operated 7.00 miles of trackage. Abandoned 1936.

MT. TAMALPAIS & MUIR WOODS RAILWAY

Organized 1913 - Steam - Standard Gauge

Located Mill Valley, Marin County. Took over the properties and operations of the Mill Valley & Mt. Tamalpais Scenic Railway. Abandoned in 1930.

MOUNT TAMALPAIS & MUIR WOODS RAILWAY - A scenic railway built from Reed on the Northwestern Pacific to the summit of Mt. Tamalpais. Trains operated by Shay locomotive to the Summit, and then passengers coasted downhill aboard gravity cars. - *Donald Duke Collection*

MUNICIPAL RAILWAY OF SAN FRANCISCO

Organized December 28, 1912 - Electric/Cable - Standard Gauge

Located San Francisco, San Francisco County. Began operations on Geary Street from Kearney Street to 33rd Avenue and Park. Purchased the Presidio Ferries Railroad in 1913. Purchased the United Railroads of San Francisco, California Street line beyond 6th Avenue to Lincoln Park in 1915. Purchased the Market Street Railway Co. September 29, 1944. Took over the operations of the California Street Cable Railway Company in 1951.

F. S. MURPHY LUMBER COMPANY

Organized 1918 - Steam - 3 ft. Gauge

Located Sloat, Plumas County. Purchased the Sloat Lumber Company trackage and extended it a distance of 6.00 miles. Sold in 1926 to the Quincy Lumber Company. Abandoned 1936.

F. S. MURPHY LUMBER COMPANY

Organized 1918 - Steam - Standard Gauge

Located Quincy, Plumas County. Purchased Quincy Lumber Co. operations in 1918. Distance 6.00 miles. Sold back to Quincy Lumber Co. in 1926. Abandoned 1955.

MYRTLE AVENUE RAILWAY COMPANY

Incorporated May 11, 1887 - Horsecar - Standard Gauge

Located Monrovia, Los Angeles County. Built from the Los Angeles & San Gabriel Valley depot north along Myrtle Avenue to Lemon Avenue. Then east on Lemon to Ivy, then along Ivy to White Oak Avenue, a distance of 1.5 miles. The line was taken over by the First National Bank of Monrovia in 1894 and operated by the bank until it was sold to Henry E. Huntington on November 14, 1901.

NEVADA COUNTY NARROW-GAUGE RAILROAD - A combination passenger and freight train pauses on Bear Creek bridge shortly before the structure was consumed by fire in 1896.

- *Hugh Tolford Collection*

N

NAPA & CLEAR LAKE RAILWAY

Organized 1911 - Electric - Standard Gauge

Located Napa, Napa County. Proposed to build to Lakeport. Distance 9.00 miles.

NAPA, DILLON'S BEACH & TOMALES RAILWAY

Organized July 22, 1905 - Electric - Standard Gauge

Located Napa, Napa County. Proposed to connect the three towns named in the organization papers. Project abandoned in 1907.

NAPA, LAKE & HUMBOLDT RAILROAD COMPANY

Organized July 1887 - Steam - Standard Gauge

Located Lakeport, Lake County. A contract was let in October 1887, to grade a roadbed between Conn and Bull's Canyon. Distance 20.00 miles. No construction work done.

NAPA & LAKEPORT RAILWAY
NAPA & LAKEPORT RAILROAD

Incorporated August 24, 1905 - Steam or Electric - Standard Gauge

Located Napa, Napa County. Proposed to build through Napa, Conn, Chiles and Napa valleys by way of Middletown and Kelseyville to Lakeport. A branch to be built to Monticello. Distance 75.00 miles. Reorganized August 20, 1908, as the Napa & Lakeport Railroad. Project abandoned in 1909.

NAPA, SACRAMENTO & RICHARDSON'S BAY COUNTY RAILROAD COMPANY

Organized 1908 - Electric - Standard Gauge

Located Petaluma, Sonoma County. Reorganization name of the Lakeport & Richardson's Bay Railroad Company.

NAPA & VACA VALLEY RAILROAD COMPANY

Incorporated February 18, 1907 - Electric - Standard Gauge

Located Vallejo, Solano County. Proposed to build via Napa Junction, Suscol and Cordelia to Vacaville. Distance 30.00 miles. Surveys begun in 1907. No construction work done. Project abandoned in 1908.

NAPA VALLEY RAILROAD COMPANY

Organized March 2, 1864 - Steam - Standard Gauge

Located Napa City, Napa County. Built from Napa Junction to Calistoga. Distance 35.00 miles. Began construction in November 1864. First section Napa to Suscol opened for service July 10, 1865. Distance 4.50 miles. Road completed January 1869. Deeded to the California Pacific Railroad Extension Company January 9, 1869. Consolidated with the Southern Pacific Co. April 14, 1898.

NAPA VALLEY WINE TRAIN, INC.

Organized December 4, 1985 - Diesel - Standard Gauge

Located Napa, Napa County. A group of investors, principally Vincent De Domenico of "Rice-A-Roni" fame, purchased the 21-mile branch of the Southern Pacific between Napa and St. Helena, with the idea of running a private passenger train into the wine country to haul tourists. Although initially considered using steam power, the line purchased four Alco FPA 4's. After months of wrangling with citizens of Napa County, Chamber of Commerce and wine growers, the Napa Valley Wine Train ran for the first time on September 16, 1989. The train is luxurious and carries a first-class dining car.

NATIONAL CITY & EL CAJON VALLEY RAILROAD COMPANY

Incorporated December 21, 1882 - Steam - 3 ft. Gauge

Located National City, San Diego County. Proposed to build to El Cajon by way of Sweetwater Valley and Spring Valley. No construction work done.

NATIONAL CITY & OTAY RAILWAY COMPANY

Organized December 27, 1886 - Steam - Standard Gauge

Located San Diego, San Diego County. Built from National City to San Diego. Opened for service June 15, 1887. Extended the road to Chula Vista. Branch built to Sweetwater Dam and La Presa. Reorganized October 12, 1888. Purchased the Otay Railroad Co. with lines from Otay to Oneonta and Tia Juana, Mexico. Total distance 28.55 miles. Leased to the Coronado Railroad, steam division, August 1, 1906. Trackage San Diego to Chula Vista and Otay electrified 1907. Consolidated with the Coronado Railroad Co. to form the San Diego Southern Railway Co. July 1, 1908.

NATIONAL CITY & OTAY RAILWAY - A train on Spring Canyon bridge near Sweetwater Dam bound for La Presa, circa 1888. Line was leased to the Coronado Railroad in 1906. - *Donald Duke Collection*

NATIONAL CITY STREET CAR COMPANY

Incorporated March 22, 1888 - Horsecar

Located National City, San Diego County. Built as a feeder line to the Coronado Railroad. Laid track from 23rd Street on McKinley Avenue, 14th Street, Hoover Avenue, 8th Street, Highland to near 2nd Street. Operated intermittently from April 1888 to March 1889. Distance 2.30 miles. Abandoned 1889.

NATIONAL REDWOOD COMPANY RAILROAD

Organized 1920 - Steam - Standard Gauge

Located Gualala, Mendocino County. Purchased the American Redwood Co. and its 22.00 miles of railroad. Extended trackage 1.00 mile. Abandoned in 1920.

NATIONAL SODA PRODUCTS COMPANY

Organized 1916 - Steam - 3 ft. Gauge

Located Keeler, Inyo County. Built 1.32 miles of trackage around plant located on Owens Lake. Abandoned in 1954.

NATOMAS CONSOLIDATED COMPANY

Steam - Standard Gauge

Located Oroville, Butte County. Quarry road around the company gravel plant.

NAVARRO RAILROAD

Organized 1874 - Steam - Standard Gauge

Located Navarro, Mendocino County. Built a logging railroad from mill to timber. Later built to Hop Flat and along Navarro River. Became Navarro Manufacturing & Railroad Company in 1886.

NAVARRO LUMBER COMPANY
NAVARRO MILL COMPANY
NAVARRO MANUFACTURING & RAILROAD COMPANY

Organized August 28, 1875 - Steam - Standard Gauge

Located Navarro Mill, Mendocino County. The Navarro Mill Co. built a logging road from mill to timber beginning in 1876. Reorganized as Navarro Manufacturing & Railroad Co. in 1886 or 1887. Extended trackage to Hop Flat along the Navarro River. Total mileage operated 8.45 miles. The Navarro Lumber Co. built along Mill Creek in 1915 to a junction with the Northwestern Pacific Railroad Albion Branch. Distance 7.10 miles. Abandoned 1920.

NEEDLES, SEARCHLIGHT & NORTHERN RAILWAY

Organized April 22, 1905 - Steam - Standard Gauge

Located Ibex, San Bernardino County. Proposed to build from a junction with the Santa Fe Railway to the mining camps at Searchlight, El Dorado Canyon and other points in Arizona.

NEVADA & CALIFORNIA LUMBER COMPANY

Organized 1873 - Steam - Standard Gauge

Located north of Truckee, Nevada County. Built 5.50 miles of logging railroad about 8 miles north of Truckee.

NEVADA-CALIFORNIA-OREGON DIVISION OF THE GREAT WESTERN RAILWAY

Organized 1985 - Diesel - Standard Gauge

Located Lakeview, Oregon. Purchased trackage of the original Nevada-California Railroad from the Southern Pacific Company Lakeview Branch January 18, 1986. Lakeview, Lake County, Oregon, to Alturas, Modoc County, California, to connect with the Southern Pacific.

NEVADA-CALIFORNIA-OREGON RAILROAD COMPANY

Incorporated March 31, 1886 - Steam - 3 ft. Gauge

Located Reno, Nevada. Planned to build to the Dallas, Oregon, on the Columbia River. Built by way of Hackstaff, Wendel and Alturas, California, to Lakeview, Oregon. Distance 235.71 miles. Section Reno northward to Goose Lake and Reno south to Aurora built by the Nevada & Oregon Railroad. Began operations October 2, 1882. Sold to Moran Brothers April 17, 1884, and operated under the name Nevada & Oregon Railroad. Transferred to the Nevada-California-Oregon Railroad Co. January 1, 1893. Branch from Plumas Junction to Mohawk obtained from Sierra Valley & Mohawk Railroad by consolidation January 1, 1915. Abandoned 1918. Section Hackstaff (now Herlong) to Reno sold to Western Pacific Railroad in 1917. Distance 64.00 miles. Section Wendel to Hackstaff abandoned in 1922. Remainder sold to Southern Pacific Co. on October 8, 1926. Distance 154.48 miles. Converted to standard gauge May 1928.

NEVADA-CALIFORNIA-OREGON RAILROAD - A narrow-gauge line proposed to build from Reno, Nevada, to the Dalles, Oregon. Actually, it was built from Reno to Lakeview, Oregon, by way of Wendel and Alturas. Sections sold to the Western Pacific and the Southern Pacific. - *Hugh Tolford Collection*

NEVADA & CALIFORNIA RAILROAD

Purchased April 17, 1884 - Steam - 3 ft. Gauge

Located Reno, Nevada. Name used by Moran Brothers to operate the Nevada & Oregon Railroad Company. Built to Oneida, California. Distance 30.10 miles. Title transferred to the Nevada-California-Oregon Railroad January 1, 1893.

NEVADA & CALIFORNIA RAILWAY COMPANY

Incorporated April 7, 1905 - Steam - 3 ft. Gauge and Standard Gauge

Located Mojave, Kern County. Built north to Owenyo as a standard gauge line. Distance 143.50 miles. Construction began February 24, 1908. Completed October 22, 1910. Took over the operations of the three-foot gauge Carson & Colorado Railway Company that had been purchased by the Southern Pacific Company in 1900. Narrow-gauge abandonments were: State Line to Benton, 7 miles, 1938; Benton to Laws, 30.70 miles, 1943; and Laws to Keeler, 71.00 miles, in 1960. Last run April 29, 1960. Standard gauge section now known as the Southern Pacific Jaw Bone Division.

NEVADA COUNTY NARROW-GAUGE RAILROAD COMPANY

Incorporated April 4, 1874 - Steam - 3 ft. Gauge

Located Colfax, Nevada County. Built from Colfax on the Southern Pacific to Nevada City. Distance 22.64 miles. Construction began February 11, 1875. Completed May 20, 1876. Opened for regular train service May 24, 1876. Converted to standard gauge from Colfax to Bear River in 1913. Distance 3.63 miles. Standard gauge third rail, for the most part, removed in 1922. Last run October 18, 1942. Last rails removed April 29, 1943.

NEVADA COUNTY TRACTION COMPANY

Incorporated March 29, 1901 - Electric - Standard Gauge

Located Grass Valley, Nevada County. Built from Boston Ravine up Mill Street to East Main Street, then over Spring Hill to Glenbrook and on to Town Talk. Entered Nevada City over Sacramento Street to Broad Street. Distance 5.00 miles. Began construction June 1, 1901. Open for traffic September 9, 1901. Abandoned January 16, 1925.

NEVADA, GRASS VALLEY & COLFAX RAILROAD

Organized in 1870 - Steam - Narrow-Gauge

Located Grass Valley, Nevada County. Surveys made in the 1870's. No construction work done.

NEVADA & OREGON RAILROAD

Incorporated June 5, 1880 - Steam - 3 ft. Gauge

Located Reno, Nevada. Built north to Goose Lake and south to Aurora. Reorganized April 25, 1881. Built to Oneida just over the California state line. Sold to Moran Brothers April 17, 1884. Transferred to the Nevada-California-Oregon Railroad January 1, 1893.

NEVADA PACIFIC RAILWAY

Chartered May 1889 - Steam - Standard Gauge

Located Nevada. Proposed to build to the Utah Central Railroad in Utah and to Daggett, San Bernardino County, California, by way of Ash Meadows. No construction work done.

NEVADA SOUTHERN RAILWAY COMPANY

Incorporated December 15, 1892 - Steam - Standard Gauge

Located Goffs, San Bernardino County. Built northward from a junction with the Santa Fe Railway to Manvel (now Barnwell). Distance 29.40 miles. Construction began January 1893. Attachment filed by Atlantic & Pacific Railroad February 12, 1894. Foreclosure sale October 16, 1895. Acquired by California Eastern Railway Co. April 17, 1896. Deeded to the Santa Fe Railway on July 1, 1902. Abandoned in 1923.

NEWELL CREEK RAILROAD

Built 1887 - Steam - Narrow-Gauge

Located Newell Creek, Santa Cruz County. Built from mill in Dougherty to above Newell Creek mill and on to timber.

NEWELL CREEK RAILROAD

Incorporated 1906 - Steam - 3 ft. Gauge

Located Boulder Creek, Santa Cruz County. Built from Felton into the woods. Distance 7.00 miles. Owned by the California Timber Company. Abandoned in 1910 or 1911.

GEORGE H. NEWELL, INC.

Organized 1907 or 1908 - Steam - Standard Gauge

Located Scotia, Humboldt County. Operated 1.00 mile of trackage. Abandoned 1909 or 1910.

NEWHART LUMBER & MILLING COMPANY

Organized 1922 - Steam - Standard Gauge

Located Willits, Mendocino County. Operated 1.00 mile of trackage built in 1923. Abandoned 1926.

NEWPORT BEACH ELECTRIC RAILWAY

Organized 1903 - Electric - Standard Gauge

Located Santa Ana, Orange County. Proposed to build to Newport Beach. Laid a few feet of track on October 3, 1903 on East Fifth Street to protect the franchise in Santa Ana.

NEWPORT WHARF & LUMBER COMPANY

Incorporated June 5, 1889 - Steam - Standard Gauge

Located Newport Beach, Orange County. Purchased the Santa Ana Railroad on November 19, 1892. Sold to the Santa Ana & Newport Railway on February 11, 1893. Sold to the Southern Pacific Co. November 23, 1899. Abandoned except for 2.66 miles of track deeded to the Pacific Electric Railway in 1933.

NEW YORK & PENNSYLVANIA REDWOOD COMPANY

Organized 1907 - Steam - Standard Gauge

Located Hardy, Mendocino County. Took over the operations and property of the C.A. Hooper Co. Operated 5.00 miles of trackage. Abandoned 1911.

NIBLEY - STODDARD LUMBER COMPANY

Organized 1913 - Steam - Standard Gauge

Located Cromberg, Plumas County. Built three miles of track from mill to timber. Abandoned 1930.

NILAND, BLYTHE & SEELEY ELECTRIC RAILWAY

Organized August 15, 1914 - Electric - Standard Gauge

Located Niland, Imperial County. Proposed to build an electric railway to Blythe, Riverside County.

NINE LUMBER COMPANY

Organized 1915 - Steam - 3 ft. and Standard Gauge

Located Bray, Siskiyou County. Built and operated 8.00 miles of trackage of both 3 ft. and standard gauge. Abandoned 1919.

NINTH STREET ELECTRIC RAILWAY

Franchise granted July 1, 1903 - Electric - 3 ft. 6 in Gauge

Located Los Angeles, Los Angeles County. Franchise granted to build on Ninth Street. No construction work done.

NORTH BEACH & MISSION RAILWAY COMPANY

Horsecar - 5 ft. Gauge

Located San Francisco, San Francisco County. Built from the post office (Kearney and Clay streets) to Mission Dolores by way of Kearney, Third and Mission streets. Consolidated with the Market Street Railway Company in 1893.

NORTH BEACH & MISSION RAILWAY - Built from the San Francisco Post Office to Mission Dolores. Became a part of the Market Street Railway in 1893 and the line electrified. - *Donald Duke Collection*

NORTH CAROLINA GOLD MINING COMPANY

Organized 1902 - Steam - Narrow-Gauge

Located Oroville, Butte County. Surveys begun in 1902 for a railroad along the North Fork of the Feather River with the view of mining several miles of riverbed.

NORTH COAST LUMBER COMPANY

Organized 1913 - Steam - Standard Gauge

Located Fort Bragg, Mendocino County. Built 2.00 miles of trackage in 1914. Abandoned 1916.

NORTH FORK & MINERET RAILROAD

Charter filed January 6, 1893 - Steam - 3 ft. Gauge and Standard Gauge

Located Fresno, Fresno County. Proposed to build 10 miles of road from a point on the North Fork of the San Joaquin River northeasterly through Fresno County. Purpose to haul timber to the river. Surveys completed March 1893. No construction work done.

NORTH PACIFIC COAST RAILROAD COMPANY

Rechartered December 16, 1871 - Steam - 3 ft. Gauge

Located Sausalito, Marin County. Incorporated in 1869 as the San Francisco & Humboldt Bay Railroad. Rechartered December 16, 1871. Purchased the San Rafael & San Quentin Railroad in 1875. Distance 3.50 miles. Purchased Northwestern Railroad Co. in 1887. Distance 7.50 miles. Built to Duncan Mills in Sonoma County in 1878. Distance 75.25 miles. Sold to the North Shore Railroad in 1902. Was partially electrified. Merged into the Northwestern Pacific Railroad in 1907.

NORTH PACIFIC COAST RAILROAD - A narrow-gauge common carrier railroad that built north from Sausalito to San Anselmo and on to Cazadero. The NPC was the first railroad in America to develop the cab-in-front steam locomotive. - *Donald Duke Collection*

NORTH PACIFIC COAST RAILROAD EXTENSION COMPANY

Organized December 6, 1882 - Steam - 3 ft. Gauge

Located Alameda Point, Marin County. Built to Corte Madera. Began construction in 1883. Distance 5.37 miles. Opened for service April 26, 1884. Operations taken over by the North Pacific Coast Railroad. Deeded to North Shore Railroad in 1902. Became part of the Northwestern Pacific Railroad on January 8, 1907.

NORTH PACIFIC NARROW-GAUGE RAILWAY COMPANY

Surveyed 1873 - Steam - 3 ft. Gauge

Located Sausalito, Marin County. Surveys made to Tomales. No construction done.

NORTH SHORE RAILROAD COMPANY

Incorporated January 11, 1902 - Steam - 3 ft. Gauge

Located Sausalito, Marin County. Took over the properties of the North Pacific Coast Railroad. A total of 92.60 miles of trackage. Main line from Sausalito to Cazadero. Distance 80.93 miles. Sections were converted to standard gauge and electrified. First electric service began August 20, 1903, between Sausalito and Mill Valley. Consolidated into Northwestern Pacific Railroad on January 8, 1907.

NORTH SIDE HORSE RAILROAD COMPANY

Incorporated June 16, 1875 - Horsecar - 3 ft. Gauge

Located San Jose, Santa Clara County. Built from First and St. John streets to Fourteenth Street (now 17th Street). Began operations in October 1875. Sold to the People's Horse Railroad April 22, 1882. Sold to San Jose & Santa Clara Railroad April 23, 1882.

NORTH & SOUTH BEACH RAILROAD COMPANY

Organized June 15, 1862 - Horsecar - Narrow-Gauge

Located San Francisco, San Francisco County. Proposed to build from Fourth and Battery streets around Telegraph Hill and back to Powell and Kearney streets.

NORTH STAR COMPANY

Began construction January 1906 - Electric - 3 ft. Gauge

Located Nevada City, Nevada County. Built an electric railway from Central Shaft to the North Star Mill and then to the cyanide plants. Distance 2.50 miles.

NORTH WESTERN RAILROAD COMPANY OF CALIFORNIA

Incorporated August 19, 1885 - Steam - 3 ft. Gauge

Located Duncan Mills, Sonoma County. Built to Ingrams (Cazadero). Distance 7.41 miles along Austin Creek. Became part of the North Shore Railroad. Consolidated into the Northwestern Pacific Railroad January 8, 1907.

NORTHERN CALIFORNIA LUMBER COMPANY RAILROAD

Organized 1903 - Steam - 3 ft. Gauge - Standard Gauge

Located Korbel, Humboldt County. Organized to take over the operations of the Humboldt Lumber Co. and the Riverside Mill & Lumber Co. Abandoned 1956.

NORTHERN CALIFORNIA RAILROAD COMPANY

Incorporated September 6, 1884 - Steam - Standard Gauge

Located Marysville, Yuba County. Successor to California Northern Railroad Co. Took over operations of the trackage from Marysville to Oroville January 8, 1885. Sold to the Northern California Railway February 1, 1889.

NORTHERN CALIFORNIA RAILROAD COMPANY

Organized October 5, 1927 - Steam - Standard Gauge

Located Crescent Mills, Plumas County. Proposed to build to Westwood. Distance 31.00 miles. 14.00 miles of logging road was to be purchased from the Red River Lumber Co. This was trackage from Westwood to the south end of Lake Almanor. Trackage was to be built from Crescent Mills to a junction with the Indian Valley Railroad. Project abandoned in June 1929.

NORTHERN CALIFORNIA RAILWAY COMPANY

Incorporated September 3, 1888 - Steam - Standard Gauge

Located Marysville, Yuba County. Purchased the Northern California Railroad Co., Marysville to Oroville. Distance 25.97 miles. Built from Marysville to Knights Landing. Distance 27.75 miles. Began construction in 1889. Completed in 1891. Consolidated with the Southern Pacific Co. April 14, 1898. Abandoned in 1945.

NORTHERN ELECTRIC COMPANY

Incorporated June 14, 1905 - Electric - Standard Gauge

Located Chico, Butte County. Built to Sacramento by way of Oroville Junction. Distance 90.50 miles. Controlled the Marysville & Yuba City Street Railroad Co. and the Shasta Southern Railway Co. Acquired the Chico Electric Railway Co., operating 5.14 miles of street railway in Chico. Deeded to the Northern Electric Railway Co. on December 2, 1907. Sold to the Sacramento Northern Railroad April 18, 1918.

NORTHERN ELECTRIC RAILWAY COMPANY

Incorporated September 19, 1907 - Electric - Standard Gauge

Located Chico, Butte County. Organized to take over the properties of the Northern Electric Co., December 2, 1907. Purchased the Shasta Southern Railway Co. January 18, 1907. Took over the operations of the Sacramento Terminal Co. May 15, 1909, distance 5.73 miles; the Sacramento & Woodland Railroad Co. June 13, 1912, distance 17.30 miles; and the West Side Railroad in 1912, distance .498 miles. Purchased the properties of the Vallejo & Northern Railroad Co. in December 1912. Sold to the Sacramento Northern Railroad June 28, 1918.

NORTHERN ELECTRIC RAILWAY - Built a high-speed electric inter-urban railway between Sacramento and Chico, with a branch line to Woodland. Became a part of the Sacramento Northern Railroad in 1918. - *Donald Duke Collection*

NORTHERN ELECTRIC RAILWAY COMPANY, MARYSVILLE & COLUSA BRANCH

Incorporated May 6, 1910 - Electric - Standard Gauge

Located Heyman (Colusa Junction), Yuba County. Built to Colusa. Distance 22.93 miles. Construction work done from December 1911 to June 1913. Operated under lease by Northern Electric Railway Co. Sold to the Sacramento Northern Railroad Co. June 30, 1918.

NORTHERN RAILWAY COMPANY

Incorporated July 19, 1871 - Steam - Standard Gauge

Located West Oakland, Alameda County. Built to a point near Martinez. Distance 31.03 miles. Construction began August 16, 1876. Completed January 9, 1878. Built from Benicia to Suisun. Distance 16.33 miles. Opened for traffic December 28, 1879. Built Woodland to Tehema. Distance 100.74 miles. Completed September 27, 1882. Became the Northern Railway Consolidated May 15, 1888. This resulted from a consolidation of the Amador Branch Railroad Co., Berkeley Branch Railroad Co., Sacramento & Placerville Railroad Co., San Joaquin Valley & Sierra Nevada Railroad Co., Santa Rosa & Carquinez Railroad Co., Shingle Springs & Placerville Railroad Co., Vaca Valley & Clear Lake Railroad Co., West Side & Mendocino Railroad Co., and Winters & Ukiah Railway Company. Consolidated with the Southern Pacific Co. April 14, 1898.

NORTHERN RAILWAY COMPANY CONSOLIDATED

Incorporated May 15, 1888 - Steam - Standard Gauge

Located West Oakland, Alameda County. This second Northern Railway Co. resulted from the consolidation of the Northern Railway Co. of 1871, Sacramento & Placerville Railroad Co., Shingle Springs & Placerville Railroad Co., West Side & Mendocino Railroad Co., San Joaquin Valley & Sierra Nevada Railroad Co., Vaca Valley & Clear Lake Railroad, Amador Branch Railroad Co., Santa Rosa & Carquinez Railroad Co., Berkeley Branch Railroad, Winters & Ukiah Railway Co., and the Woodland, Capay & Clear Lake Railroad Company. Approximately 376.00 miles of trackage, including 40.00 miles of 3 ft. gauge were consolidated. Consolidated with the Southern Pacific Company, Northern California Railway and California Pacific Railroad Company to form the Southern Pacific Railroad Company April 14, 1898. This formed the sixth corporation of the same name.

NORTHERN REDWOOD LUMBER COMPANY

Incorporated 1903 - Steam - 3 ft. 9 1/4 in. Gauge and Standard Gauge

Located Korbel, Humboldt County. Took over the operations of the Humboldt Lumber & Mill Co. at Korbel and the Riverside Mill & Lumber Co. at Eureka. Extended the narrow-gauge logging rails from Korbel to woods. Distance 26.00 miles. Obtained ownership of Arcata & Mad River Railroad. Sold to Simpson Redwood Company in 1957. Abandoned in 1960.

NORTHWESTERN PACIFIC ACQUIRING COMPANY

Organized July 1984 - Diesel - Standard Gauge

Acquired the trackage of the Northwestern Pacific from Eureka to Willits. Transferred to the Eureka Southern Railroad October 31, 1984.

NORTHWESTERN PACIFIC RAILROAD COMPANY

Incorporated January 8, 1907 - Steam and Electric - 3 ft. Gauge and Standard Gauge

Located Sausalito, Marin County. Resulted from consolidation of Northwestern Pacific Railway Co. and the following companies: The San Francisco & North Pacific Railway, distance 166.38 miles; the North Shore Railroad, distance 39.91 miles; the San Francisco & Northwestern Railway Co., distance 52.27 miles; Eureka & Klamath Railroad, distance 26.68 miles; and the Fort Bragg & Southeastern Railroad Co., distance 23.87 miles. Total mileage 402.46 miles. In time, 42 different railroads were incorporated, merged or consolidated to make up the present company. Completed from Sausalito to Eureka, a distance of 284.10 miles, October, 23, 1914. All narrow-gauge operations ceased March 30, 1930. Electric operations ceased in 1942.

NORTHWESTERN PACIFIC RAILWAY COMPANY

Incorporated November 24, 1906 - Steam - Standard Gauge

Located Sausalito, Marin County. Organized to take over the properties of the Eureka & Klamath Railroad and the Humboldt Railroad Company on December 7, 1906. Consolidated with the San Francisco & Eureka Railway October 15, 1907. Final agreement between the Atchison, Topeka & Santa Fe Railway Co. and the Southern Pacific Co. was reached with the resulting incorporation of the Northwestern Pacific Railroad Company.

NORTHWESTERN REDWOOD COMPANY

Organized 1901 - Steam - Standard Gauge

Located Willits, Mendocino County. Built from mill to timber. Distance 16.00 miles. Abandoned 1929.

NORTHWESTERN REDWOOD LUMBER COMPANY

Organized 1903 - Steam - Standard Gauge

Located Williams, Colusa County. Built from mill to Camp 13 and then on to timber in 1904. Section from timber to Camp 13 abandoned in 1909. Section from Camp 13 to Williams abandoned in 1924

NORTHWESTERN STREET RAILWAY

Incorporated August 15, 1909 - Electric - Standard Gauge

Located San Bernardino, San Bernardino County. Proposed to build to Rialto. Requested a franchise from the San Bernardino City Council September 1909. Project abandoned in October 1909, because of refusal of a franchise.

NOYO & PUDDING CREEK RAILROAD

Organized 1881 - Steam - Standard Gauge

Located Fort Bragg, Mendocino County. Built from mill to woods. Sold to the Fort Bragg Railroad Company in 1885. Extended about 10.00 miles. Sold to California Western Railroad & Navigation Company on June 30, 1905. Extended to Willits and junction with the Northwestern Pacific Railroad. Became California Western Railroad Company on December 19, 1947.

NORTHWESTERN PACIFIC RAILROAD - Resulted from the consolidation of 42 short railroads in Marin, Sonoma and Mendocino counties. The northern end was owned by the Santa Fe, thus resulting in a partnership with the Santa Fe/Southern Pacific for ownership. This photograph shows the Sausalito-Eureka train leaving the Sausalito ferry terminal. - *W.C. Whittaker*

OAKLAND TRACTION COMPANY - A scene in downtown Oakland at the corner of Broadway and 14th Street in 1906. In this scene, electric car No. 318 is operating on Broadway and is bound for San Pablo Ave. Car No. 309 is a Kelley-type car and is going east on 14th Street. - *Erle C. Hanson*

O

OAKDALE & SONORA RAILROAD

Organized 1875 - Steam - Standard Gauge

Located Oakdale, Stanislaus County. Proposed to build from the terminus of the Stockton & Visalia Railroad to Sonora, Tuolumne County.

OAKDALE WESTERN RAILWAY COMPANY

Incorporated June 24, 1904 - Steam - Standard Gauge

Located Oakdale, Stanislaus County. Built to Riverbank. Construction work done during 1904 and 1905. Began service January 1905. Sold to the Santa Fe Railway December 28, 1911.

OAKLAND, ALAMEDA & LAUNDRY FARM RAILWAY COMPANY

Organized 1887 - Steam 1888-1895 - Electric 1895-1936 - Standard Gauge

Located Alameda, Alameda County. Began operations as the Alameda County Railway Company. Ran steam trains from Fruitvale to Laundry Farm Canyon via Leona Heights. Sold to the California Railway in 1890. Sold to Oakland Traction Company in 1901. Was electrified in 1895. Became part of the Key System Transit Company on June 6, 1923. Abandoned June 10, 1936.

OAKLAND & ANTIOCH RAILWAY COMPANY

Incorporated January 13, 1909 - Electric - Standard Gauge

Located Concord, Contra Costa County. Built from Bay Point to Walnut Creek by way of Concord. Opened for traffic May 4, 1911. Purchased the Oakland & Bayshore Railway Company December 1912. Transferred to the Oakland, Antioch & Eastern Railway in 1912. Sold to the San Francisco - Sacramento Railroad Company on January 26, 1920.

OAKLAND & ANTIOCH RAILWAY - An interurban built from Oakland to Walnut Creek by way of Concord in 1911. Was later extended to Sacramento in 1920 as the Oakland, Antioch & Eastern Railway. - *Charles Smallwood Collection*

OAKLAND, ANTIOCH & EASTERN RAILWAY

Incorporated March 28, 1911 - Electric - Standard Gauge

Located Oakland, Alameda County. Took over properties of the Oakland & Antioch Railway Company. Built from Oakland to Bay Point by April 7, 1913. Opened for traffic to Sacramento on September 3, 1913. Sold to the San Francisco-Sacramento Railroad Company on January 26, 1920. Sold to the Sacramento Northern Railroad on January 1, 1929.

OAKLAND & BAY SHORE RAILWAY COMPANY

Incorporated January 5, 1911 - Electric - Standard Gauge

Located Oakland, Alameda County. Organized by the Oakland & Antioch Railway to obtain a franchise to build in Oakland along Shafter Avenue to 40th Street. Built the section of track to Temescal Canyon. Distance 7.00 miles. Became part of the Oakland & Antioch Railway in 1912. Became part of the Sacramento Northern Railway January 1, 1929.

OAKLAND & BERKELEY RAPID TRANSIT DISTRICT

Incorporated July 24, 1889 - Electric - Standard Gauge

Located Oakland, Alameda County. Began operations May 12, 1891. Operated the first electric streetcars in Alameda County. Built from Oakland to Berkeley by way of Grove Street and Shattuck Avenue to the University of California campus. Branch built from 40th and Grove streets east to Opal Street and then north on Opal to 41st Street. East on 41st Street to Howe Street and north on Howe Street to St. Mary's Cemetery. Completed in 1892. Was reorganized as Oakland Consolidated Street Railway in 1890. Taken into the Oakland Transit Company in 1898.

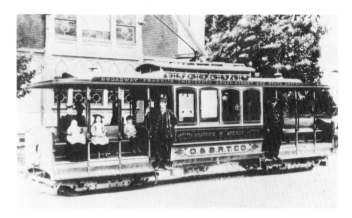

OAKLAND & BERKELEY RAPID TRANSIT - Built the first electric line between Oakland and Berkeley in 1889. Was reorganized as the Oakland Street Railway in 1890, and taken into the Oakland Transit Company in 1898. - *Harre Demoro Collection*

OAKLAND, BROOKLYN & FRUITVALE RAILWAY

Organized about 1850 - Horsecar - 5 ft. Gauge

Located Oakland, Alameda County. Constructed 2.45 miles of horsecar street railway. Electrified and operations taken over by the Oakland Railway Company.

OAKLAND CENTRAL RAILROAD

Organized 1870 - Steam - Standard Gauge

Located Oakland, Alameda County. Proposed to build to Richmond.

OAKLAND CONSOLIDATED STREET RAILWAY COMPANY

Organized 1890 - Electric - Standard Gauge

Located Oakland, Alameda County. Took over the operations of the Oakland & Berkeley Rapid Transit Company on May 12, 1891. Taken into the Oakland Transit Company in 1898. Became part of the Key System. Abandoned in 1948.

OAKLAND & EAST SIDE RAILROAD COMPANY

Incorporated March 6, 1902 - Steam - Standard Gauge

Located Oakland, Alameda County. Built to Richmond. Distance 11.32 miles. Acquired 24.50 miles of graded narrow-gauge roadbed from the California & Nevada Railroad Company, Oakland to San Pablo and Orinda Park to Bryant. About half of the right-of-way was sold in exchange for land for an Oakland terminal. Construction began in March 1903. Opened for service March 16, 1904. Sold to the Santa Fe Railway December 28, 1911.

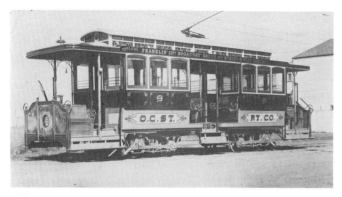

OAKLAND CONSOLIDATED STREET RAILWAY - Absorbed the street railway operations of the Oakland & Berkeley Rapid Transit Co. in 1891 and operated several streetcar lines in and around Oakland and Berkeley. Was made part of the Oakland Transit Co. in 1889. - *Harre Demoro Collection*

OAKLAND, MARTINEZ & ALHAMBRA RAILWAY & FERRY COMPANY

Organized September 4, 1911 - Electric - Standard Gauge

Located Martinez, Contra Costa County. Organized as a subsidiary company of the Oakland, Antioch & Eastern Railway to build between Oakland and Martinez by way of Walnut Creek and Alhambra Valley. Distance 13.00 miles. A wharf was to be built at Martinez and ferry service to be established between Martinez and Benicia.

OAKLAND & MARYSVILLE RAILROAD COMPANY

Incorporated October 28, 1904 - Steam - Standard Gauge

Located Oakland, Alameda County. Proposed to build through the counties of Alameda, Contra Costa, Solano and Yolo to Sacramento and then to Marysville from a point on the Oakland waterfront. Distance 135.00 miles. No construction work done.

OAKLAND PAVING COMPANY

Organized 1873 - Steam - 3 ft. Gauge

Located Oakland, Alameda County. Built a short 3 ft. gauge quarry road from the processing plant to quarry. Sold in 1904 to Blake & Bilger Company. Abandoned in 1923.

OAKLAND RAILROAD COMPANY
OAKLAND CABLE RAILWAY

Organized 1864 - Horsecar - 3 ft. Gauge

Located Oakland, Alameda County. Began operations as a horsecar line from First and Broadway out Telegraph Avenue to about 36th Street on October 30, 1869. Rechartered as the Oakland Railroad Company January 27, 1888. Began construction of a cable car line on Broadway and San Pablo Avenue. Changed the horsecar line from five-foot gauge to three-foot gauge. Oakland Cable Railway was the name used for the operation of the San Pablo-Broadway cable line. Though owned by the Oakland Railroad Company, the cars were lettered Oakland Cable Railway. The original Broadway-Telegraph Avenue line had steam dummies from Temescal to Sather Gate during the day. Horse power was used at night. The Broadway-Telegraph line was electrified January 4, 1893. The company also built electric lines in Berkeley on Telegraph, Shattuck, University, Oxford, Cedar, Spruce and Rose to make a loop in North Berkeley. Sold to Oakland Transit Company on March 29, 1901.

OAKLAND & SAN FRANCISCO TERMINAL COMPANY

Incorporated November 24, 1893 - Steam/Electric - 3 ft. 6 in. Gauge and Standard Gauge

Located Oakland, Alameda County. Proposed to build a wharf at Oakland and to operate two ferry boats to San Francisco. Trackage was to extend to a junction with the Oakland Consolidated Railway. The California & Nevada Railroad was to be extended to Walnut Creek and rebuilt to standard gauge. This was the first company set up by the Borax Smith Interests to build a ferryboat-electric railway system in the Bay Area.

OAKLAND & SAN JOAQUIN RAILROAD

Incorporated May 1887 - Steam - Standard Gauge

Located Oakland, Alameda County. Proposed to build through Antioch, Contra Costa County, by way of Lion Creek Ravine, through Redwood Canyon, Moraga and Ygnacio valleys and by the foothills of Mt. Diablo. Distance 35.00 miles.

OAKLAND & SAN JOSE RAILWAY COMPANY

Incorporated November 18, 1901 - Electric - Standard Gauge

Located Oakland, Alameda County. Planned to build to San Jose by way of Hayward where branch lines could connect Santa Clara, Saratoga and Los Gatos. Became part of the Key System.

OAKLAND, SAN LEANDRO & HAYWARD ELECTRIC RAILWAY COMPANY
OAKLAND, SAN LEANDRO & HAYWARD ELECTRIC RAILWAY, CONSOLIDATED

Organized 1891 - Electric - Standard Gauge

Located Oakland, Alameda County. Began operations May 7, 1892. Consolidated with the Twenty-third Avenue Electric Railway to form the Oakland, San Leandro & Hayward Electric Railway, Consolidated May 8, 1894. Consolidated with the Oakland Transit Company to become the Oakland Transit Consolidated on March 20, 1902.

OAKLAND TERMINAL RAILROAD

Organized 1935 - Steam - Standard Gauge

Located Oakland, Alameda County. Set up by the Railway Realty & Equipment Company, Ltd. to handle freight movements previously handled by Key System, Ltd. over portions of what later became A, B and C lines. Also Key System, Ltd. freight-only tracks on 26th Street and on the waterfront from Keel Station to Albers. Although most of this trackage was electrified, most of the operations were by steam power. Sold to Santa Fe Railway and Western Pacific Railroad.

OAKLAND TOWNSHIP RAILROAD COMPANY

Incorporated January 4, 1881 - Steam - 3 ft. Gauge

Located Oakland, Alameda County. Built from the center of San Antonio Creek bridge between Alameda and Oakland to 14th and Franklin streets by way of Webster Street. Distance .90 miles. Began operations May 30, 1881. Consolidated with the South Pacific Coast Railway on May 23, 1887. Leased to the Southern Pacific Company July 1, 1887. Abandoned on September 28, 1989.

OAKLAND TRANSIT COMPANY
OAKLAND TRANSIT CONSOLIDATED
OAKLAND TRACTION CONSOLIDATED
OAKLAND TRACTION COMPANY

Chartered March 1898 - Electric - Standard Gauge

Located Oakland, Alameda County. Oakland Transit Company resulted from the consolidation of the Oakland Consolidated Street Railway Company, Central Avenue Railway Company, Piedmont & Mountain View Railway Company, East Oakland Street Railway Company and the Highland Park & Fruitvale Railroad. Purchased the Oakland Railroad Company on March 29, 1901. Consolidated with the Oakland, San Leandro & Hayward Electric Railway, Consolidated in March 1902, to form the Oakland Transit Consolidated. Oakland Traction Consolidated was the result of a consolidation of the Oakland Transit Consolidated and Webster Street & Park Railway on September 30, 1904. Consolidation of the Oakland Traction Consolidated and the Berkeley Traction Company on November 8, 1906, resulted in the Oakland Traction Company. Consolidated into the San Francisco-Oakland Terminal Railways on March 12, 1912. This was the first company to use the term Key System.

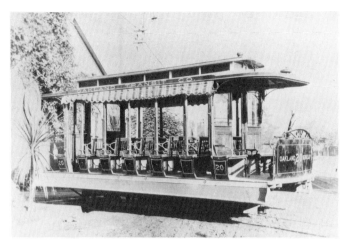

OAKLAND TRANSIT CO. - A consolidation of five local street railway firms, forming the Oakland Transit Consolidated. Consolidated into the San Francisco-Oakland Terminal Railway (Key System) in 1912. - *Harre Demoro Collection* (BELOW) Consolidation of Berkeley Traction on November 8, 1906, resulted in the formation of the Oakland Traction Co. - *Donald Duke Collection*

OAK VALLEY LUMBER COMPANY

Organized 1920 - Steam - Standard Gauge

Located Comptonville, Yuba County. Built 7.00 miles of logging railroad.

OCCIDENTAL MILLING COMPANY

Organized 1880 - Steam - Standard Gauge

Located Eureka, Humboldt County. Built from Eureka Slough to timber. Distance 6.00 miles. Deeded to the McKay & Company in 1891. Extended 4.50 miles. Abandoned 1934.

OCEAN AIR LINE RAILROAD COMPANY

Incorporated May 24, 1888 - Steam or Electric - Standard Gauge

Located Los Angeles, Los Angeles County. Proposed to build to Santa Monica and then along the coast to Port Ballona, Redondo, Wilmington and Long Beach. No construction work done.

OCEAN BEACH RAILROAD COMPANY

Organized 1888 - Steam Dummy - Standard Gauge

Located Roseville, San Diego County. Built to Ocean Beach. Distance 3.50 miles. Began operations April 23, 1888. Operated for only a few months. Became part of the Point Loma Railroad in 1907 when they took over the right-of-way.

OCEAN BEACH RAILWAY COMPANY

Chartered February 11, 1885 - Electric - Standard Gauge

Located San Francisco, San Francisco County. Consolidated with the Market Street Railway Company in 1893.

OCEAN SHORE & EASTERN RAILROAD COMPANY

Incorporated March 1, 1907 - Electric - Standard Gauge

Located Santa Cruz, Santa Cruz County. Proposed to build southeast to Watsonville. Distance 20.00 miles. No construction work done. Company dissolved November 30, 1910.

OCEAN SHORE RAILROAD, INC.

Incorporated November 16, 1934 - Steam - Standard Gauge

Organized and incorporated in Nevada to rebuild the abandoned Ocean Shore Railroad along the Pacific Coast from San Francisco to Santa Cruz. Still a corporate structure in 1970.

OCEAN SHORE RAILWAY COMPANY
OCEAN SHORE RAILROAD COMPANY

Incorporated May 18, 1905 - Steam - Electric - Standard Gauge

Located San Francisco, San Francisco County. Proposed to build south from 12th and Mission streets in San Francisco to Santa Cruz following as nearly as possible the shoreline of the Pacific Ocean. Distance 80.26 miles. Grading began September 17, 1905, at Spring Valley Ranch twelve miles south of San Francisco. First revenue train operated from Santa Cruz to Swanton on May 16, 1906. First revenue train operated from San Francisco to Tobin on October 2, 1907. Reorganized as the Ocean Shore Railroad Company on October 9, 1911. Abandoned northern section on October 10, 1920. Abandoned the southern section on October 24, 1920 and sold trackage to San Vincent Lumber Company on October 27, 1920. Railroad was steam operated except for 2.40 miles of electrification in San Francisco where franchise required electric operation. Track that was not sold to San Vincent Lumber Company was abandoned October 27, 1920.

OCEAN SHORE RAILROAD - A standard gauge railroad connecting San Francisco with Santa Cruz, following the shoreline of the Pacific. Line was steam operated except for trackage within the city of San Francisco. - *W.C. Whittaker Collection*

OCEANSIDE COAST MOTOR RAILROAD

Incorporated 1887 - Steam - Standard Gauge

Located Encinitas, San Diego County. Proposed to build to Oceanside on the California Southern Railway (Santa Fe). 1,000 ft. of grade completed in Oceanside in 1887. No rails were laid.

OLD MISSION CEMENT COMPANY

Built November 1912 - Steam - 3 ft. Gauge

Located San Juan, San Benito County. Built from cement plant and terminus of the San Juan Pacific Railway to a quarry in San Juan Canyon. Distance 4.00 miles. Sold to Pacific Portland Cement Company in 1927. Ceased operations in 1929.

OLIVER BROTHERS SALT COMPANY

Organized 1893 - Gasoline Engine - Narrow-Gauge

Located near Hayward, Alameda County. Operated around the salt evaporation pans.

OMNIBUS RAILROAD COMPANY
OMNIBUS CABLE COMPANY

Organized July 1, 1862 - Horsecar - Standard Gauge

Located San Francisco, San Francisco County. The Omnibus Railroad Company built a horsecar line along Second Street to the Mission. Extended the road along Folsom Street to California and Montgomery streets. Ran on Ellis Street from Market Street to Broderick Street via Oak and Stanyan to Haight. Ran on Post Street from Market to Leavenworth and 10th Street to Howard Street. Reorganized as the Omnibus Cable Company in 1886. Sold to the Market Street Railway Company in 1899. Deeded to United Railroads of San Francisco in 1902. Became part of the Municipal Railway of San Francisco in 1944.

ONTARIO & SAN ANTONIO HEIGHTS RAILROAD COMPANY

Incorporated September 3, 1888 - Horsecar - Standard Gauge

Located Ontario, San Bernardino County. Built from California Street to San Antonio Heights along the center line of Euclid Avenue. Distance 8.50 miles. Began operations November 1, 1889. Electrified in 1895. Extended to San Antonio Park July 4, 1907. Track completed between Upland and Claremont in 1909. Completed to Pomona, terminating on Garey Avenue near Park Avenue in January 1911. Sold to the Pacific Electric Railway Company March 19, 1912. Abandoned October 6, 1928.

ORANGE GROVE STREET RAILWAY COMPANY

Incorporated January 5, 1888 - Horsecar - 3 ft. Gauge

Located Pomona, Los Angeles County. Began construction October 20, 1887. Completed March 16, 1888. Began operations April 14, 1888. Built along Washington Avenue (Dudley Street) then east on San Bernardino County Road (Orange Grove Avenue) to Wisconsin Street, south on Wisconsin to Holt Avenue and across Holt diagonally and south on Rebecca to Second Street then east on Second Street to Reservoir Avenue. An extension was built to the bridge over San Jose Creek at Ganesha Park by way of Park Drive. Distance 3.75 miles. Rails removed September 10, 1896.

ORANGE, MC PHERSON & EL MODENA STREET RAILWAY

Incorporated February 23, 1887 - Horsecar - Standard Gauge

Located Orange, Orange County. Built to McPherson. Distance 4.50 miles. Began operations January 1, 1889. Abandoned in 1891. Rails sold to Terracina & Redlands Street Railway Company.

ORANGE, McPHERSON & EL MODENA STREET RAILWAY - A horsecar line that ran east on Chapman Avenue to McPherson and El Modena, a distance of 4.5 miles. First operated in 1889 and was abandoned in 1891. - *First American Title Insurance Company*

OREGON COAST & EASTERN RAILROAD

Organized January 1906 - Steam - Standard Gauge

Located Eureka, Humboldt County. Proposed to build from Eureka north through the coast counties of California and Oregon by way of Coos Bay and Tillamook to Portland, Oregon.

OREGON EASTERN RAILWAY COMPANY

Incorporated August 21, 1905 - Steam - Standard Gauge

Located Weed, Siskiyou County. Built northward to Chiloquin, Oregon. Completed September 1, 1926. Formed the Cascade Line of the Shasta Route of the Southern Pacific. Purchased the California Northeastern Railway on December 18, 1905.

OREGON & EUREKA RAILROAD COMPANY

Incorporated August 14, 1903 - Steam - Standard Gauge

Located Eureka, Humboldt County. Resulted from a reorganization of the Hammond Lumber Company and the Eureka & Klamath River Railroad. Trackage ran from Sonoma to Camp 5. Distance 17.55 miles. Proposed to build north to Trinidad. This section completed by the Northwestern Pacific Railroad. Leased to the Northwestern Pacific Railroad on December 7, 1906. Became part of the Northwestern Pacific Railroad on July 1, 1911.

OREGON & PACIFIC RAILROAD

Organized December 1904 - Steam - Standard Gauge

Located Grants Pass, Oregon. Proposed to build to Crescent City, California, by way of Wilderville, Kirby and Takiloma. Distance 92.00 miles. Grading on roadbed began in February 1905.

OREGON SOUTHERN RAILROAD

Organized 1907 - Steam - Standard Gauge

Located Thrall, Siskiyou County. In 1905 the Weyerhaeuser Timber Company purchased the Klamath Lake Railroad and renamed the railroad the Oregon Southern Railroad in 1907. Leased the trackage to the Siskiyou Electric Power & Light Company during 1912 and 1913. Trackage out of service during the years 1913 to 1916. Sold to the California-Oregon Company in 1916. Abandoned in 1942.

ORIENTAL & PACIFIC RAILROAD COMPANY

Incorporated March 7, 1902 - Steam - Standard Gauge

Located San Diego, San Diego County. Proposed to build to Yuma, Arizona. Distance 175.00 miles. Organizational plans called for the taking over of the properties of the Los Angeles, San Diego & Yuma Railway Company. Received by deed the wharf and terminal facilities of this company. No construction work was done.

OROVILLE & BECKWOURTH RAILROAD

Incorporated May 12, 1888 - Steam - Standard Gauge

Located Oroville, Butte County. Began construction for a railroad to Beckwourth.

ORO DAM CONSTRUCTORS RAILROAD

Organized October 1962 - Diesel - Standard Gauge

Located Oroville Dam, Butte County. Built from the dam site to quarry. Main line trackage 11.65 miles. Total trackage 19.25 miles. Began operations October 1, 1963. Junction made with the Western Pacific Railroad at Zephyr Siding.

OROVILLE & NELSON RAILROAD COMPANY

Incorporated January 12, 1907 - Steam - Standard Gauge

Located Oroville, Butte County. Proposed to build northwest to Nelson. Distance 12.00 miles. No construction work done. Deeded to the Southern Pacific Company July 1917.

OROVILLE & VIRGINIA CITY RAILROAD COMPANY

Incorporated April 12, 1867 - Steam - Standard Gauge

Located Oroville, Butte County. Surveys were made up the North Fork of the Feather River and over Beckwourth Pass to connect with the Central Pacific Railroad at Truckee Meadows. Grading began March 27, 1869, between Thompson Flat and Morris Ravine in Plumas County. Project abandoned in 1870. Franchise relinquished in 1905.

OSTRICH FARM RAILWAY

Incorporated July 24, 1886 - Steam - Standard Gauge

Located Los Angeles, Los Angeles County. Built to the Ostrich Farm (Griffith Park). Taken into the Los Angeles County Railroad and extended to Santa Monica. Consolidated into the Los Angeles & Pacific Railroad on April 29, 1895, and electrified. Became a part of the Pacific Electric Railway Company in 1911.

OTAY RAILROAD COMPANY

Incorporation filed September 30, 1887 - Steam - Standard Gauge

Located Otay, San Diego County. Incorporated to build to the Monument, International Boundary Line with Mexico. Proposed to build from Otay to Oneonta with a branch to Tia Juana on the California side. Merged with National City & Otay Railway Company on October 12, 1888. Construction completed in December 1888.

OUTER HARBOR DOCK & WHARF COMPANY

Incorporated 1908 - Steam - Standard Gauge

Located San Pedro Harbor, Los Angeles County. Organized to perform switching service in the San Pedro area of the Los Angeles Harbor. Sold to Outer Harbor Terminal Company on July 1, 1928. Abandoned December 1955.

OUTER HARBOR TERMINAL RAILWAY COMPANY

Incorporated July 29, 1927 - Steam - Standard Gauge

Located San Pedro, Los Angeles County. Acquired all of the railroad facilities of the Outer Harbor Dock & Wharf Company July 1, 1928. Abandoned in December 1955.

OUTER HARBOR TERMINAL RAILWAY - A switching railroad that operated in the Outer Harbor section of San Pedro harbor. The railroad was sold to Outer Harbor Terminal Co. in 1928, and abandoned in 1955. - *Donald Duke*

OVERFAIR RAILWAY

Organized 1915 - Steam - 19 in. Gauge

Located San Francisco, San Francisco County. Operated around the grounds of the Panama-Pacific International Exposition.

OVERFAIR RAILWAY - A 19-inch railway line that operated around the Panama-Pacific International Exposition held at San Francisco in 1915. In the above view, MacDermot (man who built locomotives) stands beside No. 1500. (BELOW) A passenger train operating around the exposition. - *Both Harre Demoro*

OVERLAND PACIFIC RAILWAY COMPANY

Organized 1894 - Steam - Standard Gauge

Located Fort Bragg, Mendocino County. Proposed to build by way of Willits to the Mount Vernon coal mines. A branch was to be built from Willits to Ukiah. Project abandoned in 1895.

OWENS RIVER VALLEY ELECTRIC RAILWAY COMPANY

Chartered November 17, 1910 - Electric - 3 ft. Gauge

Located Bishop, Inyo County. Proposed to build to Round Valley, distance 12.00, and Bishop to Big Pine, distance 16.00 miles. Surveys completed March 1911. Grading began June 18, 1911 between Bishop and Laws. Distance 4.50 miles. Project abandoned 1912.

PACIFIC COAST STEAMSHIP COMPANY - This company employed the steam dummy "Senator Perkins" to haul passengers from the shore out to the steamship dock at the end of the wharf, a distance of approximately a half-mile. - *Donald Duke Collection*

P

PACIFIC & ATLANTIC RAILROAD COMPANY

Incorporated September 6, 1851 - Steam - Standard Gauge

Located San Jose, Santa Clara County. Proposed to build to San Francisco. Name changed to San Francisco & San Jose Railroad in 1859. Reincorporated August 18, 1860. Construction work was done during the years 1860 to 1864. Sold to the Southern Pacific Co. on October 12, 1870.

PACIFIC AVENUE STREET RAILWAY
PACIFIC AVENUE RAILROAD

Organized 1877 - Horsecar - Narrow-Gauge

Located Santa Cruz, Santa Cruz County. Purchased the Santa Cruz & Felton Railroad and extended it along Mission Street to the Pope House. In 1880 extended tracks along the beach, a distance of .25 miles. Became the Pacific Avenue Railroad in 1885. Electrified and became the Santa Cruz, Garfield Park & Capitola Electric Railroad in 1891.

PACIFIC CABLE RAILWAY COMPANY

Cable - 3 ft. 6 in. Gauge

Located Los Angeles, Los Angeles County. Sold to the Los Angeles Consolidated Electric Railway Company October 4, 1893. Was designated as the Cable Division of the Los Angeles Consolidated Electric Railway.

PACIFIC CEMENT & AGGREGATES

Electric - 3 ft. Gauge

Located Davenport, Santa Cruz County. Operated 3.00 miles of quarry road.

PACIFIC CEMENT PLASTER COMPANY

Organized 1905 - Mule Power - 3 ft. Gauge

Located Funston, near Amboy, San Bernardino County. Built to gypsum beds in Bristol Lake. Distance 2.50 miles. Sold to the Consolidated Pacific Cement Plaster Company in April 1909. Rebuilt for steam power operation after 1913. Sold to the U.S. Gypsum Company September 2, 1919. Abandoned in 1924.

PACIFIC COAST AGGREGATES CORPORATION

Organized 1906 - Steam - Standard Gauge

Located Carbona, San Joaquin County. Electrified in 1918. Operated in and around gravel quarry. Abandoned 1922.

PACIFIC COAST BORAX COMPANY
BABY GAUGE RAILROAD

Constructed 1914 - Gas Engine - 2 ft. Gauge

Located Ryan, Inyo County. Built to Widow Mine. Distance 5.25 miles. Ceased operations 1946.

PACIFIC COAST LINE RAILWAY COMPANY

Incorporated August 24, 1911 - Steam - Standard Gauge

Located Portland, Oregon. Proposed to build southward to Humboldt Bay, near Eureka, California. No construction work done.

PACIFIC COAST RAILROAD
PACIFIC COAST RAILWAY COMPANY

Organized May 20, 1881 - Steam - 3 ft. Gauge

Located San Luis Obispo, San Luis Obispo County. Organized to build an extension of the San Luis Obispo & Santa Maria Valley Railroad. Built from end of track in San Luis Obispo southward to Arroyo Grande. Completed October 12, 1881. Became the Pacific Coast Railway Company by merger of the Pacific Coast Railroad and the San Luis Obispo & Santa Maria Valley Railroad September 25, 1882. Trackage extended southward to Los Alamos was completed October 11, 1882. Extended to Los Olivos November 16, 1887.

Branch line built from Santa Maria to Betteravia February 1898. An electrified section was built from Suey Ranch to Union Sugar Company and completed April 15, 1906. Distance 14.00 miles. Branch built to Guadalupe completed April 17, 1909. Electrified section converted to steam operation in 1928. Total miles operated 85.00. Section Los Olivos to Los Alamos abandoned 1936. Section San Luis Obispo to southern end of track abandoned December 20, 1941. Trackage from San Luis Obispo to Port San Luis Obispo sold to the Port San Luis Obispo Transportation Company February 28, 1942. Abandoned October 19, 1942.

PACIFIC COAST RAILWAY - A narrow-gauge line built from San Luis Obispo to Arroyo Grande, with a branch line to Port San Luis, and another from Santa Maria to Guadalupe. No. 105 was photographed at San Luis Obispo. - *Donald Duke*

PACIFIC COAST REDWOOD LUMBER COMPANY

Steam

Located Albion, Mendocino County. Abandoned 1920.

PACIFIC COAST STEAMSHIP COMPANY

Purchased 1875 - Horse Power - Narrow-Gauge

Located San Diego, San Diego County. Purchased the trackage of the Pacific Mail Steamship Company. Located foot of Fifth Avenue. Distance .33 miles. Rebuilt to standard gauge and employed steam dummy operations between end of wharf and shore. Service discontinued about 1917.

PACIFIC DISTRIBUTING COMPANY

Organized 1918 - Steam - 30 in. Gauge

Located Lang, Los Angeles County. Built from refinery at Lang to Soda Lake. Distance 7.00 miles. Construction began November 8, 1923. Abandoned 1935.

PACIFIC ELECTRIC LAND COMPANY

Chartered June 9, 1903 - Electric - Standard Gauge

Located Los Angeles. Owned 58.11 miles of track. Leased to the Pacific Electric Railway Company December 10, 1910. Controlled the San Bernardino Valley Traction Company and the Redlands Central Railway Company.

PACIFIC ELECTRIC RAILWAY COMPANY OF ARIZONA
PACIFIC ELECTRIC RAILWAY COMPANY OF CALIFORNIA
PACIFIC ELECTRIC RAILWAY COMPANY

Began operations 1898 - Electric - Standard Gauge

Located Los Angeles, Los Angeles County. The Pacific Electric Railway Company of Arizona began operations with the purchase of the Fifth Street Railway. Became part of the Pacific Electric Railway Company of California by incorporation November 12, 1901. The present Pacific Electric Railway Company was incorporated September 1, 1911. Sixty-five companies were merged into this company. Passenger service transferred by sale to the Metropolitan Coach Lines in 1954. Freight lines merged into the parent Southern Pacific Company in 1965.

PACIFIC ELECTRIC RAILWAY - Sixty-five railroads were merged to form the Pacific Electric on September 1, 1911. In this view, No. 1028 is bound for Pasadena as it passes through El Sereno, California. - *Donald Duke*

PACIFIC ENGINEERING & CONSTRUCTION COMPANY

Organized December 12, 1914 - Steam - Standard Gauge

Located Eureka, Humboldt County. Leased the railroad of the Bayside Lumber Company to haul gravel and rock from Jacoby Creek to build government jetty in Humboldt Bay. Concluded lease in 1915.

PACIFIC GAS & ELECTRIC COMPANY

Began operations 1906 - Steam - Electric - Standard Gauge

Located Bartle, Siskiyou County. Purchased the properties of the Sacramento Electric Gas & Railway Company. Extended trackage from Bartle on the McCloud River Railroad to a powerhouse on the Pitt River. Became an integral part of the Pacific Gas & Electric Company in 1915. Street railway operations sold to Sacramento City Lines in 1943. Abandoned July 4, 1947.

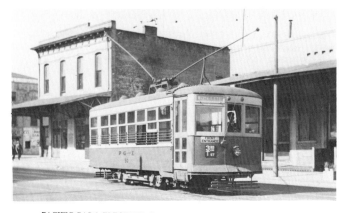

PACIFIC GAS & ELECTRIC - Operated a system of streetcar lines in and around Sacramento from 1915 to 1943, when the property was sold to Sacramento City Lines. Rail service was abandoned in 1947. - *Charles Smallwood Collection*

PACIFIC GOLD MINE RAILROAD

Steam

Located in Placerville. 1,200 feet long.

PACIFIC & GULF TERMINAL RAILROAD

Organized March 16, 1906 - Steam - Standard Gauge

Located Los Angeles, Los Angeles County. Proposed to build to San Pedro. Distance 25.00 miles. Project abandoned in 1907.

PACIFIC LUMBER COMPANY RAILROAD

Incorporated February 26, 1869 - Steam - Standard Gauge

Located Scotia, Humboldt County. Built in various stages to Alton and on to Camp 9. Distance 15.13 miles. Part of the trackage was sold to the San Francisco & Northwestern Railroad May 15, 1903. This section sold to the Northwestern Pacific Railroad June 26, 1903. The remainder extended from Scotia to timber. Trackage rights obtained to Freshwater and trackage built to timber. Operating mileage 34.55 miles.

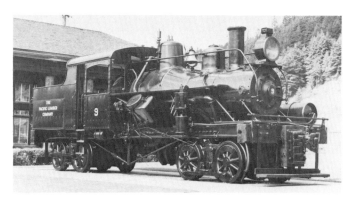

PACIFIC LUMBER CO. - Built 34.5 miles of logging railroad out of Scotia in Humboldt County. Part of the logging railroad went to form the Northwestern Pacific Railroad. Road used standard steam locomotives, Shays and Heislers. - *Donald Duke*

PACIFIC LUMBER & WOOD COMPANY

Began operations September 1, 1878 - Steam - 3 ft. Gauge

Located Nevada County. Built along the west side of Juniper Creek at Clinton near the Truckee River. The railroad was known as the Clinton Narrow-Gauge Railroad. Operated 10.35 miles of trackage by 1892. Abandoned 1901.

PACIFIC MAIL STEAMSHIP COMPANY

Incorporated in the 1850's - Horse Power - Narrow-Gauge

Located San Diego, San Diego County. Built a narrow-gauge horse-powered line from end of wharf to shore at the foot of Fifth Avenue. Distance .33 miles. Sold to the Pacific Coast Steamship Company in 1875. Rebuilt to standard gauge and began steam dummy operation in 1882. Service discontinued about 1917.

PACIFIC PORTLAND CEMENT COMPANY

Organized 1924 - Steam - 3 ft. Gauge

Located Plaster City, Imperial County. Purchased the trackage of the Imperial Gypsum Company from a junction with the San Diego & Arizona Eastern Railroad to quarry. Distance 15.00 miles. Sold to the U.S. Gypsum Company in 1946.

PACIFIC PORTLAND CEMENT COMPANY

Organized 1927 - Steam - 3 ft. Gauge

Located San Juan, San Benito County. Purchased the Old Mission Cement Company. Operated from cement plant to quarry in San Juan Canyon. Distance 4.00 miles. Ceased operations in 1929.

PACIFIC PORTLAND CEMENT CONSOLIDATED

Began operations 1911 - Steam

Located Auburn, Placer County. Built to quarry on the American River. Abandoned 1941.

PACIFIC RAILROAD COMPANY

Chartered December 20, 1889 - Steam - 3 ft. Gauge

Located San Francisco, San Francisco County. Chartered in Colorado. Proposed to build from Santa Cruz north along the coast to San Francisco.

PACIFIC RAILROAD & STEAMSHIP COMPANY

Incorporated January 29, 1909 - Steam - 3 ft. 6 in. Gauge

Located Watsonville, Santa Cruz County. Successor to the Watsonville Transportation Company. Operated from Watsonville to Port Watsonville on Monterey Bay. Distance 6.00 miles. Operations suspended October 1, 1910.

PACIFIC RAILROAD & STEAMSHIP COMPANY

Incorporated January 27, 1909 - Steam - Standard Gauge

Located Watsonville, Santa Cruz County. Proposed to build to a point on Monterey Bay north of Point Goodall. Distance 5.00 miles.

PACIFIC RAILWAY COMPANY

Incorporated September 9, 1889 - Cable - 3 ft. 6 in. Gauge

Located Los Angeles, Los Angeles County. Began operations June 8, 1889 over Grand Avenue line, Main and Arcadia to Jefferson Street. Distance 3.50 miles. East First Street line, First Street from Spring to Evergreen, opened August 3, 1889. Distance 2.50 miles. East Los Angeles line, Main and Arcadia to Broadway and Lincoln Park, opened November 2, 1889. West Seventh Street line went from Seventh Street to Grand to Alvarado. Total mileage operated 10.10 miles. Sold to the Los Angeles Consolidated Electric Railway in 1893. Cable car lines electrified. Became part of the Los Angeles Railway Company.

PACIFIC RAILWAY COMPANY - Operated 3.5 miles of cable car trackage in downtown Los Angeles. Mileage increased to 10.10 miles and was purchased by the Los Angeles Consolidated Electric Railway and route was electrified. - *Huntington Library*

PACIFIC ROCK SALT COMPANY

Organized 1918 - Steam - 3 ft. Gauge

Located Saltus, near Amboy, San Bernardino County. Operated from salt works to salt pits on Bristol Lake. Reorganized as California Rock Salt Company in 1921.

PACIFIC SOUTHWESTERN RAILROAD COMPANY

Organized October 20, 1922 - Steam - Standard Gauge

Located near Lompoc, Santa Barbara County. Built from White Hills Junction to White Hills. Distance 3.95 miles. Received permission from the California Railroad Commission to begin construction December 1, 1922. Deeded to the Southern Pacific Company in 1924.

PACIFIC & SAN BERNARDINO RAILROAD COMPANY

Incorporated September 23, 1868 - Steam

Located Anaheim, Orange County. Proposed to build to San Bernardino. Project abandoned 1870.

PACIFIC STATE STEEL COMPANY

Located Niles, Alameda County. Industrial road.

PAJARO & SANTA CRUZ RAILROAD COMPANY

Incorporated April 11, 1884 - Steam - Standard Gauge

Located Santa Cruz, Santa Cruz County. Organized to take over the Santa Cruz Railroad from the Pacific Improvement Company. Trackage ran from Pajaro (now Watsonville) to Santa Cruz. Distance 21.20 miles. On June 3, 1884, the second Pajaro & Santa Cruz Railroad Company was incorporated and consolidated with the first Pajaro & Santa Cruz Railroad Company and the Loma Prieta Railroad Company. Consolidated with the Southern Pacific Company May 14, 1888. Built from Loma Prieta to Monte Vista in 1888. Distance 2.00 miles. This section abandoned in 1901. Loma Prieta to Aptos abandoned in 1928.

PAJARO VALLEY RAILWAY
PAJARO VALLEY CONSOLIDATED RAILROAD COMPANY
PAJARO VALLEY EXTENSION RAILROAD

Incorporated December 31, 1890 - Steam - 3 ft. Gauge

Located Watsonville, Monterey County. Began by building a railroad toward Monterey Bay. Constructed 14.00 miles of track. Reorganized as Pajaro Valley Consolidated Railroad Company in December 1897. Built from Spreckels to Moss Landing. Distance 17.00 miles. Completed line to Watsonville. Distance 27.00 miles. Branch line from Spreckels to Salinas. Distance 5.00 miles. Line abandoned August 1, 1929. Pajaro Valley Extension Railroad was the name of the company that surveyed a 10.50 mile extension.

PALMDALE RAILROAD

Organized and built in 1885 or 1886 - Steam - Horsecar

Located Palmdale, Riverside County. Proposed to build a steam operated road from Seven Palms (now Garnet) on the Southern Pacific to the desert around Palm Springs. Upon completion, a horsecar was used.

PALO ALTO & SUBURBAN RAILWAY COMPANY

Incorporated December 5, 1903 - Electric - Standard Gauge

Located Palo Alto, San Mateo County. Was granted a franchise to build several lines of a city street railway in Palo Alto. No construction work done. Reincorporated as the Santa Clara Interurban Railway December 1904. Built from San Mateo through San Jose to Alum Rock Park.

PANAMA-PACIFIC INTERNATIONAL EXPOSITION TERMINAL RAILWAY COMPANY

Organized March 1913 - Electric - Standard Gauge

Located San Francisco, San Francisco County. Proposed to build an electric railway on the exposition grounds at Harbor View for the transportation of exhibits and materials. 10 miles of trackage was to be built. Application for charter made May 1, 1913.

PANOCHE VALLEY RAILROAD

Organized 1908 - Steam

Located Hollister, San Benito County. Proposed to build to the Panoche Valley. No work was done.

PARK & CLIFF HOUSE RAILROAD

Organized 1886 - Steam - 3 ft. Gauge

Located San Francisco, San Francisco County. Built the California Street steam line from Presidio Avenue along California Street and around the cliffs to Lands End Cliff House. Became part of the Ferries & Cliff House Railway Company in 1887. Became part of the first Market Street Railway by consolidation in 1893.

PARK & COAST RAILROAD COMPANY

Incorporated July 5, 1883 - Steam - Standard Gauge

Located San Francisco, San Francisco County. Built a steam railway extension of the Haight Street cable line. Distance 4.62 miles. Opened December 1, 1883. Became part of the first Market Street Railway by consolidation in 1893.

PARK & OCEAN RAILROAD

Organized 1883 - Steam Motor - Narrow-Gauge

Located San Francisco, San Francisco County. Operated a steam motor road from Haight and Stanyan streets, ran along Lincoln Way to Beach. Opened for service December 1, 1883. Converted to electric streetcar operation in 1900. Merged into the United Railways of San Francisco system in 1902.

PARK & OCEAN RAILROAD - A steam operated railroad that ran from Haight and Stanyan streets, along Lincoln Way to the beach. Was converted to electric operation in 1900. - *Harre Demoro Collection*

PARK & CLIFF HOUSE RAILROAD - Built along California Street to Lands End or the famous Cliff House. Became a part of the Ferries & Cliff House Railway in 1887. - *Harre Demoro Collection*

PARKER & COLORADO RIVER ELECTRIC RAILWAY

Organized October 1914 - Electric - Standard Gauge

Located Parker, Arizona. Resulted from the reorganization of the Colorado River Valley Electric Railway. Proposed to build to Blythe, California, Riverside County, with ferry service from Ehrenberg to the Palo Verde Valley. Final surveys completed April 1915.

PARKSIDE TRANSIT COMPANY

Organized July 7, 1906 - Electric - Standard Gauge

Located San Francisco, San Francisco County. Organized to build certain extensions in the San Francisco Parkside District. Built the Sloat Boulevard, Taraval, Twentieth Avenue and Great Highway tracks. Began operations in January 1907. Distance 3.55 miles. Began laying 4.00 miles of additional track into the Parkside District in September 1908. The completed system ran on Twentieth Avenue, T Street, Thirty-fifth Avenue and Sloat Boulevard to Ingleside. A connection was made with the United Railroad Company at H Street. Entire system opened for traffic January 1, 1909. The lines were operated as an integral part of the United Railroads of San Francisco after 1911.

PARR TERMINAL RAILROAD

Plymouth Gas Engine - Standard Gauge

Located Richmond, Contra Costa County. Operated two miles of trackage for terminal use.

PASADENA CITY RAILWAY COMPANY
PASADENA STREET RAILWAY COMPANY

Chartered March 26, 1886 - Horsecar - Standard Gauge

Located Pasadena, Los Angeles County. Built the first horsecar street railway in Pasadena. Operated from Fair Oaks Boulevard on Colorado Boulevard to Chestnut Street and on to Arroyo Seco. Distance 3.25 miles. Opened for traffic October 1, 1886. Converted to steam operation in 1888 and ran from La Pintoresca Hotel on Washington Street to Devil's Gate. Sold to Pasadena & Los Angeles Electric Railway Company in 1894.

PASADENA, LA CANADA & SAN FERNANDO RAILROAD

Incorporated 1886 - Steam - Standard Gauge

Located Pasadena, Los Angeles County. Proposed to build to the San Fernando Valley via a tunnel through the San Gabriel Mountains. The road was to connect La Canada, La Crescenta, Tujunga and Monte Vista. No construction work was done.

PASADENA & LOS ANGELES ELECTRIC RAILROAD

Incorporated April 11, 1894 - Electric - Standard Gauge

Located Pasadena, Los Angeles County. Purchased the original trackage of the Pasadena City Railway Company, also known as the Pasadena Street Railway Company. Extended the trackage to Los Angeles. Opened for through traffic May 6, 1895. All trackage electrified by 1897. Became part of the Pasadena & Pacific Railway (Arizona) November 15, 1894. Became the Los Angeles-Pacific Railroad Company June 4, 1898. Deeded to the Pacific Electric Railway Company September 1, 1911. Abandoned October 17, 1942.

PASADENA & LOS ANGELES ELECTRIC RAILROAD - Built an electric railway from Los Angeles to Pasadena which opened in 1895. The line became a part of the Los Angeles-Pacific Railroad Co. in 1898. - *Donald Duke Collection*

PASADENA, LOS ANGELES & LONG BEACH RAILROAD COMPANY

Incorporated September 12, 1887 - Electric - Standard Gauge

Located Pasadena, Los Angeles County. Proposed to build from Fair Oaks and Raymond streets down Raymond Avenue to Elm Street to Ramona at the Southern Pacific station, then through Monterey Gap to Bixby Ranch and Alamitos Ranch. From there the road would follow the coast to Long Beach. Distance 25.45 miles. No construction work was done.

PASADENA & MONTE VISTA RAILROAD COMPANY

Organized 1886 - Steam - Narrow-Gauge

Located Pasadena, Los Angeles County. Proposed to build from Pasadena north to Monk's Hill, through the Ball and Painter Tract, past Woodbury Brothers, Banbury's, and Giddings and crossing the Arroyo Seco at Devil's Gate, then west across Michigan Avenue in La Canada. The tracks would then go north around the Three Buttes and west by south through La Crescenta, La Canada and Tujunga via Monte Vista to San Fernando. Distance 22.00 miles. No construction work was done.

PASADENA & MOUNT LOWE RAILWAY COMPANY
PASADENA & MT. WILSON RAILWAY COMPANY

Incorporated January 3, 1891 - Electric - 3 ft. 6 in. Gauge

Located Altadena, Los Angeles County. Built from Lake and Calaveras streets to Rubio Canyon. A cable incline was built from Rubio Canyon to Echo Mountain. This was on a 60% grade. Distance 1,400 feet. Began operations July 4, 1893. Alpine Division from Echo Mountain to Crystal Springs completed in August 1895. Distance 4.00 miles. Reorganized as the Pasadena & Mt. Lowe Railway in 1897. Sold to the Pacific Electric Railway Company in 1902. Section Altadena to Rubio Canyon standard gauged in 1903. Abandoned in November 1939.

PASADENA & MOUNT LOWE RAILWAY - A narrow-gauge line built from Lake and Calaveras streets in Pasadena to Rubio Canyon. Was converted to standard gauge in 1903 as shown in this view taken at the Rubio Canyon terminal. - *Donald Duke Collection*

PASADENA & PACIFIC RAILWAY COMPANY OF ARIZONA
PASADENA & PACIFIC RAILWAY COMPANY

Incorporated November 15, 1894 - Electric - Standard Gauge

Located Pasadena, Los Angeles County. First incorporated in Arizona in 1894. Purchased the Pasadena & Los Angeles Electric Railroad. Purchased the Elysian Park Street Railway Company, the Los Angeles & Pacific Railway Company, the Cahuenga Valley Railroad Company and the Santa Monica & Soldiers' Home Railroad Company. Consolidated with the Pasadena & Pacific Railway Company (California) January 3, 1898, and formed the Los Angeles-Pacific Railway. Merged with the Pacific Electric Railway September 1, 1911.

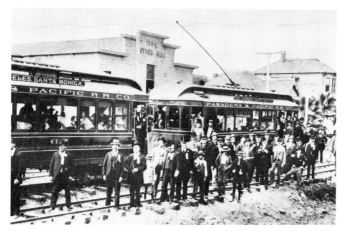

PASADENA & PACIFIC RAILWAY CO. - A consolidation of five different interurban and electric lines to form the Pasadena & Pacific Railway. In 1898 was merged to form the Los Angeles-Pacific Railway. - *Donald Duke Collection*

PASADENA RAILWAY COMPANY

Chartered February 19, 1887 - Steam - Standard Gauge

Located Pasadena, Los Angeles County. Proposed to build from Los Angeles to Mount Wilson. Distance 26.00 miles. Built from Raymond Station on the Santa Fe Railway Company to Altadena with terminal located on Lake Avenue and Calaveras Street. Completed January 31, 1888. Distance 7.00 miles. Leased to the Los Angeles, Pasadena & Glendale Railway February 28, 1889. Sold to Union Pacific Railroad Company in 1921.

PASADENA, RAMONA & LONG BEACH RAILROAD

Incorporated May 5, 1887 - Steam - Standard Gauge

Located Pasadena, Los Angeles County. Proposed to build from Shorb's Station (Alhambra) through Laguna Rancho to Downey, to the Cooperative Colony through Brockton, to south of Signal Hill and along the mesa of Alamitos to Alamitos Beach and then to Long Beach where a junction would be made with the Long Beach Railroad. No construction work done.

PASADENA RAPID TRANSIT COMPANY

Incorporated December 8, 1908 - Electric - Standard Gauge

Located Pasadena, Los Angeles County. Proposed to build a third-rail electric railway to Los Angeles by the shortest route between the two cities. The round trip to be made in 24 minutes. The title to the right-of-way of the old cycle, which extended from Pasadena to Avenue 53, was secured. Distance 6.00 miles. All trackage was to be elevated. Project abandoned in 1911.

PASADENA & WILSON'S PEAK RAILWAY

Incorporated June 15, 1887 - Steam or Cable

Located Pasadena, Los Angeles County. Proposed to build to Eaton's Canyon and then to the top of Mount Wilson. Distance 7.00 miles. 4.00 miles of grade were laid out by August 20, 1887. Project was abandoned in 1890.

PASO DE ROBLES STREET RAILWAY

Chartered June 6, 1892 - Horsecar - 3 ft. Gauge

Located Pasa Robles, San Luis Obispo County. Built 2.50 miles of street railway. Began operations August 14, 1892.

PASO DE ROBLES STREET RAILWAY - This picture postcard is the only known view of this horsecar street railway which began operation in 1892. - *Donald Duke Collection*

PASO ROBLES & CAYUCOS RAILWAY COMPANY

Incorporated December 11, 1891 - Steam - Standard Gauge

Located Paso Robles, San Luis Obispo County. Proposed to build to Cayucos. Distance 30.00 miles. No construction work done.

PATTERSON & WESTERN RAILROAD COMPANY

Began construction April 1, 1916 - Steam - 3 ft. Gauge

Located Patterson, Stanislaus County. Built from a junction with the Southern Pacific Company to Jones Station magnesite mine. Distance 28.15 miles. Ceased operations August 14, 1920. Applied for abandonment February 11, 1921.

PENINSULAR RAILROAD COMPANY

Organized September 1887 - Steam - Standard Gauge

Located San Diego, San Diego County. Organized as a successor company to the San Diego & International Railroad Company. In 1888 it was proposed to take over the Coronado Railroad for an entrance into San Diego and either to extend it to the border at Tijuana or use the trackage of the National City & Otay Railroad. Some track construction was done from San Quentin, Baja California, Mexico, northward in 1892. Distance 17.50 miles.

PENINSULAR RAILWAY COMPANY
PENINSULAR RAILROAD COMPANY

Incorporated June 30, 1909 - Electric - Standard Gauge

Located Santa Clara Valley, Santa Clara County. Resulted from the consolidation of the Peninsular Railroad Company, the Santa Clara Interurban Railroad and the San Jose-Los Gatos Interurban. Operated in San Jose, Saratoga, Los Gatos, Campbell, Cupertino, Monte Vista and Palo Alto. Although controlled by the Southern Pacific Company it was an independent company and formed no part of the Southern Pacific Railroad Company. Abandoned October 1, 1934. Company discontinued by disincorporation in 1935.

PENINSULAR RAILWAY CO. - An interurban railway that operated in the San Jose, Los Gatos and Palo Alto region of the San Francisco Peninsula. It was a wholly-owned Southern Pacific property, but independently operated. - *Donald Duke Collection*

PEOPLE'S RAILROAD COMPANY

Organized 1904 - Electric or Steam

Located San Diego, San Diego County. Made surveys through Mission Valley in 1905.

PEOPLE'S RAILROAD

Proposed 1883 - Steam - 3 ft. Gauge

Located Visalia, Tulare County. Proposed to build to Fresno. Survey work done in 1884. Project abandoned in 1885.

PEOPLE'S RAILROAD OF SAN JOSE
PEOPLE'S HORSE RAILROAD COMPANY

Franchise granted February 26, 1877 - Horsecar - 3 ft. Gauge

Located San Jose, Santa Clara County. Franchise granted for the Southeast Side Horse Railroad Company. Construction work was completed April 25, 1877. Franchise and organization transferred to People's Horse Railroad Company with the same ownership. Built along First Street, out St. John, Fifth, Washington, Seventh, Empire and 14th to Berzessa Road, then to the city of Santa Clara. Was also known by the name People's Railroad of San Jose. Purchased Northside Horse Railroad April 22, 1882. Sold to San Jose & Santa Clara Railroad April 23, 1882.

PEOPLE'S WHARF COMPANY

Organized December 1868 - Horse Power - Narrow-Gauge

Located San Luis Obispo, San Luis Obispo County. Built from the end of wharf in San Luis Obispo Bay to warehouse. Distance .25 miles. Completed September 1869.

PEPPERS - COTTON LUMBER COMPANY

Organized 1920 or 1921 - Steam - Standard Gauge

Located Macdoel, Siskiyou County. Built from mill to timber. Distance 12.00 miles.

PERRIS & LAKEVIEW RAILWAY COMPANY

Incorporated November 1, 1898 - Steam - Standard Gauge

Located Lakeview, Riverside County. Built to Lakeview Junction. Distance 8.02 miles. Sold to the California, Arizona & Santa Fe Railway Company December 28, 1911, and leased to the Atchison, Topeka & Santa Fe Railway Company. Abandoned February 15, 1937.

PERRIS & SAN JACINTO RAILROAD

Organized March 7, 1887 - Steam - Standard Gauge

Located Perris, Riverside County. This company was chartered to build a railway line from Perris to an unknown point in the San Jacinto Valley. The railroad was completed by the California Central Railway Company on April 30, 1888. On April 23, 1887 it was renamed the San Jacinto Valley Railroad Company by the board of directors. The 29-mile line was consolidated with the Southern California Railway Company on November 7, 1889. Became a part of the Santa Fe Railway

PESCADERO RAILWAY & IMPROVEMENT COMPANY

Organized 1907 - Steam - Standard Gauge

Located Pescadero, San Mateo County. Proposed to build from a junction with the Ocean Shore Railroad up Pescadero Creek. Distance 8.00 miles. No construction work done.

PETALUMA & CLOVERDALE RAILROAD COMPANY

Organized 1869 - Steam - Standard Gauge

Located Cloverdale, Sonoma County. Proposed to be a branch of the Vallejo & Sonoma Valley Railroad running from Cloverdale to Healdsburg. No construction work was done.

PETALUMA & COAST RAILWAY

Incorporated April 3, 1912 - Electric - Standard Gauge

Located Liberty, Sonoma County. Proposed to build to Bloomfield and then to the Pacific Coast near Bodega. Distance 18.00 miles.

PETALUMA & HAYSTACK RAILROAD COMPANY

Chartered April 18, 1862 - Horse Power

Located Petaluma, Sonoma County. Built to Haystack Landing on Petaluma Creek. Distance 2.50 miles. Horse power was used at first. A steam locomotive to run on log rails was obtained in 1864. Sold to the Sonoma & Marin Railroad in 1875.

PETALUMA & HEALDSBURG RAILROAD COMPANY

Organized 1865 - Steam - Standard Gauge

Located Petaluma, Sonoma County. Proposed to build to Healdsburg. Failed to raise sufficient capital for construction. Company disbanded in 1867.

PETALUMA RAILROAD COMPANY

Organized February 21, 1914 - Electric

Located Petaluma, Sonoma County. Proposed to build an electric railway from Taylor Station to Graton, Occidental and Camp Meeker. Preliminary surveys began March 1914. Distance 7.00 miles.

PETALUMA & SANTA ROSA ELECTRIC RAILWAY COMPANY
PETALUMA & SANTA ROSA RAILROAD COMPANY

Incorporated June 20, 1903 - Electric - Standard Gauge

Located Petaluma, Sonoma County. Built to connect Petaluma, Santa Rosa, Sebastopol and Forestville. Distance 38.00 miles. Began construction in

March 1904. Consolidated the Union Railway (Santa Rosa), the Santa Rosa Street Railway, the Petaluma Street Railway and the Central Street Railway into one company. Reorganized as the Petaluma & Santa Rosa Railroad Company October 29, 1918. Sold to the Northwestern Pacific Railroad in 1923. Ended electric operations January 24, 1947. Abandoned May 1984, except for 1.40 miles retained by the Northwestern Pacific Railroad.

PETALUMA & SANTA ROSA RAILROAD - An electric interurban line built to connect Petaluma with Santa Rosa, Sebastopol and Forestville. Operated freight service with electric locomotives. Was sold to the Northwestern Pacific in 1923. - *Harre Demoro Collection*

PETALUMA, SEBASTOPOL & RUSSIAN RIVER RAILROAD

Organized February 1, 1889 - Steam - Standard Gauge

Located Petaluma, Sonoma County. Proposed to build northwest to Sebastopol and then to Guerneville. Distance 26.50 miles. Further extensions into Mendocino County were contemplated. Project abandoned in November 1889.

PETALUMA STREET RAILWAY

Horsecar - Standard Gauge

Located Petaluma, Sonoma County. Began operations as a mile-long horsecar street railway between Petaluma and West Petaluma. Sold to the Petaluma & Santa Rosa Railway June 20, 1903. Sold to the Northwestern Pacific Railroad in 1923.

HERMAN PETERSON LUMBER COMPANY

Organized 1900 or 1901 - Steam

Located Rush Creek, Fresno County. Built from mill to timber. Distance 2.00 miles.

PICKERING LUMBER COMPANY

Organized May 1923 - Steam - Standard Gauge and 3 ft. Gauge

Located Macdoel, Siskiyou County. Built in 1915. Built from mill to timber. Distance 8.00 miles. Leased to Hovey & Walker in 1929. Located Hackamore, Modoc County. Built in 1929. Standard gauge operation. Ceased operations in 1930. Relocated Standard and Tuolumne, Tuolumne County. Organized in 1920. Standard gauge section built into the Tuolumne region. Incorporated the Hetch-Hetchy & Yosemite Valley Railway as a common carrier over the narrow-gauge section in 1926. Sold to the West Side Lumber Company in 1934. A standard gauge section purchased from the Sugar Pine Railroad in 1920. Sold to Pickering Lumber Corp. in 1934.

PICKERING LUMBER CORPORATION

Organized 1934 - Steam - Standard Gauge

Located Standard, Tuolumne County. Organized to acquire the holdings of the Pickering Lumber Company. Took over the standard gauge operations of the older company. Standard to Ralph over the tracks of the Sierra Railway. Ralph to Skull Creek. Distance 75.00 miles.

PIEDMONT CABLE COMPANY

Organized 1890 - Cable - Standard Gauge

Located Oakland, Alameda County. Reorganized as the Consolidated Piedmont Cable Company in 1893. Built the Oakland Avenue cable line to Piedmont and the Broadway cable line north of 14th Street to the cemetery. Had a horsecar line on 14th Street in Oakland which was later electrified, and a cable line on Washington Street. After foreclosure sale, the company was reorganized as the Piedmont & Mountain View Railway Company April 1, 1895. This company electrified all lines. Noted for combined electric and cable operation of the Oakland Avenue line. Cars had electric motor on one end and a cable grip truck on the other. Consolidated with the Oakland Transit Company in 1898.

PICKERING LUMBER CO. - A logging company with two bases of operation. One in Siskiyou and the other in Tuolumne County. This train brings a string of logs down from Schoettgen Pass to the mill at Standard. - *Donald Duke*

PIEDMONT & MOUNTAIN VIEW RAILWAY COMPANY

Organized April 1, 1895 - Electric - Standard Gauge

Located Oakland, Alameda County. A reorganization after foreclosure sale of Consolidated Piedmont Cable Company. Consolidated with Oakland Transit Company in 1898.

PINE RIDGE LUMBER COMPANY

Organized 1908 - Steam - Standard Gauge

Located Toll House, Fresno County. Built 2.00 miles of track. Abandoned 1910.

PIONEER BOX COMPANY

Organized 1916 or 1917 - Steam - Standard Gauge

Located Mt. Shasta, Siskiyou County. Built from mill to timber. Distance 9.00 miles. Reorganized as Pioneer Box & Lumber Company in 1923. Sold to Mt. Shasta Pine Manufacturing Company in 1928. Abandoned in 1936.

PIONEER BOX & LUMBER COMPANY

Organized 1923 - Steam - Standard Gauge

Located Mt. Shasta, Siskiyou County. Took over the operations of the Pioneer Box Company. Sold to the Mt. Shasta Manufacturing Company in 1928. Abandoned 1936.

PITT RIVER RAILROAD

Built 1921 - Steam - Standard Gauge

Located Bartle, Siskiyou County. This was the name given to the Mt. Shasta Corporation Construction Company Railroad built from Bartle Spur on the McCloud River Railroad to Powerhouse No. 1 on Pitt River.

PITTSBURG COAL & MINING COMPANY
PITTSBURG RAILROAD COMPANY
PITTSBURG & BLACK DIAMOND RAILROAD
PITTSBURG RAILWAY COMPANY

Incorporated January 14, 1862 - Steam - Standard Gauge

Located Pittsburg Landing, two miles from Pittsburg on the San Joaquin River, Contra Costa County. Built to Somersville. Distance 5.33 miles. Built by Pittsburg Coal & Mining Company. Completed February 1866. Named Pittsburg Railroad Company. Name changed to Pittsburg & Black Diamond Railroad in 1880. Reorganized as Pittsburg Railway Company June 30, 1911. Ceased operations November 30, 1911. Abandoned in 1916.

PLACERVILLE & LAKE TAHOE RAILROAD

Organized 1903 - Steam - Standard Gauge

Located Placerville, El Dorado County. Construction began in 1903 from Placerville on the Southern Pacific Railroad to Camino. Distance 8.05 miles. Operations discontinued in 1909. Sold to the Camino, Placerville & Lake Tahoe Railroad Company January 1912. Trackage extended from Camino to Pino Grande and then to Tallac. Distance 65.00 miles. Section from Camino to Tallac was narrow-gauge.

PLACERVILLE & SACRAMENTO VALLEY RAILROAD COMPANY

Incorporated June 12, 1862 - Steam - Standard Gauge

Located Folsom Junction, Sacramento County. Built to Shingle Springs. Distance 26.20 miles. Deeded to the Sacramento & Placerville Railroad Company in 1877. Consolidated into the Northern Railway Company May 15, 1888. Consolidated with the Southern Pacific Company April 14, 1898.

PLATT MILL COMPANY

Began operations 1867 - Horse

Located Stewart's Point, Sonoma County. Built a tramway from mill to timber. Sold to Clipper Mill Company.

PLEASURE BEACH & LOS ANGELES BELT RAILWAY COMPANY

Incorporated June 12, 1888 - Steam - Standard Gauge

Located San Pedro, Los Angeles County. Proposed to build from San Pedro to Santa Monica and then to Los Angeles. Distance 6.00 miles. Some right-of-way was obtained in 1888. Surveys completed in 1889. No construction work done. Project abandoned in 1889.

POINT ARENA RAILWAY

Organized September 1889 - Steam

Located Arena Cove, Mendocino County. Proposed to build to a point on the north fork of the Garcia River. Distance 10.00 miles.

POINT LOMA ELECTRIC RAILWAY COMPANY POINT LOMA RAILROAD COMPANY

Organized January 1907 - Electric - Standard Gauge

Located San Diego, San Diego County. Organized to build an electric railway from San Diego to Point Loma. Reorganized as Point Loma Railroad Company July 7, 1908. To build from the end of San Diego Electric Railway's line at India and Winder streets to Roseville and over the rails of the defunct Roseville & Ocean Beach Railroad right-of-way to Ocean Beach. Route to return via a loop. Built 8.20 miles of track. Construction and operation agreements made with San Diego Electric Railway Company. Began operations from India and Winder streets to Ocean Beach May 1, 1909. South scenic loop completed July 4, 1909. Made connection with the Bay Shore Railroad in Ocean Beach in 1916. Application filed for discontinuance of service in 1918. Not granted. Sold to the San Diego Electric Railway Company in 1922.

POLLARD & DODGE COMPANY

Organized 1900 - Steam - Standard Gauge

Located Newberg, Mendocino County. Operated 2.00 miles of trackage. Abandoned in 1901.

POLLARD LUMBER COMPANY

Organized 1906 - Steam - Standard Gauge

Located Westport, Mendocino County. Operated from mill to timber. Distance 3.20 miles. Trackage was built by the California Lumber Company in 1891. The road was not in continuous operation until 1906 when it was purchased by Pollard Lumber Company. Leased to the Westport Lumber & Railroad Company from 1908 to 1910. Abandoned in 1910.

POMONA & ELSINORE RAILROAD COMPANY

Incorporated April 13, 1887 - Steam - Standard Gauge

Located Pomona, Los Angeles County. Proposed to build to Elsinore through Chico Ranch. Distance 42.00 miles. Surveys completed in February 1887. Roadbed graded for 4.00 miles by November 1888. Ties and rail purchased for 25.00 miles of track February 1888. 30.00 miles of grading completed by January 3, 1888. Project abandoned in 1889.

POMONA HEIGHTS STREET RAILROAD COMPANY

Franchise granted September 8, 1887 - Horsecar - Standard Gauge

Located Pomona, Los Angeles County. Built from the Southern Pacific Railroad depot south on Thomas Street to Fifth Street, then to Ellen. South on Ellen Street to Crow. West on Crow to Hamilton. From Hamilton to Phillips Boulevard. Distance 1.70 miles. Ceased operations September 17, 1890. Abandoned February 3, 1893.

POMONA STREET RAILWAY COMPANY

Franchise granted February 15, 1887 - Steam Dummy - Standard Gauge

Located Pomona, Los Angeles County. Built from Southern Pacific Railroad Station north on Gary Avenue to Orange Grove Avenue then to Azusa Road, northwest on Azusa Road to Laurel Street, north on Laurel to Railroad Street and west on Railroad Street to a shed halfway between Pine and Laurel streets. Distance 2.75 miles. Construction began February 28, 1888. Began operations April 1888. Dummy operations ceased November 1907. Sold to the Southern Pacific Company May 14, 1905. Sold to the Pacific Electric Railway Company November 1907. Abandoned 1925.

PORT COSTA BRICK WORKS

Narrow-Gauge

Located Port Costa, Contra Costa County. Industrial quarry road.

PORT ORANGE & SANTA ANA RAILROAD COMPANY

Organized May 20, 1907 - Electric - Standard Gauge

Located Santa Ana, Orange County. Proposed to build to Newport or somewhere near Newport on the Pacific Ocean.

PORT SAN LUIS TRANSPORTATION COMPANY

Organized October 31, 1941 - Steam - 3 ft. Gauge

Located San Luis Obispo, San Luis Obispo County. Purchased the tracks of the Pacific Coast Railway from San Luis Obispo to Port San Luis. Began operations February 28, 1942. Abandoned October 19, 1942.

PORTERVILLE NORTHEASTERN RAILROAD COMPANY

Incorporated August 9, 1910 - Steam - Standard Gauge

Located Porterville, Tulare County. Proposed to build from Tulare City to Springville by way of Woodville and Porterville. Built from Porterville to Springville. Distance 16.45 miles. Completed September 9, 1911. Branch built from Magnesite Junction to Magnesite, distance 2.44 miles. Completed November 15, 1912. Operations taken over by the Southern Pacific Company April 1, 1912. Trackage Springville to Clavical abandoned 1935. Clavical to Success abandoned in 1941. Complete abandonment in 1958.

POTRERO & BAY VIEW RAILROAD COMPANY

Incorporated May 1, 1866 - Horsecar - 5 ft. Gauge

Located San Francisco, San Francisco County. Proposed to build a street railway from the intersection of Post and Montgomery streets to the Bay View Race Course or to Hunter's Point. Distance to be 4.00 miles. Actual construction resulted in 1.16 miles of track. Began operations in October 1867. Consolidated into the Market Street Railway Company.

POWELL STREET RAILWAY

Chartered 1884 - Cable - 3 ft. 6 in. Gauge

Located San Francisco, San Francisco County. Franchise was granted to the California Street Cable Railroad Company. A steam dummy extension became the Ferries & Cliff House Railway Company. The cable car section became the Powell Street Railway. Merged with the first Market Street Railway in 1893. Present operations included in the Municipal Railway of San Francisco's cable division.

PRESIDIO & FERRIES RAILROAD

Construction began 1880 - Horsecar - 5 ft. Gauge

Located San Francisco, San Francisco County. Chartered January 6, 1882. Built a combination horsecar, steam dummy line and cable car that ran from the Ferry Building to Harbor View via Presidio. Distance 7.63 miles. Electrified in 1906. Sold to the Municipal Railway of San Francisco December 11, 1913.

PRESIDIO & FERRIES RAILROAD - Built a combination of horsecar, cable car and steam dummy lines from the Ferry Building to Harbor View via Presidio. Cable lines included approximately 3.5 miles of double-track railway. - *Harre Demoro Collection*

PUDDING CREEK LUMBER COMPANY RAILROAD

Organized 1886 - Steam - Standard Gauge

Located Glen Blair, Mendocino County. Built from mill to woods. Distance 5.00 miles. Sold in 1903 to Glen Blair Redwood Company. Abandoned 1928. Dismantled 1941.

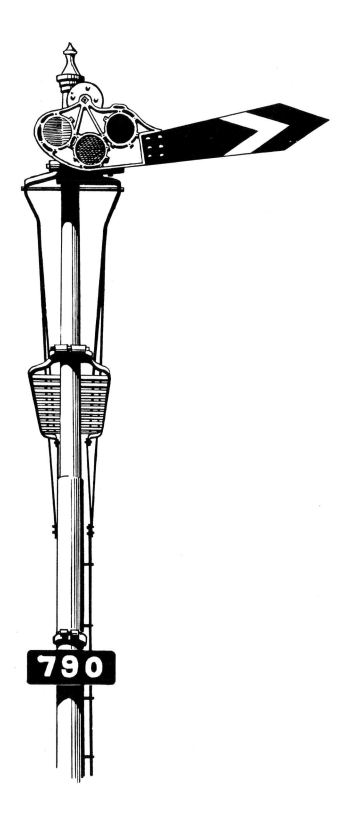

QUINCY RAILROAD - A northern California short line which operated from a Western Pacific connection at Quincy Junction to downtown Quincy, a distance of six miles. In this scene a 2-6-2 tank engine is entering Quincy in 1954. - *Art Lloyd*

Q

QUARRY PRODUCTS, INC.

Organized June 1963 - Diesel - Standard Gauge

Located Richmond, Contra Costa County. Took over the operations of the Blake Brothers Company quarry, processing plant and railroad.

QUINCY LUMBER COMPANY

Organized 1916 - Steam - Standard Gauge

Located Quincy, Plumas County. Built from Quincy to Butterfly and Meadow Valley. Distance 3.00 miles. Sold to the F.S. Murphy Lumber Company in 1918. Resold to Quincy Lumber Company in 1926. Abandoned 1955.

QUINCY LUMBER COMPANY

Organized 1926 - Steam - 3 ft. Gauge

Located Sloat, Plumas County. Purchased the properties of the F.S. Murphy Lumber Company. 8.00 miles of track. Abandoned 1936.

QUINCY RAILROAD COMPANY
QUINCY & EASTERN RAILWAY COMPANY
QUINCY WESTERN RAILROAD COMPANY

Organized 1908 - Steam - Standard Gauge

Located Quincy, Plumas County. Organized as the Quincy & Eastern Railway Company to build from Quincy to Quincy Junction on the Western Pacific Railroad. Distance 6.00 miles. Reorganized as the Quincy Western Railroad July 8, 1908, and began construction. Sold to the F.S. Murphy Lumber Company in 1917. Renamed the Quincy Railroad Company.

RIVERSIDE & ARLINGTON RAILWAY - An electrified horsecar line that operated the 6.56 miles between Riverside and Arlington. This California-type car, open at both ends, also ran to Riverside's Polo Grounds. - *Fred Schneider Collection*

R

RAINBOW MILL & LUMBER COMPANY

Organized 1918 or 1919 - Steam - Standard Gauge

Located Sisson, Siskiyou County. Built from mill to timber. Distance 12.50 miles. Ceased operations in 1921.

RAMONA & SAN BERNARDINO RAILROAD COMPANY

Incorporated April 14, 1888 - Steam - Standard Gauge

Located Alhambra, Los Angeles County. Proposed to build from Ramona (Shorb) eastward to Crafton. Distance 71.00 miles. Deeded to the Southern Pacific Company May 14, 1888. Completed November 1892.

N. B. RANDAL SAWMILL

Organized 1935 - Steam - Standard Gauge

Located Fiddletown, Amador County. Built from mill to timber. Distance 20 miles. Ceased operations 1938.

RANDSBURG RAILWAY COMPANY

Incorporated May 18, 1897 - Steam - Standard Gauge

Located Johannesburg, Kern County. Built from a junction with the Santa Fe Railway at Kramer northward to Johannesburg. Distance 28.64 miles. Construction began October 2, 1897. Opened for traffic January 5, 1898. Leased to the Santa Fe Railway April 30, 1903. Deeded to the Santa Fe Railway December 26, 1911. Abandoned December 30, 1933. Tracks removed in 1934.

RATON & SANTA CRUZ RAILROAD COMPANY

Incorporated October 8, 1902 - Steam - Standard Gauge

Located Raton, New Mexico. Proposed to build across New Mexico, Arizona and California to Santa Cruz on the Pacific Ocean.

RAYMOND GRANITE COMPANY

Standard Gauge

Located Knowles, Madera County. Quarry road.

RAYMOND RAILROAD

Organized 1883 - Steam - Standard Gauge

Located Alhambra, Los Angeles County. Proposed to build a street railroad from Shorb Station (Alhambra) on the Southern Pacific Railroad to Raymond Station on the Los Angeles & San Gabriel Valley Railroad. Taken over by the San Gabriel Valley Rapid Transit Railway in 1891 and built a branch from West Alhambra to the Raymond Hotel. Sold to the Southern Pacific Company. Abandoned in the 1960's.

READ TIMBER & LUMBER COMPANY

Organized 1906 - Steam - 3 ft. Gauge

Located Emigrant Gap, Placer County. Built from mill to timber. Distance 30.00 miles. Construction began in 1907. Ceased operations in 1918.

RED BLUFF & FALL RIVER RAILROAD COMPANY

Incorporated March 16, 1906 - Steam - Standard Gauge

Located Red Bluff, Tehama County. Proposed to build northeast to Fall River Mills by way of Shingletown. Distance 40.00 miles.

RED RIVER LUMBER COMPANY
RED RIVER RAILROAD

Organized 1912 - Steam - Electric - Standard Gauge

Located Westwood, Lassen County. Built south and west including the area of the present Lake Almanor. Extended trackage west of Chester. Electrified that section of track between Chester and Westwood and organized it as the Red River Railroad in 1927. Extended logging trackage again from Chester to Poison Lake. 95.00 miles of logging road was steam operated. 17.00 miles of trackage under electric operation. All properties were sold in 1944. Section Westwood to Chester became Almanor Railroad. Westwood section toward north sold to the Fruit Grower's Supply.

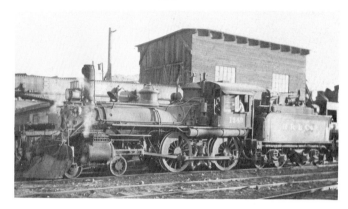

RED RIVER LUMBER - A logging railroad with 95 miles of electric and steam railroad lines operated around the Westwood and Chester area of Lassen County. Line was handled with vintage steam power. - *Donald Duke Collection*

RED ROCK RAILROAD

Organized 1908 - Steam - Standard Gauge

Located Cantil Siding, Kern County. Built by the Southern Pacific Company from Cantil Siding, 23.00 miles north of Mojave, through Red Rock Canyon. Completed January 1909. Distance 9.10 miles. Dismantled December 1910.

REDDING & RED BLUFF RAILWAY COMPANY

Incorporated February 23, 1906 - Standard Gauge

Located Chico, Butte County. Proposed to build to Redding. Acquired some right of ways and surveys were made. No construction. Sold to Shasta Southern Railway Company July 1906.

REDDING, AFTERTHOUGHT & NORTHWESTERN RAILWAY COMPANY

Incorporated April 1, 1907 - Electric - Standard Gauge

Located Bella Vista, Shasta County. Proposed to build to Ingot. Distance 18.00 miles. Surveys completed April 7, 1908.

REDLANDS CENTRAL ELECTRIC RAILWAY COMPANY

Incorporated April 26, 1907 - Electric - Standard Gauge

Located Redlands, San Bernardino County. Proposed to build from Citrus and Orange streets in Redlands in an easterly direction to Crafton and from Citrus and Orange streets to Riverside. Construction began June 17, 1907, on Brookside Avenue from San Mateo Street northeasterly to West Citrus Avenue, and easterly on West Citrus to Orange Street, and on West Citrus Avenue from 6th Street to the eastern city limits of Redlands at Wabash Street. Trackage on East Citrus Avenue from Orange Street to 6th Street. Two blocks were owned by Redlands Street Railway Company. Total mileage 3.513 miles. Began operations February 4, 1908. Sold to Southern Pacific Company November 10, 1910. Consolidated with Pacific Electric Railway Company September 1, 1911.

REDLANDS CENTRAL RAILWAY COMPANY

Incorporated May 1, 1907 - Electric - Standard Gauge

Located Redlands, San Bernardino County. Built to Riverside and Crafton. Distance 25.00 miles. Sold to the Pacific Electric Railway Company September 1, 1911.

REDLANDS CENTRAL RAILWAY - A suburban electric line that built from Redlands to Riverside and Crafton. Line became a part of the Pacific Electric system in 1911. - *Donald Duke Collection*

REDLANDS STREET RAILWAY

Organized 1887 - Horsecar - Standard Gauge

Located Redlands, San Bernardino County. Operated a 3.00 mile long horsecar street railway. Electrified in April 1899. Consolidated with the San Bernardino Valley Traction Company July 5, 1903. Became part of the Pacific Electric Railway Company September 1, 1911.

REDLANDS STREET RAILWAY COMPANY

Franchise granted January 6, 1888 - Horsecar - Standard Gauge

Located Redlands, San Bernardino County. Incorporated March 22, 1888. Began construction in April 1888. Began operations May 23, 1889. Electrified in 1899. Began electric operations December 23, 1899. Operations were over San Bernardino Avenue from Tennessee Street through the business district and Smiley Heights to Terracina, Cajon and Cypress streets to Country Club and on Citrus Avenue from Orange Street to 6th Street. Distance 8.923 miles. Consolidated with San Bernardino & Highland Electric Railway Company and the San Bernardino Valley Traction Company June 6, 1903, to form San Bernardino Valley Traction Company. Consolidated into the Pacific Electric Railway Company September 1, 1911.

REDLANDS STREET RAILWAY - A horsecar line organized in 1888 that operated around the streets of downtown Redlands and carried passengers into the residential sections. Formed a part of San Bernardino Valley Traction in 1903. - *Donald Duke Collection*

REDLANDS UNIVERSITY RAILWAY

Organized July 1911 - Electric - Standard Gauge

Located Redlands, San Bernardino County. Proposed to build a street railway from Redlands to the University. Distance 2.00 miles. Application for charter made September 15, 1911. Plans taken over by the Pacific Electric Railway Company July 1920. Line to be built up Brockton Avenue to University Street.

REDLANDS & YUCAIPA ELECTRIC RAILWAY COMPANY

Organized 1907 - Electric - Standard Gauge

Located Redlands, San Bernardino County. Proposed to build 11.00 miles of electric street railway in Redlands and then to build southward through the canyon to the Yucaipa benchlands and then on a direct line to the Oak Glen Mountain resort. Distance 19.50 miles. One mile of surveying and grading done in 1907. Began surveys January 26, 1907. Ground-breaking May 29, 1907. Project abandoned in 1913.

REDONDO BEACH RAILWAY COMPANY

Incorporated April 23, 1888 - Steam - Standard Gauge

Located Redondo Beach, Los Angeles County. Built from Inglewood to Redondo Beach. Distance 10.77 miles. Leased to the California Central Railway Company and began service April 16, 1888. Merged with the California Southern Railroad Company and California Central Railway Company to form the Southern California Railway Company November 7, 1889.

REDONDO & HERMOSA BEACH RAILROAD COMPANY

Incorporated February 21, 1901 - Electric - Standard Gauge

Located Redondo Beach, Los Angeles County. Built to Hermosa Beach. Sold to the Los Angeles, Hermosa Beach & Redondo Railway Company March 12, 1902. Merged into the Pacific Electric Railway September 11, 1911.

REDONDO RAILWAY COMPANY

Chartered 1889 - Steam - 3 ft. Gauge

Located Redondo, Los Angeles County. Purchased the Rosecrans Rapid Transit Railway. Built from 48th Street to Arlington Avenue. Incorporated April 1, 1889. Began operations in 1890. Distance 1.47 miles. Built from Los Angeles to Strawberry Park. Extended to Redondo after being sold to the Los Angeles & Redondo Railway Company in April 1896. Total distance operated 17.70 miles. Electrified in 1902. Standard gauged in 1909. Sold to the Pacific Electric Railway Company September 1, 1911.

REDONDO RAILWAY - A narrow-gauge line constructed from downtown Los Angeles to Redondo. In 1896 it became a part of the Los Angeles & Redondo Railway. Line was electrified in 1902 and converted to standard gauge in 1909. - *Donald Duke Collection*

REDWOOD CITY RAILWAY

Organized January 1913 - Electric - Standard Gauge

Located Redwood City, San Mateo County. Proposed to build a street railway. Distance 4.50 miles.

REDWOOD COAST RAILWAY COMPANY

Organized 1985 - Diesel - Standard Gauge

Located Eureka, Humboldt County. Organized by the Great Western Tours to operate passenger service over the Eureka Southern Railroad from Eureka to Willits. First run was made May 17, 1985.

REDWOOD LUMBER COMPANY

Organized 1911 - Steam - Standard Gauge

Located Fort Ross, Sonoma County. Purchased the properties of the Ft. Ross Land Company in 1911. 1.00 mile of track laid. Abandoned 1912 or 1913.

REDWOOD MANUFACTURING COMPANY

Organized about 1910 - Steam - Narrow-Gauge

Located Black Diamond, Contra Costa County. Built about twelve miles of track.

REDWOOD RAILROAD

Organized 1883 - Steam - Standard Gauge

Located Mendocino, Mendocino County. Built 4.25 miles of trackage. Abandoned in 1886.

REED TIMBER & LUMBER COMPANY

Organized May 31, 1879 - Steam - Standard Gauge

Located Albion, Mendocino County. Built 15.00 miles of logging road up Albion Canyon.

L.C. REYNOLDS LUMBER COMPANY

Steam - Standard Gauge

Located Shingletown, Shasta County. Logging road. Ceased operations in 1905 or 1906.

RICHARDSON BROTHERS

Organized 1875 - Steam - 7 ft. 2 in. Gauge

Located Marlis Creek near Truckee, Placer County. Began by using log rails. Built 1.50 miles of trackage from woods to pond. Converted from ox power to steam power and built 3.00 miles of trackage. Ceased operations in 1890.

RICHARDSON BROTHERS

Organized 1889 - Steam - Narrow-Gauge

Located Stewart's Point, Sonoma County. Built from mill to timber along the South Fork of the Gualala River.

RICHMOND BELT RAILROAD

Incorporated August 19, 1902 - Steam - Standard Gauge

Located Richmond, Contra Costa County. Built from Richmond Transfer to just beyond Winehaven. Distance 4.75 miles. Began operations in 1905. Leased jointly by the Southern Pacific Company and the Santa Fe Railway December 14, 1905.

RICHMOND RAILWAY & NAVIGATION COMPANY

Organized April 24, 1907 - Electric - Standard Gauge

Located Richmond, Contra Costa County. Built an electric street railway from the Southern Pacific Company depot in Richmond to a ferryboat connection in South Richmond. Franchise sold to the East Shore & Suburban Railway October 1, 1907. Became part of the Oakland Traction Company in 1910.

RICHMOND SHIPYARD RAILWAY

Organized 1943 - Electric - Standard Gauge

Located Richmond, Contra Costa County. Operated part of the Key System trackage from Richmond to Kaiser Shipyard for the United States Maritime Commission during World War II. Ceased operations in 1945.

RIVERSIDE & ARLINGTON RAILWAY COMPANY

Incorporated August 13, 1887 - Horse Power/Electric - Standard Gauge

Located Riverside, Riverside County. Proposed to build to Arlington. Grading began October 1887. Began operations December 11, 1888. Distance 6.56 miles. Purchased Riverside Railway Company May 3, 1895. Purchased Hall's Addition Street Railway Company June 11, 1895. Began electrification 1898. Completed electrification April 11, 1899. Control taken over by Los Angeles Interurban Railway Company December 1, 1904. Consolidated with the Pacific Electric Railway Company February 29, 1911.

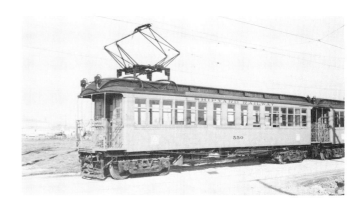

RICHMOND SHIPYARD RAILWAY - The attack on Pearl Harbor brought on the development of Kaiser Shipyards at Richmond. Lacking adequate transportation to haul a mass of workers to the shipyard, the United States Maritime Commission authorized the Key System to construct and operate an interurban line from the end of their San Pablo streetcar line to Richmond. Due to the scarcity of rolling stock, old wooden Third Avenue Elevated Railway cars from New York City were acquired. (ABOVE) A six-car train rolls on San Pablo Avenue bound for Richmond. (BELOW) One of the ornate Third Avenue Elevated cars with its brass platform railings. - *Both Charles D. Savage*

RIVERSIDE & ARLINGTON RAILWAY - A horsecar line operating in the streets of Riverside beginning in 1888. Began electric operation by converting horsecars to electric cars in 1898. Taken over by Henry E. Huntington's Los Angeles Inter-Urban Railway in 1904. - *Fred Schneider Collection*

RIVERSIDE ELECTRIC RAILWAY COMPANY

Organized May 1898 - Electric - Standard Gauge or 3 ft. Gauge

Located Riverside, Riverside County. Bid for a franchise to build an electric street railway May 23, 1898.

RIVERSIDE LUMBER COMPANY

Organized September or October 1902 - Steam

Located on Mad River, Humboldt County. Built from the mouth of Canyon Creek up Mad River to Simpson Creek. Surveys completed October 10, 1902. Road completed January 1903. Distance 4.50 miles.

RIVERSIDE RAILWAY COMPANY

Incorporated October 15, 1886 - Horsecar - 42 in. Gauge

Located Riverside, Riverside County. Built 3.243 miles of horsecar line in the City of Riverside. Sold to the Riverside & Arlington Railway May 3, 1895.

RIVERSIDE MILL & LUMBER COMPANY

Organized 1889 - Steam - Standard Gauge

Located Eureka, Humboldt County. Built from mill to tidewater. Distance 8.00 miles. Sold to the Northern Redwood Lumber Company 1903.

RIVERSIDE PORTLAND CEMENT COMPANY

Organized 1923 - Steam - Standard Gauge

Located Oro Grande, San Bernardino County. Took over the operations of the Gold State Portland Cement Company. Trackage extended from mill to quarry. Distance 3.25 miles. Rail operations ceased May 1, 1928. Scrapped 1941.

RIVERSIDE - REDLANDS INTERURBAN RAILWAY

Organized April 12, 1912 - Electric - Standard Gauge

Located Riverside, Riverside County. Filed a petition for a certificate to construct an electric railway to Redlands. Project abandoned in 1913.

RIVERSIDE, RIALTO & PACIFIC RAILROAD COMPANY

Incorporated January 15, 1911 - Electric - Standard Gauge

Located Riverside, Riverside County. Incorporated as a successor company of the Crescent City Railway Company. Original trackage from Riverside to Crestmore was built under 1911 incorporation. The extension to Bloomington and Rialto was built without incorporation. Total distance operated 9.585 miles. Application made for charter to include the whole road made January 3, 1915. Leased to the Pacific Electric Railway.

RIVERSIDE, SANTA ANA & LOS ANGELES RAILWAY COMPANY

Incorporated September 29, 1885 - Steam - Standard Gauge

Located Riverside, Riverside County. Built from Highgrove on the California Southern Railroad to Riverside January 8, 1886. Distance 3.30 miles. Extended to Arlington March 15, 1886. Distance 6.70 miles. Merged into the California Central Railway Company May 31, 1887. Completed over a period of time. Prado to Rincon June 27, 1887. Distance 12.80 miles. Orange to Santa Ana September 15, 1887. Distance 20.10 miles. Orange to Redondo Junction August 12, 1888. Distance 29.50 miles. Total distance built 72.40 miles. Taken over by the Southern California Railway November 7, 1889. Became Santa Fe Railway January 17, 1906.

ROBERTS LUMBER COMPANY

Organized 1900 - Steam - Standard Gauge

Located Loyalton, Sierra County. Built 5.00 miles of logging road. Sold to Clover Valley Lumber Company in 1917. Abandoned in 1957.

ROCKPORT REDWOOD COMPANY

Organized 1938 - Steam - Standard Gauge

Located Rockport, Mendocino County. Purchased the operations of the Southern Redwood Corporation and the Finkbind-Guild Company. Abandoned 1940.

ROSECRANS RAPID TRANSIT RAILWAY

Completed November 1, 1887 - Electric - Standard Gauge

Located Los Angeles, Los Angeles County. Built from Exposition Park in Los Angeles to Rosecrans. Distance 6.00 miles. Ceased operations in 1888. Sold to the Redondo Railway Company April 19, 1889. Sold to the Pacific Electric Railway Company September 1, 1911.

ROSEVILLE & OCEAN BEACH RAILROAD COMPANY
OCEAN BEACH RAILROAD

Application for franchise August 31, 1887 - Steam - Standard Gauge

Located Roseville, San Diego County. Proposed to build from San Diego to Ocean Beach on Point Loma by way of Roseville. Built from Roseville to Ocean Beach. Distance 3.50 miles. Opened for traffic with first train running April 17, 1888, using steam dummy engine of the Pacific Coast Steamship Company. Operated only for a few months.

ROSEVILLE & OLD TOWN RAILROAD

Chartered 1886 - Steam - Standard Gauge

Located San Diego, San Diego County. Proposed to build from the Pacific Coast Steamship wharf in San Diego to Old Town. Built 1.00 mile of track and operated a steam dummy locomotive.

ROUGH & READY ISLAND RAILROAD

Constructed 1945 - Diesel - Standard Gauge

Located Naval Communications station on Rough and Ready Island adjoining the Port of Stockton, San Joaquin County. Began operations July 6, 1945.

ROYAL CONSOLIDATED MINES

Electric - Narrow-Gauge

Located Hodson, Calaveras County. Operated an electric industrial and quarry road.

RUSSIAN RIVER LAND & LUMBER COMPANY

Organized 1877 - Steam - 3 ft. Gauge

Located Duncan's Mill, Sonoma County. Built from mill to timber.

PACIFIC ELECTRIC RAILWAY - When E.H. Harriman to over control of the Pacific Electric from Henry E. Huntington he invisioned a subway running from dowtown Los Angeles Vineyard, Hollywood and Beverly Hills. What was built in 1 was an underground terminal with a large office build complex above, plus a mile-long subway entrance to the Subw Terminal Building at 417 South Hill Street. In this scene Hollywood Boulevard car enters the terminal tracks of Subway Terminal Building. - *Donald Duke*

SAN DIEGO & ARIZONA EASTERN RAILWAY - The daily passenger train is climbing through Carriso Gorge, a rock-strewn ravine of tremendous scope in the Laguna Mountains, approximately 100 miles east of downtown San Diego. The grade of the line, as shown in the background, and the cant of the passenger cars on this train illustrates SD&AE's profile. - *Hugh Tolford Collection*

SACRAMENTO, AUBURN & NEVADA RAILWAY COMPANY

Incorporated August 17, 1852 - Steam - 5 ft. 3 ½ in. Gauge

Located Sacramento, Sacramento County. Proposed to build from Sacramento to Nevada City by way of Negro Bar. Project abandoned by 1853. First railroad to be incorporated in California.

SACRAMENTO BELT RAILROAD

Incorporated June 29, 1906 - Steam - Standard Gauge

Located Sacramento, Sacramento County. Proposed to build a belt line railroad along the crest of the river levee on the city water front. Surveys completed October 1906. Grading began January 1907. Project abandoned 1907.

SACRAMENTO BRICK COMPANY

3 ft. Gauge

Located Sacramento, Sacramento County. Used to haul brick and clay on the company property.

SACRAMENTO CITY LINES

Organized 1943 - Electric - Standard Gauge

Located Sacramento, Sacramento County. Purchased the street railway operations of the Pacific Gas & Electric Company. Abandoned January 4, 1947.

SACRAMENTO CITY LINES - A streetcar changes ends at the terminal of the No. 6 - "Oak Park Line." The operation was formerly the Pacific Gas & Electric Co. streetcar company. It was purchased by National City Lines whose purpose was to convert the system to bus operation. Streetcar service was abandoned January 4, 1947. - *Harre Demoro Collection*

SACRAMENTO CITY STREET RAILWAY COMPANY

Horsecar - 5 ft. Gauge

Located Sacramento, Sacramento County. Operated 9.00 miles of street railway.

SACRAMENTO & EASTERN RAILWAY COMPANY

Incorporated November 28, 1911 - Electric - Standard Gauge

Located Sacramento, Sacramento County. Proposed to build to Folsom by way of Sycamore. No construction work done. Conveyed to the Northern Electric Railway Company in February 1913.

SACRAMENTO ELECTRIC, GAS & RAILWAY COMPANY
SACRAMENTO ELECTRIC, POWER & LIGHT COMPANY ELECTRIC RAILWAY

Organized 1896 - Electric - Standard Gauge

Located Sacramento, Sacramento County. The Sacramento Electric, Gas & Railway Company purchased the Sacramento Electric, Power & Light Company Electric Railway in June 1896. This company had purchased the Sacramento City Street Railway Company some years before. Sold to the Pacific Gas & Electric Company in 1906. Integrated into the Pacific Gas & Electric Company in 1915. Street railway operations sold to Sacramento City Lines in 1943. Abandoned January 4, 1947.

SACRAMENTO, FAIR OAKS & ORANGEVALE RAILROAD COMPANY

Incorporated 1895 - Steam - Standard Gauge

Located Sacramento, Sacramento County. Proposed to build a railroad 20.00 miles long for the Sacramento & Orangevale Colonization Company. Project abandoned in 1897.

SACRAMENTO - FOLSOM ELECTRIC RAILWAY COMPANY

Incorporated May 9, 1911 - Electric - Standard Gauge

Located Sacramento, Sacramento County. Proposed to build to Folsom. Distance 22.50 miles. Sold to the Northern Electric Railway Company February 26, 1913. This was a probable paper reorganized change of name for the Sacramento & Eastern Railway Company.

SACRAMENTO INTERURBAN RAILWAY

Chartered March 3, 1912 - Electric - Standard Gauge

Located Sacramento, Sacramento County. Proposed to build to Roseville by way of Fair Oaks and Orangevale. Distance 13.00 miles. Project abandoned October 1, 1914, and the directors of the company filed notice of dissolution of the company with the Secretary of State.

SACRAMENTO & LAKE TAHOE RAILROAD COMPANY

Incorporated October 6, 1905 - Electric - Standard Gauge

Located Sacramento, Sacramento County. Proposed to build to Lake Tahoe by way of Folsom and Placerville. Distance 125.00 miles. Three branches were to be built, each to be 20.00 miles long. One was to be built to Auburn. The main line was to have been along the route of the present Highway 50. Project abandoned in 1906.

SACRAMENTO NORTHERN RAILROAD COMPANY

Incorporated June 20, 1918 - Electric - Standard Gauge

Located Sacramento, Sacramento County. Organized to acquire and operate all properties owned by the Northern Electric Railway Company, Sacramento Terminal Company, Sacramento & Woodland Railroad Company, and the Marysville & Colusa Branch. Distance 160.78 miles. Sold to the Sacramento Northern Railway Company November 4, 1925.

SACRAMENTO NORTHERN RAILWAY COMPANY

Incorporated August 29, 1921 - Electric - Standard Gauge

Located Sacramento, Sacramento County. Acquired the properties of the Sacramento Northern Railroad Company November 4, 1925. Wholly-owned miles of trackage was 157.044. Sacramento to Chico. Total mileage including leased lines was 160.555 miles. Control transferred to the Western Pacific Railroad Company July 8, 1925.

SACRAMENTO NORTHERN RAILWAY - Operating 157 miles of interurban railroad from Key Pier to Chico, the Sacramento Northern ran fast trains and offered parlor car-dining service. In this scene a two-car deluxe train pauses in the streets of Sacramento in 1917. - *Donald Duke Collection*

SACRAMENTO & OAKLAND RAILROAD

Organized February 5, 1903 - Steam - Standard Gauge

Located Oakland, Alameda County. Proposed to build by way of Alameda, Solano, Yolo and Sacramento counties to a point near Sacramento. A branch was to be built in a westerly direction to Richmond, distance 25.00 miles, and a branch to Martinez, distance 10.00 miles.

SACRAMENTO, PLACER & NEVADA RAILROAD

Incorporated August 16, 1852 - Steam - 5 ft. 3 ½ in. Gauge

Located Folsom, Sacramento County. Proposed to build from Folsom to Auburn in Placer County and then on through Nevada City and eastward over the Sierra Nevada Mountains. Construction began in 1861. Rails reached Auburn Station, about six miles below Auburn proper, in 1862. First train over road September 22, 1862. Abandoned in 1864.

SACRAMENTO & PLACERVILLE RAILROAD COMPANY

Incorporated April 19, 1877 - Steam - Standard Gauge

Resulted from the consolidation of the Sacramento Valley Railroad Company and the Folsom & Placerville Railroad. Operated over trackage between Sacramento and Shingle Springs. Distance 49.10 miles. Consolidated into the Northern Railway Company. Consolidated with the Southern Pacific Company April 14, 1898.

SACRAMENTO REGIONAL TRANSIT AUTHORITY

Organized July 1979 - Electric - Standard Gauge

Located Sacramento, Sacramento County. The state of California's House

SACRAMENTO RTA - Operates over 18.3 miles of track between Watt Avenue (I-80) and Butterfiled, with a single track loop running through downtown Sacramento. - *Fred Schneider*

Appropriations Committee approved $3.6 million in September 1979 for preliminary engineering. The former Sacramento Northern right-of-way was obtained from Sacramento along I-80 to Watt Avenue. A single track loop was established through the downtown and capitol area. The Southern Pacific branch to Butterfield was obtained from downtown to Butterfield. Service was established in 1987.

SACRAMENTO & SAN JOAQUIN VALLEY RAILROAD COMPANY

Incorporated October 17, 1899 - Steam - Standard Gauge

Located Stockton, San Joaquin County. Proposed to build from Sacramento south to Stockton. Surveys for this road completed December 1899. Distance 65.00 miles. Resurveyed May 11, 1900, to build from Stockton north to Sacramento by way of Freeport and along the Sacramento River Valley. Distance 50.00 miles. Project abandoned in 1902.

SACRAMENTO & SIERRA RAILWAY COMPANY

Incorporated 1911 - Electric - Standard Gauge

Located Sacramento, Sacramento County. Proposed to build to Lake Tahoe by way of Orangevale, Georgetown and Jackson Springs. Distance 126.00 miles. Right-of-way secured by May 1, 1909. Survey crews reached Georgetown from Sacramento July 3, 1909. Surveys completed December 18, 1909. Project abandoned in 1911.

SACRAMENTO SHORT LINE RAILWAY COMPANY

Incorporated 1911 - Electric - Standard Gauge

Located Oakland, Alameda County. Proposed to build to Sacramento by way of Richmond and around San Pablo to Napa Junction. No construction work done. Sold to San Francisco-Oakland Terminal Railways March 21, 1912.

SACRAMENTO SOUTHERN RAILROAD COMPANY

Incorporated June 8, 1902 - Steam - Standard Gauge

Located Sacramento, Sacramento County. Built south to Walnut Grove. Distance 24.30 miles. Construction work began January 1906. Completed March 17, 1912. Title transferred to the Central Pacific Railway February 29, 1912. Company dissolved March 4, 1916. Extension from Walnut Grove to Isleton built by the Southern Pacific Company. Opened for traffic September 14, 1929. Distance 7.80 miles. Section Isleton to Mokelumne River opened for service in 1931. This section abandoned in 1951. The remainder now known as the Walnut Grove branch of the Southern Pacific Company.

SACRAMENTO TERMINAL COMPANY

Incorporated September 17, 1908 - Electric - Standard Gauge

Located Sacramento, Sacramento County. The Northern Electric Railway Company built 5.73 miles of trackage between 1901 and 1909. 2.67 miles of track were jointly owned with the Central California Traction Company. Sold to the Sacramento Northern Railway June 28, 1918.

SACRAMENTO & VALLEJO RAILROAD COMPANY

Incorporated January 16, 1907 - Steam - Standard Gauge

Located Sacramento, Sacramento County. Proposed to build southwest to Vallejo. Distance 60.00 miles. Surveys begun April 1907. Project abandoned December 1907.

SACRAMENTO VALLEY & EASTERN RAILWAY

Incorporated November 8, 1906 - Steam - Standard Gauge

Located Pitt, Shasta County. Built from a junction with the Southern Pacific Company to Bully Hill by way of the Pitt River, Squaw Creek and Towne Creek. Distance 14.83 miles. Ceased operations 1917. Abandoned 1932.

SACRAMENTO VALLEY ELECTRIC RAILWAY

Organized December 1912 - Electric - Standard Gauge

Located Red Bluff, Tehama County. Proposed to build southward through Corning, Orland, Willows, Woodland and Dixon to Rio Vista in Solano County. No construction work was done.

SACRAMENTO VALLEY & HUMBOLDT BAY RAILROAD COMPANY

Incorporated January 1887 - Steam - Standard Gauge

Located Red Bluff, Tehama County. Proposed to build to a point on Humboldt Bay. Distance 130.00 miles. A branch from Oak Creek to Paskenta was also proposed. Project abandoned.

SACRAMENTO VALLEY, LAKE & MENDOCINO RAILROAD

Incorporated February 24, 1886 - Steam - Standard Gauge

Located Woodland, Yolo County. Proposed to build through the Capey Valley into Lake County and then to Fort Bragg on the Pacific Coast. Preliminary survey completed July 1886. Project abandoned.

SACRAMENTO VALLEY RAILROAD COMPANY

Organized August 4, 1852 - Steam - 5 ft. 3 ½ in. Gauge

Located Sacramento, Sacramento County. Survey to Folsom made in 1854. Construction began February 12, 1855. Grading started on the levee at Front and "L" streets in Sacramento. First rail laid August 9, 1855. Track reached Alder Creek January 1, 1856. Distance 18.00 miles. Reached Negro Bar January 22, 1856. First train reached Folsom February 22, 1856. Distance 22.90 miles. Original plan called for road to continue on to Marysville. Consolidated with the Folsom & Placerville Railroad August 19, 1877. Consolidated with Northern Railway Company May 15, 1888. Consolidated into the Southern Pacific Company April 14, 1898.

SACRAMENTO VALLEY RAILROAD - California's first railway began operation in 1856 between Sacramento and Folsom, a distance of 22.90 miles. The *L.L. Robinson* was one of several locomotives to operate over the line. - *Gerald Best Collection*

SACRAMENTO VALLEY WEST SIDE ELECTRIC RAILWAY

Incorporated August 31, 1911 - Electric - Standard Gauge

Located San Francisco, San Francisco County. Incorporated to construct a railroad line from Sacramento to Rio Vista, a distance of 35 miles. The road was wholly-owned by the Sacramento Northern Railway. Was absorbed into the Sacramento Northern system on November 4, 1925.

SACRAMENTO & WOODLAND RAILROAD COMPANY

Incorporated July 20, 1911 - Electric - Standard Gauge

Located Sacramento, Sacramento County. Built to Woodland. Distance 16.73 miles. Construction work done between September 1911 and July 1912. Began operations July 4, 1912. Sold to the Sacramento Northern Railroad Company June 28, 1918.

SACRAMENTO & YOLO BELT LINE COMPANY

Incorporated May 1, 1910 - Steam or Electric - Standard Gauge

Located Sacramento, Sacramento County. Proposed to build a belt line railroad within the corporate limits of the city of Sacramento and in the county of Yolo.

SALINAS RAILWAY COMPANY

Organized 1897 - Steam - 3 ft. Gauge

Located Salinas, Monterey County. Built to Spreckels. Distance 5.00 miles. Abandoned in 1900.

SALMON CREEK RAILROAD

Organized 1883 - Steam - 3 ft. Gauge

Located Whitesboro, Mendocino County. Built from mill to timber on Salmon Creek. Distance 10.00 miles. Abandoned in 1894.

SALMON CREEK EXTENSION RAILROAD

Incorporated December 3, 1896 - Steam - Standard Gauge

Located Salmon Creek, Mendocino County. Built from mill to timber. Distance 7.00 miles. Some sections of the Salmon Creek Railroad were used. Abandoned in 1902 or 1903.

SALT LAKE & LOS ANGELES RAILROAD COMPANY

Incorporated June 11, 1888 - Steam - Standard Gauge

Located Los Angeles, Los Angeles County. Proposed to build from Rattlesnake Island (San Pedro) to Los Angeles and then up the Arroyo Seco to Pacoima Pass and San Gabriel Canyon and then east to the California state border. Surveys began September 29, 1887. Survey through Arroyo Seco completed in November 1887. Deeded to the Union Pacific Railroad Company February 29, 1888. Project abandoned in 1889.

SALT LAKE, NEVADA & CALIFORNIA RAILROAD

Organized 1889 - Steam - Standard Gauge

Located Salt Lake, Utah. Proposed to build to a point somewhere on the Pacific Coast. This project was under the control of the Wyoming, Salt Lake & California Railroad Company. Project abandoned in 1890.

SALT POINT RAILROAD

Built 1871 or 1872 - Horse Power - 5 ft. Gauge

Located Miller's Gulch, just north of Salt Point Landing, Sonoma County. Built a horse drawn, wooden rail tramway from lumber to mill. Ceased operations in 1877. Moved to Rockport on Cottoneva Creek, Mendocino County.

SAN ANTONIO & HOLT AVENUE RAILROAD COMPANY

Horsecar - 3 ft. 6 in. Gauge

Located Pomona, Los Angeles County. Operated a horsecar railway. Distance 2.23 miles.

SAN BERNARDINO, ARROWHEAD & WATERMAN RAILROAD COMPANY

Incorporated October 28, 1887 - Horsecar/Steam - 3 ft. 6 in. - Standard Gauge

Located San Bernardino, San Bernardino County. Obtained a franchise to build from 7th and "A" streets to Harlem Hot Springs in November 1887. Obtained a franchise for a horsecar line from 7th and "A" streets to downtown San Bernardino and the Santa Fe Depot. Constructed a steam powered road to Harlem Hot Springs. Began construction 12, 1888. Opened for traffic June 19, 1888. Horsecar line construction began in July 1888. Completed November 1888. Steam operation from Harlem Hot Springs to 3rd and "E" streets in San Bernardino began in January 1891. Horsecar line abandoned January 1894. Steam section sold to Kohn Brothers November 30, 1895. Began standard gauging the trackage November 13, 1902. Became San Bernardino & Highland Electric Railway Company April 4, 1903. Consolidated into the Pacific Electric Railway Company September 1, 1911.

SAN BERNARDINO & BEAR VALLEY RAILROAD

Organized April 1887 - Steam - 3 ft. 6 in. Gauge

Located San Bernardino, San Bernardino County. Proposed to build to Bear Valley north of San Bernardino. No construction work done.

SAN BERNARDINO CENTRAL RAILROAD COMPANY

Incorporated March 8, 1888 - Steam - Standard Gauge

Located San Bernardino, San Bernardino County. Proposed to build to Elsinore by way of Highgrove and Corona. Distance 27.00 miles. Surveys completed April 13, 1888. Right-of-way secured April 24, 1888. Project abandoned in 1889.

SAN BERNARDINO & EASTERN RAILWAY COMPANY

Incorporated August 11, 1890 - Steam - Standard Gauge

Located San Bernardino, San Bernardino County. Built from Highland Junction to Mentone. Distance 12.88 miles. Leased to the Southern California Railway in 1891. Became part of the Santa Fe Railway January 17, 1906.

SAN BERNARDINO & HIGHLAND ELECTRIC RAILWAY COMPANY

Incorporated February 18, 1903 - Electric - Standard Gauge

Located San Bernardino, San Bernardino County. Proposed to build to Highland and then to Redlands with branch lines in and about the streets of these cities. Distance 15.00 miles. Purchased the San Bernardino, Arrowhead & Waterman Railroad Company. Merged with the Redlands Street Railway Company and San Bernardino Valley Traction Company to form the San Bernardino Valley Traction Company June 6, 1903. Consolidated into the Pacific Electric Railway Company September 1, 1911.

SAN BERNARDINO INTERURBAN RAILWAY COMPANY

Incorporated November 30, 1906 - Electric - Standard Gauge

Located San Bernardino, San Bernardino County. Proposed to build 48.00 miles of electric railway in San Bernardino County. Purchased from the San Bernardino Valley Traction Company a franchise for a route from First and Main streets in Riverside to the county line by way of Colton Avenue. Construction work began in March 1909. Work completed in 1910. Distance 3.64 miles. Became part of the Riverside & Arlington Railway August 7, 1911. Sold to the Pacific Electric Railway Company September 1, 1911.

SAN BERNARDINO & LOS ANGELES RAILWAY COMPANY

Incorporated October 1892 - Steam - Standard Gauge

Located San Bernardino, San Bernardino County. Proposed to build to Los Angeles through Morengo Pass. Distance surveyed 75.00 miles. No construction work done and the project was abandoned in 1893.

SAN BERNARDINO & LOS ANGELES RAILWAY COMPANY

Incorporated November 22, 1886 - Steam - Standard Gauge

Located San Bernardino, San Bernardino County. Built to Mud Springs (San Dimas) to join the Los Angeles & San Gabriel Valley Railroad. Distance 40.10 miles. First train April 25, 1887. Merged into the California Central Railway Company May 31, 1887. Became part of the Southern California Railway November 7, 1889. Now part of the Santa Fe Railway Company.

SAN BERNARDINO MOUNTAIN ELECTRIC RAILROAD

Surveyed November 20, 1896 - Electric - Standard Gauge

Located Highland, San Bernardino County. Surveyed a route for an electric railway to Fregolda Park. Distance 13.50 miles. Project abandoned in 1898.

SAN BERNARDINO MOUNTAIN RAILROAD

Organized May 21, 1914 - Electric or Steam - Standard Gauge

Located Victorville, San Bernardino County. Proposed to build in a northwesterly direction from a point 1.50 miles north of Leon Station on the Santa Fe Railway to the San Bernardino Mountains. It would have crossed the Mojave Northern Railroad in the vicinity of Bell Mountain.

SAN BERNARDINO & REDLANDS RAILROAD COMPANY

Incorporated January 19, 1888 - Steam Motor - 3 ft. Gauge

Located San Bernardino, San Bernardino County. Originally known as the East San Bernardino Railroad. Built from 3rd Street between "E" and "F" streets in San Bernardino along the public highway, along Rialto Avenue eastward to Waterman Avenue, south on Waterman Avenue to Central Avenue then east to Tippecanoe Avenue and south on Tippecanoe Avenue crossing the Santa Ana River to San Bernardino Avenue. The road turned south off San Bernardino Avenue onto Mountain View to Cottonwood Road and then southeasterly to Motor Junction. Distance 7.246 miles. From Motor Junction to Orange Street, Redlands, by third rail on the Southern Pacific right-of-way. Distance 2.874 miles. Total distance 10.12 miles. Railroad completed May 17, 1888. Opened to service on June 4, 1888. Ownership passed to the Southern Pacific Company on June 17, 1891. Ceased operation except for a daily franchise run during November 1906. Application for abandonment of the line made February 15, 1915. Abandoned May 14, 1915.

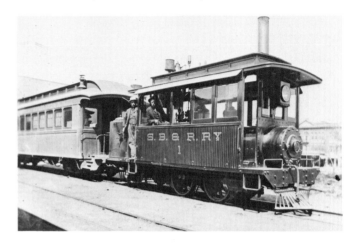

SAN BERNARDINO & REDLANDS RAILROAD - A motor road operating between San Bernardino and Redlands. Ownership passed to the Southern Pacific in 1891. *- Donald Duke Collection*

SAN BERNARDINO & SAN DIEGO RAILWAY COMPANY

Incorporated November 20, 1886 - Steam - Standard Gauge

Located Santa Ana, Orange County. Proposed to build from Santa Ana south to a junction with the California Southern Railroad Company north of Oceanside. Merged into the California Central Railway Company May 31, 1887. Extended from Santa Ana to San Juan Capistrano May 31, 1887. Extended to Fallbrook (Los Angeles Junction) August 12, 1888. Distance 49.50 miles. Became part of the Southern California Railway Company November 7, 1889. Now part of the Santa Fe Railway.

SAN BERNARDINO STREET RAILWAY

Organized April 3, 1875 - Horsecar - Narrow-Gauge

Located San Bernardino, San Bernardino County. Proposed to build a street railway from the nearest point on the Southern Pacific Company to the city. Distance 3.75 miles.

SAN BERNARDINO URBAN RAILWAY COMPANY

Incorporated January 1, 1907 - Electric - Standard Gauge

Located San Bernardino, San Bernardino County. Proposed to build to Rialto.

SAN BERNARDINO VALLEY RAILWAY COMPANY

Incorporated January 12, 1887 - Steam - Standard Gauge

Located San Bernardino, San Bernardino County. Proposed to build to Mentone. Merged into the California Central Railway Company May 31, 1887. The latter company built from San Bernardino to Mentone by way of Victoria, Gladysta and Redlands. Began operations December 31, 1887. Became part of the Southern California Railway Company on November 7, 1889. Became part of the Santa Fe Railway Company. Abandoned 1959.

SAN BERNARDINO VALLEY TRACTION COMPANY

Organized 1900 - Electric - 3 ft. 6 in. Gauge

Located San Bernardino, San Bernardino County. Merged with the Redlands Street Railway Company and the San Bernardino & Highlands Electric Railway Company July 5, 1903. Sold to the Pacific Electric Railway Company September 1, 1911.

SAN BERNARDINO VALLEY TRACTION COMPANY

Incorporated June 8, 1901 - Electric - Standard Gauge

Located San Bernardino, San Bernardino County. Built to Colton. Began construction December 1901. Completed March 1902. Began first electric streetcar operations in San Bernardino February 22, 1902. Began operations to Colton in April 1902. Line east on 7th Street to cemetery opened for service in April 1902. Line to Urbita Springs completed in 1902. Road completed to Orange and Cajon streets in Redlands March 16, 1903. Total mileage operated 13.806 miles. Merged with San Bernardino & Highland Electric Railway Company and Redlands Street Railway Company to form the San Bernardino Valley Traction Company on July 5, 1903. Sold to the Pacific Electric Railway Company on September 1, 1911.

SAN BERNARDINO VALLEY TRACTION COMPANY

Incorporated June 6, 1903 - Electric - Standard Gauge

Located San Bernardino, San Bernardino County. Resulted from the consolidation of the Redlands Street Railway Company, the San Bernardino & Highland Electric Railway Company and the San Bernardino Valley Traction Company. Mileage operated 28.729. Consolidated into the Pacific Electric Railway Company September 1, 1911.

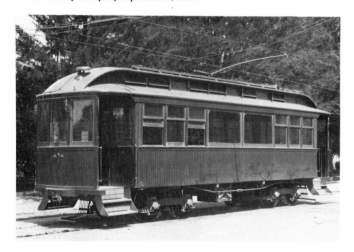

SAN BERNARDINO VALLEY TRACTION - An interurban line that built to Colton in 1902 and Redlands in 1903, operating with 13.8 miles of track. Sold to the Pacific Electric Railway in 1911. - *Donald Duke Collection*

SAN BUENAVENTURA & SOUTHERN PACIFIC RAILROAD COMPANY

Organized 1875 - Steam - Standard Gauge

Located San Buenaventura (now Ventura), Ventura County. Proposed to build through the Santa Clara Valley to a junction with the Southern Pacific Company near Lyon's Station.

SAN DIEGO & ARIZONA RAILWAY COMPANY
SAN DIEGO & ARIZONA EASTERN RAILWAY COMPANY

Incorporated December 15, 1906 - Steam - Standard Gauge

Located San Diego, San Diego County. Proposed to build to Yuma, Arizona. Took over the franchises and surveys of the San Diego Eastern Railway Com-

pany. Adopted a route through Baja California, Mexico and Carriso Gorge. Opened to Tijuana and Agua Caliente, Mexico, in 1910. El Centro in Imperial Valley to be the terminus. Took over the Southern Pacific Company tracks from El Centro to Seeley. Opened for service San Diego to Campo September 19, 1916. Distance 61.10 miles. Through passenger service from San Diego to El Centro began December 1, 1919. Distance 148.10 miles. Purchased the San Diego & South Eastern Railway Company November 1, 1917. Operation effective December 15, 1917, including the electric interurban line from San Diego to Chula Vista. The San Diego Electric Railway continued to operate this section. Electric operations abandoned to National City in 1925. All electric operations over all trackage discontinued January 1930. Partnership of the Spreckels interests and the Southern Pacific Company dissolved and reorganized by the Southern Pacific Company February 1, 1933. This reorganization resulted in the formation of the San Diego & Arizona Eastern Railway Company. Passenger service, San Diego to El Centro, discontinued January 11, 1951. Southern Pacific abandoned the line in 1977 except for 18.00 miles of track between Plaster City and El Centro. The line from San Diego to Tijuana taken over by the county of San Diego and is operated by the Metropolitan Transit System.

SAN DIEGO & ARIZONA RAILWAY - John D. Spreckels completed the impossible railroads from San Diego to El Centro and a connection with the Southern Pacific in 1919. In this view a SD&A train stands in the yard at San Diego. - *Donald Duke Collection*

SAN DIEGO & ARIZONA EASTERN RAILROAD COMPANY

Organized November 1979 - Diesel - Standard Guage

Located San Diego, San Diego County. The San Diego Metropolitan Transit board purchased the Southern Pacific's San Diego & Arizona Eastern Railway Company between San Diego and Plaster City, with a branch line to El Cajon from San Diego. A total distance of 145.7 miles. The San Diego Metropolitan Transit Board, not wishing to engage in freight service, contracted out the freight service to Kyle Railway with a ten-year contract to run from 1979 to 1989. Freight handling would be conducted at night between San Diego and Tijuana and San Diego to El Cajon so as not to interfere with passenger operations.

SAN DIEGO BAY SHORE RAILROAD COMPANY

Organized July 12, 1871 - Steam - Standard Gauge

Located San Diego, San Diego County. Organized to take over the franchise and lands of the San Diego & Gila, Southern Pacific & Atlantic Railroad Company in the transfer of this property to the Texas & Pacific Railway Company.

SAN DIEGO BAY TERMINAL RAILWAY COMPANY

Incorporated January 23, 1904 - Steam - Standard Gauge

Located San Diego, San Diego County. Proposed to build 5.00 miles of railway in the city of San Diego for terminal facilities. Project abandoned in 1904.

SAN DIEGO CABLE CAR & LAND COMPANY

Incorporated November 1, 1887 - Cable Car - Standard Gauge

Located San Diego, San Diego County. Purchased the exclusive rights for a cable car system similar to the Market Street lines in San Francisco. Formed the San Diego Cable Railway Rights Company January 4, 1888. Obtained franchises for cable car line on "E" Street, Third Avenue and Ninth Avenue in San Diego. No construction work was done.

SAN DIEGO CABLE RAILWAY COMPANY

Incorporated August 18, 1889 - Cable - 3 ft. 6 in. Gauge

Located San Diego, San Diego County. Was also known as the San Diego Cable Car Company and the San Diego Cable Tramway Company. Took over the franchise of the Electric Rapid Transit Company. Built a single track with turnouts from "L" Street on Sixth Avenue, "C" Street, Fourth Avenue, University Avenue, Normal Street and Park Blvd. to Adams Avenue, Mission Valley Bluffs. Distance 4.70 miles. Began operations June 7, 1890, on the downtown cable from the power house to Fourth Avenue and Spruce Street to "L" Street. Opened to the Bluffs in July 1890. Into receivership in 1892. Last run October 15, 1892. Assets sold to Citizen's Traction Company at a foreclosure sale March 11, 1896.

SAN DIEGO CENTRAL RAILROAD COMPANY

Incorporated November 5, 1886 - Steam - Standard Gauge

Located San Diego, San Diego County. Proposed to build through the "back country" of San Diego County. To build from the 22nd Street depot of the California Southern Railroad in San Diego by way of Chollas Valley, El Cajon, Poway, and Escondido to a junction with the California Southern Railroad south of Oceanside. Merged into the California Central Railway Company May 31, 1887. Construction done by the California Central Railway Company from Escondido Junction to Escondido. Opened for service December 31, 1887. Distance 21.30 miles. Some grading was done out of San Diego and a lead built to the San Diego Wharf. Deeded to the Southern California Railway November 7, 1889.

SAN DIEGO CABLE RAILWAY - The firm built a 4.7-mile single track line with turnouts in San Diego. Organized in 1889 and went into receivership in early 1892, making its last run during October 1892. Sold to Citizens Traction Co. at a foreclosure sale in 1896. - *Donald Duke Collection*

SAN DIEGO & COLORADO RIVER RAILROAD COMPANY

Organized 1880 - Steam - Standard Gauge

Located San Diego, San Diego County. Organized by E.W. Morse and the San Diego Railroad Commission to build a city-owned railroad to connect with the Atlantic & Pacific Railroad at Needles. No construction work done.

SAN DIEGO & CUYAMACA RAILWAY COMPANY

Incorporated September 10, 1887 - Steam - Narrow-Gauge

Located San Diego, San Diego County. Proposed to build to Cuyamaca Lake by way of El Cajon, Viegans with a loop by way of Julian. No construction work done. Superseded by the San Diego, Cuyamaca & Eastern Railway Company March 10, 1888.

SAN DIEGO & CUYAMACA RAILWAY COMPANY

Incorporated July 19, 1909 - Steam - Standard Gauge

Located San Diego, San Diego County. Successor to the San Diego, Cuyamaca

& Eastern Railway Company. Operated from San Diego to Foster. Distance 25.40 miles. Consolidated with the San Diego Southern Railway to form the San Diego & South Eastern Railway Company March 20, 1912. Sold to San Diego & Arizona Railway Company November 1, 1917.

SAN DIEGO, CUYAMACA & EASTERN RAILWAY COMPANY

Incorporated March 10, 1888 - Steam - Standard Gauge

Located San Diego, San Diego County. Result of the reorganization of the San Diego & Cuyamaca Railway. Built from the foot of Ninth Avenue in San Diego on Commercial Street through Mt. Hope Cemetery, El Cajon, to Lakewood. Began operations March 30, 1889. Extended to Foster February 13, 1890. Total 25.40 miles. Planned to extend by way of Warner's Ranch, San Felipe to a junction with the Southern Pacific Railroad Company main line in Imperial Valley between Frink and Dos Palmos with a branch to Julian. Operated a McKeen gasoline-mechanical drive motor car beginning in 1908. Reorganized as the San Diego & Cuyamaca Railway Company July 19, 1909.

SAN DIEGO, CUYAMACA & EASTERN RAILWAY - A short line railroad built from downtown San Diego to El Cajon and Lakewood. Was later extended to Foster as shown in this view in 1890. - *Donald Duke Collection*

SAN DIEGO & DEL MAR RAILROAD
SAN DIEGO & OCEAN RAILROAD COMPANY

Organized 1889 - Steam - Standard Gauge

Located San Diego, San Diego County. Franchise granted under the name of San Diego & Ocean Railroad. Construction was to be done under the name of San Diego & Del Mar Railroad. Final operating name San Diego & Del Mar Railroad. Merged into the San Diego & Eastern Terminal Railway Company February 1889.

SAN DIEGO & EASTERN TERMINAL RAILWAY COMPANY

Incorporated February 7, 1889 - Steam - Standard Gauge

Located San Diego, San Diego County. Proposed to build from Market (then "H" Street) in San Diego to Roseville, Ocean Beach, La Jolla to Del Mar, taking over the Del Mar & San Diego Railway Company and the Roseville & Ocean Beach Railroad Company. Laid some track on Atlantic Street, (now Pacific Coast Highway) in San Diego. Purchased some secondhand equipment. Grading completed to Roseville by June 1889. Taken over by the Los Angeles, San Diego & Yuma Railway Company April 23, 1889.

SAN DIEGO - EASTERN RAILWAY COMPANY

Organized 1901 - Steam - Standard Gauge

Located San Diego, San Diego County Organized by the San Diego Chamber of Commerce to build from San Diego to Imperial Valley and the Colorado River. Raised a fund and made surveys by way of Dulzura Pass. Acquired some right-of-way. Franchise and properties sold to the San Diego & Arizona Railway Company in 1906.

SAN DIEGO, EL CAJON & ESCONDIDO RAILWAY COMPANY

Organized September 30, 1909 - Electric - Standard Gauge

Located San Diego, San Diego County. Obtained franchises for an electric railway from San Diego through Balboa Park to Escondido by way of La Mesa, El Cajon, Lakeside and Poway. 40.00 miles of right-of-way were secured. Considerable grading was done from San Diego east.

SAN DIEGO & EL CAJON VALLEY INTERURBAN RAILWAY COMPANY

Incorporated February 6, 1909 - Electric - Standard Gauge

Located San Diego, San Diego County. Proposed to build through La Mesa Springs, El Cajon, Bostonia, Lakeside, Morton, San Pasqual, and Bernardo to Escondido. Distance 65.00 miles. Grading began January 1911. Completed to La Mesa September 9, 1911.

SAN DIEGO ELECTRIC RAILWAY COMPANY

Incorporated November 30, 1891 - Electric - Standard Gauge

Located San Diego, San Diego County. Acquired the assets of the San Diego Street Car Company which owned and operated a system of horsecar lines and the trackage of the City Park Belt Motor Road. Converted most horsecar lines to electric operations and laid additional trackage. Electric operations began September 21, 1892. Last horsecar ran June 1896. Acquired Citizen's Traction Company properties and converted the cable cars to electric operations March 23, 1898. Rebuilt the section from Fifth and University Avenue to Mission Cliff to standard gauge and abandoned the remainder. Took over the Orange Avenue electric line from the Coronado Railroad July 1, 1908. Purchased the South Park & East Side Railway Company road and equipment May 27, 1909. Operated the Point Loma Railroad and the San Diego & South Eastern Railway electric interurban service. Acquired the Point Loma Railroad and Bay Shore Railroad in 1922. Built lines to Ocean, Mission and La Jolla beaches in 1924. Sold to National City Lines March 1, 1948. Reorganized as San Diego Transit System September 9, 1948. Abandoned rail service April 23, 1949.

SAN DIEGO ELECTRIC RAILWAY - Formed in 1891 as an outgrowth of several street railways. In this view an array of single- and double-deck cars at Fifth and H streets in downtown San Diego in 1892. - *Frederick W. Reif Collection*

SAN DIEGO, EL PASO & ST. LOUIS RAILROAD

Organized February 1909 - Steam - Standard Gauge

Located El Paso, Texas. Proposed to build northeast through southeastern New Mexico to the Red River, and then westward to San Diego, California. Preliminary estimates of the first 180.00 miles began in July 1909. Surveys completed from El Paso, Texas, east by way of Hope, New Mexico, and Artesia then northeast to Vernon, Texas. Completed October 1909.

SAN DIEGO & ELSINORE RAILROAD COMPANY

Incorporated December 10, 1887 - Steam - Standard Gauge

Located San Diego, San Diego County. Proposed to build to Elsinore where a junction would be made with the Pomona & Elsinore Railroad. The route proposed was from San Diego to Elsinore by way of Old Town, Mission Valley, El Cajon, Ballena, Warner's Ranch and Oak Grove. No construction work was done.

SAN DIEGO, FORT YUMA & ATLANTIC RAILWAY COMPANY

Incorporated January 4, 1894 - Steam - Standard Gauge

Located San Diego, San Diego County. Proposed to build to a junction with the Southern Pacific Company at Fort Yuma, Arizona.

SAN DIEGO & GILA, SOUTHERN PACIFIC & ATLANTIC RAILROAD COMPANY

Organized November 1854 - Steam - Standard Gauge

Located San Diego, San Diego County. Proposed to build from San Diego Bay to Fort Yuma on the Colorado River by way of Mission Valley, Santa Ysabel and Warner's Ranch. Subsidies and franchises were donated to the company. The Civil War in 1861 ended all hopes of construction. Revived in 1868 to transfer the assets to the Memphis, El Paso & Pacific Railroad Company. Assets were transferred to the Texas & Pacific Railway Company including right-of-way and depot grounds in August 1872. The financial panic of 1873 prevented construction. One-half of the lands donated were recovered to be transferred as a subsidy to the California Southern Railroad Company, an Atchison, Topeka & Santa Fe Railroad subsidiary, in 1880. The other half of the property eventually became the property of the Southern Pacific Company.

SAN DIEGO & IMPERIAL VALLEY RAILROAD

Formed October 15, 1984 - Diesel - Standard Gauge

Located San Diego, San Diego County. Took over the operations of the San Diego & Arizona Eastern Railroad from the Kyle Railways, who were unsuccessful in their operation of the railroad from 1979 to 1984. Operations leased to RailTex of San Antonio, Texas, October 1984, and name changed to San Diego & Imperial Valley Railroad. The eastern terminus is Plaster City. Distance 128.90 miles. Distance now in operation 45.00 miles, including two sections: San Diego to Garcia, Mexico, and San Diego to El Cajon.

SAN DIEGO & IMPERIAL VALLEY RAILROAD

Organized 1989 - Diesel - Standard Gauge

Located San Diego, San Diego County. An organization formed by RailTex of San Antonio, Texas, to operate the former San Diego & Arizona Eastern Railroad, operated by Kyle Railways from 1979 to 1989. The line runs from San Diego to Plaster City, a distance of 130 miles, with a branch to El Cajon, a distance of 15.7 miles. The road handles only freight and operates at night over the El Cajon branch and line from San Diego to Tijuana. During the daylight hours these routes are used by the electrified San Diego Trolley system.

SAN DIEGO & INTERNATIONAL RAILROAD COMPANY

Organized 1887 - Steam - Standard Gauge

Located National City, San Diego County. Proposed to build south to Ensenada, Mexico, by way of the Tijuana River Valley. A subsidiary of the International Development Company. Superseded by the Peninsular Railroad Company in September 1887.

SAN DIEGO & LOS ANGELES RAILROAD COMPANY

Incorporated February 1870 - Steam - Standard Gauge

Located San Diego, San Diego County. Surveyed a route from Old Town in San Diego to Los Angeles in 1872. No construction work done.

SAN DIEGO METROPOLITAN TRANSIT DEVELOPMENT BOARD
SAN DIEGO METROPOLITAN TRANSIT DISTRICT

Study began 1976 - Electric - Standard Gauge

Located San Diego, San Diego County. Purchased from the Southern Pacific Company the 108 miles of right-of-way of the San Diego & Arizona Eastern Railway in 1976. Electrified 15.90 miles of track from San Diego to San Ysidro, on the Mexican border. Began operations July 26, 1981. Became the Metropolitan Transit System. Took over the San Diego & Arizona Eastern line to El Cajon and electrified it. The El Cajon line began operation in 1986. At this writing, a line from the Santa Fe station in downtown San Diego north to Old Town is in various stages of construction.

SAN DIEGO & MISSION VALLEY RAILWAY COMPANY

Organized November 1887 - Steam - Standard Gauge

Located San Diego, San Diego County. Proposed to build from Old Town in San Diego, up Mission Valley to Grantville with a branch up Murphy Canyon to the mesa (Kearny). No construction work done.

SAN DIEGO & NORTHEASTERN RAILWAY

Incorporated May 1889 - Steam - Standard Gauge

Located San Diego, San Diego County. Proposed to build to Escondido. No construction work done. Project abandoned in 1890.

SAN DIEGO & OLD TOWN RAILROAD COMPANY

Organized August 1886 - Electric - Standard Gauge

Located San Diego, San Diego County. Built to Old Town Plaza. Authorized the Electric Rapid Transit Street Car Company to install overhead wire and operate electric motors under the Henry System. Track was constructed from Broadway in San Diego out Kettner Blvd., then Artic Street to Old Town. Distance 3.00 miles. Opened with a steam dummy October 9, 1887. Electric motors started service November 19, 1887. Motors and overhead wires removed in December 1887. Steam service temporarily discontinued in January 1888. Combined with the San Diego & Pacific Beach Railway Company to form the San Diego, Old Town & Pacific Beach Railway Company April 21, 1888.

SAN DIEGO, OLD TOWN & PACIFIC BEACH RAILWAY COMPANY

Incorporated April 21, 1888 - Steam - Standard Gauge

Located San Diego, San Diego County. Took over the trackage of the San Diego & Old Town Street Railroad Company and the San Diego & Pacific Beach Railway Company operations from Morena to Pacific Beach. Closed the gap between Old Town and Morena, crossing the California Southern Railway tracks and bridging the San Diego River. Through train service from San Diego to Pacific Beach began April 26, 1888. Track extended to Ocean Front, later Braemar, in 1889. Total mileage 9.20 miles. Consolidated with the San Diego, Pacific Beach & La Jolla Railway Company to form the Los Angeles & San Diego Beach Railway Company April 1, 1906.

SAN DIEGO & PACIFIC BEACH RAILWAY - A steam dummy railroad built from Morena Station on the California Southern to Pacific Beach. - *Donald Duke Collection*

SAN DIEGO, PACIFIC & EASTERN RAILROAD COMPANY

Organized January 1895 - Steam - Standard Gauge

Located San Diego, San Diego County. Proposed to build from San Diego by way of Old Town, and also from San Diego northeasterly to a junction point and then to the El Cajon Valley, Santa Maria Valley, presumably via Warner's Pass to San Felipe Grant, with a branch to Poway and Escondido. Extensions

were to be made year by year to connections with Southern Pacific, Atlantic & Pacific, Santa Fe, Denver & Rio Grande, Union Pacific and others. No bonds. It was to be financed by railroad men investing a small portion of their monthly pay. Endorsed by Eugene V. Debs and the Brotherhood of Locomotive Engineers. No construction done.

SAN DIEGO, PACIFIC BEACH & LA JOLLA RAILWAY COMPANY

Incorporated April 3, 1889 - Steam - Standard Gauge

Located La Jolla, San Diego County. Built from Ocean Front, the terminus of the San Diego, Old Town & Pacific Beach Railway Company to La Jolla. Distance 4.50 miles. Operated the San Diego, Old Town & Pacific Beach Railway using steam motors. Formal opening to La Jolla May 15, 1894. Lacking a franchise, track was extended to Prospect Street in La Jolla, a distance of 1,400 feet, in one night. Both railways were merged into the Los Angeles & San Diego Beach Railway Company April 1, 1906.

SAN DIEGO, PACIFIC BEACH & LA JOLLA RAILWAY - Built from the end of track of the San Diego, Old Town & Pacific Beach Railway line to La Jolla in 1894. This view shows one of the electric cars at the J.G. Brill plant in Philadelphia. - *Donald Duke Collection*

SAN DIEGO & PACIFIC BEACH RAILWAY COMPANY

Organized August 1887 - Steam Dummy - Standard Gauge

Located Morena, San Diego County. Proposed to extend the Electric Rapid Transit Street Car Company tracks to Pacific Beach. Distance 4.5 miles. Plans disrupted by the removal of the electrical equipment from the San Diego & Old Town Railway in December 1887. Built trackage from Morena Station on the California Southern Railroad to Pacific Beach. Service with a steam dummy began January 20, 1888. Merged the San Diego & Old Town Street Railroad Company with the San Diego, Old Town & Pacific Beach Railway to form the San Diego & Pacific Beach Railway Company on April 21, 1888.

SAN DIEGO & PHOENIX RAILROAD COMPANY

Incorporated April 13, 1893 - Steam - Standard Gauge

Located Otay Valley, San Diego County. Proposed to construct a railroad from the end of the water pumping plant spur of the Coronado Railroad in Otay Valley, up the Valley, over Otay Mesa to cross the international boundary 6.00 miles east of Tijuana, then across Baja California, Mexico, reentering the United States at Yuma and then on to Phoenix. Some grading was done in the Otay Valley and a mile or so of track was laid by June 1893. Project abandoned in 1894.

SAN DIEGO, PHOENIX & GALVESTON RAILROAD COMPANY

Incorporated 1890 - Steam - Standard Gauge

Located San Diego, San Diego County. Proposed to build from San Diego Bay to the eastern boundary of California at the Colorado River and then on to Yuma, Arizona.

SAN DIEGO, RIVERSIDE & LOS ANGELES RAILWAY COMPANY

Incorporated March 7, 1912 - Electric - Standard Gauge

Located San Diego, San Diego County. Acquired the right-of-way and franchise of the San Diego, El Cajon & Escondido Railway. Proposed to build from San Diego to Los Angeles by way of Escondido and Riverside. Application for a charter made March 7, 1912. Work on roadbed began January 3, 1913.

SAN DIEGO & SAN BERNARDINO RAILROAD COMPANY

Incorporated November 15, 1871 - Steam - Standard Gauge

Located San Diego, San Diego County. Proposed to build from Middletown in San Diego to San Bernardino by way of Mission Valley, the Mormon line from Salt Lake City. Expected to connect with the extension of the Utah Southern Railroad. About 5.00 miles of grading was done in San Diego.

SAN DIEGO & SOUTH EASTERN RAILWAY COMPANY

Chartered March 2, 1912 - Electric - Standard Gauge

Located San Diego, San Diego County. Organized to merge the San Diego & Cuyamaca Railway Company and the San Diego Southern Railway Company, including the electric division of the latter operated from San Diego to Otay, into one company. Sustained heavy damage in the floods of January 1916. Most of the original National City and Otay track was abandoned. The electric division was transferred to former Coronado Railroad track between National City and Chula Vista and a new connecting track was laid. An agreement provided for the San Diego Electric Railway Company to operate the interurban line, which was cut back to Chula Vista. Sold to the San Diego & Arizona Railway Company November 1, 1917.

SAN DIEGO SOUTHERN RAILWAY - Proposed to build from San Diego to Ensenada, Baja, California. Took over the National City & Otay and the steam division of the Coronado Railroad. This scene shows a train pulling alongside the San Diego Gas & Electric power plant. - *Donald Duke Collection*

SAN DIEGO & SOUTH EASTERN RAILWAY - An interurban line that ran from downtown San Diego to National City, Chula Vista and the Mexican border. Became a part of the San Diego & Arizona Railway in 1917. - *Donald Duke Collection*

SAN DIEGO SOUTHERN RAILWAY COMPANY

Organized January 1908 - Steam - Electric - Standard Gauge

Located San Diego, San Diego County. Chartered February 2, 1908. Proposed to build from San Diego to Ensenada, Baja California, Mexico. Also to build to Coronado, Sweetwater Valley, La Presa, Jamacha Valley and Lakeside. Took over the National City & Otay Railway Company, including the electric interurban railway from San Diego to National City, Chula Vista and Otay and its steam division from San Diego to Tijuana, La Presa and Sweetwater Dam, also the steam division of the Coronado Railroad Company Belt Line, July 1, 1908. Consolidated with the San Diego & Cuyamaca Railway Company to form the San Diego & South Eastern Railway Company March 20, 1912. Sold to the San Diego & Arizona Railway Company November 1, 1917.

SAN DIEGO & SOUTHERN UTAH RAILROAD

Incorporated 1875 or 1876 - Steam - Standard Gauge

Located San Diego, San Diego County. Proposed to build northward to a junction with the Los Angeles & Independence Railway and then on across Southern Nevada to join the Utah Southern Railroad.

SAN DIEGO STREET CAR COMPANY

Incorporated April 22, 1886 - Horsecar - Standard Gauge

Located San Diego, San Diego County. Began horsecar street railway operations

on Fifth Avenue July 3, 1886. Built and operated other lines for a total of 8.50 miles. Operated coordinated service with the City Park Belt Motor Road. Obtained a franchise for a steam motor road on "N" Street (now Commercial Street) for the San Diego end of the Coronado Railroad's belt line. Forced into receivership and was sold to the San Diego Electric Railway Company January 30, 1892.

SAN DIEGO STREET RAILROAD COMPANY

Organized 1880

Located San Diego, San Diego County. Some work was done on this road from the west boundary of National Ranch to Old Town, Roseville and La Playa in December 1880. Not completed.

SAN DIEGO TRANSIT SYSTEM

Organized March 1, 1948 - Electric - Standard Gauge

Located San Diego, San Diego County. Purchased the San Diego Electric Railway Company March 1, 1948. Retained the original name until reorganization as the San Diego Transit System September 9, 1948. All remaining streetcar lines were changed over to bus operations. Last rail runs were made April 24, 1949.

SAN DIEGO UNION DEPOT & TERMINAL RAILWAY COMPANY

Organized April 20, 1888 - Steam - Standard Gauge

Located San Diego, San Diego County. Surveyed for a double-track road from La Playa on Point Loma, toward Roseville to Middletown in San Diego. Proposed to establish a Union Depot at the foot of Fifth Avenue in San Diego. No construction work was done.

SAN DIEGO UNION RAILWAY & SHIP TERMINAL COMPANY

Incorporated December 1903 - Electric - Standard Gauge

Located San Diego, San Diego County. Acquired 23 acres of waterfront on San Diego Bay to build a union depot and steamship wharf. This company also had an interest in the proposed San Diego to Phoenix, Arizona, line. No construction work was done.

SAN DIEGO & UTAH SOUTHERN RAILROAD COMPANY

Incorporated May 1876 - Steam - Standard Gauge

Located San Diego, San Diego County. A reorganization of the San Diego & Southern Utah Railroad. Proposed to build from San Diego to San Bernardino and then westward to the head of navigation of the Colorado River at Callville, Arizona, where a connection with the Utah Southern Extension Railroad was to be made.

SAN DIEGO & YUMA RAILROAD

Incorporated June 1893 - Steam - Standard Gauge

Located San Diego, San Diego County. Name given to an extension of the Coronado Railroad. Grading began June 18, 1893.

SAN DIEGO, YUMA & PHOENIX RAILWAY COMPANY

Surveyed June 2, 1893 - Steam - Standard Gauge

Located Phoenix, Arizona. Surveyed the right-of-way from Phoenix to San Diego by way of Yuma.

SAN FERNANDO VALLEY RAILROAD COMPANY

Standard Gauge

Located San Fernando Valley, Los Angeles County. This was a Southern Pacific Company project to be built in the San Fernando Valley. It was not incorporated and was abandoned.

SAN FRANCISCO & ALAMEDA RAILROAD COMPANY

Incorporated March 25, 1863 - Steam - Standard Gauge

Located Alameda, Alameda County. Built from High Street (Melrose Station) in Alameda to the Old Alameda Point (now the Naval Air Station). Provided ferry service to Davis Street in San Francisco. Began service August 25, 1864. Consolidated with the San Francisco & Alameda Railroad Company October 15, 1864. This consolidation consisted of the first San Francisco & Alameda Railroad Company and the San Francisco, Alameda & Stockton Railroad. Consolidated with the San Francisco & Oakland Railroad Company to form the San Francisco, Oakland & Alameda Railroad Company June 29, 1870. Deeded to the Central Pacific Railroad August 22, 1870. Now part of the Southern Pacific Company East Bay trackage.

SAN FRANCISCO, ALAMEDA & STOCKTON RAILROAD COMPANY

Incorporated December 8, 1863 - Steam - Standard Gauge

Located Alameda, Alameda County. Proposed to build to Hayward. Distance 11.50 miles. Graded 6.50 miles of roadbed. Consolidated with the San Francisco & Alameda Railroad Company October 15, 1864. Completed from Lincoln Junction to Hayward August 24, 1865. Abandoned 1869.

SAN FRANCISCO & ATLANTIC RAILROAD COMPANY

Incorporated June 19, 1892 - Steam - Standard Gauge

Located San Francisco, San Francisco County. Proposed to build through Alameda, Contra Costa, San Joaquin, Stanislaus, Merced, Fresno, Tulare, Kern and Los Angeles counties. Estimated trackage to be built was 500 miles. The route from Oakdale to Stockton was to be along the east side of the San Joaquin Valley. The surveys of the Stockton, Fresno & Southern Railroad were acquired.

SAN FRANCISCO BAY RAILROAD COMPANY

Incorporated September 25, 1868 - Steam - Standard Gauge

Located Niles, Alameda County. Built to East Oakland. Distance 22.50 miles. Began construction June 1869. Completed October 1869. Consolidated into the Western Pacific Railroad Company November 2, 1869. Consolidated with the Central Pacific Railroad of California June 23, 1870.

SAN FRANCISCO BAY AREA RAPID TRANSIT DISTRICT

Created July 25, 1951 - Electric - 5 ft. 6 in. Gauge

Located San Francisco, San Francisco County. Created by the California Legislature with a nine county Commission to study long-range transit problems. Approved by voters of three counties November 6, 1962. Right-of-way acquisition began November 27, 1963. First rail laid on Diablo test track January 19, 1965. First test run made July 12, 1965. First passenger run September 11, 1972, Oakland to Fremont.

SAN FRANCISCO & BAY COUNTIES RAILWAY COMPANY

Incorporated February 2, 1908 - Electric - Standard Gauge

Located Oakland, Alameda County. Merged with the San Francisco, Oakland & San Jose Railway February 23, 1908, to form the San Francisco, Oakland & San Jose Consolidated Railway. Became part of the East Shore & Suburban Railway Company December 16, 1904.

SAN FRANCISCO BELT RAILROAD

Incorporated June 1892 - Steam - Standard Gauge

Located San Francisco, San Francisco County Built a belt railroad and union depot in San Francisco. Connected the north end of Powell Street with the Southern Pacific Company freight wharves at the foot of Second and the depot at Third and Townsend streets. Became the State Belt Railroad of California.

SAN FRANCISCO BRIDGE COMPANY

Organized 1892 - Steam - Standard Gauge

Located Oakland, Alameda County. Owned by the Atlantic, Gulf & Pacific Company. Built to haul dirt from the tideland canal that made Alameda an island, linking the Estuary with San Leandro Bay.

SAN FRANCISCO & BUENOS AIRES RAILROAD COMPANY

Organized 1876 - Steam - Standard Gauge

Located San Francisco, San Francisco County. Proposed to build through Southern California, Mexico, the Central American states and South America, to Valparaiso or Concepcion, and on to Buenos Aires. The main line would pass through Fort Yuma on the Colorado River, through Sonora and Sinoloa to Mazatlan, then to Tehuantepec. From Tehuantepec the line would pass through the states of Guatemala, San Salvador, Honduras and Costa Rica, over the Cordilleras to Panama, from Panama to Lima, to Valparaiso or Concepcion, and then by the Cumbre or Antuco Pass across the Andes to Buenos Aires. Distance 7,200 miles by way of Concepcion, 6,940 miles by way of Valparaiso. Estimated cost $578,250,000.

SAN FRANCISCO & CLEAR LAKE RAILWAY COMPANY

Incorporated September 1892 - Steam - Standard Gauge

Located San Francisco, San Francisco County. Proposed to build northward through Napa and Lake counties to Clear Lake. Distance 90.00 miles. No construction work done.

SAN FRANCISCO & CLEAR LAKE RAILROAD

Organized September 7, 1900 - Steam - Standard Gauge

Located Clear Lake, Lake County. Proposed to build from Lower Lake, at the south end of Clear Lake, to Vallejo on San Pablo Bay by way of Sonoma Valley, Tobe and Napa. Steamers to operate from San Pablo Bay to San Francisco. Distance 86.00 miles. No construction work done.

SAN FRANCISCO, CLEAR LAKE & HUMBOLDT RAILROAD

Organized 1887 - Steam - Standard Gauge

Located Napa, Napa County. Proposed to build to Clear Lake. Distance 73.00 miles. Project abandoned same year after grading 17.00 miles of roadbed.

SAN FRANCISCO & CLEAR LAKE NARROW-GAUGE RAILROAD COMPANY

Organized 1883 - Steam - 3 ft. Gauge

Located Clear Lake, Lake County. Built from Soda Creek to Millikin Creek in 1883.

SAN FRANCISCO & COLORADO RAILWAY

Organized 1908 - Steam - Standard Gauge

Located San Francisco, San Francisco County. Proposed to build from San Francisco to the Colorado River by way of Hollister. Project abandoned in 1910.

SAN FRANCISCO & COLORADO RIVER RAILROAD COMPANY

Incorporated January 16, 1883 - Steam - 3 ft. Gauge

Located Alameda, Alameda County. Proposed to build from San Antonio Creek to the Colorado River at the 35th parallel. It was proposed to cross the Colorado River below Needles. Built from the Alameda Mole to Alameda Junction, a distance of 2.60 miles. Began operations March 15, 1884. Consolidated into the South Pacific Coast Railway on May 23, 1887.

SAN FRANCISCO & DENVER RAILROAD COMPANY

Incorporated August 5, 1892 - Steam - Standard Gauge

Located San Francisco, San Francisco County. Proposed to build from a point on San Francisco Bay in Alameda County in a general easterly and southerly direction to the state line between California and Nevada. Distance to be about 300 miles. No construction work was done.

SAN FRANCISCO & EASTERN RAILROAD

Chartered December 18, 1891 - Steam - Standard Gauge

Located San Francisco, San Francisco County. Proposed to build from Alameda Bay south through Hanford and Tejon Pass to Rogers in Kern County. Distance 380 miles. A branch was to be built from Hanford to Indian Wells in Kern County. Distance 100.00 miles. Project abandoned in 1892.

SAN FRANCISCO ELECTRIC RAILWAYS

Incorporated February 17, 1909 - Electric - Standard Gauge

Located San Francisco, San Francisco County. Acquired the Parkside Transit Company and the projected Visitation Valley Line. Leased to the United Railroads of San Francisco in 1910. Always operated as part of the United Railroads of San Francisco.

SAN FRANCISCO & EUREKA RAILWAY

Incorporated March 15, 1903 - Steam - Standard Gauge

Located Willits, Mendocino County. Incorporated to build the California Northwestern Railroad from Willits to Eureka. Proposed to build to Eureka, a distance of 200 miles. Survey was made from Willits through the main canyon of the Eel River. 100 ft. of track was constructed to comply with the law. Surveys extended from Eureka to Crescent City and to Grants Pass, Oregon. Deeded to the Northwestern Pacific Railway Company October 15, 1907. Became part of the Northwestern Pacific Railroad January 8, 1907.

SAN FRANCISCO & EUREKA RAILWAY COMPANY

Incorporated July 5, 1902 - Steam - Standard Gauge

Located Eureka, Humboldt County. Proposed to build to Dyerville by way of Alton and Route Creek. Distance 70 miles. No work done.

SAN FRANCISCO & GREAT EASTERN RAILROAD

Incorporated June 12, 1906 - Steam - Standard Gauge

Located Marysville, Yuba County. Proposed to build to Downieville. Distance 60.00 miles. Project abandoned.

SAN FRANCISCO & GREAT SALT LAKE RAILROAD COMPANY

Incorporated May 23, 1892 - Steam - Standard Gauge

Located San Francisco, San Francisco County. Charter granted to build a railroad to the California state line by way of Oroville and Beckwourth Pass. Distance to be about 230.00 miles. Survey from San Francisco to Stockton completed July 29, 1892. Survey to Oroville completed October 28, 1892. Project abandoned in 1894.

SAN FRANCISCO & HUMBOLDT BAY RAILROAD COMPANY

Organized March 2, 1868 - Steam - 3 ft. Gauge

Located Petaluma, Sonoma County. Took over the plans of the Sonoma County Railroad to build to Healdsburg by way of Santa Rosa. Completed 10.00 miles

of trackage by October 10, 1869. Conveyed to the San Francisco & North Pacific Railroad November 17, 1869. Consolidated with the Northwestern Pacific Railroad January 7, 1907.

SAN FRANCISCO, IDAHO & MONTANA RAILWAY

Organized January 2, 1905 - Steam or Electric - Standard Gauge

Located Boise, Idaho. Proposed to build from San Francisco to Butte, Montana, by way of Marysville, Oroville, Fredonyer Pass and Susanville in California; Old Camp, McGarry, Mason and Winnemucca in Nevada; and then by way of Caldwell, Boise, Salmon City from the Jordan Valley in Idaho to Butte, Montana. Distance 923.00 miles. Surveys completed by October 1906. Project abandoned in 1908.

SAN FRANCISCO & LAKE COUNTY RAILROAD COMPANY

Incorporated June 1886 - Steam - Standard Gauge

Located Rutherford, Napa County. Proposed to build northerly through Napa and Lake counties to some convenient point on Clear Lake and then to the northern boundary of Lake County. Distance 109.00 miles.

SAN FRANCISCO & LOS ANGELES AIRLINE RAILROAD

Incorporated February 1908 - Steam - Standard Gauge

Located San Francisco, San Francisco County. Proposed to build a direct railroad to Los Angeles that would be 80 miles shorter than any existing railroad.

SAN FRANCISCO MARGINAL RAILROAD

Organized November 29, 1890

Located San Francisco, San Francisco County. Proposed to build a marginal road along the waterfront in San Francisco from Lombard Street to Pacific Street and then to Powell Street.

SAN FRANCISCO MARKET STREET RAILROAD

Organized in 1859 - Steam Dummy - 5 ft. 6 in. Gauge

Located San Francisco, San Francisco County. Built to Mission Dolores from Third and Kearny streets along Market Street and Valencia Street. A branch was extended to Hayes Valley. Sold in 1866 to the San Francisco & San Jose Railroad. Converted to standard gauge in 1866.

SAN FRANCISCO & MARYSVILLE RAILROAD COMPANY

Incorporated November 9, 1857 - Steam - Standard Gauge

Located Marysville, Yuba County. Acquired the surveys and title of the Marysville & Benicia Railroad that had been organized to build to Benicia or any point on the Sacramento River at or near Knights Ferry. Some construction work was done in 1859. Sold to the California Pacific Railway January 10, 1865. Became part of the Southern Pacific Company April 14, 1898.

SAN FRANCISCO & NAPA RAILWAY COMPANY

Incorporated November 27, 1903 - Steam - Standard Gauge

Located Wingo, Sonoma County. Proposed to build from San Francisco to Napa by way of San Rafael. 50.00 miles of roadbed were surveyed and considerable grading was done by March 1905. Actual construction was in two separate sections that made up 10.70 miles of operating railroad: Wingo to Ramal, distance 2.08 miles, Bunchli to Union, distance 8.62 miles. Completed in 1905. Operated by the California & Northwestern Railroad. Operations later taken over by the Northwestern Pacific Railroad under trackage rights until July 19, 1906. Sold to the Southern Pacific Company August 12, 1911. Entire trackage abandoned in 1936 and 1939.

SAN FRANCISCO, NAPA & CALISTOGA RAILWAY COMPANY

Incorporated November 10, 1911 - Electric - Standard Gauge

Located San Francisco, San Francisco County. Organized to purchase the San Francisco, Vallejo & Napa Valley Railroad. Operated from San Francisco to Vallejo ferry, from ferry to Calistoga. Distance 71.60 miles. Reorganized as the

San Francisco & Napa Valley Railroad Company September 3, 1935. Abandoned 1956.

SAN FRANCISCO & NAPA VALLEY RAILROAD COMPANY

Incorporated September 3, 1935 - Electric - Standard Gauge

Located San Francisco, San Francisco County. Incorporated as a successor in reorganization of the San Francisco, Napa & Calistoga Railway Company. Diesel operation began in 1942. The Mare Island Freight Line in Solano County was sold to the United States Navy August 14, 1956. The trackage in Napa County between county line and Napa Junction was abandoned in 1956. Corporation dissolved September 15, 1957.

SAN FRANCISCO & NORTH PACIFIC RAIL ROAD COMPANY
SAN FRANCISCO & NORTH PACIFIC RAILROAD COMPANY
SAN FRANCISCO & NORTH PACIFIC RAILWAY COMPANY

Incorporated November 17, 1869 - Steam - 3 ft. and Standard Gauge

Located Petaluma, Sonoma County. The San Francisco & North Pacific Rail Road Company took over the properties of the Sonoma County Railroad and the San Francisco & Humboldt Bay Rail Road Company. Built 10.00 miles of track northward from Petaluma. Completed from Donahue Landing to Santa Rosa January 1, 1870. Consolidated with the Sonoma & Marin Railroad and the Fulton & Guerneville Railroad to form the San Francisco & North Pacific Railroad Company July 12, 1877. Consolidated with the Cloverdale & Ukiah Railroad, the San Francisco & San Rafael Railroad and the Marin & Napa Railroad to form the San Francisco & North Pacific Railway Company. All narrow-gauge trackage was standard gauged by April 9, 1890. Main line ran from Tiburon to Ukiah. All properties leased to the California Northwestern Railroad March 17, 1899. Consolidated into the Northwestern Pacific Railroad January 8, 1907.

SAN FRANCISCO & NORTHERN RAILROAD COMPANY

Incorporated April 9, 1880 - Steam

Located San Rafael, Marin County. Incorporated to consolidate the holdings of the North Pacific Coast Railroad Company and the San Rafael & San Quentin Railroad.

SAN FRANCISCO NORTHERN RAILWAY
SAN FRANCISCO & NORTHERN RAILWAY COMPANY

Incorporated February 5, 1912 - Electric - Standard Gauge

Located Santa Rosa, Sonoma County. Proposed to build southward to Pt. San Quentin. Distance 42.00 miles. The San Francisco & Northern Railway Company was a reorganization of the original company March 21, 1914, to take over the franchise of the San Francisco Northern and to build a road to succeed the Petaluma & Santa Rosa Railroad and to build an electric railway which would afford a direct service between Petaluma and Healdsburg with a steamer connection at Petaluma for San Francisco.

SAN FRANCISCO & NORTHWESTERN RAILROAD COMPANY

Organized May 9, 1903 - Steam - Standard Gauge

Located Eureka, Humboldt County. Organized by the Santa Fe. Purchased the properties of the Eel River & Eureka Railroad Company from Arcata to Shively. Purchased the California Midland Railroad Company July 7, 1903, and the California & Northern Railway Company March 22, 1904. Purchased some trackage from the Pacific Lumber Company Railroad through Scotia. All properties were leased to the Northwestern Pacific Railroad January 8, 1907.

SAN FRANCISCO, OAKLAND & ALAMEDA RAILROAD COMPANY

Incorporated June 29, 1870 - Steam - Standard Gauge

Located Oakland, Alameda County. Resulted from a consolidation of the San Francisco & Oakland Railroad Company and the San Francisco & Alameda Railroad Company. Operated over trackage from Oakland Wharf to East Oakland and Alameda by way of Melrose and San Leandro to Hayward. Distance 20.50 miles. Consolidated with Central Pacific Railroad August 22, 1870.

SAN FRANCISCO & OAKLAND RAILROAD COMPANY

Incorporated October 21, 1861 - Steam - Standard Gauge

Located Oakland, Alameda County. Built a steam transit line from Broadway down 7th Street to the Oakland Mole. Began construction August 2, 1862. Track extended to LaRue's Wharf and San Antonio (now Brooklyn) by 1865. Began operations September 2, 1863. Consolidated with San Francisco & Alameda Railroad Company to form San Francisco, Oakland & Alameda Railroad Company. Purchased San Antonio Steam Navigation Company operating from the Oakland Wharf to San Francisco in March 1865. Consolidated with the Central Pacific Railroad August 23, 1870.

SAN FRANCISCO, OAKLAND & OTTAWA RAILROAD COMPANY

Organized 1885 - Steam - Standard Gauge

Located San Francisco, San Francisco County. A company proposed by the Central Pacific Railroad.

SAN FRANCISCO, OAKLAND & SAN JOSE RAILWAY COMPANY

Organized June 12, 1902 - Electric - Standard Gauge

Located San Francisco, San Francisco County. Resulted from a consolidation of the Oakland & San Jose Railway and the San Francisco & Piedmont Railway. The original incorporation of the Oakland & San Jose Railway provided for a line between Oakland and San Jose. Distance 50.00 miles. Branches were to be built to Los Gatos, distance 15.00 miles, to Saratoga, distance 15.00 miles and a branch north to Santa Clara, distance 3.00 miles. A total of 83.00 miles to be built. The San Francisco & Piedmont Railway was incorporated to run an opposition ferry system between Oakland and San Francisco, including an electric tunnel railroad, with its terminus near Goat Island in San Francisco Bay. Distance 17.00 miles. The San Francisco, Oakland & San Jose Railway Company merged with the San Francisco & Bay Counties Railway to form the San Francisco, Oakland & San Jose Consolidated Railway Company in 1903.

SAN FRANCISCO-OAKLAND TERMINAL RAILWAYS

Incorporated March 12, 1912 - Electric - Standard Gauge

Located San Francisco, San Francisco County. Resulted from a consolidation of the San Francisco, Oakland & San Jose Consolidated Railway, the East Shore & Suburban Railway Company, the Oakland Traction Company, and the California Railway. This was the first company to use the term "Key System", which was applied to its ferry and electric operations. The train and ferry service was referred to as the "Key Division." The streetcar lines were referred to as the "Traction Division." Abandoned in December 1920.

SAN FRANCISCO & OCEAN SHORE RAILROAD COMPANY

Organized 1884 - Steam - Standard Gauge

Located San Francisco, San Francisco County. Proposed to build south along the Pacific Coast to Santa Cruz and then eastward to Denver, Colorado. This was the name of the holding company that purchased the right-of-way for the United States Central Railroad.

SAN FRANCISCO PENINSULA RAILWAY

Organized December 1913 - Electric - Standard Gauge

Located San Francisco, San Francisco County. Proposed to build to Monterey by way of Watsonville. Distance 100.00 miles. Made application for a charter in January 1914. Project abandoned July 1914.

SAN FRANCISCO & PIEDMONT RAILWAY COMPANY

Incorporated January 10, 1902 - Electric - Steam -Standard Gauge

Located Oakland, Alameda County. Organized to build a tunnel under San Francisco Bay to Goat Island. The road was to begin at a point near the Island of Yerba Buena. Actual construction resulted in a railroad to connect Oakland, Piedmont and Leona Heights. Deeded to the San Francisco, Oakland & San Jose Railway Company in 1902.

SAN FRANCISCO RAILROAD COMPANY

Incorporated July 29, 1904 - Electric - Standard Gauge

Located San Francisco, San Francisco County. Proposed to build a street railroad from the foot of Market Street to Ocean Beach. Distance 10.00 miles.

SAN FRANCISCO RAILWAY & FERRY COMPANY

Incorporated August 14, 1902 - Electric - Standard Gauge

Located Oakland, Alameda County. Proposed to build through Alameda, Berkeley, Hayward and San Leandro to San Jose. Distance 145.00 miles. No construction work done.

SAN FRANCISCO - SACRAMENTO RAILROAD COMPANY

Incorporation January 2, 1920 - Electric - Standard Gauge

Located San Francisco, San Francisco County. Built to Sacramento. Distance 93.10 miles. Acquired the Oakland & Antioch Railway Company, the Oakland, Antioch & Eastern Railway Company and the San Ramon Valley Railroad Company January 26, 1920. Conveyed to Sacramento Northern Railway Company December 31, 1928.

SAN FRANCISCO-SACRAMENTO RAILROAD - An amalgamation of the Oakland & Antioch, the Oakland, Antioch & Eastern and the San Ramon Valley Railroad in order to form the San Francisco-Sacramento Railroad in 1920. Became the Sacramento Northern in 1928. A train at 40th and Shafter Street in Oakland. - *Donald Duke Collection*

SAN FRANCISCO & SACRAMENTO RAILROAD COMPANY

Organized June 1856 - Steam - Standard Gauge

Located San Francisco, San Francisco County. Proposed to build from Benicia to Sacramento. Distance 52.00 miles. Trains were to connect with bay steamers at Benicia for journey to San Francisco.

SAN FRANCISCO & SAN JOAQUIN RAILROAD

Organized 1890 - Steam - Standard Gauge

Located Bakersfield, Kern County. Secured right-of-way from Tejon Pass near Bakersfield through the San Joaquin Valley. Surveys reached Antioch June 14, 1890. Project abandoned in 1892.

SAN FRANCISCO & SAN JOAQUIN VALLEY RAILWAY COMPANY

Incorporated February 26, 1895 - Steam - Standard Gauge

Located Stockton, San Joaquin County. Built to Bakersfield by May 27, 1898. Built to Point Richmond on San Francisco Bay by 1900. Completed and opened for service July 1, 1900. Distance 374.60 miles. Conveyed to the Santa Fe Railway April 1, 1901.

SAN FRANCISCO & SAN JOAQUIN VALLEY RAILWAY - Built from Stockton to Bakersfield in 1898 as competition to the Southern Pacific. Was taken over by the Santa Fe Railway and extended from Stockton to Oakland. - *Donald Duke Collection*

SAN FRANCISCO & SAN JOSE RAILROAD COMPANY

Incorporated August 18, 1860 - Steam - Standard Gauge

Located San Francisco, San Francisco County. Built to San Jose from 16th and Valencia streets through Bernal Cut to San Bruno, Daly City, Union Park, Colma and Palo Alto to San Jose. Construction began July 15, 1861. Opened for traffic to Palo Alto September 18, 1863. Completed to San Jose January 16, 1864. Consolidated into original Southern Pacific Railroad Company March 1869. Consolidated with California Southern Railroad Company and the Santa Clara & Pajaro Valley Railroad Company October 12, 1870, to form the Southern Pacific Company.

SÁN FRANCISCO & SAN MATEO RAILWAY COMPANY
SAN FRANCISCO & SAN MATEO ELECTRIC RAILWAY COMPANY

Incorporated July 29, 1891 - Electric - Standard Gauge

Located San Francisco, San Francisco County. Built from Market and Stuart streets to 30th Street. Began operations in 1892 as the first electric street railway in San Francisco. A branch line reached Golden Gate Park in 1893. Deeded to the San Francisco & San Mateo Electric Railway Company April 11, 1895. Taken into the United Railroads of San Francisco May 18, 1901. Extended the tracks from Baden southward to San Mateo. Acquired by the Municipal Railway of San Francisco September 29, 1944.

SAN FRANCISCO - SAN MATEO RIGHT-OF-WAY COMPANY

Incorporated May 16, 1914 - Electric - Standard Gauge

Located San Mateo, San Mateo County. Chartered to secure a right-of-way for an electric railroad to be built down the Peninsula from San Francisco to Palo Alto, which was to be sold to a railroad company to build a competing system or retained for a San Mateo electric railway.

SAN FRANCISCO, SAN MATEO & SANTA CRUZ RAILROAD

Incorporation papers filed 1875 - Steam - Standard Gauge

Located San Francisco, San Francisco County. Proposed to build to the boundary of Santa Cruz and San Mateo by way of Spanishtown and Pescadero. Project abandoned in 1876.

SAN FRANCISCO & SAN RAFAEL RAILROAD COMPANY

Incorporated 1882 - Steam - Standard Gauge

Located San Rafael, Marin County. Built to Tiburon as a narrow-gauge railroad by 1883. Standard gauged in 1889. Sold to the San Francisco & North Pacific Railroad in 1889. Leased to the California Northwestern Railway September 20, 1898. Consolidated with the Northwestern Pacific Railroad January 8, 1907.

SAN FRANCISCO & SANTA CLARA VALLEY RAILROAD COMPANY

Chartered July 1892 - Steam - Standard Gauge

Located San Francisco, San Francisco County. Elected a board of directors August 19, 1892. No construction work was done.

SAN FRANCISCO & SOUTHERN RAILROAD COMPANY

Organized 1904 - Steam - Standard Gauge

Located Santa Cruz, Santa Cruz County. Proposed to build through Pescadero and Half Moon Bay to San Francisco.

SAN FRANCISCO & STOCKTON RAILROAD COMPANY

Incorporated August 1890 - Steam - Standard Gauge

Located San Francisco, San Francisco County. Proposed to build through the counties of Alameda, Contra Costa and San Joaquin to Stockton. Distance 75.00 miles. Project abandoned in 1891.

SAN FRANCISCO, STOCKTON & BAKERSFIELD RAILROAD
SAN FRANCISCO, STOCKTON & SAN JOAQUIN RAILROAD

Organized September 1894 - Steam - Standard Gauge

Located San Francisco, San Francisco County. The name San Francisco, Stockton & Bakersfield Railroad was given to a project planned by the officers of the San Francisco Traffic Association for a railroad through the San Joaquin Valley. The organization name was changed to San Francisco, Stockton & San Joaquin Railroad October 12, 1894.

SAN FRANCISCO, TAMALPAIS & BOLINAS RAILWAY COMPANY

Incorporated September 6, 1889 - Steam - 3 ft. Gauge

Located Mill Valley, Marin County. Built from Almonte. Distance 1.74 miles. Completed October 13, 1889. Began service March 17, 1892. Deeded to the North Pacific Coast Railroad Company April 22, 1892. Became part of the North Shore Railroad Company March 7, 1902. Consolidated into the Northwestern Pacific Railroad Company January 8, 1907.

SAN FRANCISCO TERMINAL RAILWAY

Incorporated 1902 - Steam - Standard Gauge

Located San Francisco, San Francisco County. This railway was a combination ferry and railroad service in and around the city of San Francisco. The railroad portion of the project would run a line from Oakland to San Jose and included would be five branch lines. (1.) Ferry service from San Francisco to Oakland, with the Alameda & San Joaquin Railroad near the junction of Alameda and San Joaquin counties, for a total of 60 miles of track. (2.) Rail service from Hayward to San Jose, for a distance of 35 miles of track. (3.) Rail service from Alameda to San Leandro, a distance of 10 miles of track. (4.) Rail service from Oakland to Berkeley, a distance of 10 miles of track. (5.) Rail service from Hayward to Dumbarton Point, on San Francisco Bay. This last rail link would give the railroad access to tidewater. A further goal was the acquisition of the Alameda & San Joaquin Railroad. No construction or acquisitions made.

SAN FRANCISCO TERMINAL RAILWAY & FERRY COMPANY

Organized 1899 - Steam - Standard Gauge

Located Oakland, Alameda County. Purchased by the Western Pacific Railroad Company December 6, 1903.

SAN FRANCISCO & TRANSBAY RAILROAD COMPANY

Organized March 1910 - Electric - Standard Gauge

Located Niles, Alameda County. Proposed to build to Dumbarton and crossing the bay with connections to Redwood City and on to Woodside to San Francisco. A branch was to be built from Dumbarton to Warm Springs.

SAN FRANCISCO TRANSIT COMPANY

Organized 1900 - Electric - Standard Gauge

Located San Francisco, San Francisco County. Organized to build an electric street railway in San Francisco. Application made for a charter November 1, 1901. Application refused in 1902.

SAN FRANCISCO TRANSIT COMPANY

Incorporated June 3, 1922 - Steam - Standard Gauge

Located Carquinez Straits, Contra Costa County. Organized to build trackage across the bridge at this point.

SAN FRANCISCO & VACA VALLEY RAILWAY

Organized January 19, 1906 - Steam - Standard Gauge

Located San Francisco, San Francisco County. Proposed to establish boat service from San Francisco to Vallejo and then build a railroad into the Napa Valley. Project abandoned in 1908.

SAN FRANCISCO, VALLEJO & NAPA VALLEY ELECTRIC RAILWAY & STEAMSHIP COMPANY
SAN FRANCISCO, VALLEJO & NAPA VALLEY RAILROAD COMPANY
SAN FRANCISCO & NAPA VALLEY RAILROAD

Incorporated June 5, 1906 - Electric - Standard Gauge

Located Vallejo, Solano County. Organized to extend the Vallejo, Benicia & Napa Railroad up the Napa Valley. Proposed to build from Vallejo to Winters by way of Benicia, Fairfield, Suisun, Cordelia and Dixon. Total distance to be 110 miles. Grading began January 1907, on Main, Alameda and Pennsylvania streets and Solano Avenue in Vallejo to the county road in Benicia. Completed and opened for traffic to Yountville September 1907. Reorganized as the San Francisco, Vallejo & Napa Railway Company November 10, 1911. Reorganized and renamed San Francisco & Napa Valley Railroad. Dissolved as a corporation September 15, 1957.

SAN FRANCISCO & WASHOE RAILROAD COMPANY

Incorporated 1864 - Steam - Standard Gauge

Located Placerville, El Dorado County. Surveys were made in 1862 to build a railroad to Virginia City, Nevada by way of a route around the south end of Lake Tahoe.

SAN FRANCISCO & WEST SHORE RAILROAD
WEST SHORE & VALLEY RAILROAD

Proposed in 1895 - Steam - Standard Gauge

Located San Francisco, San Francisco County. Proposed to build to Santa Cruz as the West Shore & Valley Railroad and then over the Pacheco Pass and down the west side of the valley to Tulare.

SAN GABRIEL VALLEY NARROW-GAUGE RAILROAD

Organized August 18, 1883 - Steam - Narrow-Gauge

Located Los Angeles, Los Angeles County. Proposed to build to Pasadena and on to Mud Springs in San Bernardino County. Right-of-way taken over by the Los Angeles & San Gabriel Valley Railroad Company. Incorporated August 30, 1883. Merged into the California Central Railway Company May 31, 1887. Became part of the Santa Fe Railway Company in June 1904.

SAN GABRIEL VALLEY RAPID TRANSIT RAILWAY COMPANY

Incorporated July 29, 1887 - Steam - 3 ft. Gauge

Located Los Angeles, Los Angeles County. Built from Aliso Street to Shorb and on to Monrovia, distance 16.00 miles. Section Shorb to Monrovia opened May 18, 1888, distance 11.00 miles. Shorb to Aliso Street in Los Angeles opened for service August 21, 1888, distance 6.00 miles. Branch Alhambra to Raymond opened for traffic in 1889, distance 1.50 miles. Standard gauged in June 1892. Operated by Los Angeles Terminal Railway Company from June 12, 1892, to June 12, 1893. Sold to Pacific Improvement Company February 15, 1894. Conveyed to Southern Pacific Company October 2, 1894. Section Shorb to Los Angeles sold to Los Angeles Inter-Urban Railway May 12, 1904. Rest of trackage abandoned in 1943. Tracks removed in 1944.

SAN JACINTO, LAKEVIEW & NORTHERN RAILROAD COMPANY

Organized January 3, 1898 - Steam - Standard Gauge

Located Lakeview, Riverside County. Proposed to build from Lakeview Junction on the Southern California Railway (Santa Fe) to Lakeview. Distance 10.20 miles. Surveys completed May 1898. Properties deeded to the Southern California Railway Company.

SAN JACINTO & MURRIETA RAILROAD COMPANY

Organized 1886 - Steam - Standard Gauge

Located Riverside, Riverside County. Proposed to build a railroad from Riverside through Box Canyon to San Jacinto. A branch line was to be built from a point mid-way between Riverside and San Jacinto and extended to the hot springs at Murrieta.

SAN JACINTO VALLEY RAILWAY COMPANY

Incorporated March 7, 1887 - Steam - Standard Gauge

Located Perris, Riverside County. Built to San Jacinto. Distance 29.00 miles. Opened for traffic April 30, 1888. Sold to the California Central Railway 1887. Consolidated with the Southern California Railway Company November 7, 1889. Now part of the Santa Fe Railway.

SAN JOAQUIN DELTA RAILROAD

Incorporated May 1911 - Electric - Standard Gauge

Located Stockton, San Joaquin County. Proposed to build across the Delta country to a point in Contra Costa County.

SAN JOAQUIN & EASTERN RAILROAD COMPANY

Chartered March 16, 1912 - Steam - Standard Gauge

Located El Prado, Fresno County. Built from a junction with the Southern Pacific Company, Friant Branch, to Cascada (now Big Creek). Distance 55.92 miles. Construction began February 16, 1912. Completed July 10, 1912. Regular train service began August 1, 1912. Took over the operations of the Big Creek Railroad in 1913. Passenger service discontinued May 30, 1930. Ceased operations August 15, 1933. Corporation dissolved September 25, 1936.

SAN JOAQUIN & SIERRA NEVADA RAILROAD COMPANY

Incorporated March 28, 1882 - Steam - 3 ft. Gauge

Located Bracks Landing, San Joaquin County. Built through Lodi to Valley Springs, distance 40.30 miles. Completed in 1885. Bracks Landing to Woodbridge, distance 10.59 miles. Abandoned 1897. Consolidated into the Northern Railway Company May 15, 1888. Standard gauged 1897. Consolidated with Southern Pacific Company April 14, 1898. Extended 8.00 miles easterly from Valley Springs in 1925 or 1926. 4.00 miles of trackage from Kentucky Home purchased from Calaveras Cement Company April 28, 1929.

SAN JOAQUIN RAILROAD COMPANY

Organized 1851 - Steam - Standard Gauge

Located Stockton, San Joaquin County. Proposed to build to Sonora. Stock was issued abroad and after capital raised for construction, the project was abandoned.

SAN JOAQUIN & TULARE RAILROAD

Surveyed 1873 - Steam - 3 ft. Gauge

Located Stockton, San Joaquin County. Proposed to build to Visalia. Distance 175.80 miles. No construction work was done after the survey was made.

SAN JOAQUIN VALLEY COAL COMPANY

Organized October 1886 - Horsecar - Standard Gauge

Located near Coalinga, Fresno County. Built to the coal mines. Distance 3.90 miles. Ceased operations in 1893. Tracks taken up in 1896.

SAN JOAQUIN VALLEY ELECTRIC RAILWAY COMPANY

Incorporated November 1, 1908 - Electric - Standard Gauge

Located Stockton, San Joaquin County. Proposed to build to Modesto. Distance 35.00 miles. Grading completed to Ripon April 30, 1910. Received a franchise to build into Modesto January 3, 1911. Received a franchise to build along McKinley Avenue from Stockton to French Camp April 1911. Roadbed completed to Stockton from Modesto December 1911.

SAN JOAQUIN VALLEY RAILROAD COMPANY

Incorporated February 5, 1868 - Steam - Standard Gauge

Located Lathrop, San Joaquin County. Proposed to build a railroad from Stockton to the Colorado River. Distance 480 miles. Constructed trackage from Lathrop to the Stanislaus River. Distance 11.30 miles. Construction work done in 1869 and 1870. Before being placed in operation, the company consolidated into the Central Pacific Railroad August 22, 1870.

SAN JOAQUIN VALLEY RAILROAD COMPANY

Incorporated March 4, 1891 - Steam - Standard Gauge

Located Fresno, Fresno County. Built to Pollasky (now Friant). Distance 24.10 miles. Opened for traffic January 20, 1892. Conveyed to the Pacific Improvement Company December 14, 1893. Transferred to the Southern Pacific Railroad Company December 19, 1893. Now the Southern Pacific Company Friant Branch.

SAN JOAQUIN VALLEY WESTERN RAILROAD COMPANY

Incorporated February 18, 1907 - Electric - Standard Gauge

Located Fresno, Fresno County. Proposed to build across the San Joaquin Valley to the Pacific Ocean. Reorganized April 6, 1907, and stated that the route would be from Fresno to Watsonville by way of Mendota, Tres Pinos, Hollister and Chittenden. Distance 140.00 miles. Two branch lines of 40 miles each were to be built, one to Hanford and one to Coalinga. Ground broken for construction May 1, 1907.

SAN JOAQUIN VALLEY & YOSEMITE RAILROAD COMPANY

Incorporated February 15, 1886 - Steam - Standard Gauge

Located Berenda, Madera County. Built to Raymond. Distance 21.00 miles. Construction completed in 1886. Consolidated with the Southern Pacific Company May 14, 1888. Section of trackage east of Daulton abandoned in 1942. Trackage Berenda to Daulton abandoned in 1956.

SAN JOSE & ALMADEN RAILROAD COMPANY

Incorporated March 2, 1886 - Steam - Standard Gauge

Located Lick, Santa Clara County. Built to New Almaden. Distance 7.70 miles. Opened for service November 16, 1886. Consolidated with the Southern Pacific Company May 14, 1888. Line beyond Alamitos abandoned 1934. Tracks removed in 1936.

SAN JOSE & ALMADEN RAILWAY COMPANY

Organized 1911 - Electric - Standard Gauge

Located San Jose, Santa Clara County. Proposed to build to Almaden. Construction work from San Jose to Hacienda began January 1912. Project abandoned February 1, 1915.

SAN JOSE & ALUM ROCK PARK RAILWAY

Franchise granted April 6, 1891 - Horsecar - 3 ft. Gauge

Located San Jose, Santa Clara County. Began operations as a horsecar line from San Jose, building toward Alum Rock Park. Was quickly converted to a steam motor road on July 7, 1894. Tracks reached Alum Rock Park in 1896. Sold to the San Jose & Santa Clara Railway in 1898 and the line was electrified. Was sold to the San Jose Railroad during March 1912 and converted to standard gauge by 1914. Was later operated by Southern Pacific controlled Peninsular Railway. Service was discontinued to Alum Rock Park on April 15, 1939, when the San Jose Railroad discontinued service.

SAN JOSE & ALVISO RAILROAD

Incorporated August 30, 1895 - Steam - Standard Gauge

Located San Jose, Santa Clara County. Proposed to build to Alviso on San Francisco Bay. A fleet of steamers were to run from Alviso to Oakland, Vallejo, Berkeley and other bay points. No construction work done.

SAN JOSE & CONGRESS SPRINGS RAILROAD

Franchise granted August 18, 1901 - Electric - Standard Gauge

Located San Jose, Santa Clara County. Proposed to build to Saratoga and Congress Springs. Distance 17.00 miles. Contract for poles and ties let in November 1901. Project abandoned in 1902.

SAN JOSE - LOS GATOS INTERURBAN RAILWAY

Incorporated May 6, 1903 - Electric - Standard Gauge

Located San Jose, Santa Clara County. Built to Los Gatos by way of Vasona. Construction work began July 11, 1903. City service began December 1, 1903. Interurban service began January 1, 1904. Deeded to the Peninsular Railway Company June 30, 1909. Abandoned 1934.

SAN JOSE RAILROAD COMPANY
SAN JOSE RAILWAY COMPANY

Incorporated September 1894 - Horsecar - Electric - 3 ft. Gauge

Located San Jose, Santa Clara County. Began operations as the San Jose Railroad Company, a horsecar line on First Street. Became San Jose Railway Company in 1889. Electrified in 1903. Merged with the Market Street & Willow Glen Railroad and reincorporated as the San Jose Railroad December 22, 1909. Began conversion to standard gauge in 1910. Local service discontinued April 15, 1939.

SAN JOSE RAILROADS

Chartered December 27, 1909 - Electric - Standard Gauge

Located San Jose, Santa Clara County. This company resulted from the consolidation of the street railways of San Jose and vicinity purchased by the Southern Pacific Company in 1910. Purchased the San Jose & Santa Clara Railroad March 15, 1919. Distance 29.44 miles. Sold to the Pacific City Lines April 1, 1939. Street railway service ended April 15, 1939.

SAN JOSE RAILROADS - The Southern Pacific Company purchased several street railways in 1910 and merged them into the San Jose Railroads. This company operated streetcar service in the San Jose area. - *Charles Smallwood*

SAN JOSE & SANTA CLARA COUNTY RAILROAD COMPANY

Incorporated December 13, 1905 - Electric - 3 ft. Gauge

Located San Jose, Santa Clara County. Resulted from a reorganization of the San Jose & Santa Clara Railroad. Changed to standard gauge operations April 13, 1906.

SAN JOSE & SANTA CLARA RAILROAD

Chartered July 9, 1868 - Horsecar - 3 ft. Gauge

Located San Jose, Santa Clara County. Built from First and Santa Clara streets to Franklin and Main streets in Santa Clara. Distance 4.5 miles. First run made November 1, 1868. Regular service established November 4, 1868. Steam dummy engine tried July 11, 1871. Returned to horse power in October 1871. Purchased People's Horse Railroad April 23, 1882. Purchased North Side Horse Railroad Company April 22, 1882. Electrification began October 5, 1887. Electric service began in July 1888. Returned to horsecar operations in October 1888. Re-electrified in 1890. Became Santa Clara County Railroad Company December 13, 1905. Sold to the Southern Pacific Company April 7, 1911. Abandoned in 1939.

SAN JOSE & SANTA CLARA RAILROAD COMPANY

Chartered July 9, 1868 - Horsecar - 3 ft. Gauge

Located San Jose, Santa Clara County. Built 9.67 miles of horsecar street railway between San Jose and Santa Clara. Electrified in 1889. Electrification was not accepted after the test. Horsecars were again placed in operation. Electric operation was begun again in 1892 and the trackage was standard gauged. Purchased the San Jose & Alum Rock Park Railway in 1898. Deeded to the Municipal Railway of San Francisco. Abandoned in 1939.

SAN JOSE, SARATOGA & LOS GATOS INTERURBAN RAILROAD

Incorporated October 17, 1902 - Electric - Standard Gauge

Located San Jose, Santa Clara County. Proposed to build to Saratoga and Los Gatos. Construction began in January 1903. Reincorporated as the San Jose - Los Gatos Interurban Railway Company May 1903. Construction resumed June 13, 1903. Began operations May 19, 1904. Line completed to Los Gatos April 9, 1904. Became part of the Peninsular Railway of California June 9, 1909. Abandoned October 1, 1934.

SAN JOSE, SARATOGA & LOS GATOS RAILROAD

Organized 1901 - Electric - Standard Gauge

Located San Jose, Santa Clara County. Built to Saratoga. Construction work done from June to October 1903. Consolidated into the San Jose - Los Gatos Interurban Railway. Extended to Los Gatos April 9, 1904.

SAN JOSE SHORT LINE RAILWAY

Organized February 1, 1911 - Electric - Standard Gauge

Located San Jose, Santa Clara County. Organized to build a railroad from San Jose to an undisclosed destination.

SAN JOSE SOUTHERN RAILROAD COMPANY

Incorporated September 6, 1890 - Steam - Standard Gauge

Located San Jose, Santa Clara County. Proposed to build southward to Los Angeles. Surveys began September 1890. Convention with the officials of counties that the road would pass through was held in San Jose September 20, 1890. Project abandoned in 1891.

SAN JOSE STREET RAILWAY

Franchise granted October 1903 - Electric - Standard Gauge

Located San Jose, Santa Clara County. Constructed 5.50 miles of street railway in San Jose. Became part of the San Jose Railroads in December 1909.

SAN JOSE TERMINAL RAILWAY COMPANY

Incorporated September 2, 1911 - Electric - Standard Gauge

Located San Jose, Santa Clara County. Proposed to build to Alviso. Distance

12.00 miles. To connect with ferryboats and freight boats to the Ferry Building in San Francisco. Almost the entire line was graded by November 1912. Project abandoned January 1, 1913.

SAN JOSE TRACTION COMPANY

Organized 1907 - Electric - Standard Gauge

Located San Jose, Santa Clara County. Organized to build parallel lines to harass the San Jose Railroad Company. Sold to the Southern Pacific Company April 7, 1911. No construction work was done by the original company.

SAN JUAN PACIFIC RAILROAD

Incorporated May 4, 1907 - Steam - Standard Gauge

Located San Juan, San Benito County. Built from a junction with the Southern Pacific Company to a cement plant by way of San Juan. Distance 7.94 miles. Began operations September 1907. Deeded to the California Central Railroad Company May 21, 1912. The San Juan Pacific Railroad was dissolved July 2, 1932. The California Central Railroad ceased operations December 1937. Abandoned in 1943.

SAN JUAN SOUTHERN RAILWAY COMPANY

Incorporated August 3, 1907 - Steam - Standard Gauge

Located San Juan, San Benito County. Proposed to build from San Juan Junction on the San Juan Pacific Railroad to Hollister. Distance 5.55 miles. No construction work done.

SAN LORENZO FLUME & TRANSPORTATION COMPANY
SANTA CRUZ & FELTON RAILROAD COMPANY

Organized October 1874 - Steam - 3 ft. Gauge

Located Santa Cruz, Santa Cruz County. Organized to build a railroad to Felton with an eight mile lumber flume from Felton to the vicinity of Alcorn's old place near Turkey Flat. A 900 ft. tunnel was built through the chalk walls of Mission Hill to Santa Cruz.

SAN LORENZO VALLEY RAILROAD

Incorporated May 20, 1861 - Steam - Narrow Gauge

Located Santa Cruz, Santa Cruz County. Proposed to build from Santa Cruz up the San Lorenzo River to a point known as "Turkey Flat" where Boulder Creek, Bear Creek and the river all came together. Distance 16.25 miles. Right-of-way legal problems held up construction. Work began in 1868 with a new route plan. It would build from Santa Cruz to Felton with a line being extended to Turkey Flat at a later date. Legal problems over timber in the right-of-way delayed construction until January 1874, at which time the railroad was broke and released its franchise and ceased to exist.

SAN LUIS & SAN JOAQUIN RAILROAD

Chartered July 29, 1892 - Steam - Standard Gauge

Located San Luis Obispo, San Luis Obispo County. Proposed to build in a northerly direction to a point near El Morro or Morro Bay.

SAN LUIS OBISPO RAILROAD COMPANY

Organized January 30, 1873 - Steam - 30 in. Gauge

Located San Luis Obispo, San Luis Obispo County. Proposed to build from San Luis Obispo to join John Harford's Railroad. Project abandoned in 1874.

SAN LUIS OBISPO & SANTA MARIA RAILROAD

Organized 1873 - Steam - Narrow-Gauge

Located San Luis Obispo, San Luis Obispo County. Proposed to build to steamer landing on the bay at Avila then to Arroyo Grande. Distance 36.00 miles. Construction began in 1874. Completed San Luis Obispo to Avila in 1875. Distance 9.00 miles.

SAN LUIS OBISPO & SANTA MARIA VALLEY RAILROAD

Organized March 2, 1874 - Steam - 3 ft. Gauge

Located San Luis Obispo, San Luis Obispo County. Proposed to build from San Luis Bay to the valley of the Santa Maria River and then on to Santa Barbara. Purchased John Harford's Railroad. Built from Avila on San Luis Obispo Bay to San Luis Obispo. Opened for traffic in September 1876. Distance 10.75 miles. Merged with the Pacific Coast Railroad to become the Pacific Coast Railway in September 1882.

SAN LUIS OBISPO STREET RAILWAY COMPANY

Chartered June 13, 1887 - Horsecar - 3 ft. Gauge

Located San Luis Obispo, San Luis Obispo County. Built 2.50 miles of horsecar street railway. Sold to the West Coast Land Company February 1, 1890. Became San Luis Street Railway in 1901.

SAN LUIS REY VALLEY RAILROAD COMPANY

Surveyed 1888 - Steam - Standard Gauge

Located San Luis Rey River Valley, San Diego County. No construction work was done.

SAN LUIS VALLEY INTERURBAN RAILWAY

Incorporated December 12, 1908 - Electric - Standard Gauge

Located Del Norte, Siskiyou County. Proposed to build easterly to Center. Also to build from Monte Vista to Center and to the location of the Devil's Gate Reservoir and from Center to Saguache.

SAN MATEO BEACH RAILWAY

Electric-Standard Gauge

Located San Mateo, San Mateo County. Proposed to build to San Mateo Beach.

SAN PABLO RAILROAD COMPANY

Began operations 1871 - Horsecar - Standard Gauge

Located Oakland, Alameda County. Operated from First and Broadway to 14th Street (then San Pablo Avenue) to Park Avenue. Consolidated with the Oakland Railroad Company January 27, 1888. Changed to 3 ft. gauge and made into a cable operated street railway. Sold to the Oakland Transit Company March 29, 1901.

SAN PABLO & TULARE RAILROAD COMPANY

Incorporated July 19, 1871 - Steam - Standard Gauge

Located Martinez, Contra Costa County. Built to Tracy. Distance 46.51 miles. Began construction September 1876. Completed in 1878. Consolidated with Southern Pacific Company May 14, 1888.

SAN PABLO & TULARE RAILWAY COMPANY

Steam - Standard Gauge

Located Martinez, Contra Costa County. Proposed as an industrial line to connect with the Southern Pacific at Martinez and the Santa Fe at its Alhambra bridge crossing Alhambra Canyon, a distance of 2.5 miles. Proposed Ozai Yard in Martinez to handle freight cars.

SAN PABLO & TULARE EXTENSION RAILROAD COMPANY

Incorporated February 7, 1887 - Steam - Standard Gauge

Located Tracy, San Joaquin County. Projected to build from Tracy via "west side" to a point in Kern County. Distance 260 miles. Graded roadbed from Tracy to a point near Los Banos. Distance 65.00 miles. Consolidated with Southern Pacific Company May 14, 1888. Construction from Tracy to Los Banos completed November 1, 1889.

SAN PEDRO, LOS ANGELES & SALT LAKE RAILROAD COMPANY

Organized 1889 - Steam - Standard Gauge

Located Los Angeles, Los Angeles County. Incorporated March 20, 1901. Purchased the Los Angeles Terminal Railway Company in 1900. Built from Los Angeles to Riverside from a junction with the Atchison, Topeka & Santa Fe Railway. Distance 59.70 miles. Obtained trackage rights over the Santa Fe

133

to Daggett. Distance 99.30 miles. Built from Daggett to the California state line. Extended to Salt Lake City, Utah. First through passenger trains started May 2, 1905. The name San Pedro was dropped from the original name when that city became part of Los Angeles in 1916. Deeded to the Union Pacific Railway Company January 1, 1922, because of full stock ownership.

SAN PEDRO, LOS ANGELES & SALT LAKE RAILROAD - Purchased the Los Angeles Terminal in 1900 and then built east from Los Angeles toward Salt Lake. Building west from Salt Lake, the rails joined in Nevada. Name was changed to Los Angeles & Salt Lake Railroad when San Pedro became a part of Los Angeles. - *Donald Duke Collection*

SAN PEDRO, LOS ANGELES & UTAH RAILWAY COMPANY

Incorporated October 11, 1888 - Steam - Standard Gauge

Located Los Angeles, Los Angeles County. Proposed to build from San Pedro through Los Angeles and Pasadena and then north through Kern, San Bernardino and Inyo counties to the California state line. Distance 275.00 miles. No construction work done.

SAN PEDRO STREET RAILWAY

Organized April 7, 1914 - Electric - Standard Guage

Located Los Angeles, Los Angeles County. Built from Aliso Street to Ninth Street on San Pedro Street. Distance 1.37 miles. Completed May 1, 1914. Deeded to Los Angeles County.

SAN RAFAEL & SAN ANSELMO VALLEY RAILROAD

Incorporated August 22, 1913 - Electric - Standard Gauge

Located San Rafael, Marin County. Proposed to build 2.75 miles of street railway in San Rafael and then westerly by way of San Anselmo to Fairfax. Distance 5.85 miles. Beach storage battery cars were to be used. Reorganized October 19, 1914.

SAN RAFAEL & SAN QUENTIN RAILROAD COMPANY

Incorporated February 25, 1869 - Steam - Standard Gauge

Located San Rafael, Marin County. Built to Point San Quentin. Distance 2.10 miles. Began operations in March 1871. Leased to the North Pacific Coast Railroad March 11, 1875 for 43 years. Changed to 3 ft. gauge in April 1875. Consolidated into the Northwestern Pacific Railroad January 8, 1907. Lease expired June 26, 1928.

SAN RAMON VALLEY RAILWAY COMPANY

Incorporated March 16, 1912 - Electric - Standard Gauge

Located Walnut Creek, Contra Costa County. Built to Danville. Distance 8.00 miles. Began operations on March 2, 1914. Leased to Oakland, Antioch & Eastern Railway Company upon completion. Tracks taken up March 31, 1924.

SAN RAMON VALLEY RAILROAD COMPANY

Incorporated April 25, 1888 - Steam - Standard Gauge

Located Avon, Contra Costa County. Proposed to build to Pleasanton. Distance 35.00 miles. No construction work done. Consolidated with the Southern Pacific Company May 14, 1888. Built from Avon to San Ramon. Distance 19.70 miles. Completed in 1891. Built from San Ramon to Rodum. Distance 10.10 miles. Completed February 7, 1909.

SAN VINCENTE MILL & LUMBER COMPANY

Organized 1908 - Steam - Standard Gauge

Located Little Creek, Santa Cruz County. Built from mill to timber. Distance 2.55 miles. Purchased the trackage of the Ocean Shore Railroad from Folger to mill on Little Creek in 1920. Distance 2.10 miles. Purchased southern section of the Ocean Shore Railroad from Folger to Santa Cruz in 1920. Distance 14.40 miles. Railroad abandoned in 1923.

SANTA ANA BEACH & ROCKY POINT RAILWAY

Organized 1885 - Steam - Standard Gauge

Located Newport Beach, Orange County. The railway proposed to build from the terminus of the Santa Ana & Newport Railroad, near Newport Wharf, to the Balboa Peninsula across from Corona del Mar. A total distance of 5.00 miles. No construction work undertaken. The right-of-way was used by the Los Angeles Inter-Urban Railway in 1905, and later formed a part of the Pacific Electric system. Trackage was extended to the end of the jetty at the harbor entrance in 1918. Abandoned in 1939.

SANTA ANA, FAIRVIEW & PACIFIC RAILROAD COMPANY

Incorporated December 28, 1887 - Steam - Narrow Gauge

Located Santa Ana, Orange County. Proposed to build to Newport by way of Fairview through Gospel Swamp to Rocky Point. Built from the corner of Fourth and Broadway streets in Santa Ana to West Street and then south to Edinger Street where it crossed fields in a southwesterly direction to the present intersection of Harbor Boulevard and Talbert Avenue, then south to Fairgrove and on to the northern boundary of the Banning Tract. Distance 4.00 miles. Began operations to Fairgrove on July 2, 1888. Ceased operations in 1891.

SANTA ANA, LONG BEACH & COAST RAILWAY COMPANY

Incorporated August 8, 1887 - Steam - Standard Gauge

Located Santa Ana, Orange County. Proposed to build from Rattlesnake Island opposite San Pedro to Long Beach by way of Garden Grove and Westminster. Began securing right-of-way August 12, 1887. Project abandoned in 1888.

SANTA ANA & LONG BEACH RAILROAD COMPANY

Incorporated October 31, 1888 - Steam - Standard Gauge

Located Santa Ana, Orange County. Proposed to build to Long Beach. Distance 20.00 miles. Project abandoned September 27, 1890. Reorganized June 6, 1902. Proposed to build an electric railway along the original survey. Distance to be 24.50 miles. No construction work done.

SANTA ANA & LONG BEACH RAILROAD COMPANY

Incorporated August 1, 1901 - Electric - Standard Gauge

Located Long Beach, Los Angeles County. Proposed to build either an electric or steam railroad to Santa Ana. Stock purchased by the Pacific Electric Railway Company December 31, 1902.

SANTA ANA & LONG BEACH RAILROAD & IMPROVEMENT COMPANY

Incorporated October 29, 1888 - Steam - Standard Gauge

Located Santa Ana, Orange County. Proposed to build to Long Beach. No construction work done.

SANTA ANA & NEWPORT RAILWAY COMPANY

Incorporated October 16, 1886 - Steam - Standard Gauge

Located Santa Ana, Orange County. Built 11.00 miles to pier in Newport on the Pacific Ocean. Grading completed January 12, 1889. Road opened for traffic October 13, 1891. Sold to Southern Pacific June 30, 1900. Abandoned 1907.

SANTA ANA & NEWPORT RAILWAY COMPANY

Incorporated November 7, 1892 - Steam - Standard Gauge

Located Santa Ana, Orange County. Took over the operation of the Santa Ana Railroad Company on February 11, 1893. Trackage from Santa Ana to Newport Beach. Distance 11.71 miles. Built from Newport Beach to Smeltzer. Distance 10.75 miles. Construction done in part under its own name and in part by the predecessor companies: Santa Ana Railroad Company, Newport Wharf & Lumber Company and the Santa Ana & Westminster Railway Company. Began construction between Newport and Smeltzer in 1897. Completed November 11, 1897. Sold to the Southern Pacific Company November 23, 1899. Section from Huntington Beach to Wiebling, a distance 2.66 miles, sold to the Pacific Electric Railway Company in 1933. Balance of line abandoned in 1933.

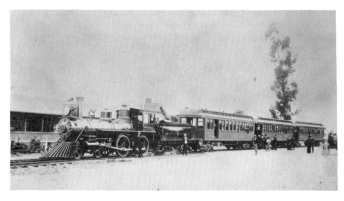

SANTA ANA & NEWPORT RAILWAY - Built from Santa Ana to Newport Beach in 1893, a distance of 11.7 miles. Operated the wharf in Newport and handled mostly lumber to Santa Ana. - *First American Title Insurance Company*

SANTA ANA & ORANGE MOTOR COMPANY

Organized 1896 - Steam - Standard Gauge

Located Santa Ana, Orange County. Built to Orange. Distance 5.60 miles. Began operations with two self-propelled upright steam boiler engines, one converted to a gas engine later. Merged with the Santa Ana, Orange & Tustin Street Railway Company. Became part of the Interurban Railway Company in 1901. Electrified in 1908. Sold to the Pacific Electric Railway Company in 1910. Abandoned in 1930.

SANTA ANA, ORANGE & TUSTIN STREET RAILWAY COMPANY

Incorporated March 30, 1886 - Horsecar - 2 ft. 6 in. Gauge

Located Santa Ana, Orange County. Built to Tustin. Opened for traffic December 22, 1886. Began operations to Orange, November 29, 1889. Converted to standard gauge and steam operation in 1893. Merged with the Santa Ana & Orange Motor Company in 1896. Became part of the Interurban Railway Company in 1901. Deeded to the Pacific Electric Railway Company in 1910. Abandoned in 1930.

SANTA ANA RAILROAD COMPANY

Incorporated August 23, 1889 - Steam - Standard Gauge

Located Santa Ana, Orange County. Built to Newport. Distance 11.71 miles. Began operations July 30, 1891. Sold to the Newport Wharf & Lumber Company November 19, 1892. Sold to the Santa Ana & Newport Railway Company February 11, 1893. Deeded to the Southern Pacific Company. Section from Huntington Beach to Wiebling, a distance of 2.66 miles, sold to the Pacific Electric Railway in 1933. Balance of line abandoned in 1933.

SANTA ANA & TUSTIN MOTOR RAILWAY COMPANY

Incorporated May 2, 1888 - Steam - Standard Gauge

Located Santa Ana, Orange County. Proposed to build to Tustin. Distance 6.00 miles. Project abandoned in 1889.

SANTA ANA VALLEY & PACIFIC RAILROAD

Organized January 12, 1889 - Steam - Narrow-Gauge

Located Fairview, Orange County. Organized to extend the Santa Ana, Fairview & Pacific Railroad to the ocean. Project abandoned in 1890.

SANTA ANA & WESTMINSTER RAILWAY COMPANY

Incorporated August 5, 1890 - Steam - Standard Gauge

Located Santa Ana, Orange County. Proposed to build to Westminster. Distance about 9.00 miles. Only a short section on Second Street in Santa Ana was built to hold the franchise. Sold March 28, 1899 to the Santa Ana & Newport Railway Company.

SANTA BARBARA CONSOLIDATED ELECTRIC COMPANY

Organized April 7, 1903 - Electric - 3 ft. 6 in. Gauge

Located Santa Barbara, Santa Barbara County. Purchased the Santa Barbara Street Railway, a 2.50 mile long horsecar street railway. Electrified the railway. Reorganized as the Santa Barbara & Suburban Railway February 21, 1912. Trackage standard gauged. Abandoned October 1, 1929.

SANTA BARBARA & SOUTHERN PACIFIC RAILROAD COMPANY

Incorporated October 1879 - Steam - Standard Gauge

Located Santa Barbara, Santa Barbara County. Proposed to build to Newhall where a junction could be made with the Southern Pacific Company. Distance surveyed 86.00 miles.

SANTA BARBARA STREET RAILWAY

Incorporated 1897 - Horsecar - 3 ft. 6 in. Gauge

Located Santa Barbara, Santa Barbara County. Began operations as a horsecar street railway. Built 2.50 miles of street railway. Sold to the Santa Barbara Consolidated Electric Company October 1, 1896. Operations electrified. Reorganized as the Santa Barbara & Suburban Railway February 21, 1912. Standard gauged. Abandoned October 1, 1929.

SANTA BARBARA & SUBURBAN RAILWAY COMPANY

Incorporated February 21, 1912 - Electric - Standard Gauge

Located Santa Barbara, Santa Barbara County. Resulted from the reorganization of the Santa Barbara Consolidated Electric Company. Abandoned October 1, 1929.

SANTA BARBARA & SUBURBAN RAILWAY - A reorganization of the Santa Barbara Consolidated Electric Co. Was later taken over by the Southern California Edison Company who operated the line until 1929.

SANTA CATALINA ISLAND COMPANY

Organized 1910 or 1911 - Cable Car

Located Avalon, Santa Catalina Island, Los Angeles County. Built a 1,000 ft. electric-driven cable car line.

SANTA CLARA & ALVISO RAILROAD COMPANY

Proposed 1875 - Steam - Standard Gauge

Located Santa Clara, Santa Clara County. Proposed to build to San Jose and then on to deep water near Alviso.

SANTA CLARA BELT RAILROAD

Incorporated 1889 - Steam - Standard Gauge

Located Santa Clara, Santa Clara County. Proposed to build to Saratoga and San Jose. Distance 12.50 miles. Project abandoned in 1890.

SANTA CLARA INTERURBAN RAILROAD COMPANY

Incorporated December 20, 1904 - Electric - Standard Gauge

Located San Jose, Santa Clara County. Built from San Mateo to San Jose. Amended its charter January 12, 1907 to build an electric railway from San Mateo to Alum Rock Park near San Jose and to pass through Redwood City, Menlo Park, Palo Alto, Mayfield, Mountain View, Sunnyside, Santa Clara and San Jose. Consolidated with the Peninsular Railway Company June 30, 1909. Abandoned in 1934.

SANTA CLARA & PAJARO VALLEY RAILROAD COMPANY

Incorporated January 2, 1868 - Steam - Standard Gauge

Located San Jose, Santa Clara County. Built to Gilroy. Distance 30.00 miles. Consolidated with the Southern Pacific Company (original), San Francisco & San Jose Railroad Company and the California Southern Railroad Company to form the present Southern Pacific Company. Opened for traffic to Gilroy March 13, 1869.

SANTA CLARA VALLEY ELECTRIC RAILWAY & POWER COMPANY

Incorporated October 1901 - Electric - Standard Gauge

Located Oxnard, Ventura County. Franchise granted to build an electric railway to Port Hueneme to give street railway service to both cities. Trackage was to be extended from Oxnard to El Rio and then to Saticoy and Santa Paula. Franchise transferred to the Bakersfield & Ventura County Railway in March or July of 1908. Reorganized and deeded to the Ventura County Railway Company in 1910.

SANTA CLARA VALLEY MILL & LUMBER COMPANY

Organized 1886 or 1887 - Steam - 3 ft. Gauge

Located Boulder Creek, Santa Cruz County. Built 7.20 miles of trackage. Abandoned in 1920.

SANTA CLARA VALLEY RAILROAD

Organized October 1875 - Steam - Standard Gauge

Located Oakland, Alameda County. Took over the surveys of the California Narrow-Gauge Railroad & Transportation Company and proposed a standard gauge railroad rather than 3 ft. gauge to run from Dumbarton Point, Alameda County, to Santa Cruz by way of Alviso, Santa Clara County, and then to San Jose. Project abandoned in 1877.

SANTA CLARA VALLEY RAILROAD

Incorporated September 14, 1895 - Steam - Standard Gauge

Located San Jose, Santa Clara County. Proposed to build to a point on San Francisco Bay near Alviso. Distance 8.00 miles. Project abandoned in 1895.

SANTA CLARA VALLEY RAILROAD

Organized 1971 - Diesel - Standard Gauge

Located Alameda, Alameda County. Incorporated to build from Dumbarton Point on San Francisco Bay to Santa Cruz. Proposed to build from Santa Cruz into the Santa Clara Valley through the Santa Cruz Mountains. The winter rains of 1975-76 did so much damage that the railroad was abandoned.

SANTA CLARA VALLEY RAILWAY

Organized July 11, 1902 - Steam - Standard Gauge

Located Santa Clara, Santa Clara County. Proposed to build to Port Hueneme by way of Bakersfield. Distance 115 miles. Road to be converted to electric operation after traffic and revenues were proved. Project abandoned in 1903.

SANTA CLARA VALLEY RAILWAY & NAVIGATION COMPANY

Incorporated March 22, 1895 - Steam - Standard Gauge

Located Gilroy, Santa Clara County. Proposed to build north to San Jose and then on to Palo Alto. A branch was to be built to Los Gatos and another branch to Alviso. Distance 75.00 miles. No construction work was done.

SANTA CRUZ, BIG TREES & PACIFIC RAILWAY COMPANY

Steam - Standard Gauge

Located Santa Cruz, Santa Cruz County. Began operations as part of the Southern Pacific Railroad Company October 13, 1875, as the Santa Cruz & Felton Railroad. Section Santa Cruz to Olympia sold to Santa Cruz, Big Trees & Pacific Railway Company. Distance 8.87 miles.

SANTA CRUZ, BIG TREES & PACIFIC RAILWAY COMPANY

Agreement to purchase February 1, 1985 - Diesel -Standard Gauge

Located Santa Cruz, Santa Cruz County. Purchased from Southern Pacific Transportation Company trackage from Santa Cruz to Olympia via Roaring Camp. Distance 8.85 miles.

SANTA CRUZ, CAPITOLA & WATSONVILLE RAILROAD

Incorporated October 1902 - Electric - Standard Gauge

Located Santa Cruz, Santa Cruz County. Proposed to build to Watsonville. Distance 22.00 miles. Some construction work done in Santa Cruz to Woodrow Avenue. Sold to Union Traction Company of Santa Cruz October 8, 1904, and consolidated with the Santa Cruz Electric Railway.

SANTA CRUZ COUNTY RAILROAD

Organized February 3, 1866 - Steam - Narrow-Gauge

Located Santa Cruz, Santa Cruz County. Proposed to build from the headwaters of the San Lorenzo River through the Santa Cruz Mountains to Saratoga and Mountain View.

SANTA CRUZ ELECTRIC RAILWAY

Electric - 3 ft. 2 in. Gauge

Located Santa Cruz, Santa Cruz County. Operated 8.00 miles of street railway. Also operated the Pacific Avenue Railroad.

SANTA CRUZ ELECTRIC RAILWAY - An old picture postcard showing one of the trolley cars operating on Pacific Avenue and passing Casa del Rey Hotel. - *Donald Duke Collection*

SANTA CRUZ & FELTON RAILROAD

Organized 1875 - Horsecar

Located Santa Cruz, Santa Cruz County. Built on Pacific Avenue to the wharf. Began operations in 1876. Sold to Pacific Avenue Street Railroad.

SANTA CRUZ & FELTON RAILROAD COMPANY

Incorporated November 13, 1874 - Steam - 3 ft. Gauge

Located Santa Cruz, Santa Cruz County. Built to "Old Felton" by way of the San Lorenzo River. Began operations October 13, 1875. Completed to Lumber Mill in 1887. Distance 1.50 miles. This section, known as Dougherty Extension Railroad, was operated by the Dougherty Lumber Company. Original 7.80 miles taken into the Southern Pacific Company May 23, 1887. Standard gauged in 1906.

SANTA CRUZ, GARFIELD PARK & CAPITOLA ELECTRIC RAILROAD

Organized 1890 - Electric

Located Santa Cruz, Santa Cruz County. Took over the Pacific Avenue Railroad in Santa Cruz and began operations in 1891 from the bridge west on Walnut Avenue and by way of Mission, Young Love and Garfield (now Woodrow Street) to the cliffs. Became Santa Cruz Electric Railway. Consolidated with the Union Traction Company of Santa Cruz in 1904. Abandoned January 15, 1926.

SANTA CRUZ LUMBER COMPANY

Organized 1923 - Steam - Standard Gauge

Located Pescadero Creek, Santa Cruz County. Built from Mill in Saratoga Gap, at the headwaters of Pescadero Creek north of Big Basin State Park, to timber. Began construction April 15, 1930, from mill northwestward along Pescadero Creek. Distance 7.55 miles. Ceased operations in 1950. Abandoned in 1951. Mill closed in 1972.

SANTA CRUZ PORTLAND CEMENT COMPANY

Incorporated 1905 - Steam - Standard Gauge

Located Davenport, Santa Cruz County. Construction work began October 1905, from cement plant to quarry. Began operations in 1906. Distance 3.00 miles. Rebuilt in 1923. Changed to 3 ft. gauge and electrified. Sold to the Pacific Coast Aggregates March 14, 1956. Ceased operations August 27, 1970.

SANTA CRUZ RAILROAD

Incorporated June 18, 1873 - Steam - 3 ft. Gauge

Located Santa Cruz, Santa Cruz County. Built eastward 8.00 miles through Soquel, skirting Monterey Bay and then southeastward to Watsonville and Pajaro. Distance 21.20 miles. Opened for traffic May 18, 1876. Sold to the Pacific Improvement Company October 1, 1881. Standard gauged in 1883. Transferred to the Pajaro & Santa Cruz Railroad Company April 11, 1884. Consolidated with the Southern Pacific Company May 14, 1888.

SANTA CRUZ & WATSONVILLE RAILROAD COMPANY

Organized 1871 - Steam - 3 ft. Gauge

Located Santa Cruz, Santa Cruz County. Proposed to build to Watsonville from the east bank of the San Lorenzo River, opposite Santa Cruz. Distance 20.00 miles. Before work began, it was sold to the Santa Cruz Railroad June 18, 1873.

SANTA FE & LOS ANGELES HARBOR RAILROAD COMPANY

Incorporated April 20, 1922 - Steam - Standard Gauge

Located Wilmington, Los Angeles County. Built to El Segundo. Distance 12.70 miles. Completed December 31, 1924. Deeded to the Santa Fe Railway December 31, 1924.

SANTA FE & SANTA MONICA RAILWAY COMPANY

Incorporated April 4, 1892 - Steam - Standard Gauge

Located Santa Monica, Los Angeles County. Built to Inglewood. Distance 9.056

SANTA FE AVENUE RAILWAY - A steam dummy streetcar line operating on Santa Fe Avenue to Vernon. Became a part of the Los Angeles Railway. - *Donald Duke Collection*

miles. Opened to traffic June 18, 1892. Leased to the Southern California Railroad June 18, 1892. Sold to the Los Angeles-Pacific Railroad Company March 21, 1902. Electrified and put into service October 18, 1902, as the Inglewood Line. Merged with the Pacific Electric Railway Company.

SANTA FE AVENUE RAILWAY

Organized 1891 - Steam - 3 ft. 6 in. Gauge

Located Los Angeles, Los Angeles County. Built along Santa Fe Avenue from Los Angeles to Vernon. Became part of the Los Angeles Railway.

SANTA FE CONNECTING RAILROAD COMPANY

Proposed 1929 - Steam - Standard Gauge

Located San Bernardino County. Proposed to operate from Crucero on the Union Pacific Railroad to Newberry on the Santa Fe Railway, and to use Union Pacific Railroad tracks through Afton Canyon. Total operating mileage to be 36.25 miles. This was to be a part of the proposed Mid-Pacific Railroad.

SANTA FE PACIFIC RAILROAD COMPANY

Corporation formed June 16, 1897 - Steam - Standard Gauge

Located Los Angeles, Los Angeles County. A reorganization of the Atchison, Topeka & Santa Fe Railway Company and the assets of the Atlantic & Pacific Railroad Company. A total of 806.58 miles of trackage was involved. 562.58 miles were owned and 244.00 miles were leased. This trackage included 562.58 miles from Isleta, New Mexico, to Needles, California, owned and 242 miles from Needles to Mojave leased from the Santa Fe Railway and the Southern Pacific Company. 2.00 miles from Bakersfield to Kern Junction leased from the San Francisco & San Joaquin Valley Railway Company acquired from Atlantic & Pacific Railroad Company through foreclosure June 24, 1897. Conveyed to the Atchison, Topeka & Santa Fe Railway Company July 1, 1902.

SANTA FE PACIFIC - A holding company of the Santa Fe Railroad which took over the assets of the Atlantic & Pacific Railroad. Trackage included 562 miles from Islets, New Mexico to Needles, California. Very few locomotives carried the SFP name. - *Donald Duke Collection*

SANTA FE - SOUTHERN PACIFIC CORPORATION

Memorandum May 15, 1980 - Diesel - Standard Gauge

Located San Francisco, San Francisco County. Directors of the Santa Fe and Southern Pacific jointly embraced a memorandum of intent to merge on May 15, 1980. No formal application was made to the stockholders, the various state railroad commissions or the Interstate Commerce Commission. Under the proposed merger the Santa Fe was to take over the Southern Pacific. However, the courtship ended 26 months later when alleged personality conflicts developed between the chairmen of the two roads.

SANTA FE - SOUTHERN PACIFIC CORPORATION

Memorandum September 27, 1983 - Diesel - Standard Gauge

Located San Francisco, San Francisco County. In 1983 the merger between the Santa Fe and Southern Pacific was on again. An agreement in principle was announced between Santa Fe Industries and the Southern Pacific Company on September 27, 1983. The two railroads would become subsidiaries of a holding company to be called the Santa Fe - Southern Pacific Corporation. The scope of the merger would include the railroad, real estate, construction companies, pipelines, trucking companies, forest products, mining and financial services. The merger plan was submitted to stockholders and to the Interstate Commerce Commission. On July 24, 1986, the application was rejected by a 4 to 1 vote. The commission ordered the holding company to divest itself of one or both railroads. The Southern Pacific was sold to Philip Anschutz in 1984.

SANTA FE TERMINAL COMPANY OF CALIFORNIA

Incorporated February 23, 1899 - Steam - Standard Gauge

Located San Francisco, San Francisco County. Built .05 miles of trackage. Owned terminal facilities and floating equipment. Operated by San Francisco & San Joaquin Valley Railway Company until March 31, 1902. Operated under lease by the Santa Fe Railway Company March 31, 1902 to July 24, 1912. Conveyed to the Santa Fe Railway Company July 24, 1912.

SANTA MARIA VALLEY RAILROAD COMPANY

Organized July 14, 1911 - Steam - Standard Gauge

Located Santa Maria, Santa Barbara County. Leased 3.62 miles of trackage from the Southern Pacific Company between Guadalupe and Betteravia Junction. Built trackage from Betteravia to Santa Maria. Branches from Stowell to Air Base, Suey to Rosemary and Rex to Gates. Completed in 1911. Total mileage operated 14.80 miles.

SANTA MARIA VALLEY RAILROAD - Built a short line railroad from Betteravia to Santa Maria with an extension to Gates. Branches were later built to an air base and Rosemary Farms. - *Donald Duke*

SANTA MONICA CANYON RAILROAD COMPANY

Organized 1904 - Electric - Standard Gauge

Located Santa Monica, Los Angeles County. Incorporated September 23, 1905. Consolidated with the Los Angeles Pacific Railroad Company of California October 12, 1903. Sold to the Pacific Electric Railway Company in 1910.

SANTA MONICA & NORTHERN RAILWAY COMPANY

Incorporated March 11, 1907 - Electric - Standard Gauge

Located Santa Monica, Los Angeles County. Consolidated into the Los Angeles Pacific Railroad of California. Became part of the Los Angeles Pacific Company March 30, 1907. Sold to the Pacific Electric Railway Company in 1910.

SANTA MONICA OUTLOOK RAILROAD

Organized September 1887 - Steam - Standard Gauge

Located Santa Monica, Los Angeles County. Proposed to build from the front entrance of the Arcadia Hotel, along Ocean Avenue to the entrance to Santa Monica Canyon. The line would run up the canyon a distance of 1.00 mile to Santa Monica Heights - a new real estate development. Terminus would be at the east end of the tract. Project abandoned.

SANTA MONICA & SOLDIERS HOME RAILROAD COMPANY

Incorporated May 8, 1891 - Horsecar - Narrow-Gauge

Located Santa Monica, Los Angeles County. Sold to the Pasadena & Pacific Railway Company June 17, 1895. Electrified 1896. Sold to the Los Angeles & Pacific Railway of California in 1897. Sold to the Pacific Electric Railway in 1910.

SANTA MONICA SURF LINE RAILWAY COMPANY

Incorporated September 24, 1890 - Steam - Standard Gauge

Located Santa Monica, Los Angeles County. Proposed to build to Port Ballona. Distance 4.00 miles. Right-of-way secured in November 1890. Project abandoned in 1892.

SANTA MONICA WHARF & TERMINAL RAILWAY COMPANY

Incorporated June 16, 1890 - Steam - Standard Gauge

Located Santa Monica, Los Angeles County. Proposed to build from the terminus of the Los Angeles & Pacific Railway to a point on the Ballona Division of the Southern California Railway and then to a terminus of the Los Angeles & Independence Railroad. Distance 10.95 miles. Project abandoned.

SANTA ROSA & BENICIA CENTRAL RAILWAY

Organized December 1886 - Steam - Standard Gauge

Located Santa Rosa, Sonoma County. Proposed to build to Benicia. Trackage would nearly parallel the tracks of the San Francisco & North Pacific Railroad branch.

SANTA ROSA & CARQUINEZ RAILROAD COMPANY

Incorporated March 26, 1887 - Steam - Standard Gauge

Located Santa Rosa, Sonoma County. Partially constructed a railroad from Napa Junction to Santa Rosa. Consolidated with the Northern Railway Company May 15, 1888. Construction began in May 1887. Completed May 31, 1888. Distance 36.70 miles. Consolidated with the Southern Pacific Company April 14, 1898. Trackage from Schellville to Santa Rosa abandoned in 1936. 9.79 miles of trackage sold to the Northwestern Pacific Railroad Company in 1936.

SANTA ROSA CITY RAILROAD

Chartered June 5, 1877 - Horsecar - 3 ft. 6 in. Gauge

Located Santa Rosa, Sonoma County. Began as a horsecar street railway operation in June 1878. This company was held in common ownership with the Union Street Railway.

SANTA ROSA & CLEAR LAKE RAILROAD COMPANY

Organized 1911 - Electric - Standard Gauge

Located Kellogg, Sonoma County. Proposed to build northward to Lakeport by way of Middletown and Kelseyville. Distance 35.35 miles. Grading begun December 1911. Project abandoned.

SANTA ROSA & LAKE COUNTY SCENIC RAILWAY COMPANY

Proposed September 19, 1908 - Electric - 2 ft. 6 in. Gauge

Located Santa Rosa, Sonoma County. Proposed to build to Clear Lake by way of Knights Valley, Pine Flat and Lower Lake to an undetermined point on Clear Lake. No work done.

SANTA ROSA & NAPA RAILROAD

Organized 1879 - Steam - Standard Gauge

Located Santa Rosa, Sonoma County. Proposed to build to Napa Junction on the California Pacific Railroad by way of Sonoma. Distance 38.00 miles.

SANTA ROSA NORTHERN RAILROAD

Incorporated April 8, 1906 - Electric - Standard Gauge

Located Santa Rosa, Sonoma County. Incorporated by the Petaluma & Santa Rosa Railroad Company. Proposed to build from a junction with the Petaluma & Santa Rosa Railroad to Healdsburg and then up Dry Creek Valley. Abandoned in 1907 after some grading had been done.

SANTA ROSA, SEBASTOPOL & GREEN VALLEY RAILROAD

Organized April 1887 - Steam - Standard Gauge

Located Santa Rosa, Sonoma County. Built to Sebastopol. Distance 7.14 miles. Leased to the California Northwestern Railway in 1898. Sold to the Northwestern Pacific Railway Company in 1907.

SANTA ROSA & SONOMA COUNTY ELECTRIC RAILWAY COMPANY

Incorporated December 1896 - Electric - 3 ft. Gauge

Located San Francisco, San Francisco County. Proposed to build from the Embarcadero to either Santa Rosa or Calistoga or both. Surveys began February 1897. No construction work was done.

SANTA ROSA STREET RAILWAY COMPANY

Chartered June 5, 1877 - Horsecar - 3 ft. 6 in. Gauge

Located Santa Rosa, Sonoma County. Built 1.62 miles of horsecar street railway from the station on the San Francisco & North Pacific Railroad. Sold to the Union Street Railways in 1902. Became part of the Northwestern Pacific Railway Company in 1923.

SANTA ROSA STREET RAILWAYS

Organized 1902 - Electric - 3 ft. 6 in. Gauge

Located Santa Rosa, Sonoma County. Consolidated the Santa Rosa Street Railway Company, the Union Street Railway and the Central Street Railway. Sold to the Petaluma & Santa Rosa Railroad September 28, 1903. Became part of the Northwestern Pacific Railway Company in 1923.

SANDERSON & PORTER LUMBER COMPANY

Organized 1910 - Steam - 3 ft. Gauge

Located Sonora, Tuolumne County. Built and operated 16.00 miles of trackage.

SANGER LUMBER COMPANY

Organized 1885 - Steam - Standard Gauge and 3 ft. Gauge

Located Sanger, Fresno County. Built from Padre on the Southern Pacific Railroad to Saw Mill at Sanger. Standard Gauge. Operated the Sequoia Railroad 3 ft. gauge from 1896 to 1907. Was taken over by the Hume-Bennett Lumber Company in 1908. Renamed Sanger Lumber Company in 1917. Ceased operations in 1918. Leasee operations from time to time from 1918 to 1930. Abandoned in 1930.

SAUSALITO INCLINE STREET RAILWAY

Organized June 6, 1914 - Electric Cable - Standard Gauge

Located Sausalito, Marin County. Proposed to build from the Bay Front to the Heights 1,000 ft. above Sausalito. To use compensating cable cars. The power station to be located at the top of the incline. Received a certificate of public convenience to operate October 1, 1914. Right-of-way secured from Water Street over Oak Street and to the summit of the hill. Distance 2,900 ft.

M. J. SCANLON LUMBER COMPANY

Organized 1923 - Steam - Narrow-Gauge

Located Massack, Plumas County. Built from mill to timber. 6.00 miles. Abandoned 1926.

GEORGE SCHAFFER LUMBER COMPANY

Organized 1886 - Steam - Narrow-Gauge

Located Martins Creek, 6 miles south of Truckee, Placer County. Built from mill to timber. Distance 2.00 miles.

SCOTT VALLEY RAILWAY

Incorporated October 2, 1905 - Steam - Standard Gauge

Located Yreka, Siskiyou County. Proposed to build southwesterly through Scott Valley to a point on the Pacific Ocean, either at Del Norte or Humboldt counties, and also from Yreka to Montague. Distance 150.00 miles. Project abandoned.

SCOTTS CREEK RAILWAY

Incorporated July 1, 1908 - Electric - Standard Gauge

Located Scotts Creek, Santa Cruz County. Proposed to build from Scotts Branch on the Ocean Shore Railway to Vincente. Distance 2.30 miles.

SECOND STREET CABLE RAILROAD COMPANY

Incorporated March 12, 1885 - Cable - 3 ft. 6 in. Gauge

Located Los Angeles, Los Angeles County. Built on Second Street from Spring Street to Belmont Street. Opened for service October 8, 1885. This was the first cable car line in Los Angeles. Destroyed by flood December 24, 1889. Sold to the Belt Line Railroad Company in December 1890. Converted to electric operation. Began electric operations December 17, 1890. Deeded to Los Angeles Consolidated Electric Railway Company November 3, 1891. Sold to the Los Angeles Railway Company August 18, 1895.

SECOND STREET CABLE RAILROAD - Built on Second Street in downtown Los Angeles between Spring and Belmont. The line was the first cable car operation in Los Angeles. This scene shows the cable barn and powerhouse at 2nd and Boylston streets. - *Donald Duke Collection*

SECOND STREET RAILROAD COMPANY

Franchise granted September 8, 1887 - Horsecar - 3 ft. 6 in. Gauge

Located Pomona, Los Angeles County. Built from Garey Avenue to Reservoir Avenue on East Second Street. Distance 1.00 mile. Construction began September 17, 1887. Began operations October 27, 1887. Sold to the Orange Grove

Street Railway Company January 3, 1888. Tracks removed September 10, 1896.

SEQUOIA RAILROAD
Organized 1891 - Steam - Horse Power - 3 ft. Gauge

Located Kings River Lumber Company, Fresno County. Built a horse power gravity logging road from the Upper Mill or Mill Flat Creek Mill to timber. Distance 1.00 mile. Steam operations were built from mill, two miles west of the horse power line. Distance 2.00 miles. Rebuilt in 1892 from Upper Mill to timber. Distance 6.70 miles. Began operations in 1893. Extended to Converse Basin by means of an incline over Hoist Ridge by 1897. Road taken over by the Sanger Lumber Company in 1897. Abandoned 1908. Trackage and rolling stock moved to the Hume-Bennett Lumber Company operations at Hume Lake, Fresno County. Ceased operations 1917. Operated from time to time by lease until abandonment in 1930.

T.R. SHANNON COMPANY
Organized 1930 - Steam

Located Carlotta, Humboldt County. Operated 4.00 miles of trackage from 1940 to 1942 or 1943.

SHARPE ARMY DEPOT RAILROAD
Established 1941 - Diesel - Standard Gauge

Located Lathrop, San Joaquin County. The United States Army Materials Command established its west coast materials center at Lathrop, six miles south of Stockton, in 1941. The depot contains 46 miles of track inside the installation and is connected to the Western Pacific.

SHASTA COMMERCIAL COMPANY
Organized 1915 - Steam - Narrow-Gauge

Located Terry Mills, Shasta County. Operated 10.00 miles of narrow-gauge railroad. Began operations in 1916. Ceased operations in 1919.

SHASTA MINERAL BELT RAILROAD
Organized January 1902 - Steam - Standard Gauge or Narrow-Gauge

Located Shasta County. Proposed to build a railroad to service all the mineral, lumbering and agricultural facilities in the county and to join with all of the existing railroads and all railroads that may be built in the future. No construction work was done.

SHASTA SOUTHERN RAILWAY COMPANY
Incorporated July 17, 1906 - Standard Gauge

Located Hamilton, Glenn County. Built to Monroeville. Distance 3.75 miles. Acquired the properties of the Redding & Red Bluff Railroad Company. Sold to the Northern Electric Railway Company January 18, 1907. Abandoned in 1913.

SHASTA SPRINGS SCENIC RAILROAD
Organized 1888 - Cable

Located Shasta Springs Resort, Shasta County. Built a short funicular road up the bluff from the Southern Pacific Depot to the grounds of the Shasta Springs Resort.

SHASTA, TRINITY & HUMBOLDT RAILROAD
Organized January 1901 - Steam - Standard Gauge

Located Eureka, Humboldt County. Proposed to build east about 100 miles through Trinity and Shasta counties to a connection with the Southern Pacific Railroad Company in the Sacramento Valley. Project abandoned in 1902.

SHAVER LAKE LUMBER COMPANY
Organized 1919 - Steam - Standard Gauge

Located Shaver, Fresno County. Purchased the Shaver Lake Railroad and the Fresno Lumber & Irrigation Company. Trackage extended from Dawn on the San Joaquin & Eastern Railway to Shaver Lake. Abandoned 1927.

SHASTA SPRINGS SCENIC RAILROAD - A short cable incline railway was built from the Southern Pacific depot to the Shasta Springs Resort on the mountain above.
- Donald Duke Collection

SHAVER LAKE RAILROAD
Organized 1907 - Steam - Standard Gauge

Located Shaver, Fresno County. Resulted from the purchase of the Fresno Lumber & Irrigation Company holdings by the Southern California Edison Company. Trackage extended from Dawn on the San Joaquin & Eastern Railway to Shaver. Distance 6.00 miles. Sold in 1919 to Shaver Lake Lumber Company. Extended 6.00 miles to timber. Abandoned in 1927.

J.G. SHEBLEY COMPANY
Organized 1908 - Steam - Narrow-Gauge

Located Colfax, Placer County. Operated 8.00 miles of trackage.

SHELL OIL COMPANY
Steam - Standard Gauge

Located Watson, Los Angeles County. Built from a junction with the Pacific Electric Railway Company to the company oil loading docks.

SHINGLE SPRINGS & PLACERVILLE RAILROAD
Incorporated May 10, 1887 - Steam - Standard Gauge

Located Shingle Springs, El Dorado County. Built to Placerville. Distance 10.60 miles. Opened for traffic March 29, 1888. Consolidated into the Northern Railway Company May 15, 1888. Consolidated with the Southern Pacific Company April 14, 1898.

SIERRA COUNTY RAILROAD
Organized May 1911 - Electric - Steam - Standard Gauge or 3 ft. Gauge

Located Sacramento, Sacramento County. Organized to build a railroad connecting the towns of Sierra, Wyandotte, Banker and Nord with Sacramento or some other large city. No construction work done.

SIERRA & EASTERN RAILROAD COMPANY
Incorporated January 19, 1906 - Steam - 3 ft. Gauge

Located Bakersfield, Kern County. Proposed to build from Tehachapi east to Searchlight, Lincoln County, Nevada. Distance 200 miles. No construction work done.

SIERRA IRON & QUINCY RAILROAD COMPANY
Incorporated 1867 - Steam - 3 ft. Gauge

Located Quincy, Plumas County. Proposed to build a railroad from Quincy through the Mohawk Valley and over Beckwourth Pass. Some grading was done and an office building erected. Project abandoned in 1873.

SIERRA LUMBER COMPANY

Incorporated October 4, 1878 - Steam - Meter Gauge

Located Lyonsville, Tehama County. Plans were made in September 1880 to build a meter gauge logging railroad. Construction began in March 1881. Built to Yellow Jacket Mill on Antelope Creek. Distance 14.00 miles. In 1896, a second meter gauge railroad was built from the Providence Mill on Big Chico Creek, Butte County, through Chico Canyon towards Soda Springs. Distance 6.35 miles. Built a standard gauge switching and connecting road with the Southern Pacific Company in Chico in 1901. Sold to Diamond Match Company March 19, 1907.

SIERRA LUMBER COMPANY

Organized 1881 - Steam - 39 1/2 in. Gauge

Located Lyonsville, Tehama County. Built from mill to timber. Distance 26.00 miles. Abandoned in 1907.

SIERRA MADRE STREET RAILWAY COMPANY

Incorporated August 7, 1887 - Mule Car - Narrow-Gauge

Located Sierra Madre, Los Angeles County. Built from the Santa Anita Station on the California Central Railway Company (Santa Fe) along Baldwin Avenue, Central Avenue and Grand View Avenue to Sierra Madre. Distance 1.50 miles. Plans were made to extend the tracks to Santa Anita Canyon April 24, 1889. Tracks were not laid down and the whole line was abandoned in 1890 or 1891.

SIERRA NEVADA WOOD & LUMBER COMPANY

Organized 1896 - Steam - Standard Gauge and 3 ft. Gauge

Located Truckee, Nevada County. Built to Hobart Mills and then on to timber. Section from Truckee to Hobart Mills standard gauge. Distance 6.50 miles. Section from Hobart Mills to woods 3 ft. gauge. Distance 8.10 miles. Completed 1899. Became Hobart Estate Company in 1917. Trackage extended to the woods 23.50 miles by 1923. Section Hobart to Truckee became Hobart Southern Railroad Company in 1923. This trackage was standard gauge. Distance 6.50 miles. All trackage abandoned December 1, 1937.

SIERRA PACIFIC RAILROAD

First train May 7, 1986 - Diesel - Standard Gauge

Located Susanville, Lassen County. Leased Southern Pacific's Susanville Branch which ran from Wendel to the Eagle Lake Lumber Company mill, a distance of 23 miles. Lease was to run for a period of five years with a renewal. Line operated under contract with the Quincy Railroad.

SIERRA PACIFIC RAILROAD COMPANY

Incorporated September 18, 1896 - Steam - 3 ft. Gauge

Located Stockton, San Joaquin County. Proposed to build to Jackson in Amador County. Distance 50.00 miles. Branches were to be built to San Andreas, Camp Seco and Plymouth Rock mine in Calaveras County. No construction work done.

SIERRA PACIFIC RAILROAD COMPANY

Organized September 23, 1906 - Steam - Standard Gauge

Located Globe, Tulare County. Proposed to build southwest through Success and Worth to Plano and Porterville, then northwest by way of Woodville and Tulare to Tagus, then west by way of Hanford, Armona, Lemoore and Huron to Coalinga. Then over the Coast Range Mountains to Port Hanford on San Luis Obispo Bay by way of Paso Robles, Templeton and Santa Margarita. Distance 193.00 miles. One branch to be built from Tagus northeast to Visalia then northwest by way of Reedley, Orosi and Sanger to Fresno. Distance 70.00 miles. A branch from Tagus south to Bakersfield. Distance 60.00 miles. Project abandoned.

SIERRA RAILWAY COMPANY OF CALIFORNIA
SIERRA RAILROAD COMPANY

Incorporated February 27, 1897 - Steam - Standard Gauge

Located Oakdale, Stanislaus County. Built to Tuolumne County by 1900. Distance 55.00 miles. Foreclosure sale March 31, 1937 resulted in the present Sierra Railroad Company. Section Jamestown to Angels Camp built 1902. Abandoned 1932. Present operating mileage 57.43 miles.

SIERRA RAILROAD - Built from Oakdale to Jamestown in 1900, a distance of 55 miles. Extensions to Tuolumne and Angels Camp were built in 1902. In this scene a train rolls along the line near Cooperstown. - *Donald Duke*

SIERRA & SAN FRANCISCO POWER COMPANY

Steam - Standard Gauge

Located Schoettgen Pass, Tuolumne County. Built from Pickering Lumber Company Railroad to powerhouse. Distance 12.35 miles.

SIERRA SUGAR PINE COMPANY

Organized December 1, 1912 - Steam - Standard Gauge

Located Triant, Sonoma County. Proposed to build in the North Forks country to Chiquita. Distance 100 miles.

SIERRA VALLEY RAILROAD COMPANY
SIERRA VALLEY & MOHAWK RAILROAD COMPANY
SIERRA & MOHAWK RAILWAY COMPANY

Incorporated October 1, 1885 - Steam - 3 ft. Gauge

Located Quincy, Plumas County. On October 1, 1885, the Sierra Valley & Mohawk Railroad Company was chartered to build from a junction with the Nevada & California Railroad (later the Nevada-California-Oregon Railroad Company) to Quincy. Built from Junction to Kirby's Mill in 1889. Distance 23.10 miles. Reorganized January 5, 1895, as the Sierra Valley Railroad Company. Opened for traffic June 1, 1895. Sold to the trustee of the Nevada-California-Oregon Railroad Company under foreclosure January 3, 1909. Rechartered as the Sierra & Mohawk Railway Company June 11, 1911. Consolidated with the Nevada-California-Oregon Railroad Company January 1, 1915, and became their Sierra Valley Branch. Total mileage built 39.40 miles. Abandoned April 16, 1918.

SIERRAVILLE LUMBER COMPANY

Organized 1952 - Standard Gauge

Located Sierra City, Sierra County. Built from mill to timber. Distance 13.00 miles. Abandoned 1954.

SILVER LAKE RAILROAD

Steam - Standard Gauge

Located Silver Lake, San Bernardino County. Proposed to build from a junction with the Tonopah & Tidewater Railroad at Silver Lake west to Iron Mountain via the Crackerjack Mine and the Bonanza Mine. Distance 12.00 miles. No work was done.

SIMON'S BRICK COMPANY

Gas Engine - 2 ft. Gauge

Located Montebello, Los Angeles County. Built from plant to quarry along Washington Blvd. Distance 3.46 miles. Abandoned 1952.

SIMPSON LOGGING COMPANY

Organized 1950 - Standard Gauge

Located near Arcata, Humboldt County. Purchased the Arcata Branch of the Hammond Lumber Company for trackage connection between mill and the Northwestern Pacific Railroad.

SISKIYOU ELECTRIC POWER & LIGHT COMPANY

Organized 1912 - Steam - Standard Gauge

Located Thrall, Siskiyou County. Leased the trackage of the Oregon Southern Railroad from a junction with the Southern Pacific Company to the power house. Distance 20.45 miles. Lease terminated in 1913. Railroad out of service from 1913 to 1916. Sold to the California-Oregon Power Company in 1916. Abandoned in 1942.

SISKIYOU LUMBER COMPANY

Organized 1920 - Steam - Standard Gauge

Located Mt. Hebron, Siskiyou County. Built from mill to timber. Distance 12.00 miles. Abandoned in 1930.

SISSON MILL & LUMBER COMPANY
SISSON LUMBER COMPANY

Organized 1889 - Steam - Narrow-Gauge

Located Sisson, Siskiyou County. Built from mill to timber. Distance 3.00 miles. Reorganized as the Sisson Lumber Company in 1895. Began building from Upton to the timber near the McCloud River. A total of 15.00 miles of track in use.

SLOAT LUMBER COMPANY

Organized 1917 - Steam - 3 ft. Gauge

Located Sloat, Plumas County. Built 3.00 miles of track. Sold to the F.S. Murphy Lumber Company. Track extended 3.10 miles in 1918. Sold to the Quincy Lumber Company in 1926. Abandoned in 1936.

RALPH L. SMITH LUMBER COMPANY

Organized 1943 - Steam - Standard Gauge

Located Canby, Modoc County. Took over the properties of the Big Lake Lumber & Box Company. Operated over the trackage of the Canby Railroad Company. Distance 10.00 miles. Abandoned in 1948. Tracks removed in 1951.

SONOMA COUNTY RAILROAD COMPANY

Incorporated January 10, 1868 - Steam - Standard Gauge

Located Petaluma, Sonoma County. Proposed to build to Healdsburg by way of Santa Rosa with a branch to Bloomfield. Some grading work was done but no track was laid. Sold to the San Francisco & North Pacific Railroad Company November 17, 1869.

SONOMA & LAKE COUNTY ELECTRIC RAILWAY COMPANY

Incorporated March 1, 1907 - Electric - Standard Gauge

Located Lakeport, Lake County. Proposed to build from Cloverdale to Lakeport. A branch was to be built to Kelseyville. Distance 27.00 miles for total railroad mileage. Surveys completed May 27, 1907.

SONOMA & LAKE COUNTY RAILROAD

Proposed August 10, 1907 - Electric - Standard Gauge

Located Lakeport, Lake County. Planned to build to Cloverdale by way of Highland Springs, Saratoga, Adams Springs and Hartlett. Distance 26.75 miles. No work done.

SONOMA & LAKE COUNTY RAILWAY

Organized February 1909 - Electric - Standard Gauge

Located Santa Rosa, Sonoma County. Proposed to build to Lakeport by way of Cloverdale and Preston. Franchise granted July 1, 1909. Franchise sold to the Highland Pacific Railroad Company in September 1909.

SONOMA LAND & LUMBER COMPANY

Organized 1892 - Steam - Standard Gauge

Located Guerneville, Sonoma County. Purchased the holdings of the Guerne-Murphy Lumber Company. Abandoned in 1902.

SONOMA MAGNESITE RAILROAD

Built 1914 - 2 ft. Gauge

Located Magnesia, Sonoma County. Built to the west side of East Austin Creek, on the Cazadero Branch of the Northwestern Pacific Railroad. Total mileage was 10 miles of track. Abandoned in 1920.

SONOMA & MARIN RAILROAD

Incorporated November 13, 1874 - Steam - 3 ft. Gauge

Located Petaluma, Sonoma County. Proposed to build to San Rafael. Took over the right-of-way of the Contra Costa Navigation Company March 23, 1875. Built as far as Novato. Sold and rebuilt as a standard gauge railroad to San Rafael October 17, 1876. Distance 21.50 miles. Consolidated into the San Francisco & North Pacific Railroad July 12, 1877. Consolidated into the Northwestern Pacific Railroad January 8, 1907.

SONOMA, MENDOCINO & HUMBOLDT RAILROAD COMPANY

Incorporated July 12, 1895 - Steam - Standard Gauge

Located Healdsburg, Sonoma County. Proposed to build north through Dry Creek and Anderson Valley to Eureka, Humboldt County. Distance 170.00 miles. Branches were to be built from Fort Bragg to the coal fields at Round Valley. Surveys were begun July 26, 1895. Project abandoned in 1897.

SONOMA, NAPA JUNCTION & VALLEJO RAILROAD

Organized January 1879 - Steam - Standard Gauge

Located Sonoma, Sonoma County. Proposed to build southeast to a junction with the Napa Valley Branch of the California Pacific Railroad. Distance 14.75 miles.

SONOMA & SANTA ROSA RAILROAD COMPANY

Incorporated March 3, 1881 - Steam - 3 ft. Gauge

Located Sonoma, Sonoma County. Built to Glen Ellen. Distance 6.53 miles. Began operations August 15, 1882. Conveyed to the Sonoma Valley Railroad January 30, 1885. Consolidated into San Francisco & North Pacific Railway December 19, 1888. Consolidated into Northwestern Pacific Railroad January 8, 1907.

SONOMA VALLEY EXTENSION RAILROAD

Incorporated July 1887 - Steam - Standard Gauge

Located Glen Ellen, Sonoma County. Proposed to build to Santa Rosa. Distance 16.00 miles.

SONOMA VALLEY PRISMOIDAL RAILROAD
SONOMA VALLEY RAILROAD COMPANY

Incorporated February 18, 1875 - Steam - Single Rail "A" Frame

Located Sonoma, Sonoma County. Built from Sonoma to Sonoma Creek. Construction was a single elevated "A" frame. Distance 3.50 miles. Reincorporated July 24, 1876, as the Sonoma Valley Railroad Company. Built north from Wingo Station, to Schellville, Vineburg and Sonoma. Built south from Wingo Station to "Sonoma Landing" near Petaluma Creek on San Pablo Bay. Consolidated with the Sonoma & Santa Rosa Railroad Company to form the Sonoma Valley Railroad Company in 1885. Built to 3 ft. gauge. Sold to the San Francisco & North Pacific Railroad Company in March 1899. Standard gauged. Sold to the Northwestern Pacific Railroad Company in 1907.

SONORA BELT LINE RAILROAD COMPANY

Incorporated July 1, 1907 - Electric or Steam - Standard Gauge

Located Sonora, Tuolumne County. Proposed to build a belt line railroad in and about the town of Sonora. Electric power was to be used if possible. Distance 2.15 miles.

SONORA-GROVELAND RAILWAY

Organized April 1907 - Steam

Located Sonora, Tuolumne County. Proposed to build south from Sonora to Groveland by way of Quartz and Algerine. No construction work done.

SOUTH BAY RAILROAD & LAND COMPANY

Built 1875 - Steam

Located south end of Humboldt Bay, Humboldt County. Built up Salmon Creek to Milford Mill & Lumber Company. Distance 5.00 miles. After the area was logged off, railroad was transferred to Freshwater Slough and named Humboldt Logging Railway. Sold to Excelsior Redwood Company.

SOUTH BEACH & MISSION RAILWAY COMPANY

Began operations December 24, 1862

Located San Francisco, San Francisco County. Operated from Montgomery and California streets to near Mission Dolores.

SOUTH-EAST-SIDE HORSE RAILROAD COMPANY

Incorporated March 14, 1877 - Horsecar - 3 ft. Gauge

Located San Jose, Santa Clara County. Built from Second and St. John streets to Reed and Ninth streets. Distance 1.50 miles. Began operations April 25, 1877. Sold to the People's Horse Railroad Company in March 1877. Sold to the San Jose & Santa Clara Railroad Company April 23, 1882.

SOUTH PACIFIC COAST RAILROAD COMPANY

Incorporated March 25, 1876 - Steam - 3 ft. Gauge

Located Newark, Alameda County. Proposed to build to the Colorado River. Built southward to Felton in Santa Cruz County. Opened for service to Los Gatos June 1, 1876. Completed to Felton May 15, 1880. Distance 45.30 miles. Operated a horsecar street railway between Newark and Centerville. Began operations February 18, 1882. Abandoned May 29, 1909. Section from Newark to Felton consolidated into the South Pacific Coast Railway May 23, 1887.

SOUTH PACIFIC COAST RAILWAY COMPANY

Incorporated May 23, 1887 - Steam - 3 ft. Gauge

Located Newark, Alameda County. Operated from Newark to Felton. Consolidated the South Pacific Coast Railroad Company, Santa Cruz & Felton Railroad Company, Bay & Coast Railway Company, Oakland Township Railroad, the San Francisco & Colorado River Railroad Company, Felton & Pescadero Railroad and the Almaden Branch Railroad to form the South Pacific Coast Railway Company. Leased to the Southern Pacific Company July 1, 1887. Standard gauged by June 30, 1909. Abandoned 1940.

SOUTH PACIFIC COAST RAILWAY - A narrow-gauge railroad running between Alameda pier to Santa Cruz by way of San Jose. In this scene a train enters the town of Wright after it leaves the Summit Tunnel. - *Donald Duke Collection*

SOUTH SAN DIEGO & IMPERIAL BEACH RAILWAY COMPANY

Incorporated December 1, 1908 - Gasoline Motor - Standard Gauge

Located South San Diego, San Diego County. Purchased the South San Diego Railway Company. Extended the trackage to Imperial Beach. Approximately 2.00 miles. Operated a coordinated ferry, launch and railroad between San Diego and South San Diego. Distance 9.00 miles. Gasoline motor car operated to Imperial Beach by 1910. Sold to the Mexico & San Diego Railway in 1912.

SOUTH SAN DIEGO RAILWAY COMPANY

Organized 1907 - Gasoline Motor - Standard Gauge

Located South San Diego, San Diego County. Built to the Boat Landing. Taken over by the South San Diego & Imperial Beach Railway in December 1908.

SOUTH SAN FRANCISCO BELT RAILWAY

Incorporated November 20, 1907 - Steam - Standard Gauge

Located South San Francisco, San Francisco County. Purchased the trackage of the South San Francisco Land & Improvement Company to Bruno Point. This property used and owned by the Western Meat Company. Serviced by the Southern Pacific Company. Deeded to the Southern Pacific Company December 3, 1945.

SOUTH SAN FRANCISCO LAND & IMPROVEMENT COMPANY

Built 1891 - Steam - Standard Gauge

Located South San Francisco, San Francisco County. Built to Bruno Point. Leased to the Western Meat Company in 1903. Purchased by the Western Meat Company March 1, 1907. Sold to the South San Francisco Belt Railway November 20, 1907. Total mileage 3.08 miles. Serviced by the Southern Pacific Company. Deeded to the Southern Pacific Company December 3, 1945.

SOUTH SAN FRANCISCO RAILROAD & POWER COMPANY

Incorporated January 1, 1903 - Electric - Standard Gauge

Located South San Francisco, San Francisco County. Built from Holy Cross to Chestnut. Distance 1.00 mile. Built from South San Francisco to Lepsic Junction. Distance 1.50 miles. Began operations December 31, 1903. Holy Cross section abandoned in 1904. Section to Lepsic Junction sold to the Market Street Railway in 1909. Abandoned in 1938.

SOUTH SIDE STREET RAILWAY

Chartered May 16, 1888 - Horsecar - 3 ft. 6 in. Gauge

Located Santa Rosa, Sonoma County. Built 2.00 miles of horsecar street railway. Began operations August 15, 1888. Re-chartered as Union Street Railway May 8, 1893. Became part of the Santa Rosa Street Railway December 24, 1897 and electrified. Sold to the Petaluma & Santa Rosa Railroad Company in 1903.

SOUTHERN CALIFORNIA BEACH RAILWAY

Organized September 4, 1912 - Electric - Standard Gauge

Located Santa Ana, Orange County. Proposed to build through Colton, Riverside, Santa Ana, Balboa, Laguna Beach, San Juan Capistrano and Oceanside to San Diego. Distance 150.00 miles. Project abandoned in 1914.

SOUTHERN CALIFORNIA EDISON COMPANY

Organized 1914 - Steam - Standard Gauge

Located Alhambra, Los Angeles County. The Southern California Edison Company established a large line pole and transformer storage yard at Shorb Junction on the Southern Pacific. In order to gain access to their yard the Edison Company laid approximately five miles of tracks within the yard. For years all switching was done with steam cranes. Sometime in the late 1920's a tank engine was acquired. In the 1950's this tank engine was replaced by a diesel-electric switcher. In 1978 switching within the yard was handled by the Southern Pacific and the diesel presented to the Orange Empire Trolley museum.

SOUTHERN CALIFORNIA MOTOR ROAD COMPANY

Built 1886 - Steam Dummy - 3 ft. Gauge

Located San Bernardino, San Bernardino County. Built to Colton. Distance 3.00 miles. A horsecar was used for local traffic. Incorporated October 31, 1887, to be rebuilt to standard gauge and to use steam dummy motive power. Completed to Riverside November 1, 1888. Horsecar used for local service in San Bernardino. Leased to the Southern Pacific Company in 1892. Sold under foreclosure September 15, 1895, to Pacific Improvement Company and reconstructed. Became part of the Southern Pacific Company March 5, 1898. Entire road was rebuilt. Section San Bernardino to Colton sold to Pacific Electric Railway Company in 1956.

SOUTHERN CALIFORNIA NARROW-GAUGE RAILWAY

Organized 1879 - Steam - 3 ft. Gauge

Located San Pedro, Los Angeles County. Proposed to build to Downey with branches or extensions to Pasadena, San Gabriel, Duarte, Azusa, Pomona, Rincon and Anaheim. No work done.

SOUTHERN CALIFORNIA RAILWAY COMPANY

Organized November 7, 1889 - Steam - Standard Gauge

Located Los Angeles, Los Angeles County. Formed by consolidation of the California Southern Railroad Company, distance 210.60 miles; California Central Railway, distance 258.30 miles; and the Redondo Beach Railway Company, distance 10.80 miles. Total operating mileage 479.70 miles. Leased to the Atchison, Topeka & Santa Fe Railway Company June 1, 1904. Sold to the Santa Fe Railway Company January 17, 1906.

SOUTHERN CALIFORNIA RAILWAY COMPANY

Incorporated June 8, 1892 - Steam - Standard Gauge

Located Los Angeles, Los Angeles County. Formed by consolidation of the California Southern Railroad Company. Acquired by consolidation of the Santa Fe & Santa Monica Railway Company, distance 5.42 miles; San Bernardino & Eastern Railway Company, distance 12.88 miles; and the Elsinore, Pomona & Los Angeles Railway Company, distance 7.76 miles. Constructed 6.30 miles of trackage. Consolidated with the Southern California Railway Company. Incorporated November 7, 1889. Leased to the Santa Fe Railway Company June 1, 1904. Sold to the Santa Fe Railway Company January 17, 1906.

SOUTHERN CALIFORNIA RAILWAY - A consolidation of Santa Fe Railroad lines in Southern California, including the California Southern and five other railroads, were incorporated during November 1889, and leased to the Santa Fe in 1904. In this scene a train is running westbound out of San Bernardino. - *Donald Duke Collection*

SOUTHERN CALIFORNIA RAPID TRANSIT DISTRICT METRO RAIL

Established March 1975 - Electric - Standard Gauge

Located Los Angeles, Los Angeles County. Purchased 40 acres of Santa Fe Railway property near Union Station for Metro Rail storage yard, maintenance shops and central control facility October 1984. Official groundbreaking ceremonies held September 1986. Utility relocation work began near 5th and Hill September 1986. Proposed route from Union Station to Civic center and 5th and Hill to Wilshire and Alvarado. Distance 4.40 miles.

SOUTHERN HEIGHTS & VISITATION VALLEY RAILWAY COMPANY

Located San Francisco, San Francisco County. Consolidated with the Market Street Railway Company in 1893.

SOUTHERN HUMBOLDT LUMBER COMPANY

Incorporated November 6, 1902 - Steam - Standard Gauge

Located Bear Harbor, Mendocino County. Took over the operations of the Bear Harbor Lumber Company and extended the trackage of the Bear Harbor & Eel River Railroad from Moody on Indian Creek to Andersonia on the Eel River. Distance 7.80 miles. Total mileage from Bear Harbor to Andersonia 17.50 miles. Ceased operations in 1906 or 1907. Abandoned 1940.

SOUTHERN HUMBOLDT LUMBER CO. - Took over the operations of the Bear Harbor Lumber and extended a wharf into Humboldt Bay to load lumber. - *Donald Duke Collection*

SOUTHERN OREGON LUMBER COMPANY

Organized 1928 - Steam - Standard Gauge

Located Siskiyou County. Built 8.10 miles of track. Abandoned in 1930.

SOUTHERN PACIFIC BRANCH RAILROAD COMPANY

Incorporated December 23, 1872 - Steam - Standard Gauge

Located Salinas, Monterey County. Built to Soledad. Distance 25.40 miles. Completed 1873. Consolidated with the Southern Pacific Railroad Company August 19, 1873.

SOUTHERN PACIFIC BRANCH RAILWAY COMPANY

Incorporated April 12, 1886 - Steam - Standard Gauge

Located San Miguel, San Luis Obispo County. Built to Templeton, distance 13.80 miles; and Saugus to Ellwood, distance 91.00 miles. Consolidated with the Southern Pacific Railroad Company May 14, 1888.

SOUTHERN PACIFIC COMPANY

Organized March 17, 1884 - Steam - Standard Gauge

Located San Francisco, San Francisco County. Collis P. Huntington and his associates felt the need to simplify the corporate structure of the entire Southern Pacific system. Thus on March 17, 1884, under the laws of Kentucky, the Southern Pacific Company was incorporated. All securities of the Southern Pacific Railroad Company, and its subsidiaries, were brought under one organization. In 1899, the Central Pacific Railroad was reorganized as the Central Pacific Railway, and its stock was turned over to the Southern Pacific Company.

SOUTHERN PACIFIC RAILROAD

Incorporated December 2, 1865 - Steam - Standard Gauge

Located San Francisco, San Francisco County. Consolidated October 12, 1870 with California Southern Railroad, San Francisco & San Jose Railroad and Santa Clara & Pajaro Valley Railroad to form the Southern Pacific Railroad.

SOUTHERN PACIFIC RAILROAD

Incorporated October 12, 1870 - Steam - Standard Gauge

Located San Francisco, San Francisco County. Consolidated August 19, 1873 with the Southern Pacific Branch Railroad to form the Southern Pacific Railroad.

SOUTHERN PACIFIC RAILROAD

Incorporated August 19, 1873 - Steam - Standard Gauge

Located San Francisco, San Francisco County. Consolidated December 18, 1874 with the Los Angeles & San Pedro Railroad to form the Southern Pacific Railroad.

SOUTHERN PACIFIC RAILROAD

Incorporated December 18, 1874 - Steam - Standard Gauge

Located San Francisco, San Francisco County. Consolidated May 14, 1888, with the Long Beach Railroad; Long Beach, Whittier & Los Angeles County Railroad; Los Angeles & Independence Railroad; Los Angeles & San Diego Railroad; Monterey Extension Railroad; Monterey Railroad which purchased the Monterey & Salinas Valley Railroad; Pajaro & Santa Cruz Railroad (1884), a consolidation of Pajaro & Santa Cruz Railroad which purchased the Santa Cruz Railroad; Loma Prieta Railroad; Ramona & San Bernardino Railroad; San Joaquin Valley & Yosemite Railroad; San Jose & Almaden Railroad; San Pablo & Tulare Railroad; San Pablo & Tulare Extension Railroad; San Ramon Valley Railroad; Southern Pacific Branch Railway; Stockton & Copperopolis Railroad, a consolidation of the Stockton & Visalia Railroad, and the Stockton & Copperopolis Railroad; and the Stockton & Tulare Railroad to form the Southern Pacific Railroad.

SOUTHERN PACIFIC RAILROAD - This railroad built south from Bakersfield in 1875-76, running over Tehachapi Pass and around the famous "Loop," then bound for Yuma. In this scene a train is about to enter a tunnel in Tehachapi Pass in 1876. - *Donald Duke Collection*

SOUTHERN PACIFIC RAILROAD

Incorporated May 14, 1888 - Steam - Standard Gauge

Located San Francisco, San Francisco County. Acquired by purchase or lease the San Bernardino & Redlands Railroad (lease March 14, 1892); San Gabriel Valley Rapid Transit Railway (purchase October 2 1894); and the San Joaquin Valley Railroad (purchase March 5, 1898) and was consolidated April 14, 1898, with the Northern Railway, a consolidation May 15, 1888, of the Sacramento & Placerville Railroad, a consolidation of Folsom & Placerville Railroad, Sacramento Valley Railroad and Placerville & Sacramento Railroad; Shingle Springs & Placerville Railroad; West Side & Mendocino Railroad; Northern Railway (1871); San Joaquin & Sierra Nevada Railroad; Vaca Valley & Clear Lake Railroad (which purchased Vaca Valley Railroad); Amador Branch Railway; Santa Rosa & Carquinez Railroad; Berkeley Branch Railroad; Winters & Ukiah Railway; Woodland, Capay & Clear Lake Railroad; Northern California Railway (which purchased Northern California Railroad, the former name of which was California Northern Railroad); California Pacific Railroad, a consolidation December 29, 1869, of California Pacific Railroad, a consolidation of Sacramento & San Francisco Railroad, and San Francisco & Marysville Railroad; and the California Pacific Railroad Extension (which purchased Napa Valley Railroad) to form the Southern Pacific Railroad.

SOUTHERN PACIFIC RAILROAD - Of all the types of steam locomotives used on the Southern Pacific, none were more numerous than the 4-4-0 type. Literally thousands of them were produced in the last quarter of the 19th century. The No. 1310 was built in February 1880 by the Schenectady Locomotive Works for the Southern Pacific of Arizona as the No. 8. It later became SP No. 88 and then renumbered No. 1310 in 1891. - *Guy L. Dunscomb Collection*

SOUTHERN PACIFIC RAILROAD

Incorporated April 14, 1898 - Steam - Standard Gauge

Located San Francisco, San Francisco County. Purchased the Santa Ana & Newport Railway, which purchased the Newport Wharf & Lumber Company, which purchased the Santa Ana Railroad; Santa Ana & Westminster Railway, Ventura & Ojai Valley Railroad, and Visalia Railroad and was merged March 10, 1902, with Southern Pacific Railroad of Arizona and Southern Pacific Railroad of New Mexico to form the Southern Pacific Railroad.

SOUTHERN PACIFIC RAILROAD

Incorporated March 10, 1902 - Steam - Standard Gauge

Located San Francisco, San Francisco County. And into which were merged the San Francisco & Napa Railway, Coast Line Railway, Colusa & Hamilton Railroad, Hanford & Summit Lake Railway and Porterville Northeastern Railway. Southern Pacific Railroad was merged with the Southern Pacific Company on September 30, 1955.

SOUTHERN PACIFIC RAILROAD EXTENSION

Incorporated February 21, 1888 - Steam - Standard Gauge

Located San Pedro, Los Angeles County. Built to Point Fermin. Distance 5.00 miles. Consolidated with the Southern Pacific Railroad Company May 14, 1888. Construction finished August 14, 1888.

SOUTHWESTERN PORTLAND CEMENT COMPANY

Constructed 1915 - Steam - Standard Gauge

Located Victorville, San Bernardino County. Began operations to quarry August 1916. Organized as the Mojave Northern Railroad Company in 1916. Common carrier status dissolved in 1925. Operations continued as a quarry road.

SPANISH PEAK LUMBER COMPANY

Organized 1926 - Steam - Narrow-Gauge

Located Quincy, Plumas County. Built towards Snake Lake. Distance 7.00 miles. Began as a narrow-gauge timber road but was standard gauged. Abandoned 1935.

SPRECKELS SUGAR COMPANY

Built 1929 - Steam - Standard Gauge

Located Spreckels, Monterey County. Built 3.50 miles of industrial track in and about their plant.

SOUTHERN PACIFIC COMPANY - Running nearly two hours late, the Sacramento to Los Angeles *West Coast Limited* is racing to make up time as it rolls through Rosamond, south of Mojave, at 6:30 A.M. Connecting at Sacramento with the *Klamath* (train No. 19) out of Portland, Oregon, the *West Coast Limited* apparently made a late connection. It should be noted that the *West Coast Limited* is operating in two sections this busy day as the train No. 1-60 shows this as the first of two sections in the train indicator. - *Donald Duke*

SPRING & WEST SIXTH STREET RAILROAD

Incorporated February 6, 1874 - Horsecar - Narrow-Gauge

Located Los Angeles, Los Angeles County. Began operations July 1, 1874. Built 2.50 miles of street railway. Built from the Plaza down Main Street and Spring Street to Sixth Street. Sold to the Central Railroad Company in 1884. Became part of the Los Angeles Railway Company.

SPRING & WEST SIXTH STREET RAILROAD - A horsecar line built down Main and Spring streets from the Plaza to Sixth Street. It was sold to the Central Railroad Company in 1884. - *Donald Duke Collection*

STANDARD LUMBER COMPANY

Located Standard, Tuolumne County. Purchased the Empire City Railroad in 1917. Built a total of 60.00 miles of logging road. Abandoned 1926. Built 7.00 miles of logging road in Macdoel region in 1923. Abandoned in 1926. Operated 6.00 miles of standard gauge trackage from Lyons Dam to Camp Frazier on the Sugar Pine Railway.

STANDARD OIL COMPANY

Began operations 1902 - Electric - 42 in. Gauge

Located Richmond, Contra Costa County. Operated from a pier on San Francisco Bay to oil plant. Service discontinued in 1945.

STANISLAUS RAILWAY COMPANY

Incorporated August 15, 1906 - Steam - 30 in. Gauge

Located Empire, Tuolumne County. Built from a junction with the Sugar Pine Railroad that operated over the Sierra Railroad Company between Sonora and Ralph to Empire City. Extended from near Hales Old Mill on the south fork of the Stanislaus River to the middle or main fork of the same river. Distance 16.00 miles. Sold to the Empire City Railroad in 1917.

STANISLAUS & MARIPOSA RAILROAD COMPANY

Organized 1866 - Steam - Standard Gauge

Located Stockton, San Joaquin County. Proposed to build to a junction with the Stockton & Copperopolis Railroad. Distance 10.00 miles. An extension was to reach Knights Ferry and La Grange. Distance 50.00 miles. A final extension was to be built to Fort Tejon on the southeasterly end of the San Joaquin Valley. Project abandoned in 1868.

STANLEY BROWN COMPANY

Organized 1896 - Horse Power - Gas Engine - 42 in. Gauge

Located Betteravia, Santa Barbara County. Began operations in 1905 or 1906 with a horse power railroad around the feeding pens. A Fordson tractor engine was put in operation in 1934. Distance 3.50 miles.

STATE BELT RAILROAD OF CALIFORNIA

Incorporated June 1892 - Steam - Standard Gauge

Located San Francisco, San Francisco County. Organized as the San Francisco Belt Railroad and built a belt railroad and depot in San Francisco. Connected with the Southern Pacific Company wharves at the foot of Second Street with the depot at Third and Townsend. Ownership transferred to the City of San Francisco February 7, 1969. During August 1973 Kyle Railways became the operator under contract of the line. As ocean going service moved from wharves to container terminals the lines business shrank to a few cars per day. Service discontinued in 1991.

STEARNS LUMBER COMPANY

Incorporated April 15, 1905 - Steam - Standard Gauge

Located Wendling, Mendocino County. Built from a junction with the Northwestern Pacific Albion Branch to Keene's Summit. Distance 9.00 miles. Sold in 1913 to Navarro Lumber Company. Abandoned in 1920.

STERLING BORAX COMPANY

Steam - 2 ft. Gauge

Located Lang, Los Angeles County. Operated a borax mine north of the depot toward Vasquez Rocks, circa 1912. Depth of the borax was found to be rather shallow and mine only operated for a period of three to five years.

STEWART & HUNTER LUMBER COMPANY

Organized 1880 - Steam - Standard Gauge

Located Fort Bragg, Mendocino County. Built to Ten Mile River. Distance 22.50 miles. Sold to the California Western Railroad & Navigation Company in 1905. Abandoned in 1950.

STOCKTON & BAY CITY SHORT LINE RAILROAD

Organized July 3, 1911 - Electric - Standard Gauge

Located Stockton, San Joaquin County. Proposed to build to Byron and ultimately to Antioch and Oakland. Project abandoned in 1912.

STOCKTON & BECKWITH PASS RAILROAD COMPANY

Incorporated December 1, 1902 - Steam - Standard Gauge

Located Stockton, San Joaquin County. Proposed to build to Sacramento and then on to Oroville through Butte County to the Feather River. The tracks were to follow the river to Delaney Canyon and cross the Sierra Valley to Beckwith Pass. Distance 160.00 miles. Surveys begun in May 1903. Charter forfeited in 1908.

STOCKTON BELT LINE RAILROAD COMPANY

Steam - Standard Gauge

Located Stockton, San Joaquin County. A switching company operated by the Western Pacific Railroad Company, the Southern Pacific Company and the Santa Fe Railway in the Stockton area.

STATE BELT RAILROAD OF CALIFORNIA - Connected with the Southern Pacific and serviced the wharves along San Francisco Bay. In this view a train pauses in front of the famous Ferry Building. - *Donald Duke Collection*

STOCKTON & COPPEROPOLIS RAILROAD COMPANY

Incorporated October 11, 1865 - Steam - Standard Gauge

Located Stockton, San Joaquin County. Built to Milton. Distance 25.80 miles. Construction period was from 1866 to 1871. Consolidated with the Stockton & Visalia Railroad November 17, 1877, to form the re-incorporated Stockton & Copperopolis Railroad Company. Consolidated with the Southern Pacific Railroad Company May 14, 1888.

STOCKTON ELECTRIC RAILWAY

Incorporated December 29, 1891 - Electric - Standard Gauge

Located Stockton, San Joaquin County. Purchased the Stockton Street Railway. Electrified in 1892. Sold to the Southern Pacific Company in 1905. Took over the street railway operations of the Central California Traction Company December 29, 1929. Sold to the Pacific City Lines April 1, 1939. Operations ceased in September 1941.

STOCKTON ELECTRIC RAILWAY - Operated the streetcar system within the city of Stockton. Took over the horsecar service of the Stockton Street Railway and was electrified in 1892. Became the property of the Southern Pacific in 1905 and was operated by the Central California Traction Co. - *Francis J. Goldsmith Collection*

STOCKTON, FRESNO & SOUTHERN RAILWAY

Surveyed 1889 - Steam - Standard Gauge

Located Stockton, San Joaquin County. Proposed to build southeast on the east side of the San Joaquin Valley to Visalia. Project abandoned before the survey was completed.

STOCKTON & IONE RAILROAD

Organized February 13, 1873 - Steam - Narrow-Gauge

Located Stockton, San Joaquin County. Proposed to build northwestward to Linden and then to the coal mines near Ione City, Amador County. Distance 40.00 miles. Began grading in 1874. Laid 18 miles of track in 1875. Project abandoned in 1876.

STOCKTON & LODI RAILROAD

Organized December 27, 1895 - Steam - Standard Gauge

Located Stockton, San Joaquin County. Began laying track to the mines at Corral Hollow in 1896.

STOCKTON & LODI TERMINAL RAILROAD COMPANY

Incorporated September 1895 - Steam or Electric - Standard Gauge

Located Stockton, San Joaquin County. Proposed to build to Lodi. Distance 16.00 miles. Grading completed November 29, 1895.

STOCKTON STREET RAILWAY COMPANY

Began operations April 6, 1874 - Horsecar - Standard Gauge

Located Stockton, San Joaquin County. Sold to the Stockton Electric Railway Company December 29, 1881. Electrified in 1892. Began operations on Stockton Street from Market Street to North Beach. Ceased operations September 1941.

STOCKTON TERMINAL & EASTERN RAILROAD

Incorporated October 29, 1908 - Electric - Steam - Standard Gauge

Located Stockton, San Joaquin County. Original plans called for electric operation to Jenny Lind. Distance 29.80 miles. Opened for traffic with steam power to Fine, distance 15.20 miles, September 1, 1910. Extended to Bellota March 20, 1913. Arrived at Jenny Lind on July 19, 1914.

STOCKTON TERMINAL & EASTERN RAILROAD - A short line built from downtown Stockton east to Jenny Lind. Was to be electrified, however, it remained a steam operated carrier with rail motorcars handling the passenger service. - *Donald Duke Collection*

STOCKTON & TULARE RAILROAD COMPANY

Incorporated December 2, 1887 - Steam - Standard Gauge

Located Fresno, Fresno County. Built from Famoso to Fresno by way of Exeter. Distance 102.30 miles. Completed December 24, 1890. Built Oakdale to Merced February 2, 1891. Consolidated with Southern Pacific Company May 14, 1888. Section Montpelier to Merced abandoned 1942. Distance 23.00 miles.

STOCKTON & TUOLUMNE COUNTY RAILROAD
STOCKTON & TUOLUMNE RAILWAY COMPANY

Incorporated December 1897 - Steam - Standard Gauge

Located Stockton, San Joaquin County. Organized under both names. Proposed to build eastward through Copperopolis and Sonora to Summersville. Distance 35.00 miles. Grading began in April 1898, under the name of Stockton & Tuolumne Railway Company. Project abandoned in 1899.

STOCKTON & VISALIA RAILROAD COMPANY

Incorporated December 16, 1869 - Steam - Standard Gauge

Located Peters, San Joaquin County. Built from a junction with the Stockton & Copperopolis Railroad at Peters to Oakdale. Distance 18.90 miles. Construction work was done from June to September 1871. Consolidated with the Stockton & Copperopolis Railroad Company November 17, 1877. Consolidated with the Southern Pacific Railroad Company May 14, 1888.

STONE CANYON & PACIFIC RAILROAD COMPANY

Organized July 14, 1905 - Steam - Standard Gauge

Located MacKay, Monterey County. Built eastward from a junction with the Southern Pacific Railroad Company to the Canon Consolidated Coal Company mines in Stone Canyon. Distance 21.50 miles. Completed and opened for traffic in January 1909. Became the California Coal Fields Railroad in 1920. Abandoned in 1932.

STONE & WEBER CONSTRUCTION COMPANY

Incorporated March 16, 1912 - Steam - Standard Gauge

Located El Prado, Fresno County. Built a railroad from a junction with the Southern Pacific Company to Big Creek (Cascada). Distance 56.00 miles. Began operations August 1, 1912, under the name of Big Creek Railroad. Sold to the San Joaquin & Eastern Railroad Company in 1913. Abandoned in 1933.

SUGAR PINE LUMBER COMPANY

Began construction July 15, 1923 - Steam - Standard Gauge

Located Wishon, Fresno County. Built from end of the Minarets & Western Railway to Central Camp, distance 10.80 miles, and on to timber for a total distance of 35.00 miles. Abandoned in 1936.

SUGAR PINE RAILWAY

Incorporated March 6, 1903 - Steam - Standard Gauge

Located Ralph, Tuolumne County. Built from a junction on the Sierra Railroad Company to Middle Camp. Extended trackage to Lyon's Dam in 1907. Distance 14.15 miles. Leased to the Standard Lumber Company May 23, 1918. Abandoned in 1922.

SUISUN, BERRYESSA & CLEAR LAKE RAILROAD

Organized 1869 - Steam

Located Suisun, Solano County. Proposed to build to Clear Lake. Ground broken and construction begun November 16, 1869. Project abandoned in 1871.

SUNSET WESTERN RAILWAY COMPANY
SUNSET RAILROAD COMPANY
SUNSET RAILWAY COMPANY

Incorporated March 17, 1900 - Steam - Standard Gauge

Located Gosford, Kern County. Built to Hazelton in 1901, a distance of 30.27 miles. Built from Hazelton to Maricopa in 1904. Distance 2.48 miles. The Sunset Western Railway Company was organized in 1905. Built from Pentland to Shale March 20, 1912. Distance 17.11 miles. These two companies consolidated to form the Sunset Railway Company March 20, 1912. The Sunset Railway Company is controlled one-half by the Southern Pacific Co. and the Santa Fe Railway who operate the line in five-year periods.

SUTRO RAILROAD COMPANY

Incorporated August 1894 - Electric - Standard Gauge

Located San Francisco, San Francisco County. Began operations February 1, 1896. Built between Central Avenue and Sutro Baths by way of California, First Avenue, Euclid Avenue, Clement Street, 33rd Avenue, Point Lobos Blvd. and private right-of-way. Constructed a branch on 8th Avenue from Clement Street to Fulton Street (Golden Gate Park). Sold to Sutter Street Railway Company in 1897. Merged into the United Railroads of San Francisco May 18, 1901.

SUTTER STREET RAILWAY COMPANY
SUTTER STREET RAILROAD COMPANY
SUTTER STREET WIRE CABLE RAILWAY COMPANY

Incorporated December 22, 1887 - Cable - 5 ft. Gauge

Located San Francisco, San Francisco County. The original company was the Front, Mission & Ocean Railroad. Began operations as a horsecar street railway. Converted to cable operations and began cable operations January 27, 1877. Operated for a time as Sutter Street Wire Cable Railway Company. Sutter Street Railway Company chartered November 1879. Purchased the Sutro Railroad Company in 1897. Sold to United Railroads of San Francisco May 18, 1901. Operated by the United Railroads of San Francisco as the Sutter Street Railroad. Though electrified at an early date, the section of track from Geary Street to the Ferry Building on Market Street was horsecar operated until June 3, 1913.

SWAYNE LUMBER COMPANY

Organized 1900 - Steam - Standard and Narrow-Gauge

Located Oroville, Butte County, and Truckee, Nevada County. Built in Oroville from mill to timber. Total distance 50.00 miles. Purchased the holdings of the Truckee Lumber Company, including their narrow-gauge Butte & Plumas Railway, in 1917. All trackage abandoned in 1940 .

SAN DIEGO ELECTRIC - For the 1915 Panama-Pacific International Exposition the San Diego Electric built a new line through Balboa Park complete with three large steel trestles and a terminal for the loading and unloading of fair passengers. In this scene a route No. 7 streetcar rolls toward San Diego after leaving the Balboa Park terminal. - *Donald Duke*

TONOPAH & TIDEWATER RAILROAD - Operating 169.07 miles between Ludlow and Beatty, Nevada, the Tonopah & Tidewater never did reach either location of its name. In this view, No. 9 is at Ludlow when new in 1907. Note all the pinstripes around the wheels and cab. - *Hugh Tolford Collection*

T

TECOPA RAILROAD COMPANY

Incorporated May 1909 - Steam - Standard Gauge

Located Tecopa, San Bernardino County. Built from a junction with the Tonopah & Tidewater Railroad Company to the Noonday Mine. Distance 9.50 miles. Began construction in October 1909. Built a branch to the Gunsight Mine and to Horse Springs. Distance 2.00 miles. Ceased operations in 1932. Abandoned in 1935.

TECOPA RAILROAD - An industrial line running off the Tonopah & Tidewater Railroad at Tecopa to the Noonday Mine, a distance of 9.50 miles. - *Hugh Tolford Collection*

TEHACHAPI RAILWAY COMPANY

Incorporated September 6, 1923 - Steam - Standard Gauge

Located Tehachapi, Kern County. No construction work was done and the charter was forfeited February 27, 1926.

TELEGRAPH HILL RAILROAD COMPANY

Construction began February 1884 - Cable - Narrow-Gauge

Located San Francisco, San Francisco County. Operated 1,560 feet of cable railway in 1891. Built from Powell Street up Greenwich Street.

TEMPLE & DIAMOND STREETS STEAM DUMMY RAILROAD

Construction began 1887 - Steam - Narrow-Gauge

Located Los Angeles, Los Angeles County. Built from Temple and Hoover streets to Western and Melrose Avenue. Sold to Cahuenga Valley Railroad Company April 16, 1888.

TEMPLE STREET CABLE RAILWAY COMPANY

Chartered October 31, 1885 - Cable - 3 ft. 6 in. Gauge

Located Los Angeles, Los Angeles County. Construction began December 30, 1885. Built on Temple Street from Spring Street to Hoover Street. Opened for service July 10, 1886. Consolidated with the Los Angeles & Pasadena Electric Railway Company, Pasadena & Mt. Lowe Railway Company, Pacific Electric Railway Company of Arizona, East Ninth Street Railway Company and the Brooklyn Avenue Railway Company to form the Pacific Electric Railway Company on February 28, 1902. Electrified October 2, 1902. Deeded to the Los Angeles Railway Company in October 1910. Abandoned June 20, 1946.

TERMINAL RAILWAY COMPANY

Incorporated January 30, 1867 - Steam - Standard Gauge

Located San Francisco, San Francisco County. Built an office at Fourth and Townsend streets. Some construction work proposed on December 31, 1884.

TERRACINA & REDLANDS STREET RAILWAY COMPANY

Incorporated March 5, 1892 - Mule Power - 3 ft. 6 in. Gauge

Located Redlands, San Bernardino County. Construction began in March 1892. Completed May 1892. Built from Olive and Cajon in a westerly direction along Olive Avenue to the Terracina Hotel. Distance 2.00 miles. Abandoned in 1895. Charter cancelled December 14, 1905. Properties were sold to the Pacific Electric Railway Company in 1902.

TERRY LUMBER COMPANY

Organized in 1905 or 1906 - Steam - Narrow-Gauge

Located Round Mountain, Shasta County. Built 12.00 miles of logging road. This section abandoned in 1918. Operated the standard gauge California, Shasta & Eastern Railroad from 1913 to 1920. Sold to the Red River Lumber Company in 1920. Abandoned in 1927.

TEXAS PACIFIC RAILROAD COMPANY

Projected 1870 - Steam - Standard Gauge

Proposed to build from Marshall, Texas, along the 32nd Parallel route to San Diego, California. Lands of the San Diego & Gila, Southern Pacific & Atlantic Railroad plus depot grounds in San Diego were donated to the company. Final survey adopted from San Diego via Temecula Canyon and San Gorgonio Pass to Fort Yuma. 10.00 miles of grading were done from San Diego northward. Plans were disrupted by the panic of 1875. One-half of the land subsidy was recovered to be re-deeded to the California Southern Railroad Company. The other one-half went to the Southern Pacific Railroad Company.

F.M. THATCHER LUMBER COMPANY

Organized 1916 - Steam - Standard Gauge

Located Sterling City, Butte County. Built from mill to timber. Distance 13.75 miles. Abandoned in 1923.

TIDEWATER NORTHERN RAILWAY COMPANY

Incorporated October 1, 1909 - Electric - Standard Gauge

Located Los Angeles, Los Angeles County. Proposed to build from Santa Monica along the coast to Ventura. Project abandoned in 1910.

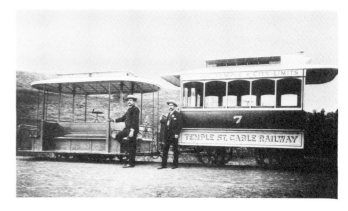

TEMPLE STREET CABLE RAILWAY - A cable car line built west out Temple Street, going from Spring to Hoover Street. Was consolidated with the Los Angeles & Pasadena Electric Railway and electrified. - *UCLA Library*

TIDEWATER NORTHERN RAILWAY COMPANY

Incorporated October 1, 1909 - Electric - Standard Gauge

Located Los Angeles, Los Angeles. Proposed to build from Santa Monica along the coast to Ventura. Project abandoned in 1910.

TIDEWATER & SOUTHERN RAILROAD COMPANY

Incorporated October 4, 1910 - Electric - Standard Gauge

Located Stockton, San Joaquin County. Proposed to build southward from Stockton to Modesto. Graded about 9.00 miles of roadbed and laid 3.50 miles of track between Turlock and Modesto. Consolidated with the Tidewater & Southern Transit Company March 11, 1912, to form the Tidewater Southern Railway Company.

TIDEWATER SOUTHERN RAILWAY COMPANY

Incorporated March 11, 1912 - Electric - Standard Gauge

Located Modesto, Stanislaus County. Resulted from a consolidation of the Tidewater & Southern Railroad Company and the Tidewater & Southern Transit Company. Opened for traffic between Taylor Street, Stockton and Modesto October 1912. Distance 32.23 miles. Section Modesto to Turlock put into operation in July 1916. Distance 16.00 miles. Operated both steam and electric motive power. First steam power put into service in 1917. Last electric interurban train ran May 26, 1932.

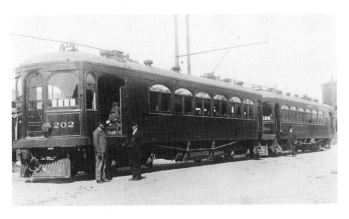

TIDEWATER SOUTHERN RAILWAY - Began life as an electric interurban line running south from Stockton to Modesto in 1912, a distance of 32 miles. A steam division was extended to Turlock in 1916. Electric service was abandoned in 1912, however, it was retained through the streets of Modesto. (ABOVE) An electric interurban train ready to leave Stockton for Modesto. - *Charles Smallwood Collection* (BELOW) A Tidewater Southern steam locomotive under electrification at Modesto. - *Donald Duke Collection*

TIDEWATER & SOUTHERN TRANSIT COMPANY

Incorporated February 16, 1912 - Electric - Standard Gauge

Located Merced, Merced County. Some construction work was done along the Merced River. Consolidated with the Tidewater & Southern Railroad Company to form the Tidewater Southern Railway Company March 11, 1912.

TONOPAH & GREENWATER RAILROAD COMPANY

Organized March 1907 - Steam - Standard Gauge.

Located Gold Center, Nevada. Proposed to build from a junction with the Las Vegas & Tonopah Railroad Company to Greenwater in Death Valley, California. No construction work done. Project abandoned in 1908.

TONOPAH & TIDEWATER RAILROAD COMPANY

Incorporated July 19, 1904 - Steam- Standard Gauge

Located Ludlow, San Bernardino County. Proposed to build to Tonopah, Nevada. Construction began August 30, 1905. The first rails were laid November 26, 1905. Reached Crucero and crossed the Los Angeles & Salt Lake Railroad (Union Pacific Railroad) February 20, 1906. Crossed the California-Nevada border in 1907. Entered Beatty, Nevada, October 30, 1907. Took over the operations of the Bullfrog-Goldfield Railroad July 1, 1908, and extended service to Goldfield and Rhyolite. Purchased the Bullfrog-Goldfield Railroad December 8, 1919. The Bullfrog-Goldfield Railroad trackage abandoned in January 1928. Section Ludlow to Crucero ceased operations December 8, 1933. Distance 25.68 miles. Total abandonment of the company authorized December 31, 1938. All operations ceased June 14, 1940. Track removal began July 18, 1942 and completed July 25, 1943.

TONOPAH & TIDEWATER RILROAD - Built north off the Santa Fe from Ludlow to Beatty, Nevada. Proposed to extend the line to Tonopah during the gold mining era. Due to lack of patronage a railroad motorcar replaced the regular passenger train. - *R.H. Kindig*

TOWLE BROTHERS & COMPANY
TOWLE BROTHERS LUMBER COMPANY

Organized 1883 - Steam - 3 ft. Gauge

Located Towle Station on the Southern Pacific Railroad and one mile east of Alta, Placer County. Built to a mill located three miles northwest of Remington Hill, Nevada County. Distance 22.00 miles. Abandoned in 1890.

TRINIDAD MILL COMPANY

Organized 1869 - Horse Tram - Narrow-Gauge

Located Trinidad, Humboldt County. The Hooper brothers formed the company and operated one of the first tram roads. Was consolidated with the Dougherty & Smith Mill in 1873 and the railroad was converted to steam operation.

TRINITY RAILWAY

Organized January 1901 - Steam - Standard Gauge

Located Trinity, Trinity County. Planned to build from the Trinity Copper Company to the Flat Creek District in Shasta County. It was to connect with the Southern Pacific Company at either Kennett, distance 6.00 miles, or Copley, distance 11.00 miles. Project abandoned in 1902.

TRONA RAILWAY COMPANY

Incorporated March 12, 1913 - Steam - Standard Gauge

Located Trona, San Bernardino County. Built from Searles Station on the

Southern Pacific Railroad to Trona. Distance 30.70 miles. Construction began September 27, 1913. Completed in March 1914. Opened for traffic September 1, 1914.

TRONA RAILWAY - Built from a siding on the Southern Pacific "Jawbone" line to Trona, a distance of 30.70 miles. Mainly an industrial road handling chemicals and borax. - *Hugh Tolford Collection* (BELOW) A rail motorcar handled passenger service from Trona to Searles Junction, a connection with the Southern Pacific. - *Donald Duke Collection*

TRUCKEE LUMBER COMPANY

Organized 1880 - Steam - 3 ft. Gauge

Located Truckee, Nevada County. Began construction of a logging railroad in 1887. Completed 10.35 miles of trackage. Ceased operations in 1912. Sold to the Swayne Lumber Company and moved to Oroville in 1917. Abandoned in 1940.

TULARE COUNTY POWER COMPANY

Organized July 25, 1911 - Electric - Standard Gauge

Located Porterville, Tulare County. Proposed to build to Lindsay on the north and Tulare on the west. This was to be a cooperative company financed by power users and ranchers in Tulare County. Project abandoned in 1912.

TULARE VALLEY & GRANT FOREST RAILROAD COMPANY

Organized 1882 - Steam - Standard Gauge or 3 ft. Gauge

Located Tulare, Tulare County. Proposed in 1882 under the name of Tulare & Grant Forest Railroad to build from Tulare eastward into the timberlands around General Grant National Park. Incorporated October 29, 1885, under the title of Tulare Valley & Grant Forest Railroad Company to build from a junction with the Southern Pacific Company near Tulare to the Sierra Nevada forests. Project abandoned in 1886 or 1887.

TULARE & GRANT FOREST RAILROAD
TULARE VALLEY & GRANT FOREST
RAILROAD COMPANY

Organized 1882 - Steam - Standard Gauge or 3 ft. Gauge

Located Tulare, Tulare County. Proposed in 1882 under the name of Tulare & Grant Forest Railroad to build from Tulare eastward into the timberlands around General Grant National Park. Incorporated October 29, 1885, under the title of Tulare Valley & Grant Forest Railroad Company to build from a junction with the Southern Pacific Company near Tulare to the Sierra Nevada forests. Project abandoned in 1886 or 1887.

TURLOCK & EASTERN RAILROAD COMPANY

Organized August 4, 1928 - Steam - Standard Gauge

Located Turlock, Stanislaus County. Proposed to build to Cortez and a junction with the Santa Fe Railway Company. Distance 5.00 miles. Project abandoned in 1929.

TURLOCK TRACTION COMPANY

Incorporated March 6, 1911 - Electric - Standard Gauge

Located Turlock, Stanislaus County. Proposed to build to Denair. Distance 4.00 miles.

TUSCAN MINERAL SPRINGS CORPORATION
ELECTRIC RAILWAY

Incorporated August 1, 1903 - Electric - Standard Gauge

Located Red Bluff, Tehama County. The Board of Supervisors granted a franchise to the Tuscan Mineral Springs Corporation to construct and operate an electric railway on public highways from Red Bluff to Tuscan Springs. Distance 9.00 miles. Construction work begun November 1, 1903.

TWENTY-THIRD AVENUE ELECTRIC RAILWAY

Electric - Standard Gauge

Located Oakland, Alameda County. Consolidated with the Oakland, San Leandro & Hayward Electric Railway Company to form the Oakland, San Leandro & Hayward Electric Railway Consolidated May 8, 1894

UNITED RAILROADS OF SAN FRANCISCO - Street railway action on Market Street, circa 1920. Portions of the line formed a part of the Market Street Railway in 1920, and was sold to the San Francisco Muncipal Railway in 1944. - *Donald Duke Collection*

U

UNION BELT LINE RAILWAY OF OAKLAND

Organized November 1906 - Steam - Standard Gauge

Located Oakland, Alameda County. Built 0.70 mile of industrial trackage in 1910. Leased to the Central Pacific Railroad in 1910, but operations were performed by the Southern Pacific Company. Sold to the Southern Pacific Company May 31, 1949.

UNION BELT RAILWAY COMPANY

Incorporated June 15, 1906 - Electric - Standard Gauge

Located Sacramento, Sacramento County. Proposed to encircle the city of Sacramento with a belt line railroad and to establish a terminal.

UNION LUMBER COMPANY

Organized 1891 - Steam - Standard Gauge

Located Fort Bragg, Mendocino County. Built from mill to timber. Purchased the properties of the Fort Bragg Redwood Company in 1891. Connected logging lines and formed the California Western Railroad & Navigation Company on July 1, 1905. Built from Shake City to Willits on December 20, 1911, thus forming a railroad line from Fort Bragg on the coast to a connection with Northwestern Pacific at Willits, a distance of 40 miles.

UNION PLANK WALK & RAILROAD COMPANY

Organized 1875 - Horse Power - Steam - 3 ft. 9 1/4 in. Gauge

Located Arcata, Humboldt County. Resulted from a reorganization of the Union Plank Walk, Rail Track & Wharf Company Railroad. Extended trackage from Arcata to Dolly Varden Mill in 1876. Distance 1.00 mile. Sold to Arcata Transportation Company. Deeded to the Arcata & Mad River Railroad Company June 22, 1881.

UNION PLANK WALK, RAIL TRACK & WHARF COMPANY RAILROAD

Incorporated December 15, 1854 - Horse Power - 3 ft. 9 1/4 in. Gauge

Located Union (Arcata), Humboldt County. Built from the end of wharf to facilities on shore. Distance 2.00 miles. Construction began December 22, 1854. Converted to steam operation in 1872, but horse power was still used. Trackage extended from Arcata to Falk, Minor's Mill and the Jolly Giant Mill in 1875. Distance 0.75 miles. Reorganized as the Union Plank Walk & Railroad Company in 1875. Extended to the Dolly Varden Mill in 1875. Distance 1.00 mile. Sold to Arcata Transportation Company June 15, 1878. Extended to Isaac Minor's Mill on Warren Creek in 1880. Distance 3.50 miles. Deeded to the Arcata & Mad River Railroad Company June 22, 1881. Extended to Korbel on the North Fork of the Mad River in 1883. Distance 5.00 miles. Branches built to Glendale and Riverside Mills in 1885. Junction made with the Northwestern Pacific Railroad Company at Korblex in 1925. Trackage from Korblex to Korbel standard gauged by use of a third rail. All narrow-gauge rails removed in 1942.

UNION STREET RAILWAY

Chartered May 8, 1893 - Electric - 3 ft. 6 in. Gauge

Located Santa Rosa, Sonoma County. Resulted from the re-chartered South Side Railway Company. Operated 4.00 miles of street railway. Sold to the Santa Rosa Street Railways December 24, 1897, and electrified. Sold to Santa Rosa Railroad Company in 1903. Became part of the Northwestern Pacific Railroad in 1923.

UNION TRACTION COMPANY OF SANTA CRUZ

Organized October 8, 1904 - Electric - 3 ft. 2 5/8 in. Gauge

Located Santa Cruz, Santa Cruz County. Resulted from the reorganization of the East Santa Cruz Railroad, a horsecar line and Santa Cruz, Capitola & Watsonville Railway. When the road was electrified the name was changed to Union Traction Company of Santa Cruz. Connected Santa Cruz, Seabright, Twin Lakes, Del Mar, Opal and Capitola. Distance 15.73 miles.

UNITED RAILROAD

Incorporated September 7, 1894 - Steam - Standard Gauge

Located Stockton, San Joaquin County. Proposed to build southwesterly through the San Joaquin Valley to Kings County and then in a southerly direction through Kern County to Bakersfield. This project was entirely distinct from the surveys of the San Francisco, Stockton & Bakersfield Railroad, but it was along an almost exact route. Project abandoned at about the same time that the San Francisco, Stockton & Bakersfield Railroad project was abandoned.

UNITED RAILROADS OF SAN FRANCISCO

Incorporated March 4, 1902 - Electric - Standard Gauge - 3 ft. 6 in. Gauge - 5 ft. Gauge

Located San Francisco, San Francisco County. Resulted from the merger of the San Francisco & San Mateo Electric Railway, Sutter Street Railway and the Sutro Railroad Company. Reorganized into the Market Street Railway Company February 16, 1921. Operations were merged into the Municipal Railway of San Francisco on September 29, 1944.

UNITED STATES CENTRAL RAILROAD
SAN FRANCISCO & OCEAN SHORE RAILROAD

Proposed 1884 - Steam - Standard Gauge

Located San Francisco, San Francisco County. Incorporation notice read, "To build to Denver, Colorado, by following the Pacific Ocean shore." Later specific plans were shown for a railroad to be built down the coast via Santa Cruz, Aptos, Corralitos and north to Watsonville to Chittenden. At Chittenden it would cross the Southern Pacific Railroad and then follow the Pajaro River to the Santa Clara Valley, pass through Pacheco Pass to the San Joaquin Valley and cross the Sierra at Yosemite. Right-of-way was secured under the company title of San Francisco & Ocean Shore Railroad. Project was abandoned by 1886.

UNIVERSITY HEIGHTS MOTOR ROAD

Planned 1886 - Steam - Standard Gauge

Located San Diego, San Diego County. Planned to build a steam motor railroad through University Heights Addition in San Diego. All construction was made by the City Park Belt Motor Road. Began operations July 7, 1888. Sold to the San Diego Electric Railway Company.

UPLAND & CLAREMONT RAILROAD

Organized 1908 - Steam - Standard Gauge

Located Upland, San Bernardino County. Proposed to build to San Bernardino and then from Upland to Los Angeles. Contract for surveys let August 1909. Project abandoned in 1910 because of lack of financial support.

U.S. BUREAU OF RECLAMATION

Organized 1938 - Steam - Standard Gauge

Located Redding, Shasta County. The government took over the Southern Pacific line between Redding to Coram, a distance of 14 miles, to haul in construction materials for the building of Shasta Dam. This required a Southern Pacific line change from Redding to Delta Junction, as the right-of-way following the Sacramento River would be under water when the dam was completed. A bypass line was surveyed by the state of California in 1935 and accepted in 1938. The bypass line was opened for traffic March 17, 1942. Once Shasta Dam was completed the Bureau of Reclamation abandoned the line from Redding to Coram.

U.S. GYPSUM COMPANY

Organized September 2, 1919 - Steam - 3 ft. Gauge

Located Amboy, San Bernardino County. Purchased the properties of the Consolidated Pacific Cement Plaster Company. Abandoned in 1924.

U.S. GYPSUM COMPANY

Organized 1946 - Steam - 3 ft. Gauge

Located Plaster City, Imperial County. Purchased the properties of the Pacific Portland Cement Company in 1946. Trackage runs from a junction with the San Diego & Arizona Eastern Railway Company north to quarry. Distance 20.50 miles.

U.S. NAVY DRYDOCKS

Organized 1940 - Steam - Standard Gauge

Located Hunters Point, San Francisco County. Built five miles of switching tracks within the U.S. Naval drydocks at Hunters Point, located south of San Francisco Bay. A railroad connection is made with the Southern Pacific at Hunters Point.

U.S. NAVY RAILROAD

Organized 1942 - Diesel - Standard Gauge

Located Inyokern, Kern County. Built from a junction with the Southern Pacific Company to China Lake and then out onto the desert.

U.S. GYPSUM - Built a narrow-gauge line 26 miles north of Plaster City toward the Salton Sea to a gypsum quarry. In the above view a steam train with a diesel on the opposite end. - *Richard Steinheimer*

Two U.S. Gypsum diesels handle a train of gypsum from the mine to the processing plant at Plaster City. - *Donald Duke*

A U.S. Gypsum diesel locomotive and a novel caboose. - *Donald Duke*

156

USAL REDWOOD COMPANY

Organized 1890 - Steam - Standard Gauge

Located Rockport, Mendocino County. Built 6.00 miles of railroad. Abandoned in 1902.

UTAH & LOS ANGELES RAILWAY COMPANY

Chartered March 2, 1894 - Steam - Standard Gauge

Located Denver, Colorado. Projected a railroad from Salt Lake City, Utah, to Los Angeles. No construction work was done.

UTAH, NEVADA & CALIFORNIA RAILROAD COMPANY

Organized 1889 - Steam - Standard Gauge

Located Utah and San Diego, San Diego County. Proposed to build from a point in Utah to San Diego. Was given an exclusive option on a railroad sub- sidy by the San Diego Railroad Extension Committee in 1890. Incorporated on February 2, 1899. Surveys were begun in April 1899. Project abandoned in 1900.

UTAH SOUTHERN RAILROAD COMPANY
UTAH SOUTHERN RAILROAD EXTENSION COMPANY

Organized 1871 - Steam - Standard Gauge

Located Salt Lake City, Utah. Chartered by Brigham Young to build a railroad from Salt Lake City to the head of navigation on the Colorado River with a link across California to San Bernardino. No construction in California. San Diego & San Bernardino Railroad would have extended it to San Diego Bay. Merged into Utah Central Railway Company in 1881. Reorganized as Oregon Short Line & Utah Northern Railroad Company in 1889 and Oregon Short Line Railroad Company in 1897. Numerous rumors of extensions to Los Angeles and San Diego appeared at intervals.

U.S. NAVY DRYDOCKS - A five-mile switching railroad within the Hunters Point Naval Drydocks of South San Francisco. A connection was made with the Southern Pacific at Hunters Point. - *Arthur Lloyd*

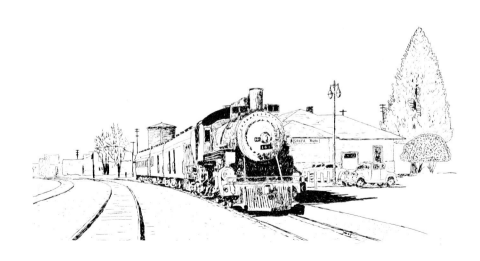

157

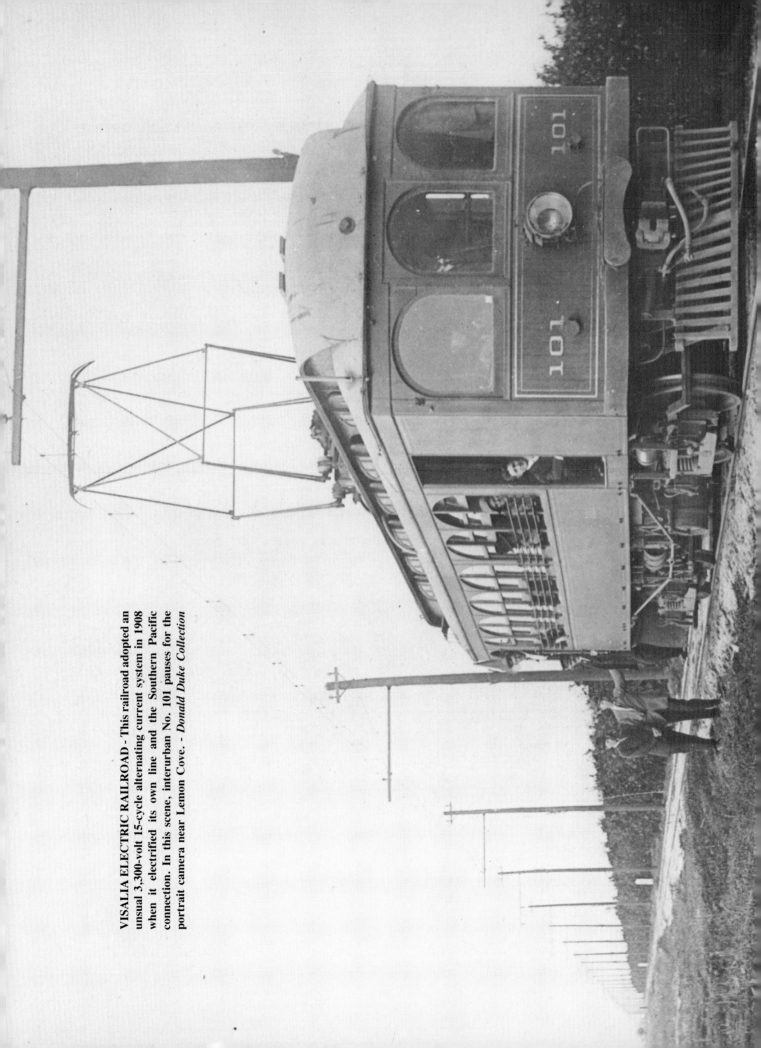

VISALIA ELECTRIC RAILROAD - This railroad adopted an unsual 3,300-volt 15-cycle alternating current system in 1908 when it electrified its own line and the Southern Pacific connection. In this scene, interurban No. 101 pauses for the portrait camera near Lemon Cove. - *Donald Duke Collection*

V

VACA VALLEY RAILROAD COMPANY

Incorporated April 12, 1869 - Steam - Standard Gauge

Located Elmira, Solano County. Built to Vacaville. Distance 4.35 miles. Began service June 1869. Sold at Sheriff's sale September 17, 1870. Extended Vacaville to Winters. Distance 13.30 miles. Opened for traffic August 26, 1875. Transferred to Vaca Valley & Clear Lake Railroad Company February 19, 1877. Consolidated into Northern Railway Company May 15, 1888. Consolidated into Southern Pacific Company April 14, 1898.

VACA VALLEY & CLEAR LAKE RAILROAD COMPANY

Incorporated February 28, 1877 - Steam - Standard Gauge

Located Elmira, Solano County. Organized to take over the operations of the Vaca Valley Railroad Company from Elmira on the California Pacific Railroad to Madison. Distance 27.40 miles. Began operations May 1, 1877. Consolidated into the Northern Railway Company May 15, 1888. Extended Madison to Rumsey. Distance 23.70 miles. Completed July 1, 1888. Consolidated into Southern Pacific Company April 14, 1898. Trackage Rumsey to Capay. Distance 18.60 miles. Abandoned April 15, 1934. Capay to Esparto abandoned July 10, 1941. Remaining trackage is known as the Southern Pacific Company, Esparto Branch. Distance 20.50 miles.

VALLEJO, BENICIA & NAPA VALLEY RAILROAD COMPANY

Incorporated April 24, 1902 - Electric - Standard Gauge

Located Vallejo, Solano County. Proposed to build to Napa then northwesterly to Lakeport in Lake County. Branches to be built from Vallejo to White Sulphur Springs and from Napa to Jackson's Soda Springs. Ground broken in Vallejo October 17, 1903. First rails laid September 16, 1904. Completed and began operations July 4, 1905, to Calistoga. Became the San Francisco, Vallejo & Napa Valley Railroad Company June 5, 1907. Merged with the San Francisco, Napa & Calistoga Railroad Company November 10, 1911. Reorganized as San Francisco & Napa Valley Railroad February 29, 1936. Dissolved as a corporation September 15, 1957.

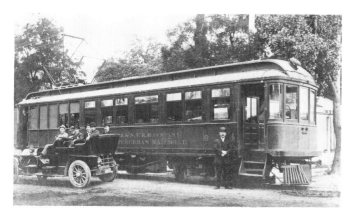

VALLEJO, BENICIA & NAPA VALLEY RAILROAD - An interurban line connecting with ferry service across San Francisco Bay to South Vallejo, then running north to Napa, St. Helena and Calistoga. - *Donald Duke Collection*

VALLEJO & NORTHERN RAILWAY COMPANY
VALLEJO & NORTHERN RAILROAD COMPANY

Incorporated 1909 - Electric - Standard Gauge

Located Sacramento, Sacramento County. Organized to build from a branch of the Northern Electric Railway Company at Woodland to Winters then on to Vacaville, Suisun and Vallejo by way of Napa Junction. Proposed to link by electric railway the Northern Electric Railway Company and San Francisco,

Vallejo & Napa Valley Railroad. Surveys were made but very little construction work was done. Reorganized as the Vallejo & Northern Railroad Company in January 1910. Some construction work was done around Vallejo and 1.80 miles of track were laid in Sacramento during the year 1911. Deeded to the Northern Electric Railway Company December 31, 1912. Part of the right-of-way was later used to connect Mare Island with the San Francisco, Napa & Calistoga Railroad Company by the Sacramento Northern Railway Company and the Napa Route as a joint project. A portion of this trackage is still operated by the United States Navy.

VALLEJO & SONOMA VALLEY RAILROAD

Proposed 1867 - Steam - Standard Gauge

Located Suscol, Sonoma County. Proposed to build to Cloverdale and Healdsburg. This organization was proposed as a substitute for the Petaluma & Healdsburg Railroad.

VALLEJO TRACTION COMPANY

Organized February 15, 1910 - Electric - Standard Gauge

Located Vallejo, Solano County. Organized to operate an electric railroad through the streets of Vallejo from Virginia Street Wharf to the northern limits of the city. Franchise granted March 9, 1910. No work done.

VALLEY RAILROAD COMPANY

Incorporated May 5, 1912 - Electric - Standard Gauge

Located Red Bluff, Tehama County. Proposed to build through Tehama County and then through Glenn, Colusa and Yolo counties to Woodland, and then to Davis and on to Dickson to connect with the Oakland, Antioch & Eastern Railroad in Solano County.

VANCE MAD RIVER RAILROAD
HUMBOLDT & MAD RIVER RAILROAD

Organized 1873 - Steam - Standard Gauge

Located Humboldt Bay (Samoa), Humboldt County. Built in 1874 to Essex. Organized under the name Vance Mad River Railroad. Rolling stock was lettered Humboldt & Mad River Railroad. Sold to the Eureka & Klamath River Railroad Company in 1896.

VANCE MAD RIVER RAILROAD - A logging line built from Sonoma to Essex in 1874. The railroad hauled some very large redwood logs as is evidenced by this photograph. - *Donald Duke Collection*

JOHN VANCE MILLING & LUMBER COMPANY

Organized 1886 - Steam - Standard Gauge

Located Samoa, Humboldt County. Built 7.00 miles of track. Sold to Vance Redwood Lumber Company in 1900.

VANCE REDWOOD LUMBER COMPANY

Organized 1900 - Steam - Standard Gauge

Located Samoa, Humboldt County. Purchased the John Vance Milling & Lumber Company properties, 7.00 miles of trackage. Extended the trackage 20.00 miles. Sold to the Hammond Lumber Company in 1912.

VENICE MINIATURE RAILWAY

Organized 1902 - Steam - 18 in. Gauge

Located Venice, Los Angeles County. Built to operate as a tourist attraction along the beach front. Abandoned 1927. Equipment moved to various places: Five Points, El Monte in 1941; Streamland Park near Whittier Narrows Dam in 1945; and Legg Lake Park near South El Monte in 1960.

VENICE MINIATURE RAILWAY - A commercial tourist railroad that operated around attractions and the boardwalk at Venice beach. - *Donald Duke Collection*

VENTURA COUNTY RAILROAD COMPANY

Incorporated May 11, 1911 - Steam - Standard Gauge

Located Oxnard, Ventura County. Purchased the Bakersfield & Ventura Railway Company. Built Oxnard to Port Hueneme, distance 5.40 miles. Extended trackage from Oxnard to Wilds, distance 3.50 miles. Branches built to Bebo, Petit and to Patterson Ranch have been abandoned.

VENTURA COUNTY RAILWAY COMPANY

Organized 1911 - Steam - Standard Gauge

Located Oxnard, Ventura County. Purchased the Bakersfield & Ventura Railway in 1911. Trackage ran from Oxnard to Port Hueneme with branches west and north to McGrath Dump, south and east to Round Mountain Dump and south to Ormond Beach Power Plant. Received by transfer the franchise of the Santa Clara Valley Electric Railway Power Company March 1902. Incorporated February 1903, as a California corporation and worked on a franchise to build from Los Angeles around Elysian Park and north along the Los Angeles River through Calabasas Pass to Triunfo and across the hills to Fillmore via Grimes Canyon. It would then follow the original survey to Sunset, then up the west side of the San Joaquin Valley over Pacheco Pass and across the Santa Clara Valley, crossing the Coast Range to Santa Cruz. First load of ties delivered at Port Hueneme in August 1903. Grading began in Oxnard December 10, 1903. All work ceased after 2.00 miles of rail had been laid by January 8, 1904. April 1905, work began on the Oxnard-Hueneme section. First train over the line took place on July 4, 1905. Road sold to Ventura County Railway Company in 1911. Passenger service discontinued December 31, 1926.

VENTURA & OJAI RAILROAD COMPANY OF CALIFORNIA

Incorporated September 25, 1896 - Steam - Standard Gauge

Located Ventura, Ventura County. Proposed to build north up the Ojai Valley to Nordhoff and then on to Hobart. Distance 30.00 miles. Right-of-way secured May 1897. Contract for construction let in August 1897. Track laying began in September 1897. Built from Ventura Junction to Nordhoff (Ojai). Distance 15.13 miles. Construction completed March 11, 1898. Opened for service May 1, 1898. Sold to the Southern Pacific Company June 27, 1899.

VENTURA & OJAI RAILWAY

Organized 1901 - Horsecar - Narrow-Gauge

Located Ventura, Ventura County. Operated from Southern Pacific depot to Main Street. June 1902, surveys made for right-of-way from Ventura to Santa Paula.

VENTURA & OJAI RAILWAY - A horsecar line operated from the Southern Pacific Ventura depot down Main Street to a park with a loop track. - *Donald Duke Collection*

VENTURA TERMINAL RAILWAY COMPANY

Incorporated 1907 or 1908 - Electric - Standard Gauge

Located Ventura, Ventura County. Proposed to build an electric railway to the cement quarries in the Matilija Valley. Distance 22.00 miles. A branch was to be built to Nordhoff (Ojai). Distance 5.00 miles.

VERDI LUMBER COMPANY

Organized 1900 - Steam - Standard Gauge

Located Verdi, Nevada. Built to Long Valley Camp, Bear Valley Camp and Lemon Canyon Camp in California. Trackage was extended beyond a junction that was made with the Boca & Loyalton Railroad. Distance 32.00 miles. Abandoned in May 1927.

VICTOR & EASTERN RAILROAD COMPANY

Incorporated July 3, 1908 - Steam - Standard Gauge

Located Victorville, San Bernardino County. Proposed to build in an easterly direction to Black Mountain. Distance 11.00 miles. This was probably the route taken by the Mojave Northern Railway.

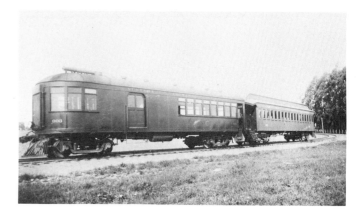

VENTURA COUNTY RAILROAD - A railroad built to serve a sugar beet mill and the agricultural fields in and around Ventura. Was proposed to build to Bakersfield, however, built west to Port Hueneme where a wharf was erected. This motor train operated between Ventura and Port Hueneme. - *Donald Duke Collection*

VIRGINIA & BEAR RIVER RAILROAD COMPANY

Organized 1853 - Steam - Standard Gauge

Located Auburn Ravine, Placer County. Proposed to build to Bear River. Could have been the first railroad organized in California. Project abandoned.

VIRGINIA CITY & FEATHER RIVER RAILROAD

Organized January 20, 1875 - Steam - Narrow-Gauge

Located Virginia City, Nevada. Proposed to build by way of Reno and Long Valley to the middle fork of the Feather River in California.

VISALIA RAILROAD COMPANY

Incorporated May 21, 1874 - Steam - Standard Gauge

Located Visalia, Tulare County. Built to Goshen Junction. Distance 7.41 miles. Construction completed August 1874. Sold to the Southern Pacific Company April 14, 1898.

VISALIA ELECTRIC RAILROAD COMPANY

Incorporated April 22, 1904 - Electric - Standard Gauge

Located Exeter, Tulare County. Built to Lemon Cove. Distance 11.00 miles. Ground broken March 15, 1905. Opened for service using Southern Pacific Railroad steam power in July 1906. Extended to Terminus on the Kaweah River in 1908. Electrified in 1908. Line Citro to Redbank opened for service in 1910. Distance 8.00 miles. Section Woodlake Junction to Elderwood opened in 1915. Section Wirts to Strathmore opened for service in 1916. Passenger service discontinued in 1924. All electric operations ceased in 1944. This company owned by the Southern Pacific Company, but operated independently.

VISALIA - TULARE RAILROAD COMPANY

Incorporated November 1887 - Steam - Standard Gauge

Located Visalia, Tulare County. Built to Tulare. Completed in October 1888. Distance 11.50 miles. Ceased operations in October 1900.

VOLCANO NORTHERN RAILWAY

Organized December 1903 - Electric - 3 ft. or Standard Gauge

Located Volcano, Amador County. Proposed to build northward. Distance 15.00 miles. Organization papers stated,"To operate an interurban electric railway for passenger and freight at the speed of 40 miles an hour." No construction work was done.

VOSS' LUMBER RAILROAD

Organized 1883 - Steam - 3 ft. Gauge

Located Greenhorn Creek Area, near Nevada City, Nevada County. Operated logging road from mill to timber. Horse-drawn and gravity road from mill to junction with the Nevada City - Red Dog road. Distance 13.00 miles. Built in 1883. Abandoned in 1894.

VISALIA ELECTRIC - Baldwin-Westinghouse box cab electric locomotive No. 601 hauls a long train of wooden boxcars through the San Joaquin Valley. This subsidiary of the Southern Pacific, had the only 15-cycle, single-phase electrification system in North America. - *Donald Duke Collection*

WESTERN PACIFIC RAILROAD - Handling a westbound stock extra, No. 256, a 2-8-8-2 type articulated leaves Keddie and crossed the Keddie "Y" bridge prior to rolling down the Feather River Canyon. - *Donald Duke*

M. S. WAGY LUMBER COMPANY

Organized 1909 - Steam - Narrow-Gauge

Located Cazadero, Sonoma County. Took over the properties of the D.H. McEwen Lumber Company. Operated 4.00 miles of trackage. Abandoned in 1910 or 1911.

WALKER - HOVEY COMPANY

Organized 1929 - Steam - Standard Gauge

Located Canby, Modoc County. Operated over the trackage of the Canby Railroad Company that built from a junction with the Southern Pacific Company south. Sold to the Big Lakes Lumber & Box Company in 1937.

WARREN CREEK RAILROAD

Organized 1880 - Steam - 4 ft. 9 1/4 in. Gauge

Located Warren Creek, Humboldt County. Built from mill to timber along Warren Creek. Mill burned in 1885. Trackage removed in 1886.

WARREN CREEK RAILROAD COMPANY

Organized 1917 - Steam - Standard Gauge

Located Warren Creek, Humboldt County. Construction work was done under the name of Granite Mountain Rock Quarry Railroad. Built to haul rock from quarry to Humboldt Bay jetties. Ceased operations in 1917.

WATERLOO MINING COMPANY

Built 1888 - Steam - 38 in. Gauge

Located near Daggett, San Bernardino County. Built from Oro Grande Mill across the river from Daggett to the Waterloo Mine with a branch to Calico Town. Tracks taken up in 1903, except for one mile used by the American Borax Company. Abandoned in 1908.

WATSONVILLE RAILROAD & NAVIGATION COMPANY

Organized 1905 - Electric - 3 ft. Gauge

Located Watsonville, Santa Cruz County. Built to a wharf on the Pacific Ocean. Distance 3.50 miles.

WATSONVILLE RAILWAY & NAVIGATION COMPANY

Incorporated April 17, 1911 - Steam - 3 ft. 6 in. Gauge

Located Watsonville, Santa Cruz County. Organized to take over the operations of the Watsonville Transportation Company. Abandoned in April 1911.

WATSONVILLE TRANSPORTATION COMPANY

Incorporated February 13, 1903 - Electric - 3 ft. 6 in. Gauge

Located Watsonville, Santa Cruz County. Built from Wall and Main streets out Wall Street to Beach Road and then along Beach Road to the ocean. Distance 6.00 miles. Opened for traffic in May 1904. Proposed to extend the road from Watsonville to Hollister. Distance 25.60 miles. This part of the project was abandoned. Sold to the Monterey, Fresno & Eastern Railroad in April 1907. Operations suspended October 1, 1910. Reorganized and deeded to the Watsonville Railway & Navigation Company April 22, 1911. Ceased operations December 1912. Abandoned in October 1913.

WEBSTER & LAKE PARK RAILROAD
WEBSTER STREET & PARK RAILWAY COMPANY

Began operations April 15, 1903 - Electric - Standard Gauge

Located Piedmont, Alameda County. Operated from Piedmont and Pleasant Valley avenues to Oakland Heights by way of Piedmont. Operated under both names before becoming part of the Key System.

WEED LUMBER COMPANY

Incorporated 1902 - Steam - Standard Gauge

Located Weed, Siskiyou County. Began operations in 1903. Built a total of 50.00 miles of logging road. Sold to the Long-Bell Lumber Company in 1905. Continued to operate as the Weed Lumber Company until 1926. Section Weed to Grass Lake sold to the California Northwestern Railway July 29, 1905. Distance 21.59 miles. Sold to the Oregon Eastern Railway December 18, 1911. Abandoned April 17, 1927. Remainder of trackage abandoned by Long-Bell Lumber Company in 1956.

WELLS LUMBER COMPANY

Organized 1953 - Diesel - Standard Gauge

Located Rio Dell, Humboldt County. Operated 5.00 miles of trackage. Abandoned 1954.

WEST COAST LAND COMPANY

Organized February 1, 1890 - Horsecar - 3 ft. Gauge

Located San Luis Obispo, San Luis Obispo County. Purchased the San Luis Obispo Street Railway Company. Operated 2.50 miles of street railway. Abandoned in 1906. Operated as San Luis Street Railway.

WEST END CHEMICAL COMPANY

Organized September 1, 1914 - Steam - 2 ft. Gauge

Located West End, San Bernardino County. Built 7.00 miles of industrial trackage in and around the West End Chemical plant.

WEST END STEAM DUMMY RAILROAD

Built 1887 - Steam - Narrow-Gauge

Located Los Angeles, Los Angeles County. Built as an extension of the Temple & Diamond Streets Steam Dummy Railroad from Western Avenue to Santa Monica Blvd. Sold April 16, 1888, to the Cahuenga Valley Railroad Company.

WEST PASADENA RAILWAY COMPANY

Organized 1887 - Horsecar - Standard Gauge

Located Pasadena, Los Angeles County. Built in 1891 a 3.50 mile long horsecar street railway on Colorado Blvd. from Fair Oaks to Vernon (U.P. Station). Purchased the Colorado Street Railway Company in 1893. Sold to the Pasadena & Los Angeles Electric Railway Company in 1894. Electrified 1894. Sold to the original Pacific Electric Railway March 1902. Abandoned in 1923.

WEST SACRAMENTO ELECTRIC COMPANY

Organized February 1, 1914 - Electric - Standard or Narrow-Gauge

Located Sacramento, Sacramento County. Organized to build electric railways and other public utilities in and about the city of Sacramento. Company dissolved September 5, 1914. Properties sold to the Pacific Gas & Electric Company.

WEST SHORE RAILROAD COMPANY

Incorporated July 12, 1895 - Steam - Standard Gauge

Located San Francisco, San Francisco County. Proposed to build a railroad southward along the Pacific Coast to Santa Cruz. Distance 70.00 miles.

WEST SIDE FLUME & LUMBER COMPANY

Organized May 31, 1899 - Steam - 3 ft. Gauge

Located Charters (now Tuolumne), Tuolumne County. Built to timber. Distance 15.00 miles. Sold 1903. Name changed to West Side Lumber Company.

WEST SIDE LUMBER COMPANY

Organized 1903 - Steam - 3 ft. Gauge

Located Tuolumne, Tuolumne County. Purchased the properties of the West Side Flume & Lumber Company. Extended the trackage into the woods. Total main line mileage 79.00 miles. Became a division of the Pickering Lumber Company in 1925. Reorganized as the West Side Lumber Company in 1934. Ceased operations in 1962.

WEST SIDE LUMBER CO. - The last all-Shay operated narrow-gauge logging railroad in the California woods. Rail enthusiasts flocked to see and photograph its trains between 1960-1962. - *Gary Allen*

WEST SIDE & MENDOCINO RAILROAD COMPANY

Organized 1886 - Steam - Standard Gauge

Located Willows, Glenn County. Proposed to build from Willows to Fruto. Distance 17.10 miles. Some construction work was done, but no operations were conducted. Consolidated into the Northern Railway Company May 15, 1888. Completed July 1, 1888. Consolidated with Southern Pacific Railroad Company April 14, 1898. Section Fruto to Kurand abandoned in 1953. Section Kurand to Willows abandoned in 1956. 2.75 miles of trackage kept by the Southern Pacific Company for a siding.

WEST SIDE RAILROAD COMPANY

Incorporated August 31, 1911 - Electric - Standard Gauge

Located Sacramento, Sacramento County. Proposed to build to Rio Vista. Distance 34.45 miles. Built 1.009 miles of trackage in West Sacramento. Built .40 miles more in 1912. Built .609 miles in 1921. Company was controlled by the Sacramento Northern Railroad Company.

WESTERN MEAT COMPANY

Organized 1903 - Steam - Standard Gauge

Located South San Francisco, San Francisco County. Leased the trackage of the South San Francisco Land & Improvement Company. Purchased the property March 1, 1907. Sold to the South San Francisco Belt Railway November 20, 1907. Total mileage 3.08 miles. Serviced by the Southern Pacific Company. Deeded to the Southern Pacific Company December 3, 1945.

WESTERN MINERAL COMPANY

Built 1895 - Mule Power - 3 ft. Gauge

Located Yermo, San Bernardino County. Built from Bartlett Mill on the north shore of Calico Dry Lake to Bartlett Mine near Calico Town. Distance 2.10 miles. Abandoned 1906 or 1907.

WESTERN NEVADA RAILROAD COMPANY

Incorporated December 12, 1879 - Steam - Standard Gauge

Located Wadsworth, Nevada. Proposed to build south to a point near Walker Lake and then on to Bodie, Mono County, California. No work was done.

WESTERN PACIFIC RAILROAD COMPANY

Incorporated December 13, 1862 - Steam - Standard Gauge

Located San Jose, Santa Clara County. Built through Niles, Tracy, Stockton and Brighton to Elvas (near Sacramento). Distance 123.45 miles. Began construction from San Jose in January 1865. Completed in December 1869. Operations taken over by the Central Pacific Railroad of California May 15, 1869.

WESTERN PACIFIC RAILWAY COMPANY
WESTERN PACIFIC RAILROAD COMPANY

Incorporated March 6, 1903 - Steam - Standard Gauge

Located Oakland, Alameda County. Organized February 6, 1903, as a connecting link between Oakland, California, and Salt Lake City, Utah, thus forming the seventh United States transcontinental route. Incorporated March 6, 1903. First spike driven at Third and Union street at Oakland, January 3, 1906. Railroad was constructed simultaneously, joining together at Keddie, California, on November 1, 1909. Line opened for through freight traffic on December 1, 1909, and on August 10, 1911 the first passenger train was run. A branch was built north from Keddie to Bieber on November 19, 1931, forming a through connection with the Pacific Northwest by way of the Great Northern Railway. Purchased the narrow-gauge Nevada-California-Oregon Railroad between the main line at Reno Junction and Reno, Nevada, in 1917, and converted to standard gauge. Operates 1,524 miles of track including branch lines. Defaulted on its bonds March 1, 1935 and trustee appointed November 14, 1935. Was reorganized as the Western Pacific Railroad Company.

WESTERN PACIFIC - Pride of the Western Pacific was its famous streamliner the *California Zephyr*, as photographed here it is rolling eastbound through Feather River Canyon in 1959. - *Bart Gregg*

WESTERN REDWOOD LUMBER COMPANY

Organized October 6, 1906 - Steam - Standard Gauge

Located Jenner, Sonoma County. Built from mill to timber. Distance 8.00 miles. Built from mill to Pacific Coast. Distance 3.00 miles. Abandoned in 1910.

WESTPORT LUMBER & RAILROAD COMPANY

Incorporated February 21, 1908 - Steam - Standard Gauge

Located Westport, Mendocino County. Took over the trackage of the California Lumber Company Railroad in 1908. Trackage also used by the Pollard Lumber Company from 1906 to 1918. Abandoned in 1919.

L. E. WHITE LUMBER COMPANY

Organized 1916 - Steam - 3 ft. Gauge

Located Elk, Mendocino County. Built from mill to timber. Distance 22.00 miles. Sold to Goodyear Redwood Company in 1916. Abandoned in 1935.

WILDWOOD, BOULDER CREEK & NORTHERN RAILROAD

Organized April 25, 1914 - Steam - 3 ft. Gauge

Located Boulder Creek, Santa Cruz County. Extended to Wildwood near the Cunningham & Company mill. Resulted from the leasing of the trackage of the California Timber Company. Trackage also known as the Dougherty Extension Railroad, Boulder Creek & Pescadero Railroad, The Dinkey Line and the Northern Extension Railroad.

WINTERS & UKIAH RAILWAY COMPANY

Incorporated August 11, 1887 - Steam - Standard Gauge

Located Winters, Yolo County. Projected from Winters northwesterly up Berryessa Valley to Clear Lake and then to Ukiah. Distance 105.00 miles. No construction work was done. Consolidated with the Northern Railway Company May 15, 1888. Consolidated into Southern Pacific Company April 14, 1898.

WOLF CREEK TIMBER COMPANY

Steam - Narrow-Gauge

Located Greenville, Plumas County. Built a logging road along Wolf Creek.

WOOD & SHELDON LUMBER COMPANY

Organized 1902 or 1903 - Steam - Standard Gauge

Located Sisson, Siskiyou County. Built from mill to timber. Distance 9.00 miles. Abandoned 1913.

WOODBRIDGE & SACRAMENTO RIVER RAILROAD

Organized 1862 or 1863 - Steam - Standard Gauge

Located Woodbridge, San Joaquin County. Proposed to build northwest to Walnut Grove and then west to the Sacramento River. No work done.

WOODLAND, CAPAY & CLEAR LAKE RAILROAD COMPANY

Incorporated July 8, 1887 - Steam - Standard Gauge

Located Woodland, Yolo County. Proposed to build from Woodland to Lakeport. Distance 97.35 miles. No construction work was done. Consolidated with Northern Railway Company May 15, 1888. Consolidated into the Southern Pacific Company April 14, 1888.

WOODLAND STREET RAILWAY COMPANY

Chartered October 1887 - Horsecar - 3 ft. Gauge

Located Woodland, Yolo County. Built 1.00 mile of horsecar street railway. Began service in May 1888.

WESTERN PACIFIC RAILROAD - A bay window caboose is about to duck in a tunnel while the head end of the eastbound train crosses overhead at Williams Loop between Keddie and Portola. By means of this loop the railroad elevated some 100 feet. Williams Loop is similar to Southern Pacific's Tehachapi Loop between Bakersfield and Mojave. - *Richard Steinheimer*

YOSEMITE VALLEY RAILWAY - This railroad built from a connection with the Southern Pacific at Merced to El Portal, a distance of 79.17 miles. Passengers were carried by carriage into the Yosemite Valley. In this scene, a Yosemite bound train stops at Snelling to pick up both passengers and unload Railway Express. Snelling was 18 miles east of Merced and along the banks of the Merced River. - *Donald Duke Collection*

Y

YELLOW ASTER MINE

Organized 1899 - Steam - Narrow-Gauge

Located Randsburg, Kern County. Built from mill to mine.

YELLOW JACKET RAILROAD

Organized 1908 - Steam - Narrow-Gauge

Located Lyonsville, Tehama County. Built from mill to timber. Distance 10.00 miles. Abandoned 1913.

YGNACIO VALLEY RAILROAD COMPANY

Incorporated January 3, 1906 - Electric - Standard Gauge

Located Oakland, Alameda County. Proposed to build to Antioch. Distance 40.00 miles. A branch was to be built to Mt. Diablo. Distance 7.00 miles. A branch was to be built from Concord to Martinez. Distance 9.00 miles. No construction work was done.

YOSEMITE LUMBER COMPANY

Incorporated 1910 - Steam - Standard Gauge

Located Merced Falls, Mariposa County. Built from a junction with the Yosemite Valley Railroad Company near El Portal, up an incline to Moss Creek. Began operations in 1912. Distance 39.45 miles. Moved across the Merced River in 1923. Closed down operations November 26, 1927. Abandoned in 1938.

YOSEMITE PARK ELECTRIC RAILWAY

Organized 1904 - Electric - Standard Gauge

Located Merced, Merced County. Franchise granted June 17, 1904. Proposed to build north to the Merced River and to follow the river into the Yosemite Park Valley. This was the first franchise ever granted by the U.S. Government for an electric railway into any government reservation. Stations were to be built every ten miles under the terms of the franchise. No construction work was done.

YOSEMITE PORTLAND CEMENT COMPANY

Incorporated 1925 - Steam - Standard Gauge

Located Emery, Mariposa County. Built from a junction with the Yosemite Valley Railroad Company to a quarry. Abandoned in June 1944.

YOSEMITE SHORT LINE RAILROAD COMPANY

Organized August 1904 - Steam - 30 in. Gauge

Located Jamestown, Tuolumne County. Proposed to build from Woods Creek in Tuolumne County to the Yosemite Valley. Distance 60.00 miles. Branch to be built from Crocker Station to the Hetch Hetchy. Distance 10.00 miles. Incorporated June 21, 1905. Construction began from a junction with the Sierra Railway Company to Jacksonville on the Hetch-Hetchy Railroad October 15, 1905. Abandoned April 20, 1906.

YOSEMITE SUGAR PINE LUMBER COMPANY

Organized 1934 - Steam - Standard Gauge

Located Merced Falls, Mariposa County. Built from Incline on the Yosemite Valley Railroad Company to Sunset Camp. Distance 40.00 miles. Abandoned 1942.

YOSEMITE VALLEY RAILROAD COMPANY
YOSEMITE VALLEY RAILWAY COMPANY

Incorporated December 19, 1902 - Steam - Standard Gauge

Located Merced, Merced County. Built to El Portal. Construction began in September 1905. Completed June 30, 1907. Distance 79.17 miles. Reorganized as the Yosemite Valley Railway Company December 23, 1935. Last run August 24, 1945.

YREKA RAILROAD
YREKA RAILROAD COMPANY
YREKA WESTERN RAILROAD COMPANY

Incorporated May 28, 1888 - Steam - Narrow-Gauge

Located Yreka, Siskiyou County. Built to Montague. Distance 7.50 miles. Standard gauged. Sold to Yreka Railroad Company April 7, 1906. Reorganized Yreka Western Railroad Company August 1933.

YREKA WESTERN RAILROAD - This line was built back in 1888 from Montague on the Southern Pacific to Yreka, a distance of 7.50 miles. A Yreka Western steam locomotive was photographed switching cars at Montague in 1969. - *Donald Duke*

YREKA & SCOTT VALLEY RAILROAD

Incorporated August 5, 1904 - Steam - Standard Gauge

Located Yreka, Siskiyou County. Proposed to build into Scott Valley. Surveys began September 1904. Project abandoned in 1905.

YUBA RAILROAD COMPANY

Incorporated November 17, 1862 - Steam - Standard Gauge

Located Lincoln, Placer County. Built to Marysville. Distance 23.90 miles. Began construction in 1866. Completed in 1868. Consolidated with the California & Oregon Railroad Company December 18, 1869. Consolidated with Central Pacific Railroad Company August 22, 1870.

YUCAIPA & OAK GLEN RAILROAD

Organized April 1908 - Electric - Standard Gauge or 3 ft. Gauge

Located Yucaipa, Riverside County. Proposed to build from Yucaipa to Roseglen resorts and later to build to Redlands. Distance 21.50 miles.

YOSEMITE VALLEY
·RAILROAD CO·

SANTA FE RAILWAY - Diesel locomotive units No. 90, Santa Fe's only Fairbanks-Morse passenger power, handles the *San Diegan* on its southbound run between Los Angeles and San Diego. The *San Diegan* was photographed at speed as it passed through Santa Fe Springs. - *Donald Duke*

SANTA FE SPRINGS

RAILWAY EXPRESS AGENCY

WESTERN UNION

12679

Appendix

California Railroads by County

This county listing of railroads includes all those carriers that either operated within a given county, or were either headquartered or organized in the listed county. Many railroads also operated in other counties that do not show on this listing. Each California Railroad listed is followed by a date of organization. All listings that appear in italic are paper railroads, or those organized, yet never built.

ALAMEDA COUNTY

Alameda Belt Line Railroad (1917)
Alameda County Railway (1887)
Alameda County Terminal Railway Co. (1889)
Alameda & Hayward Railroad (1863)
Alameda & Oakland Horsecar Railroad Co. (1870)
Alameda, Oakland & Piedmont Electric Railroad (1893)
Alameda, Oakland & Piedmont Railway (1870)
Alameda Railroad (1871)
Alameda & San Joaquin Valley Railroad (1893)
Alameda Valley Railroad Co. (1864)
BART-Bay Area Rapid Transit (1957)
Bay & Coast Railroad Co. (1877)
Berkeley Branch Railroad Co. (1876)
Berkeley Traction Co.
Blake & Bilger Co. (1904)
Broadway, Berkeley & Piedmont Railway (1876)
Broadway & Piedmont Horse Railway
Brooklyn & Fruit Vale Railroad (1875)
California & Mount Diablo Railroad (1881)
California & Nevada Railroad Co. (1881)
California Railway Co. (1890)
California Rock & Gravel Co.
Central Avenue Railroad Co. (1889)
Central Avenue Railway Co. (1889)
Claremont, University & Ferries Railroad (1891)
Consolidated Piedmont Cable Co. (1889)
Delta Finance Co.
East Bay Street Railways, Ltd., (1930)
East Bay Transit Co. (1932)
East Oakland Street Railway Co. (1890)
Emergency Transportation Co. (1918)
Fourteenth Street Railroad (1877)
Highland Park & Fruit Vale Railroad (1875)
Howard Terminal Co. (1917)
Key System
Key System, Limited (1923)
Key System Transit Co. (1923)
Key System Transit Lines (1954)
Key Terminal Railway, Ltd. (1930)
King Coal Co. (1916)
Market Street Railroad (1869)
Northern Railway Co. (1871)
Northern Railway Co. Consolidated (1888)
Oakland, Alameda & Laundry Farm Railroad (1888)
Oakland, Antioch & Eastern Railway (1911)

Oakland & Bay Shore Railway Co. (1911)
Oakland & Berkeley Rapid Transit Co. (1889)
Oakland, Brooklyn & Fruitvale Railway (1850)
Oakland Cable Railway (1888)
Oakland Central Railroad (1870)
Oakland Consolidated Street Railway Co. (1890)
Oakland & East Side Railroad Co. (1902)
Oakland & Marysville Railroad (1904)
Oakland Paving Co., (1873)
Oakland Railroad Co. (1864)
Oakland & San Francisco Terminal Co. (1893)
Oakland & San Joaquin Railroad (1887)
Oakland & San Jose Railway Co. (1901)
Oakland, San Leandro & Hayward Electric Railway Co. (1891)
Oakland, San Leandro & Hayward Electric Railway Consolidated (1892)
Oakland Terminal Railroad (1935)
Oakland Township Railroad Co. (1881)
Oakland Traction Co. (1912)
Oakland Traction Consolidated (1904)
Oakland Transit Co. (1898)
Oakland Transit Consolidated (1902)
Oliver Brothers Salt Co. (1893)
Pacific State Steel Co.
Piedmont Cable Co. (1890)
Piedmont & Mountain View Railway Co. (1895)
Sacramento & Oakland Railroad (1903)
Sacramento Short Line Railway Co. (1911)
San Francisco & Alameda Railroad Co. (1863)
San Francisco, Alameda & Stockton Railroad Co. (1863)
San Francisco & Bay Counties Railway Co. (1908)
San Francisco Bay Railroad Co. (1868)
San Francisco Bridge Co. (1892)
San Francisco & Colorado River Railroad Co. (1883)
San Francisco & Oakland Railroad Co. (1861)
San Francisco, Oakland & Alameda Railroad (1870)
San Francisco & Piedmont Railway Co. (1902)
San Francisco Railway & Ferry Co. (1902)
San Francisco Terminal Railway & Ferry Co. (1899)
San Francisco & Transbay Railroad Co. (1910)
San Pablo Railroad Co. (1871)
Santa Clara Valley Railroad (1875)
South Pacific Coast Railroad Co. (1887)
South Pacific Coast Railway Co. (1876)
Twenty-Third Avenue Electric Railroad (1894)

Union Belt Line Railway of Oakland (1906)
Webster & Lake Park Railroad (1903)
Webster Street & Park Railway Co. (1905)

AMADOR COUNTY

Amador Central Railroad Co. (1908)
Amador Railroad Co. (1893)
Ione & Eastern Railroad Co. (1904)
Ione Railroad (1875)
N.B. Randal Sawmill (1935)
Volcano Northern Railway (1903)

BUTTE COUNTY

Bechtel-Kaiser Rock Co. (1926)
Butte County Railroad Co. (1902)
Central Sacramento Valley Railroad Co. (1859)
Chico & Colusa Railroad (1875)
Chico Electric Railway Co. (1904)
Chico & Northern Railroad Co. (1903)
DeLong Mining Co. Railroad (1899)
Diamond Match Co. Railroad (1902)
Feather River & Beckwourth Pass Railroad (1868)
Feather River Pine Mills (1927)
Feather River Railway Co. (1939)
Hutchinson Lumber Co. (1923)
H.J. Kaiser Gravel Co. (1942)
Minshew Railroad (1910)
Natomas Consolidated Co. (1930)
North Carolina Gold Mining Co. (1902)
Northern Electric Co. (1905)
Northern Electric Railway Co. (1907)
Northern Electric Railway Co. - Marysville
  & Colusa Branch (1910)
Oro Dam Constructors Railroad (1962)
Oroville & Beckwourth Railroad (1888)
Oroville & Nelson Railroad Co. (1907)
Oroville & Virginia City Railroad Co. (1867)
Redding & Red Bluff Railway Co. (1906)
Swayne Lumber Co. (1900)
F.M. Thatcher Lumber Co. (1916)

CALAVERAS COUNTY

Calaveras Cement Co. (1925)
Calaveras Copper Co. (1877)
Copper Belt Railway & Power Co. (1902)
Copperopolis Copper Mining Co. (1902)
Royal Consolidated Mines

COLUSA COUNTY

Colusa & Hamilton Railroad Co. (1911)
Colusa & Lake Railway Co. (1886)
Colusa Railway Co. (1885)
Northwestern Redwood Co. (1901)
Northwestern Redwood Lumber Co. (1903)

CONTRA COSTA COUNTY

Antioch & Grangerville Railroad Co. (1880)
Antioch Railroad Co. (1899)
Antioch & Visalia Railroad (1870)
Bay Point & Clayton Railroad Co. (1906)
Black Diamond Coal & Railroad Co. (1868)
Black Diamond Railroad (1868)
Blake Brothers Co. (1914)
California Wine Association Railroad (1905)
Castro Point Railway & Terminal Co. (1911)
Cowell Portland Cement Co. (1906)
East Shore & Suburban Railway Co. (1900)
Empire Coal Mine & Railroad Co. (1877)
Hercules Powder Co. (1921)
Martinez & Concord Interurban Railway Co. (1916)
Mountain Copper Co., Ltd. (1905)
Oakland & Antioch Railway Co. (1909)
Oakland, Martinez & Alhambra Railway & Ferry Co.
  (1911)
Parr Terminal Railroad
Pittsburg & Black Diamond Railroad (1866)
Pittsburg Coal & Mining Co. (1862)
Pittsburg Railroad Co. (1911)
Pittsburg Railway Co. (1912)
Port Costa Brick Works
Quarry Products, Inc. (1963)
Redwood Manufacturing Co. (1910)
Richmond Belt Railroad (1902)
Richmond Railway & Navigation Co. (1907)
Richmond Shipyard Railway (1942)
San Francisco Transit Co. (1900)
San Francisco Transit Co. (1922)
San Pablo & Tulare Railroad Co. (1871)
San Ramon Valley Railroad Co. (1888)
San Ramon Valley Railway Co. (1912)
Standard Oil Co. (1902)

DEL NORTE COUNTY

California & Oregon Coast Railroad Co. (1903)
Crescent City, Fort Dick & Smith River Railway
  (1906)
Crescent City Mill & Transportation Co. (1855)
Crescent City & Smith River Railroad Co. (1907)
Del Norte Southern Railroad (1912)
Hobbs, Wall & Co. (1886)
Klamath-California Redwood Co. (1935)

EL DORADO COUNTY

American River, Land & Lumber Co. (1892)
Caldor Lumber Co. (1904)
California Door Co. (1917)
Camino, Placerville & Lake Tahoe Railroad (1911)
C.W. Chubbuck (1884)
R.E. Danaher Lumber Co. (1915)
C.D. Danaher Pine Co. (1904)

Diamond & Caldor Railway (1904)
El Dorado Land & Mineral Co.
El Dorado Lumber Co. Railroad (1901)
M.C. Gardner Lumber Co., (1875)
Knob Peak Lumber Co. (1951)
Lake Tahoe Railway Co. (1904)
Lake Valley Railroad Co. (1886)
Michigan-California Lumber Co. (1917)
Placerville & Lake Tahoe Railroad (1903)
San Francisco & Washoe Railroad Co. (1864)
Shingle Springs & Placerville Railroad (1887)

FRESNO COUNTY

Big Creek Railroad (1912)
Fresno & Clovis Interurban Railway (1914)
Fresno & Eastern Railroad (1911)
Fresno & Pine Ridge Railroad (1889)
Fresno City, Belmont & Yosemite Railroad (1888)
Fresno City, Belmont & Yosemite Railway Co. (1895)
Fresno City Railroad Co. (1901)
Fresno, Clovis & Acadmey Interurban Railway (1915)
Fresno, Coalinga & Monterey Railway (1913)
Fresno, Coalinga & Tidewater Co. (1911)
Fresno Copper Co. (1903)
Fresno County Railroad (1905)
Fresno Flume & Irrigation Co. (1891)
Fresno Flume & Lumber Co. (1908)
Fresno, Hanford & Summit Lake Interurban Railway (1908)
Fresno Interurban Railroad Co. (1914)
Fresno Railroad Co. (1889)
Fresno Traction Co. (1903)
Hume-Bennett Lumber Co. (1908)
Inter-Mountain Electric Railway Co. (1904)
Kings River Railway Co. (1909)
Laton & Western Railroad Co. (1910)
Minarets & Western Railway Co. (1921)
Minkler Southern Railway (1913)
North Fork & Minaret Railroad (1893)
Herman Peterson Lumber Co. (1900)
Pine Ridge Lumber Co. (1908)
Sanger Lumber Co. (1885)
San Joaquin & Eastern Railroad Co. (1912)
San Joaquin Valley Coal Co. (1886)
San Joaquin Valley Railroad Co. (1891)
San Joaquin Valley Western Railroad Co. (1907)
Sequoia Railroad (1891)
Shaver Lake Lumber Co. (1919)
Shaver Lake Railroad (1907)
Stockton & Tulare Railroad Co. (1887)
Stone & Webster Construction Co. (1912)
Sugar Pine Lumber Co. (1923)

GLENN COUNTY

Shasta Southern Railway Co. (1906)
West Side & Mendocino Railroad Co. (1886)

HUMBOLDT COUNTY

Arcata & Mad River Railroad Co. (1881)
Arcata Mill & Lumber Co. (1887)
Arcata Transportation Co. (1878)
Bayside Lumber Co. (1905)
Bayside Mill & Lumber Co. (1900)
Bayside Redwood Co. (1920)
Bendixen Shipbuilding Co. (1908)
Blue Lake Logging Co. (1928)
Bucksport & Elk River Railroad (1884)
Bucksport & Elk River Railway (1932)
M.A. Burns Manufacturing Co. (1923)
California Barrel Co. (1916)
California Midland Railway Co. (1902)
California Redwood Co. (1882)
Chandler, Henderson & Co. (1884)
Cottoneva Lumber Co. (1911)
Del Norte & Humboldt Railroad Co. (1903)
E.J. Dodge Lumber Co. Railroad (1914)
Dolbeer & Carson Lumber Co. (1884)
Eel River & Eureka Railroad Co. (1882)
Eel River, Eureka & Pacific Railroad Co. (1903)
Eel River Valley Lumber Co. (1891)
Elk River Mill & Lumber Co. (1885)
Elk River Railroad (1882)
Eureka & Eastern Railroad Co. (1902)
Eureka & Freshwater Railway (1900)
Eureka & Klamath River Railroad (1896)
Eureka Municipal Railway (1921)
Eureka & Red Bluff Railroad (1892)
Eureka Southern Railroad Co. (1983)
Eureka Street Railroad Co. (1887)
Excelsior Redwood Co. (1891)
Falk & Minor Lumber Co. (1875)
Freshwater Lumber Co. (1903)
Georgia-Pacific Corporation (1956)
Glendale Mill Co. (1893)
Glendale Railroad Co. (1902)
Granite Mountain Rock Quarry Railroad (1916)
Hammond & Little River Railroad Co. (1912)
Hammond Lumber Co. (1912)
Hammond Redwood Lumber Co. (1936)
Hardy Creek & Eel River Railroad Co. (1907)
Harpset & Spring Tramway (1876)
Heney's Railroad (1892)
Holmes-Eureka Lumber Co. Railroad (1904)
Humboldt & Eastern Railroad Co. (1908)
Humboldt Bay & Eel River Railroad (1882)
Humboldt Bay & Mad River Railroad (1875)
Humboldt Bay & Trinidad Log & Lumber Co. (1891)
Humboldt Bay & Trinidad Railroad Co. (1896)
Humboldt Cooperage Co. (1913)
Humboldt County Railroad (1903)
Humboldt Logging Co. (1885)
Humboldt Lumber & Mill Co. (1882)
Humboldt Northern Railway (1904)
Humboldt Railroad (1901)

Humboldt Redwood Co. (1929)
Humboldt, Siskiyou & Klamath Railroad (1913)
Humboldt Transit Co. (1903)
Jacoby Creek Railroad Co. (1875)
Little River Redwood Co. (1908)
Mattole Lumber Co. (1908)
McCormick & Haupman (1901)
McKay & Co. (1891)
Metropolitan Redwood Co. (1907)
Minor, Kirk & Co. (1890)
Minor Mill & Lumber Co. (1885)
George H. Newell, Inc. (1907)
Northern California Lumber Co. Railroad (1903)
Northern Redwood Lumber Co. (1903)
Occidental Milling Co. (1880)
Oregon & Eureka Railroad (1903)
Oregon Coast & Eastern Railroad (1906)
Pacific Coast Line Railway Co. (1911)
Pacific Engineering & Construction Co. (1914)
Pacific Lumber Co. Railroad (1869)
Redwood Coast Railway Co. (1985)
Riverside Lumber Co. (1902)
Riverside Mill & Lumber Co. (1889)
San Francisco & Eureka Railway Co. (1903)
San Francisco & Northwestern Railroad Co. (1903)
T.R. Shannon Co. (1930)
Shasta, Trinity & Humboldt Railroad (1901)
Simpson Logging Co. (1950)
South Bay Railroad & Land Co. (1875)
Trinidad Mill Co. (1869)
Union Plank Walk & Railroad Co. (1875)
Union Plank Walk, Rail Track & Wharf Co. Railroad
    (1854)
Vance Mad River Railroad (1873)
John Vance Milling & Lumber Co. (1886)
Vance Redwood Lumber Co. (1900)
Warren Creek Railroad (1880)
Warren Creek Railroad Company (1917)
Wells Lumber Co. (1943)

IMPERIAL COUNTY

California Development Co. (1916)
Colorado River Land Co. (1924)
Holton Inter-Urban Railway Co. (1903)
Imperial & Gulf Railroad Co. (1902)
Imperial Gypsum Co. Railway (1922)
Imperial Irrigation District Railroad (1918)
Imperial Valley Gypsum & Oil Co. (1920)
Inter-California Railway Co. (1904)
Niland, Blythe & Seeley Electric Railway (1914)
Pacific Portland Cement Co. (1924)
U.S. Gypsum Co. (1919)
U.S. Gypsum Co. (1946)

INYO COUNTY

Bonnie Claire & Ubehebe Railroad (1906)

Carson & Colorado Railroad Co. (1880)
Carson & Colorado Railway (1892)
Darwin Development Co. (1917)
Death Valley Railroad Co. (1914)
Gerstley Borax Mine Railroad
Inyo Development Co. (1885)
Lila C. Railroad (1910)
Los Angeles & Owens River Railway Co. (1906)
National Soda Products Co. (1916)
Owens River Valley Electric Railway Co. (1910)
Pacific Coast Borax Co. (1914)

KERN COUNTY

Bakersfield & Kern Electric Co. (1900)
Bakersfield & Los Angeles Railway Co. (1898)
Bakersfield & San Luis Obispo Railroad Co. (1875)
California Midland Railroad (1902)
Central Railway of California (1902)
Consolidated Salt Co. (1914)
Diamond Salt Co. (1911)
Long Beach Salt Co. (1927)
Los Angeles, Owens Valley & Utah Railroad (1893)
Midland Pacific Railroad (1901)
Mojave & Bakersfield Railroad Co. (1910)
Monolith Portland Cement Co. Railroad (1920)
Monolith Railroad (1906)
Mountain Valley & Bakersfield Railroad Co. (1901)
Mountain Valley Railroad (1900)
Nevada & California Railway Co. (1905)
Randsburg Railway Co. (1897)
Red Rock Railroad (1908)
San Francisco & San Joaquin Railroad (1890)
Sierra & Eastern Railroad Co. (1906)
Sunset Railroad Co. (1900)
Sunset Railway (1904)
Sunset Western Railway Co. (1905)
Tehachapi Railway Co. (1923)
U.S. Navy Railroad - Inyokern (1942)
Yellow Aster Mine Railroad (1899)

KINGS COUNTY

Hanford & Summit Lake Railway Co. (1910)
Kings Lake Shore Railroad (1917)
Kings River Railroad (1910)

LAKE COUNTY

Clear Lake & Northern Pacific Railroad (1889)
Clear Lake & Northern Railroad (1891)
Clear Lake Northern Railway Co. (1909)
Clear Lake & Russian River Railroad (1892)
Clear Lake Traffic Co. (1908)
Highland Pacific Railroad (1909)
Lake County Lumber & Box Co.
Napa, Lake & Humboldt Railroad Co. (1887)
San Francisco & Clear Lake Narrow-Gauge Railroad
    Co. (1883)

San Francisco & Clear Lake Railroad (1900)
Sonoma & Lake County Electric Railway Co. (1907)

LASSEN COUNTY

Fernley & Lassen Railway (1909)
Great Northern Railway (1931)
Lassen Logging Co. Railroad (1918)
Lassen Lumber & Box Co. Railroad (1918)
Red River Lumber Co. (1912)
Red River Railroad (1921)

LOS ANGELES COUNTY

Alhambra & Pasadena Street Railway Co. (1887)
Altadena Railway (1887)
American Bulk Loaders Enterprise (1954)
American Colony Railway Co. (1882)
American High Speed Rail Corp. of Los Angeles (1981)
American Rapid Transit Co. of Southern California (1887)
Angels Flight Railway Co. (1912)
Aqueduct Construction Railroad - City of Los Angeles (1907)
Arcadia & Monrovia Railway Co. (1887)
Atchison, Topeka & Santa Fe Railway Co. (1895)
Azusa, Pomona & Elsinore Railroad Co. (1895)
Ballona & Santa Monica Railroad Co. (1887)
Belt Line Railroad Co. (1890)
Brooklyn Avenue Railway
Cahuenga Valley Railroad Co. (1888)
California & Arizona Railroad (1870)
California Central Railway Co. (1887)
California Improvement Co. (1890)
California Pacific Railroad Co. (1901)
California Pacific Railway (1899)
Central & Boyle Heights Railroad Co. (1885)
Central Railroad (1884)
City Railroad Co. (1883)
City Railway Co. of Los Angeles (1910)
City Railway Co. of Pasadena (1886)
Claremont Electric Railroad Co. (1894)
Colorado Street Railway Co. (1886)
Consolidated Rock Products Co. (1924)
Court Flight Incline Railroad (1901)
Covina Electric Railroad Co. (1903)
Depot Railway of Los Angeles (1888)
East Lake Park Scenic Railway (1901)
East Los Angeles & San Pedro Street Railway Co. (1875)
East & West Street Railway Co. (1888)
Electric Rapid Transit Co. (1890)
Elysian Park Street Railway Co. (1887)
Everett Street Railway (1911)
Falkes Aerial Railway (1912)
Fifth Street Railway (1887)
Garvanza Railroad (1886)
Gladstone Street Railway Co. (1887)

Glendale & Eagle Rock Railway Co. (1909)
Glendale, Gloretta & Sunland Railway Co. (1914)
Glendale & Montrose Railway (1914)
Glendale & Verdugo Mountain Railway (1912)
Greater Pacific Railroad & Navigation Co. (1979)
Harbor Belt Line Railroad (1929)
Highland Railroad Company (1888)
Holt & San Antonio Avenue Street Railroad (1887)
Hueneme, Malibu & Port Los Angeles Railroad (1903)
Hueneme, Malibu & Southern Railway (1916)
Industrial Terminal Railway Co. (1915)
Island Mountain Railway (1900)
Long Beach & Alamitos Bay Railway Co. (1891)
Long Beach Railroad Co. (1887)
Long Beach Salt Co. (1927)
Long Beach & San Pedro Railway Co. (1888)
Long Beach, Whittier & Los Angeles County Railroad Co. (1887)
Lookout Mountain Park Land & Water Co. (1900)
Los Angeles & Aliso Street Railroad Co. (1876)
Los Angeles Board of Harbor Commissioners Railroad (1925)
Los Angeles Cable Railway Co. (1887)
Los Angeles, Carlton & Eastern Railway Co. (1888)
Los Angeles & Cerro Gordo Narrow-Gauge Railroad (1874)
Los Angeles & Coast Railroad (1874)
Los Angeles Consolidated Electric Railroad (1890)
Los Angeles County Flood Control District Railroad
Los Angeles County Railroad Co. (1887)
Los Angeles County Transit Commission (1986)
Los Angeles & Eagle Rock Valley Railroad (1887)
Los Angeles & Eastern Railroad Co. (1888)
Los Angeles Electric Railway Co. (1886)
Los Angeles & Garvanza & Eagle Rock Railroad (1888)
Los Angeles & Glendale Electric Railway Co. (1903)
Los Angeles & Glendale Railroad (1887)
Los Angeles & Glendale Steam Railway Co. (1887)
Los Angeles Harbor Department Railroad (1904)
Los Angeles Harbor Railroad (1908)
Los Angeles, Hermosa & Redondo Beach Railway Co. (1901)
Los Angeles & Hueneme Railroad (1889)
Los Angeles Incline Railway (1901)
Los Angeles & Independence Railroad Co. (1875)
Los Angeles Inter-Urban Railway Co. (1903)
Los Angeles Junction Railway Co. (1923)
Los Angeles & Long Beach Railroad (1885)
Los Angeles Metropolitan Transit Authority (1958)
Los Angeles & Mount Washington Railway Co. (1908)
Los Angeles Municipal RR & Terminal Co. (1912)
Los Angeles, Ocean Park & Santa Monica Railway Co. (1902)
Los Angeles & Ocean Railway Co. (1887)

Los Angeles Ostrich Farm Railway Co. (1886)
Los Angeles Pacific Co. (1905)
Los Angeles Pacific Railroad Co. of California (1903)
Los Angeles-Pacific Railway Co. (1898)
Los Angeles & Pacific Railway Co. (1888)
Los Angeles, Pasadena & Altadena Railroad (1894)
Los Angeles & Pasadena Electric Railway Co. (1894)
Los Angeles, Pasadena & Glendale Railway Co. (1889)
Los Angeles & Pasadena Railway Co. (1884)
Los Angeles & Pasadena Railway Co. (1888)
Los Angeles & Pasadena Rapid Transit Co. (1888)
Los Angeles-Pasadena Traction Co. (1900)
Los Angeles Railway Co. (1895)
Los Angeles Railway Co. (1910)
Los Angeles Railway Corporation (1910)
Los Angeles & Redondo Railway Co. (1896)
Los Angeles & Salt Lake Railroad Co. (1916)
Los Angeles, Salt Lake & Atlantic Railway (1889)
Los Angeles & San Diego Railroad Co. (1876)
Los Angeles & San Fernando Electric Railway Co. (1911)
Los Angeles, San Fernando & Hueneme Railroad Co. (1887)
Los Angeles, San Francisco & Salt Lake Railroad (1894)
Los Angeles, San Francisco Short Line Railroad (1908)
Los Angeles & San Gabriel Valley Railroad Co. (1883)
Los Angeles & San Joaquin Valley Railroad Co. (1913)
Los Angeles & San Pedro Railroad Co. (1868)
Los Angeles, San Pedro & Wilmington Harbor Railroad Co. (1909)
Los Angeles & Santa Monica Railroad (1873)
Los Angeles & Santa Monica Railroad Co. (1902)
Los Angeles & Santa Monica Railway Co. (1886)
Los Angeles Suburban Homes (1911)
Los Angeles Terminal Exchange, Inc. (1929)
Los Angeles Terminal Railway Co. (1890)
Los Angeles Traction Co. (1895)
Los Angeles Transit Lines (1945)
Los Angeles, Tropico & Glendale Railway Co. (1903)
Los Angeles Union Passenger Terminal Railroad (1937)
Los Angeles, Utah & Atlantic Railroad Co. (1888)
Los Angeles & Vernon Street Railway (1887)
Los Angeles-Western Railway Co. (1910)
Main & Fifth Street Railway (1888)
Main, Fifth & San Pedro Street Railway Co. (1897)
Main Street & Agricultural Park Horsecar Line (1874)
Main Street & Agricultural Park Railroad Co. (1876)
Maple Avenue Electric Railway (1887)
Mateo Street & Santa Fe Avenue Street Car Co. (1895)
Metrolink (1990)
Metropolitan Coach Lines (1953)
Metro Rail (1980)

Monrovia, Arcadia & Pasadena Railroad (1887)
Monrovia Street Railway (1888)
Montecito Railway Co. (1914)
Mount Lowe Railway (1891)
Myrtle Avenue Railway Co. (1887)
Ninth Street Electric Railway (1903)
Ocean Air Line Railroad Co. (1888)
Orange Grove Street Railroad (1888)
Ostrich Farm Railway (1886)
Outer Harbor Dock & Wharf Co. (1908)
Outer Harbor Terminal Railway Co. (1927)
Pacific Cable Railway Co. (1890)
Pacific Distributing Co. (1918)
Pacific Electric Land Co. (1903)
Pacific Electric Railway Co. (1911)
Pacific Electric Railway Co. of Arizona (1898)
Pacific Electric Railway Co. of California (1901)
Pacific & Gulf Terminal Railroad (1906)
Pacific Railway Co. (1889)
Palmdale Railroad (1885)
Pasadena City Railway Co. (1888)
Pasadena, La Canada & San Fernando Railroad (1886)
Pasadena & Los Angeles Electric Railroad (1894)
Pasadena, Los Angeles & Long Beach Railroad Co. (1887)
Pasadena & Monte Vista Railroad Co. (1886)
Pasadena & Mount Lowe Railway Co. (1893)
Pasadena & Mount Wilson Railway Co. (1891)
Pasadena & Pacific Railway Co. (1898)
Pasadena & Pacific Railway Co. of Arizona (1894)
Pasadena Railway Co. (1887)
Pasadena, Ramona & Long Beach Railroad (1887)
Pasadena Rapid Transit Co. (1908)
Pasadena Street Railway Co. (1886)
Pasadena & Wilson's Peak Railway (1887)
Pleasure Beach & Los Angeles Belt Railway (1888)
Pomona & Elsinore Railroad Co. (1887)
Pomona Heights Street Railroad Co. (1887)
Pomona Street Railway Co. (1887)
Ramona & San Bernardino Railroad Co. (1888)
Raymond Railroad (1883)
Redondo Beach Railway Co. (1888)
Redondo & Hermosa Beach Railroad Co. (1901)
Redondo Railway Co. (1889)
Rosecrans Rapid Transit Railway (1887)
Salt Lake & Los Angeles Railroad Co. (1888)
San Antonio & Holt Avenue Railroad Co.
San Fernando Valley Railroad Co.
San Gabriel Valley Narrow-Gauge Railroad (1883)
San Gabriel Valley Rapid Transit Railway Co. (1887)
San Pedro, Los Angeles & Salt Lake Railroad Co. (1899)
San Pedro, Los Angeles & Utah Railway Co. (1888)
San Pedro Street Railway (1914)
Santa Ana & Long Beach Railroad Co. (1888)
Santa Catalina Island Co. (1910)
Santa Fe Avenue Railway (1891)
Santa Fe & Los Angeles Harbor Railroad Co. (1922)

Santa Fe Pacific Railroad (1897)
Santa Fe & Santa Monica Railway Co. (1892)
Santa Monica Canyon Railroad Co. (1904)
Santa Monica & Northern Railway Co. (1907)
Santa Monica Outlook Railroad (1887)
Santa Monica & Soldiers Home Railroad Co. (1891)
Santa Monica Surf Line Railway Co. (1890)
Santa Monica Wharf & Terminal Railway Co. (1890)
Second Street Cable Railroad Co. (1885)
Second Street Railroad Co. (1887)
Shell Oil Co.
Sierra Madre Street Railway Co. (1887)
Simon's Brick Co.
Southern California Narrow-Gauge Railroad (1879)
Southern California Railway Co. (1889)
Southern California Rapid Transit District (1975)
Southern Pacific Railroad Extension (1888)
Spring & West Sixth Street Railroad (1874)
Sterling Borax Co. (1912)
Temple & Diamond Street Steam Dummy Railroad (1887)
Temple Street Cable Railway Co. (1885)
Tidewater Northern Railway (1909)
Utah & Los Angeles Railway Co. (1894)
Venice Miniature Railway (1902)
West End Steam Dummy Railroad (1887)
West Pasadena Railway Co. (1887)

MADERA COUNTY

Chowchilla Pacific Railway Co. (1913)
Madera Flume & Trading Co. (1878)
Madera Railway Co. (1903)
Madera Sugar Pine Lumber Co. (1899)
Raymond Granite Co.
San Joaquin Valley & Yosemite Railroad Co. (1886)

MARIN COUNTY

Bay Counties Electric Railroad Co. (1905)
Marin County Electric Railways (1913)
Marin & Napa Railroad Co. (1886)
Marin Shore Railroad Co. (1904)
Mill Valley & Mount Tamalpais Scenic Railway Co. (1896)
Mount Tamalpais & Muir Woods Railway (1913)
North Pacific Coast Railroad Co. (1871)
North Pacific Coast Railroad Extension Co. (1882)
North Pacific Narrow-Gauge Railway Co. (1873)
North Shore Railroad (1902)
Northwestern Pacific Railroad Co. (1907)
Northwestern Pacific Railway Co. (1906)
San Francisco & Northern Railroad Co. (1880)
San Francisco & San Rafael Railroad Co. (1882)
San Francisco, Tamalpais & Bolinas Railway Co. (1889)
San Rafael & San Anselmo Valley Railroad (1913)
San Rafael & San Quentin Railroad Co. (1869)
Sausalito Incline Street Railway (1914)

MARIPOSA COUNTY

California Peach & Fig Growers Assn. (1920)
California Peach Growers Assn. Railroad (1918)
Coulterville Lumber Co. (1948)
Hazel Green Railroad (1909)
Merced Gold Mining Co. (1894)
Yosemite Lumber Co. (1910)
Yosemite Portland Cement Co. (1925)
Yosemite Sugar Pine Lumber Co. (1934)

MENDOCINO COUNTY

Albion Lumber Co. (1891)
Albion River Railroad (1885)
Albion & Southeastern Railway (1902)
Albion & Wetherbee Co. (1880)
American Redwood Co. (1915)
Anderson & Middleton Lumber Co. (1902)
Bear Harbor & Eel River Railroad (1886)
Bear Harbor Lumber Co. (1893)
California Lumber Co. (1872)
California Western Railroad (1947)
California Western Railroad & Navigation Co. (1905)
Casper Creek Railroad (1874)
Casper & Hare Creek Railroad Co. (1885)
Casper, South Fork & Eastern Railroad (1903)
Charles Lumber Co. (1952)
Clear Lake Lumber Co. (1911)
Clear Lake Railroad & Electric Power Co. (1904)
Clear Lake Railroad Co. (1913)
Clear Lake Suspended Monorail Co. (1911)
Cleone Lumber Co. (1900)
Cleone Tramway (1901)
Dehaven Lumber Co. (1901)
Dehaven Railroad Co. (1916)
Elk Creek Railroad (1889)
Elk Redwood Co. Railroad (1934)
Empire Redwood Co. Railroad (1903)
Finkbind-Guild Co. (1926)
Fort Bragg Railroad Co. (1885)
Fort Bragg & Southeastern Railroad Co. (1903)
Garcia & Point Arena Railroad (1870)
Glen Blair Lumber Co. (1905)
Glen Blair Redwood Co. (1903)
Goodyear Redwood Co. Railroad (1916)
Greenwood Railroad Co. (1890)
Gualala Mill Co. (1884)
Gualala Milling Co. (1872)
Gualala River Railroad (1891)
A. Haun & Sons (1907)
Helm Railway (1940)
C.A. Hooper Co. (1886)
Howard Creek Lumber Co. Railroad (1916)
Irvine & Muir Lumber Co. (1906)
Little Valley Lumber Co. (1901)
Mendocino Coast Railway (1987)
Mendocino Lumber Co. (1900)

Mendocino Railroad (1875)
National Redwood Co. Railroad (1920)
Navarro Lumber Co. (1875)
Navarro Manufacturing & Railroad Co. (1886)
Navarro Mill Co. (1915)
Navarro Railroad (1874)
Newhart Lumber & Milling Co. (1922)
New York & Pennsylvania Redwood Co. (1907)
North Coast Lumber Co. (1913)
Northwestern Redwood Co. (1903)
Noyo & Pudding Creek Railroad (1881)
Overland Pacific Railway Co. (1894)
Pacific Coast Redwood Lumber Co.
Point Arena Railway (1889)
Pollard & Dodge Co. (1900)
Pollard Lumber Co. (1906)
Pudding Creek Lumber Co. Railroad (1886)
Redwood Railroad (1883)
Reed Timber & Lumber Co. (1879)
Rockport Redwood Co. (1938)
Salmon Creek Extension Railroad (1896)
Salmon Creek Railroad (1883)
San Francisco & Eureka Railway (1903)
Southern Humboldt Lumber Co. (1902)
Stearns Lumber Co. (1905)
Stewart & Hunter Lumber Co. (1880)
Union Lumber Co. (1890)
USAL Redwood Co. (1890)
Westport Lumber & Railroad Co. (1908)
L.E. White Lumber Co. (1916)

MERCED COUNTY

Foster Farms Railroad
Merced Canyon Railway (1905)
Merced Canyon Railway Co. (1909)
Tidewater & Southern Transit Co. (1912)
Yosemite Park Electric Railway (1912)
Yosemite Valley Railroad Co. (1902)
Yosemite Valley Railway Co. (1935)

MODOC COUNTY

Big Lakes Lumber Co. (1937)
Canby Railroad Co. (1929)
Conklin Mill Railroad (1935)
Crane Creek Lumber Co. (1928)
Davis Creek Lumber Co. (1931)
Goose Lake & Southern Railway Co. (1908)
Modoc Northern Railway Co. (1908)
Pickering Lumber Co. (1934)
Ralph L. Smith Lumber Co. (1943)
Walker-Hovey Co. (1929)

MONO COUNTY

Bodie & Benton Railway & Commercial Co. (1882)
Bodie Railway & Lumber Co. (1881)

Mono Lake Railway (1907)
Mono Lake Railway & Lumber Co. (1906)
Western Nevada Railroad Co. (1879)

MONTEREY COUNTY

California Coal Fields Railroad (1920)
*Del Norte, Monterey & Pacific Grove Electric Railway
    Co. (1901)*
Monterey & Del Monte Heights Railway Co. (1909)
Monterey & Eastern Railroad (1906)
Monterey Extension Railroad Co. (1888)
Monterey & Fresno Railroad Co. (1895)
Monterey, Fresno & Eastern Railway Co. (1906)
Monterey & Pacific Grove Railway Co. (1893)
Monterey & Pacific Grove Street Railway & Electric
    Power Co. (1893)
Monterey Peninsula Railroad Co. (1977)
Monterey Railroad Co. (1880)
Monterey & Salinas Valley Railroad Co. (1874)
Monterey & San Joaquin Railroad (1912)
Pajaro Valley Consolidated Railroad Co. (1897)
Pajaro Valley Extension Railroad (1898)
Pajaro Valley Railway (1890)
Salinas Railway (1897)
Southern Pacific Branch Railroad Co. (1872)
Spreckles Sugar Co. (1929)
Stone Canyon & Pacific Railroad Co. (1905)

NAPA COUNTY

Bay Counties Power Co. (1902)
California Eastern & Northern Railway (1917)
Cement, Tolenas & Tidewater Railroad Co. (1911)
Lakeport & Southern Railway (1906)
Mare Island Freight Line Co. (1919)
Napa & Clear Lake Railway (1911)
Napa, Dillon's Beach & Tomales Railway (1905)
Napa & Lakeport Railroad (1908)
Napa & Lakeport Railway (1905)
Napa Valley Railroad Co. (1864)
Napa Valley Wine Train, Inc. (1985)
San Francisco, Clear Lake & Humboldt Railroad (1889)

NEVADA COUNTY

Birch & Smart (1904)
Carson River Railroad (1867)
Fiberboard Products, Inc. (1946)
Charles H. Fowler & Co. (1910)
Greenhorn Railroad (1888)
Hassler Lumber Co. (1950)
Hobart Estate Co. (1917)
Hobart Southern Railroad Co. (1932)
Charles W. Kitts Lumber Co. (1886)
Kitts Railroad (1886)
Lake Tahoe Railway & Transportation Co. (1898)
Nevada & California Lumber Co. (1873)
Nevada County Narrow-Gauge Railroad Co. (1874)

Nevada County Traction Co. (1901)
Nevada, Grass Valley & Colfax Railroad (1870)
Nevada & Oregon Railroad (1880)
Nevada Pacific Railway (1889)
North Star Co. (1906)
Pacific Lumber & Wood Co. (1878)
Sierra Nevada Wood & Lumber Co. (1896)
Truckee Lumber Co. (1880)
Voss' Lumber Railroad (1883)

ORANGE COUNTY

Anaheim City & Interurban Railway (1912)
Anaheim, Olinda & Pomona Railroad Co. (1888)
Anaheim Railway (1870)
Anaheim-San Bernardino Railroad (1868)
Anaheim Street Railway Co. (1887)
Anaheim-Tustin Railroad
Fairview Railroad (1888)
Fullerton & Richfield Railway Co. (1910)
Inter-Urban Railway Co. (1901)
Newport Beach Electric Railway (1903)
Newport Wharf & Lumber Co. (1889)
Orange, McPherson & El Modena Street Railway (1887)
Pacific & San Bernardino Railroad Co. (1868)
Port Orange & Santa Ana Railroad Co. (1907)
San Bernardino & San Diego Railway Co. (1886)
Santa Ana Beach & Rocky Point Railway (1885)
Santa Ana, Fairview & Pacific Railroad Co. (1887)
Santa Ana & Long Beach Railroad Co. (1888)
Santa Ana & Long Beach Railroad & Improvement Co. (1888)
Santa Ana, Long Beach & Coast Railway Co. (1887)
Santa Ana & Newport Railway Co. (1892)
Santa Ana & Orange Motor Co. (1896)
Santa Ana, Orange & Tustin Street Railway Co. (1886)
Santa Ana Railroad Co. (1889)
Santa Ana & Tustin Motor Railway Co. (1888)
Santa Ana Valley & Pacific Railroad (1889)
Santa Ana & Westminster Railway Co. (1890)
Southern California Beach Railway (1912)

PLACER COUNTY

American Canyon Railroad
Auburn Branch Railroad (1858)
Auburn Street Railway (1899)
California & Oregon Railroad Co. (1868)
Clinton Narrow-Gauge Railroad (1878)
Crown Williamette Paper Co. (1924)
Eastern Extension Railroad (1860)
Giant Gap & Rubicon Railroad Co. (1907)
Lake Tahoe Narrow-Gauge Railroad (1878)
Lincoln & Gold Hill Railroad (1859)
Lincoln Northern Railroad (1907)
Lincoln, San Francisco & Eastern RR Co. (1905)
Link Belt Railway (1910)

Mountain Quarries Railroad (1909)
Pacific Portland Cement Consolidated (1911)
Read Timber & Lumber Co. (1906)
Richardson Brothers (1875)
George Schaffer Lumber Co. (1886)
J.G. Shebley Co. (1908)
Towle Brothers & Co. (1883)
Towle Brothers Lumber Co. (1885)
Virginia & Bear River Railroad Co. (1853)
Yuba Railroad Co. (1862)

PLUMAS COUNTY

Almanor Railroad Co. (1944)
Butte & Plumas Railway (1902)
California Fruit Growers Exchange (1916)
Clio Lumber Co. (1907)
Davis Box & Lumber Co. (1916)
Feather River-Crescent Mills Railroad (1902)
Feather River Lumber Co. (1915)
Graeagle Lumber Co. (1916)
Indian Valley Railroad Co. (1916)
Massack Timber & Lumber Co. (1916)
F.S. Murphy Lumber Co. (1918)
Nibley-Stoddard Lumber Co. (1913)
Northern California Railroad Co. (1927)
Quincy & Eastern Railway Co. (1908)
Quincy Lumber Co. (1916)
Quincy Railroad Co. (1917)
Quincy & Western Railroad Co. (1908)
M.J. Scanlon Lumber Co. (1923)
Sierra Iron & Quincy Railroad Co. (1867)
Sierra & Mohawk Railway Co. (1885)
Sierra Valley & Mohawk Railroad Co. (1890)
Sierra Valley Railroad Co. (1895)
Sloat Lumber Co. (1917)
Spanish Peak Lumber Co. (1926)
Wolf Creek Timber Co.

RIVERSIDE COUNTY

California Southern Railroad Co. (1914)
Chuckwalla Valley Railroad (1910)
Colorado River Valley Electric Railway Co. (1914)
Corona & Santa Fe Railway Co. (1926)
Crescent City Railway Co. (1907)
Eagle Mountain Railroad Co. (1948)
Elsinore, Pomona & Los Angeles Railway Co. (1887)
Hall's Addition Street Railway Co. (1887)
Lake Elsinore Railroad (1887)
Parker & Colorado River Electric Railroad (1914)
Perris & Lakeview Railway Co. (1898)
Perris & San Jacinto Railroad (1887)
Riverside & Arlington Railway Co (1887)
Riverside Electric Railway Co. (1898)
Riverside Railway Co. (1886)
Riverside-Redlands Interurban Railway (1912)
Riverside, Rialto & Pacific Railroad Co. (1911)
Riverside, Santa Ana & Los Angeles Railway (1885)

San Jacinto, Lakeview & Northern Railroad Co. (1898)
San Jacinto & Murrieta Railroad Co. (1886)
Yucaipa & Oak Glen Railroad (1908)

SACRAMENTO COUNTY

Amador Branch Railroad Co. (1875)
California Central Railroad Co. (1857)
California Midland Railroad Co. (1892)
California Pacific Eastern Extension Co. (1871)
California Pacific Railroad Co. (1865)
California & Yosemite Short Line Railroad (1882)
Central Pacific Railroad Co. (1870)
Central Pacific Railroad of California (1864)
Central Pacific Railway (1899)
Central Street Railway (1867)
City Omnibus Co. (1868)
City Railway (1870)
Elmhurst Street Railway Co. (1910)
Eureka Railroad Co. (1852)
Folsom & Placerville Railroad Co. (1876)
Freeport Railroad (1858)
Galt & Ione Railway Co. (1875)
Placerville & Sacramento Valley Railroad Co. (1862)
Sacramento, Auburn & Nevada Railway Co. (1852)
Sacramento Belt Railroad (1906)
Sacramento Brick Co.
Sacramento City Lines (1943)
Sacramento City Street Railway Co.
Sacramento & Eastern Railway Co. (1911)
Sacramento Electric, Gas & Railway Co. (1896)
Sacramento Electric, Power & Light Co. Electric Railway (1897)
Sacramento, Fair Oaks & Orangevale Railroad Co. (1895)
Sacramento-Folsom Electric Railway Co. (1911)
Sacramento Interurban Railway (1912)
Sacramento & Lake Tahoe Railroad Co. (1905)
Sacramento Northern Railroad Co (1918)
Sacramento Northern Railway Co (1921)
Sacramento, Placer & Nevada Railroad (1852)
Sacramento & Placerville Railroad Co. (1877)
Sacramento Regional Transit Authority (1979)
Sacramento & San Joaquin Valley Railroad Co. (1899)
Sacramento & Sierra Railway Co. (1911)
Sacramento Southern Railroad Co. (1902)
Sacramento Terminal Co. (1908)
Sacramento & Vallejo Railroad Co. (1907)
Sacramento Valley Railroad Co. (1852)
Sacramento & Woodland Railroad Co. (1911)
Sacramento & Yolo Belt Line Co. (1910)
Sierra County Railroad (1911)
Union Belt Line Railway Co. (1906)
Vallejo & Northern Railroad Co. (1910)
Vallejo & Northern Railway Co. (1909)
West Sacramento Electric Co. (1914)
West Side Railroad Co. (1911)

SAN BENITO COUNTY

California Central Railroad Co. (1912)
Lime Kiln Railroad (1892)
Old Mission Cement Co. (1912)
Pacific Portland Cement Co. (1927)
Panoche Valley Railroad (1908)
San Juan Pacific Railroad (1907)
San Juan Southern Railway Co. (1907)

SAN BERNARDINO COUNTY

Amargosa Valley Railroad Co. (1907)
American Borax Co. (1901)
American Magnesium Co. (1922)
Arizona & California Railroad Co. (1991)
Arrowhead & Waterman Railroad (1891)
Atlantic & Pacific Railroad Co. (1866)
Barnwell & Searchlight Railway Co. (1906)
Big Pine Lime & Transportation Co. (1910)
Borate & Daggett Railroad Co. (1896)
Brookings Lumber & Box Co. Railroad (1897)
California, Arizona & Santa Fe Railway Co. (1911)
California Eastern Railway Co. (1895)
California Rock Salt Co. (1921)
California Salt Co. (1950)
California Southern Extension Railroad Co. (1881)
CALTRANS - California Department of Transportation (1979)
Chino Valley Railway Co. (1888)
City Street Railroad Co. (1885)
Colorado River & Gulf Railroad (1901)
Colton & San Bernardino Railway Co. (1888)
Columbia Materials Co.
Consolidated Pacific Cement Plaster Co. (1909)
Consumer Salt Co. (1916)
Crystal Salt Co. (1909)
Daggett & Calico Railroad Co. (1885)
Death Valley Monorail Co. (1922)
Death Valley Prismodial (1922)
East San Bernardino Railroad (1888)
Epsom Salts Monorail (1922)
Golden State Portland Cement Co. (1915)
Highland Lumber Co. Railroad (1890)
Highland Railroad (1887)
Lake Arrowhead Dam Construction Co. Railroad (1905)
Leslie Salt Co. (1960)
Lone Pine Utilities Co. (1914)
Los Angeles, Daggett & Tonopah Railroad Co. (1903)
Ludlow & Southern Railway Co. (1902)
Mid-Pacific Railroad (1929)
Mojave Northern Railroad Co. (1915)
Needles, Searchlight & Northern Railway (1915)
Nevada Pacific Railway (1889)
Nevada Southern Railway Co. (1892)
Northwestern Street Railway (1909)
Ontario & San Antonio Heights Railway Co. (1888)

Pacific Cement Plaster Co. (1905)
Pacific Rock Salt Co. (1918)
Redlands Central Electric Railway Co. (1907)
Redlands Central Railway Co. (1907)
Redlands Street Railway (1887)
Redlands Street Railway Co. (1888)
Redlands University Railway (1911)
Redlands & Yucaipa Electric Railway (1907)
Riverside Portland Cement Co. (1923)
San Bernardino, Arrowhead & Waterman Railroad
    Co. (1887)
San Bernardino & Bear Valley Railroad (1887)
San Bernardino Central Railroad Co.
San Bernardino & Eastern Railway Co. (1890)
San Bernardino & Highland Electric Railway (1903)
San Bernardino Interurban Railway Co. (1906)
San Bernardino & Los Angeles Railway Co. (1886)
San Bernardino & Los Angeles Railway Co. (1892)
San Bernardino Mountain Electric Railroad (1896)
San Bernardino Mountain Railroad (1914)
San Bernardino & Redlands Railroad Co. (1888)
San Bernardino Street Railway (1875)
San Bernardino Urban Railway Co. (1907)
San Bernardino Valley Railway Co. (1887)
San Bernardino Valley Traction Co. (1900)
Santa Fe Connecting Railroad Co. (1929)
Silver Lake Railroad
Southern California Motor Road Co. (1886)
Southwestern Portland Cement Co. (1915)
Tecopa Railroad Co. (1909)
Terracina & Redlands Street Railway Co. (1891)
Tonopah & Tidewater Railroad Co. (1904)
Trona Railway Co. (1913)
U.S. Gypsum Co. (1919)
Upland & Claremont Railroad (1908)
Victor & Eastern Railroad Co. (1908)
Waterloo Mining Co. (1888)
West End Chemical Co. (1914)
Western Mineral Co. (1895)

SAN DIEGO COUNTY

Atchison, Topeka & Santa Fe Railroad Co. (1859)
Baja California & Sonora Railroad Co. (1881)
Bay Shore & Pacific Railroad Co. (1905)
Bay Shore Railroad Co. (1914)
California Southern Railroad Co. (1880)
California Southern Railroad Co. (1881)
Citizens Traction Co. (1896)
City Park Belt Motor Road (1887)
City & University Heights Motor Road (1886)
Coast Motor Co. (1889)
Coronado Beach Railroad Co. (1886)
Coronado Railroad Co. (1886)
Del Mar San Diego Railway Co. (1888)
Electric Rapid Transit Street Car Co (1887)
Enid, San Diego & Pacific Railroad Co. (1902)
Escondido Street Car Co. (1886)

S.M. Haskins (1905)
Junipero Land & Town Co. (1888)
Keller-Kerckhoff Co. (1906)
Keller & Morfey Co. (1888)
Kyle Railways (1979)
Los Angeles, Niagra & San Diego Railroad Co. (1887)
Los Angeles & San Diego Beach Railway Co. (1888)
Los Angeles, San Diego & Yuma Railroad Co. (1889)
Charles R. McCormick Lumber Co. (1910)
Memphis & El Paso Railroad Co. (1853)
Memphis, El Paso & Pacific Railroad Co. (1853)
Mesa & El Cajon Railroad Co. (1887)
Metropolitan Transit Development Board (1976)
Mexican Pacific Railroad Co. (1888)
Mexico & San Diego Railway Co. (1911)
National City & El Cajon Valley Railroad Co. (1882)
National City & Otay Railway Co. (1886)
National City Street Car Co. (1888)
Ocean Beach Railroad Co. (1888)
Oceanside Coast Motor Railroad (1887)
Oriental & Pacific Railroad Co. (1902)
Otay Railroad Co. (1887)
Pacific Coast Steamship Co. (1875)
Pacific Mail Steamship Co. (1850)
Peninsular Railroad Co. (1887)
People's Railroad Co. (1904)
Point Loma Electric Railway Co. (1907)
Point Loma Railroad Co. (1908)
Roseville & Ocean Beach Railroad Co. (1887)
Roseville & Old Town Railroad (1886)
San Diego & Arizona Eastern Railway Co. (1933)
San Diego & Arizona Eastern Railway Co. (1979)
San Diego & Arizona Railway Co. (1906)
San Diego & Bay Shore Railroad Co. (1871)
San Diego Bay Terminal Railway Co. (1904)
San Diego Cable Car & Land Co. (1887)
San Diego Cable Railway Co. (1889)
San Diego Central Railroad Co. (1886)
San Diego & Colorado River Railroad Co. (1880)
San Diego & Cuyamaca Railway Co. (1887)
San Diego & Cuyamaca Railway Co. (1909)
San Diego, Cuyamaca & Eastern Railway Co. (1888)
San Diego & Del Mar Railroad (1889)
San Diego & Eastern Terminal Railway Co. (1889)
San Diego-Eastern Railway Co. (1901)
San Diego & El Cajon & Escondido Railway Co. (1909)
San Diego, El Cajon Valley Interurban Railway Co.
    (1909)
San Diego Electric Railway Co. (1891)
San Diego, El Paso & St. Louis Railroad (1909)
San Diego & Elsinore Railroad Co. (1887)
San Diego, Fort Yuma & Atlantic Railway Co. (1894)
San Diego & Gila, Southern Pacific & Atlantic
    Railroad Co. (1854)
San Diego & Imperial Valley Railroad Co. (1984)
San Diego & International Railroad Co. (1887)
San Diego & Los Angeles Railroad Co. (1870)

San Diego Metropolitan Transit Development Board (1976)
San Diego & Mission Valley Railway Co. (1887)
San Diego & Northeastern Railway (1889)
San Diego & Ocean Railroad Co. (1889)
San Diego & Old Town Railroad Co. (1886)
San Diego, Old Town & Pacific Beach Railway (1888)
San Diego & Pacific Beach Railway Co. (1887)
San Diego, Pacific Beach & La Jolla Railway (1889)
San Diego, Pacific & Eastern Railroad Co. (1895)
San Diego & Phoenix Railroad Co. (1893)
San Diego, Phoenix & Galveston Railroad Co. (1890)
San Diego, Riverside & Los Angeles Railway Co. (1912)
San Diego & San Bernardino Railroad Co. (1871)
San Diego & South Eastern Railway Co. (1912)
San Diego & Southern Utah Railroad (1875)
San Diego Southern Railway Co. (1908)
San Diego Street Car Co. (1886)
San Diego Street Railroad Co. (1880)
San Diego Transit System (1948)
San Diego Union Depot & Terminal Railway Co. (1888)
San Diego Union Railway & Ship Terminal Co. (1903)
San Diego & Utah Railroad Co. (1876)
San Diego & Yuma Railroad (1893)
San Diego, Yuma & Phoenix Railway Co. (1893)
San Luis Rey Valley Railroad (1888)
South San Diego & Imperial Beach Railway Co. (1908)
South San Diego Railway Co. (1907)
Texas Pacific Railroad Co. (1870)
University Heights Motor Road (1886)
Utah, Nevada & California Railroad Co. (1889)

SAN FRANCISCO COUNTY

Alcatraz Island Railroad (1865)
Amtrak (1970)
Bay & Coast Railway Co. (1899)
Bayshore Railway (1904)
Belt Railroad Co. of San Francisco (1891)
Bridge Railway (1939)
California Electric Railway (1909)
California Great Trunk of the Pacific & the Atlantic Railroad Co. (1857)
California Inland Empire Railroad (1905)
California Midland Railroad (1902)
California Pacific Railroad Co. (1869)
California Pacific Railroad Extension Co. (1869)
California Rapid Transit Railroad Co. (1907)
California Street Cable Railroad Co. (1884)
California Street Railway (1878)
California Terminal Co. (1911)
California Terminal Railway Co. (1914)
Central California Railway Co. (1904)

Central Railroad Co. (1862)
City Railroad Co. (1863)
Clay Street Hill Railroad Co. (1869)
Clear Lake & Southern Railroad (1906)
Clear Lake Southern Railroad Co. (1907)
Exposition Terminal Railway Co. (1913)
Fairfax Incline Railroad Co. (1913)
Farallon Midland Railway (1880)
Ferries & Cliff House Railway Co. (1888)
Folsom Street & Fort Point Railroad & Tunnel Co. (1863)
Front Street, Mission & Ocean Railroad Co. (1862)
Geary Street Municipal Railway (1912)
Geary Street, Park & Ocean Railroad Co. (1878)
Golden Gate & Cliff House Railway
Gough Street Railroad (1910)
Inter-Urban Electric Railway Co. (1934)
Jackson, Sutter & Amador Railway Co. (1890)
Market Street Cable Railway Co. (1882)
Market Street & Fairmont Railroad Co.
Market Street Railroad Co. (1859)
Market Street Railway Co. (1893)
Martin-Murietta Carbon Co.
Metropolitan Street Railway (1891)
Monorail Rapid Transit Co. (1912)
Mount Olivet Cemetery's Electric Railway
Municipal Railway of San Francisco (1912)
North Beach & Mission Railway Co.
North & South Beach Railroad Co. (1862)
Ocean Beach Railway Co. (1885)
Ocean Shore Railroad (1911)
Ocean Shore Railway (1905)
Omnibus Cable Co. (1886)
Omnibus Railroad Co. (1862)
Overfair Railway (1915)
Pacific Railroad Co. (1889)
Panama-Pacific International Exposition Terminal Railway Co. (1913)
Park & Cliff House Co. (1886)
Park & Coast Railroad Co. (1883)
Park & Ocean Railroad (1883)
Parkside Transit Co. (1906)
Potrero & Bay View Railroad Co. (1866)
Powell Street Railway (1884)
Presidio & Ferries Railroad (1880)
Sacramento Valley West Side Electric Railway (1911)
San Francisco & Atlantic Railroad Co. (1892)
San Francisco Bay Area Rapid Transit District (1951)
San Francisco Bay Railroad Co. (1868)
San Francisco Belt Railroad (1892)
San Francisco & Buenos Aires Railroad Co. (1876)
San Francisco & Clear Lake Railway Co. (1892)
San Francisco & Colorado River Railway (1908)
San Francisco & Denver Railroad Co. 1892)
San Francisco & Eastern Railroad (1891)
San Francisco Electric Railway (1909)
San Francisco & Great Salt Lake Railroad Co. (1892)

San Francisco, Idaho & Montana Railroad Co. (1905)
San Francisco & Los Angeles Airline Railroad (1908)
San Francisco Marginal Railroad (1890)
San Francisco Market Street Railroad (1859)
San Francisco & Napa Valley Railroad Co. (1935)
San Francisco, Napa & Calistoga Railway Co. (1911)
San Francisco, Oakland & Ottawa Railroad Co. (1885)
San Francisco, Oakland & San Jose Railway Co.
   (1902)
San Francisco-Oakland Terminal Railways (1912)
San Francisco & Ocean Shore Railroad Co. (1884)
San Francisco Peninsula Railway (1913)
San Francisco Railroad Co. (1904)
San Francisco & Sacramento Railroad Co. (1856)
San Francisco-Sacramento Railroad Co. (1920)
San Francisco & San Jose Railroad Co. (1860)
San Francisco & San Mateo Electric Railway Co.
   (1895)
San Francisco & San Mateo Railway Co. (1891)
San Francisco, San Mateo & Santa Cruz Railroad (1875)
San Francisco & Santa Clara Valley Railroad (1892)
San Francisco & Stockton Railroad Co. (1890)
San Francisco, Stockton & Bakersfield Railroad (1894)
San Francisco, Stockton & San Joaquin Railroad (1894)
San Francisco Terminal Railway (1902)
San Francisco Transit Co. (1900)
San Francisco & Vaca Valley Railway (1906)
San Francisco & West Shore Railroad (1895)
Santa Fe-Southern Pacific Corporation (1980)
Santa Fe-Southern Pacific Corporation (1983)
Santa Fe Terminal Co. of California (1899)
Santa Rosa & Sonoma County Electric Railway Co.
   (1896)
South Beach & Mission Railway Co. (1862)
South San Francisco Belt Railway Co. (1907)
South San Francisco Land & Improvement Co.
   (1891)
South San Francisco Railroad & Power Co. (1903)
Southern Heights & Visitation Valley Railway Co.
Southern Pacific Company (1884)
Southern Pacific Railroad (1865)
Southern Pacific Railroad (1870)
Southern Pacific Railroad (1873)
Southern Pacific Railroad (1874)
Southern Pacific Railroad (1888)
Southern Pacific Railroad (1898)
Southern Pacific Railroad (1902)
State Belt Railroad of California (1892)
Sutro Railroad Co. (1896)
Sutter Street Railroad Co. (1887)
Sutter Street Railway Co. (1877)
Sutter Street Wire Cable Railway Co. (1879)
Telegraph Railroad Co. (1884)
Terminal Railway Co. (1867)
United Railways of San Francisco (1902)
United States Central Railroad Co. (1884)
West Shore Railroad Co. (1895)

West Shore & Valley Railroad (1895)
Western Meat Co. (1903)

SAN JOAQUIN COUNTY

Alameda & San Joaquin Valley Railroad (1895)
Central California Traction Co. (1905)
Corn Products Co.
Corral Hollow Railroad Co. (1895)
Holly Sugar Co. Railroad
Pacific Coast Aggregates Corporation (1906)
Rough & Ready Island Railroad (1945)
Sacramento & San Joaquin Valley Railroad Co. (1899)
San Francisco & San Joaquin Valley Railway Co.
   (1895)
San Joaquin Delta Railroad (1911)
San Joaquin Railroad Co. (1851)
San Joaquin & Sierra Nevada Railroad Co. (1882)
San Joaquin & Tulare Railroad (1873)
San Joaquin Valley Electric Railway Co. (1908)
San Joaquin Valley Railroad Co. (1868)
San Pablo & Tulare Extension Railroad Co. (1887)
Sharp Army Depot Railroad (1941)
Sierra Pacific Railroad Co. (1896)
Stanislaus & Mariposa Railroad Co. (1866)
Stockton & Bay City Short Line Railroad (1911)
Stockton & Beckwith Pass Railroad (1902)
Stockton Belt Line Railroad Co.
Stockton & Copperopolis Railroad Co. (1865)
Stockton Electric Railway (1891)
Stockton, Fresno & Southern Railway (1889)
Stockton & Ione Railroad (1873)
Stockton & Lodi Terminal Railroad (1895)
Stockton Street Railway Co. (1874)
Stockton Terminal & Eastern Railroad (1908)
Stockton & Tuolumne County Railway Co. (1897)
Stockton & Tuolumne Railway Co. (1899)
Stockton & Visalia Railroad Co. (1869)
Tidewater & Southern Railroad Co. (1910)
United Railroad (1894)
Woodbridge & Sacramento River Railroad (1862)

SAN LUIS OBISPO COUNTY

Camp San Luis Obispo Military Railroad (1941)
Eastern Sierra & Pacific Railroad Co. (1907)
John Harford's Railroad (1871)
Pacific Coast Railroad Co. (1881)
Pacific Coast Railway Co. (1882)
Paso De Robles Street Railway (1892)
Paso Robles & Cayucos Railway Co. (1891)
People's Wharf Company (1868)
Port San Luis Transportation Co. (1941)
San Luis Obispo Railroad Co. (1873)
San Luis Obispo & Santa Maria Valley Railroad
   (1873)
San Luis Obispo Street Railway Co. (1887)
San Luis & San Joaquin Railroad (1892)

Southern Pacific Branch Railway Co. (1886)
West Coast Land Co. (1890)

SAN MATEO COUNTY

Burlingame Railroad Co. (1914)
Burlingame Railway Co. (1911)
California Tie & Timber Co. (1929)
Campbell Redwood Lumber Co. (1917)
Easton Railroad (1913)
Palo Alto & Suburban Railway Co. (1903)
Pescadero Railway & Improvement Co. (1907)
Redwood City Railway (1913)
San Francisco-San Mateo Right-of-Way Co. (1914)
San Mateo Beach Railway

SANTA BARBARA COUNTY

Avila & Sunset Railway (1902)
Back & Forth Railroad (1967)
Consolidated Electric Co. (1896)
Johns-Manville Products Corporation
Pacific Southwestern Railroad Co. (1922)
Santa Barbara Consolidated Electric Co. (1903)
Santa Barbara & Southern Pacific Railroad Co. (1879)
Santa Barbara Street Railway (1897)
Santa Barbara & Suburban Railway Co. (1912)
Santa Maria Valley Railroad Co. (1911)
Stanley-Brown Co. (1906)

SANTA CLARA COUNTY

California Narrow-Gauge Railroad & Transportation
  Co. (1875)
California Southern Railroad Co. (1870)
First Street Railroad Co. (1871)
First Street & San Pedro Street Railway
First Street & Willow Glen Horse Railroad Co. (1874)
F.A. Hihn Lumber Co. (1876)
Market Street & Willow Glen Horse Railroad Co.
  (1876)
Molina Timber Co. (1890)
Mount Hunter Railroad (1904)
North Side Railroad Co. (1875)
Pacific & Atlantic Railroad Co. (1851)
Peninsular Railroad Co. (1909)
Peninsular Railway Co. (1911)
People's Horse Railroad Co. (1877)
People's Railroad of San Jose (1877)
San Jose & Almaden Railroad Co. (1886)
San Jose & Almaden Railway Co. (1911)
San Jose & Alum Rock Park Railway (1891)
San Jose & Alviso Railroad (1895)
San Jose & Congress Springs Railroad (1901)
San Jose-Los Gatos Interurban Railway (1903)
San Jose Railroad Co. (1894)
San Jose Railroads (1909)
San Jose Railway Co. (1903)

San Jose & Santa Clara County Railroad Co. (1905)
San Jose & Santa Clara Railroad Co. (1868)
San Jose, Saratoga & Los Gatos Interurban Co.
  (1902)
San Jose, Saratoga & Los Gatos Railroad (1901)
San Jose Short Line Railway (1911)
San Jose Southern Railroad Co. (1890)
San Jose Street Railway (1903)
San Jose Terminal Railway Co. (1911)
San Jose Traction Co. (1907)
Santa Clara & Alviso Railroad Co. (1875)
Santa Clara Belt Railroad (1889)
Santa Clara Interurban Railroad Co. (1904)
Santa Clara & Pajaro Valley Railroad Co. (1868)
Santa Clara Valley Railroad (1895)
Santa Clara Valley Railway (1902)
Santa Clara Valley Railway & Navigation Co. (1895)
South-East Side Horse Railroad Co. (1877)
Western Pacific Railroad Co. (1862)

SANTA CRUZ COUNTY

Almaden Branch Railroad Co. (1887)
Alpine Lumber Co. (1908)
Avenue Railroad (1877)
Boulder Creek & Pacific Railroad
Boulder Creek & Pescadero Railroad
California Central Railroad (1881)
California Timber Co. (1906)
Coast Line Railway Co. (1905)
Dougherty Extension Railroad (1887)
Dougherty Lumber Co. (1890)
East Santa Cruz Street Railway (1890)
Felton & Pescadero Railroad Co. (1883)
Glynn & Peterson Mill & Lumber Co. (1902)
Granite Rock Company Railroad (1900)
Loma Prieta Lumber Co. (1910)
Loma Prieta Railroad Co. (1882)
Molino Timber Co. (1890)
Newell Creek Railroad (1887)
Newell Creek Railroad (1906)
Ocean Shore & Eastern Railroad Co. (1907)
Pacific Avenue Railroad Co. (1885)
Pacific Avenue Street Railroad
Pacific Cement & Aggregates
Pacific Railroad & Steamship Co. (1909)
Pajaro & Santa Cruz Railroad Co. (1884)
San Francisco & Southern Railroad Co. (1904)
San Lorenzo Flume & Transportation Co. (1874)
San Lorenzo Valley Railroad (1861)
San Vincente Mill & Lumber Co. (1908)
Santa Clara Valley Mill & Lumber Co. (1887)
Santa Cruz, Big Trees & Pacific Railway Co. (1985)
Santa Cruz, Capitola & Watsonville Railroad (1902)
Santa Cruz County Railroad (1866)
Santa Cruz Electric Railway
Santa Cruz & Felton Railroad (1875)
Santa Cruz & Felton Railroad Co. (1874)

Santa Cruz, Garfield Park & Capitola Electric
  Railroad (1890)
Santa Cruz Lumber Co. (1923)
Santa Cruz Portland Cement Co. (1906)
Santa Cruz Railroad (1873)
Santa Cruz & Watsonville Railroad (1871)
Scotts Creek Railway (1908)
Union Traction Co. of Santa Cruz (1904)
Watsonville Railway & Navigation Co. (1911)
Watsonville Transportation Co. (1903)
Wildwood, Boulder Creek & Northern Railroad
  (1914)

SHASTA COUNTY

Anderson & Bella Vista Railroad (1909)
M.A. Brown Lumber Co. (1911)
California & Northeastern Railroad Co. (1892)
California, Shasta & Eastern Railroad Co. (1912)
Castle Crag Lumber Co. (1929)
Great Western Gold Co. (1906)
Grizzly Creek Lumber Co. (1921)
Iron Mountain Railway Co. (1895)
Mammoth Copper Co. Railroad (1906)
Redding, Afterthought & Northwestern Railway Co.
  (1907)
L.C. Reynolds Lumber Co.
Sacramento Valley & Eastern Railroad (1906)
Shasta Commercial Co. (1915)
Shasta Mineral Belt Railroad (1902)
Shasta Springs Scenic Railroad (1888)
Terry Lumber Co. (1905)
U.S. Bureau of Reclamation (1938)

SIERRA COUNTY

N.J. Blagen Lumber Co. (1922)
Boca & Loyalton Railroad Co. (1900)
Boca Mill & Ice Company
Clover Valley Lumber Co. Railroad (1917)
C.A. & Kenneth Copen (1950)
Davis-Johnson Lumber Co. (1919)
Horton Brothers Railroad (1902)
Marsh Lumber Co. (1908)
Roberts Lumber Co. (1900)
Sierraville Lumber Co. (1952)

SISKIYOU COUNTY

American Fruit Growers, Inc. (1920)
California Northeastern Railway (1905)
Coggins Brothers Lumber Co. (1899)
John Cook Lumber Co. (1892)
J.N. Durney Lumber Co. (1906)
Dwinnel Lumber Co. (1919)
Fruit Growers Supply Co. (1909)
Hovey & Walker (1929)
Johnson-Pollock Lumber Co. (1915)
Kespine Lumber Co. (1926)

Kesterson Lumber Co. (1925)
Klamath Lake Railroad Co. (1901)
Le Moine Lumber & Trading Co. (1898)
Long-Bell Lumber Co. (1926)
McCloud River Railroad Co. (1896)
Moon Lumber Co. (1921)
Mount Hebron Lumber Co. (1918)
Mount Shasta Corporation Construction Co. (1921)
Mount Shasta Pine Manufacturing Co. (1887)
Nice Lumber Co. (1915)
Oregon Eastern Railway Co. (1905)
Oregon Southern Railroad (1907)
Pacific Gas & Electric Co. (1906)
Peppers-Cotton Lumber Co. (1920)
Pickering Lumber Co. (1915)
Pioneer Box & Lumber Co. (1923)
Pioneer Box Co. (1916)
Pitt River Railroad (1921)
Rainbow Mill & Lumber Co. (1918)
San Luis Valley Interurban Railway (1908)
Scott Valley Railway (1905)
Siskiyou Electric Power & Light Co. (1912)
Siskiyou Lumber Co. (1920)
Sisson Lumber Co. (1895)
Sisson Mill & Lumber Co. (1889)
Southern Oregon Lumber Co. (1928)
Weed Lumber Co. (1902)
Wood & Sheldon Lumber Co. (1902)
Yreka Railroad (1888)
Yreka Railroad Co. (1906)
Yreka & Scott Valley Railroad (1904)
Yreka Western Railroad Co. (1933)

SOLANO COUNTY

Bender Brothers (1901)
Benicia Land & Terminal Railway Co. (1914)
California Central Narrow-Gauge Railway Co. (1873)
Napa & Vaca Valley Railroad Co. (1907)
San Francisco & Napa Valley Railroad
San Francisco, Vallejo & Napa Valley Electric Railway
  & Steamship Co. (1906)
San Francisco, Vallejo & Napa Valley Railroad Co.
  (1911)
Suisun, Berryessa & Clear Lake Railroad (1869)
Vaca Valley & Clear Lake Railroad Co. (1877)
Vaca Valley Railroad Co. (1869)
Vallejo, Benicia & Napa Valley Railroad Co. (1902)
Vallejo Traction Co. (1910)

SONOMA COUNTY

California Company (1909)
Cazadero Lumber Co. (1889)
Central Street Railway (1891)
Clear Lake Electric Railway Co. (1903)
Clipper Mill Tramway (1869)
Cloverdale & Ukiah Railroad Co. (1886)
Contra Costa Steam Navigation Co. (1852)

A.B. Davis Lumber Co. (1904)
Duncan's Mill, Land & Lumber Assn. (1880)
Fisk's Mill Railroad (1860)
Fort Ross Land Co. (1910)
Fulton & Guerneville Railroad Co. (1874)
Golden Gate Railroad Co. (1893)
Guerne & Murphy Railroad (1892)
Heald & Guerne Lumber Co. (1876)
Healdsburg Railway (1914)
J.C. Hickman & Son (1910)
Jenner Lumber Co. (1911)
Lakeport & Richardson's Bay Railroad Co. (1907)
Laton Lumber & Investment Co. (1906)
Liberty Lumber Co. (1920)
Madona Land & Lumber Co. (1877)
Marin Terminal Electric Railroad (1906)
Marin Terminal Railroad (1905)
Andrew Markham Lumber Co. (1886)
D.H. McEwen Lumber Co. (1906)
Minton Mills (1919)
Napa, Sacramento & Richardson's Bay County
   Railroad Co. (1908)
North Western Railroad Co. of California (1885)
Petaluma & Cloverdale Railroad Co. (1869)
Petaluma & Coast Railway (1912)
Petaluma & Haystack Railroad Co. (1862)
Petaluma & Healdsburg Railroad Co. (1865)
Petaluma Railroad Co. (1914)
Petaluma & Santa Rosa Electric Railway Co. (1903)
Petaluma & Santa Rosa Railroad Co. (1908)
Petaluma, Sebastopol & Russian River Railroad (1889)
Petaluma Street Railway
Platt Mill Co. (1867)
Redwood Lumber Co. (1911)
Richardson Brothers (1889)
Russian River, Land & Lumber Co. (1877)
Salt Point Railroad (1871)
San Francisco & Humboldt Bay Railroad Co. (1868)
San Francisco & Napa Railway Co. (1903)
San Francisco & Northern Railway (1912)
San Francisco & Northern Railway Co. (1914)
San Francisco & North Pacific Railroad Co. (1869)
San Francisco & North Pacific Railway Co. (1877)
Santa Rosa & Benicia Central Railway (1886)
Santa Rosa & Carquinez Railroad Co. (1887)
Santa Rosa City Railroad (1877)
Santa Rosa & Clear Lake Railroad Co. (1911)
Santa Rosa & Clear Lake Scenic Railway Co. (1908)
Santa Rosa & Napa Railroad (1879)
Santa Rosa Northern Railroad (1906)
Santa Rosa, Sebastopol & Green Valley Railroad
   (1887)
Santa Rosa Street Railway Co. (1877)
Santa Rosa Street Railways (1902)
Sierra Sugar Pine Co. (1912)
Sonoma County Railroad Co. (1868)
Sonoma & Lake County Electric Railway Co. (1907)

Sonoma & Lake County Railway (1909)
Sonoma Land & Lumber Co. (1892)
Sonoma Magnesite Railroad (1914)
Sonoma & Marin Railroad (1874)
Sonoma, Mendocino & Humboldt Railroad Co. (1895)
Sonoma, Napa Junction & Vallejo Railroad (1879)
Sonoma & Santa Rosa Railroad Co. (1881)
Sonoma Valley Extension Railroad (1887)
Sonoma Valley Prismoidal Railroad (1875)
Sonoma Valley Railroad Co. (1885)
South Side Street Railway (1888)
Union Street Railway (1893)
Vallejo & Sonoma Valley Railroad (1867)
M.S. Wagy Lumber Co. (1909)
Western Redwood Lumber Co. (1906)

STANISLAUS COUNTY

Atlas-Olympic Co. Railroad
Foster Farms Railroad
Inter-Counties Railway (1911)
Modesto & Empire Traction Co. (1911)
Modesto Interurban Railroad (1908)
Modesto Interurban Railroad Co. (1909)
Modesto, Tuolumne & Mono Railroad Co. (1900)
Modesto & Yosemite Valley Railroad Co.
Oakdale & Sonora Railroad (1875)
Oakdale Western Railway Co. (1904)
Patterson & Western Railroad Co. (1916)
Sierra Railroad Co. (1937)
Sierra Railway Co. of California (1897)
Tidewater Southern Railway Co. (1912)
Turlock & Eastern Railroad Co. (1928)
Turlock Traction Co. (1911)

TEHAMA COUNTY

Forward Brothers Lumber Co. (1941)
Red Bluff & Fall River Railroad Co. (1906)
Sacramento Valley Electric Railway (1912)
Sacramento Valley & Humboldt Bay Railroad (1887)
Sierra Lumber Co. (1878)
Sierra Lumber Co. (1881)
Tuscan Mineral Springs Corporation Electric Railway
   (1903)
Valley Railroad Co. (1912)
Yellow Jacket Railroad (1908)

TRINITY COUNTY

Copper Belt Railway & Power Co. (1902)
Trinity Railway (1901)

TULARE COUNTY

Big Four Electric Railway Co. (1912)
Kaweah & Giant Forest Railroad (1888)
People's Railroad (1883)
Porterville Northeastern Railroad Co. (1910)

Sierra Pacific Railroad Co. (1906)
Tulare County Power Co. (1911)
Tulare & Grant Forest Railroad (1885)
Tulare Valley & Grant Forest Railroad Co. (1882)
Visalia Electric Railroad Co. (1904)
Visalia Railroad Co. (1874)
Visalia-Tulare Railroad Co. (1887)

TUOLUMNE COUNTY

Dutch Mine Railroad
Empire City Railroad (1910)
Hetch-Hetchy Railroad Co. (1916)
Hetch-Hetchy & Yosemite Valley Railroad Co. (1900)
Jamestown & Yosemite Valley Railroad (1905)
McKay Lumber Co.
Pickering Lumber Corporation (1934)
Sierra & San Francisco Power Co.
Sonora Belt Line Railroad Co. (1907)
Sonora-Groveland Railway (1907)
Standard Lumber Co.
Stanislaus Railway Co. (1906)
Sugar Pine Railway (1903)
West Side Flume & Lumber Co. (1899)
West Side Lumber Co. (1903)
Yosemite Short Line Railroad Co. (1904)

VENTURA COUNTY

Bakersfield & Ventura Railway (1902)
San Buenaventura & Southern Pacific Railroad Co.
  (1875)
Santa Clara Valley Electric Railway & Power Co.
  (1901)
Ventura County Railroad Co. (1911)

Ventura County Railway Co. (1911)
Ventura & Ojai Railway (1901)
Ventura & Ojai Railroad Co. of California (1896)
Ventura Terminal Railway Co. (1907)

YOLO COUNTY

Clear Lake Railroad Co. (1908)
Elkhorn & Humboldt Railroad Co. (1875)
Sacramento Valley, Lake & Mendocino Railroad (1886)
Winter & Ukiah Railway Co. (1887)
Woodland, Capay & Clear Lake Railroad Co. (1887)
Woodland Street Railway Co. (1887)

YUBA COUNTY

California Midland Railroad Co. (1905)
California & Oregon Railroad Co. (1865)
California & Oregon Railroad Co. (1869)
Marysville & Benicia Railroad Co. (1851)
Marysville & Colusa Railroad Co. (1911)
Marysville-Colusa Railway (1912)
Marysville & Great Eastern Railroad Co. (1907)
Marysville Railroad Co. (1867)
Marysville & Susanville Railway Co. (1904)
Marysville & Yuba City Railroad Co. (1889)
Marysville & Yuba City Street Railroad Co. (1889)
Northern California Railroad Co. (1884)
Northern California Railway Co. (1888)
Northern Electric Railway Co. - Marysville & Colusa
  Branch (1910)
Oak Valley Lumber Co. (1920)
San Francisco & Great Eastern Railroad (1906)
San Francisco & Marysville Railroad Co. (1857)

Index

191

Out of State Railroads which planned to build
and terminate within California

1992 Additions

AMSTAR CORPORATION SUGAR COMPANY

Organized 1985 - Diesel - Standard Gauge

Located Manteca, San Joaquin County. Operates an in-plant switching service for its company plants at Manteca, Mendota, Spreckles and Woodland.

CARGILL

Organized 1985 - Diesel - Standard Gauge

Located Verdemont, San Bernardino County. Operates a switching service for the Cargill feed elevator located along the Santa Fe Railway north of San Bernardino.

DELTA CONSOLIDATED MINING COMPANY

Organized 1908 - Steam - Narrow-Gauge

Located Delta, Shasta County. A six and one-half mile 3-foot gauge gold mining railroad that hauled sacked concentrate from the stamp mill to the Southern Pacific transfer at Delta. The post office name for Delta was Bayles, located midway between Redding and Dunsmuir. Line abandoned in 1928.

A. L. GILBERT COMPANY

Organized 1990 - Diesel - Standard Gauge

Located Keyes, Stanislaus County. Operates a switching railroad off the Southern Pacific in order to serve A. L. Gilbert Co. and the Berry Feed & Seed Co.

HOLLY SUGAR COMPANY

Diesel - Standard Gauge

Located Brawley, Imperial County. Operates several sugar mill in-plant railroads at Hamilton City, Union City and San Francisco.

HUMBOLDT COUNTY RAILROAD

Organized 1991 - Diesel - Standard Gauge

Located Humboldt, Humboldt County. A new 165-mile railroad has been proposed to run from Humboldt Bay, over the coast range, to connect with the Southern Pacific at Redding or Red Bluff. Would be used to handle redwood lumber due to frequent washouts on the Northwestern Pacific.

JAMES RAILWAY

Organized 1980 - Diesel - Standard Gauge

Located Anita, Butte County. Operates a switching railroad for the Diamont International Corporation near Chico. Has a track connection with the Union Pacific at Anita.

LINCOLN CLAY PRODUCTS

Diesel - Standard Gauge

Located Lincoln, Madera County. Operates an in-plant railroad off the Southern Pacific at Chowchilla.

LONE STAR INDUSTRIES

Organized 1990 - Diesel - Standard Gauge

Located Lopis, Monterey County. Operates a switching railroad off the Southern Pacific at Castroville.

ORANGE COUNTY COMMUTER

Organized 1990 - Diesel - Standard Gauge

Located Santa Ana, Orange County. Orange County subsidizes three passenger trains, operated by Amtrak, between San Juan Capistrano and Los Angeles.

PENINSULA CORRIDOR JOINT POWERS BOARD

Organized 1991 - Diesel - Standard Gauge

Located San Jose, Santa Clara County. Took over the operation of CalTrain from Caltrans. Chose ATE Commuter Rail (a subsidiary of Ryder Systems) to operate the former Southern Pacific commuter operation from San Francisco to San Jose, with an extension to Gilroy.

PHILLIPS PETROLEUM

Diesel - Standard Gauge

Located Avon, Contra Costa County. Operates an in-plant switching service off the Southern Pacific at Martinez.

PORT BELT RAILROAD

Organized 1985 - Diesel - Standard Gauge

Located Westgate, Yolo County. A four-mile switching railroad jointly operated by the Southern Pacific and Union Pacific railroads. Serves an industrial area of docks and warehouses west of the Sacramento River.

PURDY COMPANY

Organized 1974 - Diesel - Standard Gauge

Located Mojave, Kern County. Operates approximately a quarter mile of railroad track within a railroad scrapping yard located along the Southern Pacific.

QUINCY RAILROAD EASTERN BRANCH RAILROAD

Organized 1991 - Diesel - Standard Gauge

Located Quincy, Plumas County. Operates the former Susanville branch of the Southern Pacific between Wendel and Susanville, on behalf of its owner the Sierra Pacific Industries.

RIVERSIDE COUNTY RAIL TRANSIT

Organized 1991 - Diesel - Standard Gauge

Located Riverside, Riverside County. This firm was started by the Riverside County Board of Supervisors to establish rail service between Riverside and the Menifee Valley area (Sun City).

ROSEBURG LUMBER PRODUCTS

Diesel - Standard Gauge

Located Red Bluff, Tehama County. Operates an in-plant switching railroad for a lumber mill off the Southern Pacific near Red Bluff.

SAN JOAQUIN VALLEY RAILWAY

Organized 1991 - Diesel - Standard Gauge

Located Exeter, Tulare County. Organized by Kyle Railways to take over the Coalinga, Exeter, Stratford and Visalia branches of the Southern Pacific in the San Joaquin Valley. Included in the operation will be the jointly owned Santa Fe/Southern Pacific Arvin and Oil City branches, and the Sunset Railway running from Bakersfield to Taft.

SAVAGE COAL TERMINAL

Organized 1985 - Diesel - Standard Gauge

Located Wasco, Kern County. Operates an in-plant switching service for an Asbury Systems Corporation coal storage facility located off the Santa Fe at Wasco.

TUSTIN CITY RAILROAD

Organized 1886 - Horsecar - Standard Gauge

Located Tustin, Orange County. Built on 4th Street to Olive Street in Tustin in 1886, then extended to the Santa Fe station in Santa Ana the following year. Abandoned in 1896 due to the lack of patronage.

TUSTIN MOTOR RAILROAD

Organized 1888 - Steam Motor - Standard Gauge

Located Santa Ana, Orange County. Proposed to build a motor railroad from Santa Ana to Tustin. A franchise was to be granted from the city center east to the depot as soon as James McFadden filed incorporation papers. By May the name of the railroad had been changed to the Santa Ana & Tustin Motor Railroad Company and articles of incorporation filed. Proposed project was abandoned in 1889.

UNION CARBIDE

Diesel - Standard Gauge

Located Pine, Marin County. Operates a short in-plant railroad off the Northwestern Pacific Railroad north of Sausalito.

YOLO SHORTLINE RAILROAD

Organized 1991 - Diesel - Standard Gauge

Located West Sacramento, Yolo County. Purchased the former Sacramento Northern Holland branch from the Union Pacific during January 1991. Operates a switching railroad along the banks of the Sacramento River from West Sacramento to the Delta Sugar Mill at Clarksburg.